$9.95
10/10/11

Bentley on Brecht

Eric Bentley

BENTLEY ON BRECHT

Third Edition

Northwestern University Press
Evanston, Illinois

PT
2603
.R397
Z5589
2008

Northwestern University Press
www.nupress.northwestern.edu

Copyright © 1981, 1987, 1999, 2008 by Eric Bentley. Northwestern University Press edition published 2008. All rights reserved.

Printed in the United States of America

10 9 8 7 6 5 4 3 2 1

Library of Congress Cataloging-in-Publication Data

Bentley, Eric, 1916–
    Bentley on Brecht / Eric Bentley. — 3rd ed.
      p. cm.
    Contains the texts of: The Brecht commentaries (1987) and The Brecht memoir
      (1990).
    Includes bibliographical references and index.
    ISBN-13: 978-0-8101-2393-9 (pbk. : alk. paper)
    ISBN-10: 0-8101-2393-2 (pbk. : alk. paper)
    1. Brecht, Bertolt, 1898–1956—Criticism and interpretation. 2. Brecht, Bertolt, 1898–
1956—Correspondence. 3. Bentley, Eric, 1916—Correspondence. I. Title.
    PT2603.R397Z5589 2008
    832.912—dc22

                                   2007043986

♾ The paper used in this publication meets the minimum requirements of the American National Standard for Information Sciences—Permanence of Paper for Printed Library Materials, ANSI Z39.48-1992.

Contents

The Brecht Memoir   373

Gallery follows page 136.

Acknowledgments and Dedications

Between the forties and the eighties, there have been many helping hands. In something like chronological order I would like to acknowledge Rosa and Herbert Kline, David Beams, Elisabeth Hauptmann, Gordon Rogoff, Heinrich Jalowetz, Stanley Burnshaw, Fritz and Elsa Cohen, Fred Jordan, Berthold Viertel (and Liesl), John Hancock, Maja Apelman, Leo and Louise Kerz, Ruth Berlau, Seymour Peck, James Laughlin, Richard Schechner, Harry Ford, Erika Munk, Caspar Neher, Kenneth Tynan, Teo Otto, John Gassner, Herbert Berghof, David Daiches, Uta Hagen, Martin Esslin, Toby Cole, John Fuegi, Isaiah Sheffer, James Lyon, Barney Rosset, Saul Elkin, Hugo Schmidt, John Dexter, and, of course, the Man himself.

—*E. B.*

New York, September 1980

In 1990 the following names were added: Joel Schechter, Elsa Lanchester, Charles Laughton, Lisa Jalowetz Aronson, and Martha Feuchtwanger.

The Brecht Commentaries were dedicated to those who sat around the dining table in the home of Rosa and Herb Kline, Hollywood, 1942.

The Brecht Memoir was dedicated to the memory of Ruth Berlau, 1906–74.

Preface
1998

See the two cranes through heaven sweeping!
The clouds give way before them, bringing
Both of them from one life to another.
At the same height, the same speed flying
Side by side together keeping
The cranes with the cloud banks are sharing
The lovely skies in which they're floating.
Neither longer than the other staying
Each sees nothing but the other rocking
In the soft wind that both are feeling
In their flight together pressing.
They are not dying, they're surviving:
Let the wind blow them toward nothing!
Now they can be touched by nothing!
Now they can be driven onward
Far from the rainstorms and the shooting
'Neath sun and moon, lost in each other!
(Sun, moon are disks that hardly differ.)
Where are you heading, you two? Nowhere.
From whom then fleeing? Everybody.
For they are lovers. Long together? No.
Not long. And very soon they'll part.
(Love stops the clock in the lover's heart.)

BENTLEY ON BRECHT SPANS THE WHOLE period from the day I first met Brecht (1942) to the present (1998), fifty-six years. Does it comprise all I have to say about him? I only know it contains most of what I *have* said about him in print.

Two earlier books of mine are subsumed here: *The Brecht Commentaries* and *The Brecht Memoir*. *The Brecht Commentaries* is a series of soundings: I lowered my weighted line into the water at different locations and did my best to measure the depth, the different depths, different at the different locations, but different also at the different times when the soundings were made.

Different also because (though the scientific metaphor may not support me now) I was a different person at the different times. The title of my second volume makes the personal factor obvious, the subjectivity of the critiques overt. *The Brecht Memoir* makes manifest what had been latent in the commentaries: this is not a detached judgment and exposition made by critic A upon writer B. Rather, it reflects an encounter of one writer with another, one person with another. Indeed a series of encounters. Even the "soundings," as people realize upon reading the memoir, were that. Hence I would not claim that my personal anecdotes sometimes rise to the rank of critical comment and analysis. I would claim—or at least I would hope—that my critical and less concrete comments reinforce and elaborate direct description of Brecht the man and Brecht the artist.

Subjectivity, here, is not an obstacle to be overcome. It is an organic part of a process shown. This is not Brecht elucidated by Bentley (though there may be elucidations in plenty along the way). Exhibited here is the *clash* of Brecht and Bentley. I don't mean hostility. Brecht is not being debunked or deplored. We see, rather, what impact he makes upon an admirer of very different background, temperament, and philosophy. He does not suffer thereby. Considering how great those differences are, he comes out of them, can it not be said? rather well.

Bentley on Brecht ends with a postscript which was originally entitled *The Eric Bentley Memoir*. Egotism? Perhaps. But the subjectivity implicit all along needed at long last to become explicit. Or so I had to conclude upon reading complaints that I had concealed from the reader the self who had so confidently (confidently!) looked Brecht in the eye.

He was just as subjective. He did not stand back from the personal relationship and evaluate the truth or untruth of what I wrote about him. In the language of his detractors, he exploited me, used me, as he exploited and used a hundred others. But I was a subjectivity too. As I saw matters, he was not exploiting me, because I could, equally, have been accused of exploiting and using him.

What was in it for me? Money, say *my* detractors, knowing that I have indeed earned money, if not from the critical essays, then from the transactions and adaptations. But little money was earned during Brecht's lifetime. What I was learning was much more than money. It was skill. Yet another reason that my Brecht writings are not "objective" is that my motive was, not to be the great critic, but to learn about playwriting and about theater in general. My periodic pronouncements upon Brecht's plays trace the history of my investigation of the playwright's craft and art.

So I became a Brechtian playwright? Not that either. I did not imitate his plays, nor did I use his theoretical writings as a guide, much less as a rationale or justification. I absorbed theater from his mode of work. But if it came to reusing his material, as I did, for instance, in the play *The Recantation of Galileo Galilei,* then it was necessary to clash with his version of things. That way I could draw upon him and at the same time, with luck, become myself.

But it is not for me to say what, for the reader, *Bentley on Brecht* adds up to. I can only report what I am aware of having put into it.

About that "mode of work." The reference is, in the first instance, the work I saw him do in the last years of his life, but more than forty years have elapsed since he died, and through most of this period I continued to absorb what was there to be absorbed, which, for me, was not his by now notorious theatrical Theory (of Gestus, of Alienation Effect, and so on) nor yet, exclusively, the practice of the Berlin Ensemble, for I was seldom in touch with it anyway. What brought me and kept me close to the spirit and essence of Brecht was the process of translating and sometimes adapting him. I translated few of the theoretical essays but a good many of the plays and not a little of the poetry.

> A plum tree stands by the garden wall
> Hard to believe, how very small
> Behind wire netting taking cover
> So nobody will knock it over.
>
> But, oh, how it would like to grow
> Ah no, ah no, ah no
> No hopes, no prospects, no, not one
> It gets too little sun.
>
> "Is it a plum tree, can you tell?
> Can it bear plums? I don't see how!"
> "No plums, no plums but mark well
> The plum tree leaves on the bough."

If there is a Brechtian quintessence, you will find it there: in the poetry. The term should not of course exclude the plays—they are dramatic poetry—but I should record here that, in recent years, if I have done any reading in the collected works of Brecht in German, and I have, it has been in the three volumes of *Gedichte*—poems. It is there that he is most often at his best, and I get the feeling that I see him there in the nude, which is to say without the accoutrements and disguises of his theater.

To the two earlier volumes, I add, in this present volume, a short piece (pages 365–72) on Brecht as poet. But *Bentley on Brecht* must remain biased the other way. A book will be written someday that does justice to Brecht as poet. This is not it. This is only the book of the encounter I characterized just now. The clash.

And that is all: it's not enough, I know
But it will tell you I was there maybe
I'm like the man with but one brick to show
Who says: this is my house that here you see.

Bentley on Brecht

THE BRECHT
COMMENTARIES

Brecht's Reputation
1998

February 10, 1998, was the one hundredth anniversary of Brecht's birth. In a longish report published one day later, the New York Times *announced that, after some bleak years, Brecht was now "back on his pedestal." And I was asked to write a follow-up piece for their Op Ed page. This piece (with minor changes) follows. The* Times *never ran it. Nor did* The Nation *or the* New Republic *to whom it was subsequently offered. It first appeared in* American Theatre, *May–June 1998.*

ONE DAY WE READ IN THE PAPER that Bertolt Brecht's reputation—as playwright, poet, whatever—has sunk to zero. Next day, or maybe next year, we read that he is back up, or maybe higher than ever, the greatest writer of the century, or since Shakespeare. He always made bitter enemies and attracted doting admirers. I think sometimes that the world is divided into those who think Brecht was no good at all and those who think he was the best ever, even that he had a kind of greatness that goes beyond the greatness of other great writers.

He himself had created this last idea. The work of his colleagues in modern theater, such as Chekhov or Pirandello, had aesthetic merit, and that was all: that was their achievement and their limitation. They were not in league with history, nor was history in league with them: the history they were attached to was a history of failure, that of the Russian bourgeoisie (Chekhov), or that of Italian fascism (Pirandello). Brecht would not offer himself to the world as just an artist of genius (i.e. possessed of aesthetic merit) but was closer to the role of prophet and guru, and much better than those, for his work embodied no mere guesses about the future and no merely personal vision but the objective truth, the true and final truth, the truth on the march toward Utopia.

In the early forties, I was taken up by Brecht as a young critic who might well be the person to establish his reputation in the whole English-speaking world—I was a British subject living, like him at the time, in America. Although America and Russia had not yet emerged as the two superpowers, he always seemed to think that they would so emerge, and as rivals—indeed as hell and heaven. He liked individual Americans but had no doubt that theirs was the evil empire. Russia was the future, and if he hadn't *seen* it work he had seen, in the Marxist-Leninist classics, the proof that it was going to work, that its success was inevitable. Except as "socialism" succeeds, he told me, his works had no future.

I did not share his politics or the philosophy behind them. It is true that many people heard of Brecht through me, and that I ranked him among the half dozen great playwrights of the past century, in other words as the equal of Chekhov and Pirandello and the rest. But that any of them should be the single transcendent genius of the century was not, for me, in the cards.

It *was* in the cards for some people and remains so today. Although the Soviet Union never returned this ardent wooer's love, the left-wing intelligentsia of Western Europe did. To date, the most ardent support for the transcendent Brecht has come from Paris, but the cities of what used to be West Germany were not far behind, nor was London, with its two "royal" theaters which, politically, have often seemed Popular Front theaters dating from the thirties.

Stalin's proclamation of a Popular Front in 1935 was the greatest propaganda coup of the twentieth century. He thereby detached maybe half the liberals in the world from their liberal affiliations and affiliated them with Moscow—and against Washington. Brecht, for his part, had never been a liberal, but now, though Moscow hardly even smiled at him, he became the darling of the fellow travelers, a large worldwide following. By the time his Berlin Ensemble visited Paris—in the midfifties—this meant he had now attained a big reputation indeed. His own dream of being the poet of a new era and a new humanity seemed to be in process of realization.

One was conscious of this fact in the mideighties when the Berlin Ensemble visited Toronto. At the conference connected with this visit, a Canadian student asked the East Berlin big shots on the dais if other kinds of drama than Brecht, other views of life than communism, were offered in their theater: was there dissidence? The big shots went into a huddle. Was there a German word for dissidence? *Ach, ja.* Answer: "There is no dissidence because there is no need for dissidence." Ergo, there was no need for other kinds of dramatists, and one icon would suffice.

Then came 1989, and the end of the Soviet Union. Must it not be the end of Bertolt Brecht, even as it was the end of the German Democratic Republic? Brecht had told me: if socialism falls, I fall, and his daughter did fall—from her position as head of the Berlin Ensemble, the Winifred Wagner of East Berlin's Bayreuth (as I had called her).

For myself, I was hopeful. Perhaps we could now put politics, with the Soviet Union, behind us. Perhaps now my own vision of Brecht—as simply poet and dramatist, not theorist, philosopher, guru, prophet, icon—would be vindicated.

I had reckoned without the Popular Front and the fellow travelers. It turned out they had survived what they fellow-traveled with. What we meet with now, in Germany in the first instance, is the belief that Ulbricht and Honecker and their men had let communism down, and so Brecht and his Brechtians (Hanns Eisler, Paul Dessau et al.) had only been LET DOWN, not discredited. This way Brecht is returned to his unique status as the transcendent one.

Not all Brecht fans talk this way, of course. The tone is different among, say, professors of literature in American universities and their student protégés. Yet the Marxism no European proletariat ever yet embraced is being desperately held on to by what one might call a cadre of American (and British and French) academics.

And there is an International Brecht Society. From what its members have published, I would gather that, though there is no commitment to Soviet communism, there is some not altogether vague acquiescence in Popular Front politics, in which the bottom line was always: no criticism of Soviet communism. Criticism of Stalin is allowed, now he is long dead and the Soviet Union has come to an end, but there is (in many quarters) still no criticism of Brecht's politics: he, too, can *now* be classed as anti-Stalinist. He is back on his pedestal because (in those quarters) Lenin is back on his.

The few Brecht scholars, such as Martin Esslin, who have been anti-Communist were always jumped on by the true-believing Brechtians, whose claim is implicitly to *own* Brecht and who automatically regard critics of his views as heretical and reactionary. Even exposure of the facts about Brecht's political career is often dismissed now as "cold-war scholarship."

But, you may interject, even if Brecht was wrong about the Soviet Union and so on, isn't it still possible he *was* a significant sage and theorist? For one of the most thoughtful and sensitive artists in our English-language theater, he was. In *The Empty Space* (1968) Peter Brook wrote: "Brecht is the key figure of our time, and all theatre work today at some point starts from or returns to his statements and achievement."

Read this sentence over a few times, and you will have less and less idea what is being said, other than that Brook thought Brecht had a lot of influence. Yet, looking back now from the year 1998, one looks in vain for *any* Brechtian elements in all the work of Brook himself.

In the second half of the twentieth century, even after 1989, Brecht has the reputation of a man of influence, but signs of that influence are often hard to seek and even more often are just the influence of Brecht the theorist—Brecht the Communist sage, head of a Marxist-Leninist think tank. In Koestlerian phrase, he is, for some, both yogi and commissar.

Still. In 1998. The other day I received a boxed set of twenty CDs from Germany: *The Selected Works of BB.* In the liner notes, a theater man is exclaiming that one must not make an aesthete of Brecht, one should not produce his plays as mere plays; they must have political resonance and urgency. Along with statements of this sort one might place the contention, often repeated over the years, that Marxism allowed Brecht to grow from the young decadent of his early twenties poetry and drama to the Stalin Prize–winner of the big plays carried across the world by the Berlin Ensemble.

Not all the people who parrot such statements are Communists, but I may be permitted to call them fellow travelers in that they decline to be critical either of communism or of Brecht. Now an uncritical attitude may be a service to a political cause, but it is not a service to a great artist. As Samuel Johnson observed long ago, we do our favorite (he had Shakespeare in mind) no service by ignoring or discounting his flaws and limitations. And to Peter Brook I would say: "No one person holds the key to our time; our theater knows no single key figure; and no single playwright has found an *unum necessarium* that all the others have missed." As to Brecht's "statements," under which heading Brook presumably includes the many theoretical volumes, there is indeed much of *practical* interest for the theater worker, but as to general ideas nothing there is world-shaking, unless you consider the world is still being shaken by Karl Marx. There are more profound thinkers than Brecht, even in the small world of German drama (such as Schiller and Hebbel).

I was reminded of all this when giving a graduate seminar on Brecht this winter [1998] at Hunter College. Before we even began, the students were throwing technical terms at me that they had picked up from old Brechtians or from the Meister's own essays—*gestus,* the *alienation effect, epic theater, dialectical theater.* They seemed to think that Brecht wrote plays to exemplify these abstractions. I told them a story *I* thought was well known, though they hadn't heard it. Back in the early twenties, Brecht plays were not getting much attention. "What you need," a friend told him, "is a theory. To make your stuff important." So Brecht went home and got himself a theory, which now is known to more people than are the plays. "We shall approach Brecht," I announced at Hunter College, "not through the theoretical essays but through the poems. This was a poet who proceeded from lyric to dramatic poetry. You can postpone your reading of the theoretical essays till later—or forever." Thus may my students discover the merit—the positive substance—of Brecht's works, as they might discover the substance of Dostoevsky's works despite his anti-Semitism and pan-Slavism or the substance of Ezra Pound's poetry despite *his* anti-Semitism and adulation of Mussolini.

The subject is not simple. The positive substance of such artists, as a recent writer on T. S. Eliot's anti-Semitism has been arguing, is not cut off from the negative substance. Recent biographies have been showing that every great artist you ever heard of had a Dark Side, be it Charles Dickens or Robert Frost. Let students learn that too. And Brecht's dark side was not the fact that he adopted an ideology different from yours or mine. Mere difference of opinion is not what is at stake: a whole cultural situation is involved. The context of Brecht, from the beginning, was an intelligentsia in extremis that found the most negative features of totalitarianism, of the right or of the left, highly seductive. Brecht did not have to abandon the nihilistic destructiveness inherent in his early work when he turned toward Moscow. Not only nineteenth-century Marxism but also twentieth-century Leninism-Stalinism was seductive—a proposition hard for American students of the 1990s to grasp, though they could easily find a neo-Marxist professor to explain it away for them.

And the man's reputation? Those who share his outlook put it excessively high. Those who don't share it put it excessively low. Perhaps such a good/bad reputation is what, as a historical figure, Brecht deserves. But if people would just see his plays and read his poetry, they would reach more interesting, more differentiated conclusions. And give him a new reputation.

The Trial of Lucullus
1943

This was the sequence. 1942: I met Bertolt Brecht and was given man-
uscripts of his to read. A little later I met a friend of Brecht's, Berthold
Viertel, who was directing scenes from Master Race *in German at the*
Barbizon Plaza in New York. I got closer to Viertel than one ever could
to Brecht himself, and learned much, too, not only of Brecht but of Karl
Kraus and others... When, in 1943, a small book by Brecht was pub-
lished by New Directions, I made sure that I got to review it in The
Nation. *It was* The Trial of Lucullus, *translated by H. R. Hays.*

IT IS CURIOUS TO WATCH THE DELAYED and erratic flow of foreign literature into English translation. Rilke came in a few years
ago like a tidal wave; then came Kierkegaard, nearly a century
late; only yesterday Stefan George arrived; today it is the turn of
Bertolt Brecht. This is an important event for all who are interested in present tendencies of poetry and the drama, though it
means reopening all those problems of poetry and the left, poetry
and propaganda, poetry and the people, which are assumed to
have passed away with the red decade. As to the drama, it is not
only the leftist brand that has disappeared; there is simply no
drama at all these days with any quality or any future in it. That
at least is one's general impression of the English-speaking

theater, and that is why, not for the first time in theater history, one turns eagerly to translations from the German.

Bertolt Brecht is one of the best living poets and one of the very few living dramatists worth mentioning. Unfortunately, however, his lyric poetry is as unsuccessful in translation as George's, yet for precisely opposite reasons: George uses a kind of poetic diction that in translation is merely precious; Brecht uses a tricky kind of colloquialism that in translation is merely commonplace. The explanation seems to be that the German language and German literature are, in some respects, at an earlier stage than English and that therefore a German poet can still adopt either a traditional poetic diction or a traditional popular style without making a fool of himself. George is indeed the leading modern in the literary tradition of Goethe and Hölderlin; Brecht, the leading *modern* in a popular tradition that goes back to Luther and Hans Sachs. I emphasize the word *modern*, for Brecht is not a pure folk poet but also the parodist of folk poetry, a sarcastic mind, superficially antiliterary, fundamentally lyrical, tough, angular, righteously indignant, all that W. H. Auden in his satiric days tried to be. But Auden's wit was always that of a clever and rather priggish undergraduate, and since a poet cannot be perpetually precocious, one guessed that he would take to religion. Brecht, on the other hand, has always been an engaging blend of introvert and extrovert, never so tender-minded that the tough exterior looked like affectation. More successfully than almost anyone else he fused the idiom and rhythm of prose with a resilient verse. In his attempt to break down the disastrous modern antithesis of highbrow and lowbrow he created out of the vernacular something we are not often vouchsafed these days—a poetic style, firm, simple, and ironic.

In the course of the past twenty years Brecht has written some six kinds of drama. He began with plays that were at once expressionistic and psychological; second, he wrote the most telling satiric librettos (for Kurt Weill and Hanns Eisler) at least since W. S. Gilbert and probably since John Gay; third, he invented a much-publicized didactic drama in which choruses, chanting to an orchestral accompaniment, purveyed a political gospel; fourth, he has scribbled some propaganda pieces close to the style and the level of current popular drama, such as *Señora Carrar's Rifles* and the script of Fritz Lang's *Hangmen Also Die;* fifth, he has attempted to present a composite picture of the Third Reich in his most ambitious project, in verse and prose, *Fear and Misery of the Third Reich,* one scene of which is shortly to be published in *The Nation;* sixth, he has attempted several historical plays whose meaning is entirely contemporary. *The Trial of Lucullus* is one of these.

The Trial of Lucullus tells how a great Roman conqueror appears after his death before a judge and jury who are to decide whether he should go to Hades or to the Elysian fields. The jury, consisting of a farmer, a teacher, a fishwife, a baker, and a courtesan, allows Lucullus to summon as witnesses the people portrayed on a frieze representing his triumphal procession. All the evidence is against Lucullus except that he brought back from the East a cherry tree, that he wept over the destruction of books, and that he encouraged good cooking. The story ends thus:

> And from the high bench they rise up
> The ancestors of the world-to-be,
> The world with many hands to take
> With many mouths to eat,
> The hard to deceive, the firmly united,
> The joyous world-to-be.
> The tribunal withdraws to consider the verdict.

The Trial of Lucullus is neither a lengthy nor a massive work. It is a short "radio play in verse," a play in which the military-heroic ideal of conquest is poignantly denounced by the common man and in which psychological distance is achieved by austerity of style and remoteness of period. There is nothing very complex about this, but since, when we hear nowadays of a "radio play in verse" by an author with propagandist intentions we forthwith prepare for the worst, a few words of explanation are in order. What are we afraid of? In the first place we fear the politics, because we associate political drama with our own abortive proletarian literature of the now despised thirties. But Brecht's political emphasis is neither a phase nor a fad: he was political in the thirties and remains political after. *The Trial of Lucullus* is not of the Mike Gold mint. One must simply recall that, from the artistic point of view, political emotion is as good a basis for a poet as any other and an excellent point of contact, at least now that the war is on, with his audience.

Our second fear is fear of poetry in drama. It is true that T. S. Eliot straightened out the theory of it for us when he observed that dramatic poetry was a specific type of work, not an arbitrary union of two modes, the dramatic and the poetic, and when in his own dramatic verse he provided a recipe—a racy, modern speech on top, a tremendous emotional pressure underneath. But the fact remains that neither Eliot nor Auden nor any of the others achieved more than an effective dialogue; the incomplete state of the brilliant "Sweeney Agonistes" bears eloquent witness to this. No more than Tennyson and Swinburne, therefore, have the moderns created a verse drama. So we are skeptical. Does Bertolt Brecht remove our doubts? Not altogether, in so slight a work as this, but at least we feel in reading *The Trial of Lucullus* the *possibility* of a modern verse drama—giving full and equal weight to both words.

Our third fear is our fear of the radio, for here too we have been disappointed. Like the cinema, the radio has been regarded as a possible means to a renewal of good popular art, but in fact both radio and cinema have become more and more commercialized, and most directors who were experimenters twenty years ago are complacent hacks today. Serious writers were slow to find the peculiar potentialities of the new mediums and continued to bring stage plays before the microphone and the camera. When the poetic radio play did arrive, it was bound to be merely the affair of special "workshops," and anyway, if Archibald MacLeish's efforts are typical, it was more bombastic and pretentious than popular. Does Brecht have a remedy for all this? Of course not. But his play is wholly conceived in terms of radio; that is, it is simply an oral time-sequence with visual imagery instead of a spectacle, with a carefully planned rhythm and a musical symmetry, with a poetry that consists of the best spoken words in the best order, with a bias or emotional prejudice that listeners share, with a tang and a hard-headedness that they can enjoy. Nevertheless, I cannot imagine the play being a commercial success. It is simple, but simplicity is itself a style, if a style very different from that of show business.

The Trial of Lucullus, then, shares the fate of most proletarian literature in that it is published by a minority press and is noticed only by the literary journals. This is not the fault of Bertolt Brecht. His difficulty is that in our time the good in art can only be popular by an accident, and even when the masses enjoy Brecht they enjoy him for what he has in common with Stefan Heym and other third-raters who write thrillers about the Nazis. The prerequisite of a great popular art, as Whitman and other realistic democrats have allowed, is a great populace and not a people drugged by opiates every bit as strong as religion. Until this condition is fulfilled, Bertolt Brecht will be important only to the intelligentsia; *after* it is fulfilled, paradoxically enough, propaganda will be gratuitous.

The Private Life of the Master Race
1944

The union of the mathematician with the poet, fervor
with measure, passion with correctness, this surely is
the ideal.

—WILLIAM JAMES

Brecht prepared a streamlined version of his Fear and Misery of the
Third Reich *for possible American production and called it* The Private
Life of the Master Race. *Viertel gave me a manuscript copy and, as
mentioned in the piece above,* The Nation *published a scene from it in
1943.* Theatre Arts *ran several scenes from it the following year along
with the following essay, which had begun as a program note at Black
Mountain College, where I had directed a staged reading of the whole
play, and which ended as an afterword to the New Directions edition of
the play. In this essay I came close to letting Brecht ghostwrite, or rather
to letting his girlfriend be the ghost, with him as the ghost of the ghost.
I certainly let Ruth Berlau talk me into overpraising the play the three
of us were busy selling to America:* Master Race. *Then there was the
anonymous essay, "What Is Epic Theater?" from Thomas Mann's magazine* Mass und Wert. *Ruth indicated that I was free to lift anything
I liked from it: it belonged to Brecht. Only later did I learn that its author was Walter Benjamin, and I arranged for a translation of it to be*

published under Benjamin's name in the Western Review *(Spring 1948)—the first Benjamin to appear in this country.*

BERTOLT BRECHT WAS BORN IN Bavaria in 1898; in due time studied medicine and the natural sciences; served in the medical corps during the First World War; subsequently decided on a literary career; was awarded the Kleist Prize for *Drums in the Night,* his first play; became the leading dramatist of the revolutionary theater in collaboration with Erwin Piscator at the Schiffbauerdam Theater, Berlin; left Germany in 1933, after his *Threepenny Opera* had enjoyed the longest run known to serious theater in Germany; lived in Denmark and Finland; finally crossed the Soviet Union and sailed for the United States on the last boat before Pearl Harbor; lives now with his wife and children in Santa Monica, California; intends, I am sure, to return to Germany after the war to continue his theatrical experiments.

Brecht is an interesting man. Though he is one of the few "workers' poets" who look even remotely like a worker, he also has many of the characteristics popularly attributed to poets. He leaves business matters to others. He almost never replies to letters, even to those that offer contracts and money. On one occasion a play of his was to be performed with some pomp and circumstance in Denmark, and performances were no longer an everyday occurrence for Brecht. He was to meet the promoters of the venture to make final arrangements. The hour of the meeting came but Brecht did not arrive. There was consternation. The production must now be postponed. Could Brecht be sick? Why had he let no one know? Finally Brecht was found, and quite unperturbed. "I had stomachache," he said. The play was never staged.

Brecht does not have the mild, comfortable ordinariness of personality that one has come to associate with modern poets. He can be quiet, embarrassed, somber, but suddenly the dark eyes flash, he jumps up from the chair and paces the room waving his cheap cigar. At such times he talks in tirades. Metaphors and anecdotes of Brechtian concreteness flow freely from his lips. His laugh is sharp and staccato. His slight body and gnome's head become important.

In Weimar days Brecht was a leader of the younger generation. In the years following the World War his work, alike tough and sophisticated, was both Ernest Hemingway and Aldous Huxley to many young Germans. Irreverent, energetic, sharp-tongued, anarchistic, Brecht hit the mood of the time. But the change came sooner to him than to his English and American compeers. Radicalism came earlier and lasted longer. For Brecht it was not the enthusiasm of a moment but a philosophy for a lifetime. Before long he was number five on the Nazi murder list.

Ten years of exile have left their mark on Brecht. His face is no longer young. It bears the imprint of suffering, for though he has escaped the Nazis personally, his thoughts are always with Germany. Some refugees have adjusted themselves to other countries, have even been fully assimilated. Not so Brecht. He seldom speaks English and that with a strong accent and halting delivery. He has not sought to maintain here the reputation he made for himself in Germany. He waits. He broods. He hopes. And he writes. His writings, as a matter of fact, include almost the only real "literature of exile" that has been written in German since Heine, for the work of other refugees is either a continuation of their former work or anti-Nazi polemic. The inner story of the refugee, the human significance of exile, has been adequately told only by Brecht. As he tells it, it is not an inspiring, not a dramatic story. Its meaning for him is summed up in a quatrain with which he prefaces some recent unpublished poems:

> Dies ist nun alles und ist nicht genug.
> Doch sagt es euch vielleicht, ich bin noch da.
> Dem gleich ich, der den Backstein mit sich trug
> Der Welt zu zeigen, wie sein Haus aussah.

That's the whole story and it's not enough.
And yet it tells you maybe: I'm still there.
I'm like the man who carried a brick with him
To show the world just what his house looked like.

The average reader knows little or no German poetry since Rilke, Stefan George, and Hugo von Hofmannsthal. This is rather like knowing no French poetry since Mallarmé, and makes it hard to explain the position of Brecht in German poetry. In the simplest terms then: he is definitely a *modern* poet—by which I mean one who benefits from the housecleaning of poetry that the Symbolists effected in France; Yeats and Eliot in England; George, Rilke, and Hofmannsthal in Germany. His versification has been influenced by Rimbaud, and he has been compared by Clement Greenberg to Apollinaire and Mayakovsky. On the other hand, Brecht uses—though for his own purposes—many traditional German elements: meter, diction, turns of phrase familiar to readers of Heine or even Hölderlin.

Much of the essential Brecht was already in the "Legend of the Dead Soldier" of 1918. Such lines as

Und die nahmen den Soldaten mit
    Die Nacht war blau und schön
Man konnte, wenn man keinen Helm aufhatte
    Die Sterne der Heimat sehn.

And they took the soldier away with them—
    A bright blue sky was on hand.
When you took your helmet off you could see
    The stars of the Fatherland.

show how counterpointing of rhythm (note the cleverly lengthened third line) is fused with a counterpointing of associations (note the interaction of ballad cliché—"Die Nacht war blau und schön" and "die Sterne der Heimat"—with "wenn man keinen Helm aufhatte"). In the past ten years, however, Brecht has worked out a new style still largely unknown because only to be found in manuscripts, rare magazines, or unavailable editions. The Brecht of the Weimar Republic was known for his brilliant songs, his tricky ballads, his mordant *jeux d'esprit*. The Brecht of Svendborg, Denmark, is ascetic, reticent, delicate, and stoically tender.

Many of the Svendborg poems are rhymeless lyrics in irregular rhythms, yet they are often utterly simple in structure, sometimes close to a quiet sort of poetic epigram:

DER ANSTREICHER SPRICHT VON KOMMENDEN GROSSEN ZEITEN

Die Wälder wachsen noch
Die Aecker tragen noch
Die Städte stehen noch
Die Menschen atmen noch

THE HOUSEPAINTER SPEAKS OF GREAT TIMES TO COME

The woods are still growing.
The fields are still bearing.
The towns are still standing.
People are still breathing.

At other times the rhythms are syncopated, the speech subtly orchestrated, the whole carefully modulated to produce the peculiarly Brechtian combination, unique in German, unusual in any language, of naturalness and stylization, fluency and staccato, suppleness and strength, oil and acid. "It should be remembered," Brecht wrote in an essay on verse technique, "that I have chiefly worked in the theater. I always thought of the spoken language.

And I devised a quite special technique for the spoken word, whether prose or verse. I called it *gestisch.*"

Gestisch is an adjective from *gestus,* which means "gesture," a metaphor that R. P. Blackmur has also applied to poetry, though not in quite the same way. Brecht observes that the gesture of the spoken word is often more effective than that of the written: "If thine eye offend thee, pluck it out" is a better gesture than the more logical "Pluck out the eye that offends thee." This simple observation is the theoretical starting point of Brecht's lyric technique. It is a rhetorical technique, and yet poetic, since his verses are not "free" in the manner of most modern poetry in irregular rhythms. Precision is the hallmark of Brecht's mind, and his rhetoric finds always the *mot juste* and the exact rhythm. When he does not write

> Wie werde ich es im Sommer kühl haben
> Mit so viel Schnee.

—but

> Wie werde ich es im Sommer kühl haben mit
> So viel Schnee.

he writes as rhetorician, metrist, and dramatist. He is not a dramatist who happens to write poems or a poet who happens to write dramas. He is a dramatic poet.

Lest all this should seem an explanation of the unknown by the still more unknown I will give one example of Brecht's later style:

TO THOSE BORN LATER

(1)

These are, indeed, dark times in which I live!
To speak without guile is foolish.

To have an unwrinkled brow bespeaks insensitivity.
To laugh is to be someone who
Has not yet received the
Frightful news.

Times in which conversation about trees is almost
    a crime
Because it includes silence concerning atrocities,
What times these are!
That man there, calmly crossing the street,
Is he perhaps beyond the reach of friends in des-
    perate need?

True, I still earn a living, but
That's an accident, believe me.
Nothing I do gives me the right to eat my fill.
I have been spared by chance.
If my luck gives out, I am lost.
Eat and drink, they tell me, be glad you have it!
But how can I eat and drink when
I take what I eat from someone who's hungry and
    when
Someone who's thirsty goes without my glass of
    water?
Yet I do eat and drink.

How I wish I were wise!
It's in old books what Wise means.
To keep out of world's strife,
To pass the short space without fear,
To survive without resort to violence,
To return good for evil,
Not to fulfill one's wishes but forget them:
This is what Wise means.

All of which I cannot do:
These are, indeed, dark times in which I live!

(2)

I came to the cities in a time of disorder
When hunger reigned there.
I came among men in a time of revolt
And I rose up with the others.
So passed the time that was given me on earth.

I ate my food between battles.
I lay down to sleep among murderers.
I made love without enthusiasm
And looked upon Nature with impatience.
So passed the time that was given me on earth.

The roads in my time led to the swamp.
Speech betrayed me to the butcher.
I could do little, but without me
Rulers would have felt more secure, or so I hoped.
So passed the time that was given me on earth.

One's powers were slight. The goal
Lay in the far, far distance.
It was clearly visible if, also, for me,
Hardly to be reached.
So passed the time that was given me on earth.

(3)

You
You who will be borne up by the flood
In which we
Went down,
Remember too,

When you speak of our weaknesses,
The dark time
You have escaped:
How,
Changing our country more often than our shoes,
We walked through the wars of the classes,
Despairing
When we saw injustice and no rebellion.

Yet this we knew;
Even hatred of baseness distorts the features.
Even anger at injustice makes the voice hoarse.
We, alas,
Who wished to prepare the grounds for kindness
Could not ourselves be kind.

But you
When things reach the point where man
Is no longer a wolf to man
Remember us with
Forbearance.

Many have enjoyed Brecht's plays and left it at that, but did these people—the crowds who flocked to *The Threepenny Opera*—really enjoy anything more than Brecht's biting wit or Kurt Weill's tunes? Brecht has a theory of drama and, if his words are not to be misread and his gestures misinterpreted, the theory must be examined—at least by those who try to judge Brecht's plays from their armchairs.

The history of drama affords many clear examples of the life and death of a form that at first satisfies the needs of the age and later does not. Greek tragedy, for instance, implies a particular attitude to the universe, and to fate in particular, and once that attitude disappeared, the art form that went with it died out. The same is true of Elizabethan tragedy. The tragic view of life has in fact only had any apparent validity at one or two points in history, and attempts to revive it at other points have only yielded such results as the music drama of Wagner and the hortatory exercises of Nietzsche.

The bourgeois epoch has had its own nontragic drama. The serious, noncomic, nontragic drama of Diderot, Lessing, Dumas *fils,* and Ibsen was the major theatrical product of the period and survives today in the well-made Broadway play. It is based on two psychological factors: the *illusion* that the actors are real people and *suspense* used as a magnet by which the interest of the audience is drawn.

This drama Brecht believes to be bankrupt. To it he opposes Epic Theater, a type that lacks the careful centralization of Ibsen, the identification of the spectator with the chief characters, the sympathy—or empathy (*Einfühlung*)—with the fortunes of the protagonist, "all the illusion," as Brecht once put it, "which whips the spectator for two hours and leaves him exhausted and full of vague recollection and vaguer hope." To *Einfühlung* Brecht opposes *Verfremdung,* the making strange or alien, a word we may roughly translate as "distancing." The drama of sympathy, pity, and intimate, largely passive suffering has sacrificed greatness in theater to naturalness, and from Aristotle's "pity and terror" the second term has been either removed or debased to mere sensationalism. We are now—audience, actor, dramatist, director—so far conditioned to the well-made play of pity, sympathy, illusion, and suspense that distance can only be secured by the most drastic means. And Brecht has been drastic.

In a play called *The Measures Taken,* presented in Europe some fourteen years ago, he offered to his audience none of the enticements and titillations that have come to be considered "good theater" but a play that is a study in the same sense as Czerny's studies for the piano, a play therefore that would help to train the audience and the actor in dramatic method (not to mention politics). The scene is a tribunal. Three comrades have returned from China to report on their activities there. In a nondescript setting, with the help of chorus and orchestra, they tell their story by acting it out before the tribunal, playing not only their own roles but those of all who enter into the narrative. This device is characteristic of the Brechtian theater.

The meaning of the device is, in a word, *Verfremdung*. The audience is put at a distance from the events related, is prevented from identifying itself with any character because each actor is all the time shifting roles; it must therefore observe what passes critically and not—as in the older theater—with such excited empathy that it ceases to be conscious of anything but narrative and excitement itself. The characters quote themselves, so to speak, in rehearsing what they formerly experienced, and just as quotation in an essay gives the quoted passage distance, allows one to see it in the different light of a new context, so quotation of whole episodes imparts the required distance to the action of a play. From the simple "quotations" of *The Measures Taken* is but a step to the "quotations" of *The Private Life of the Master Race,* notably in "The Chalk Cross," where the worker gives his real opinions while pretending to act out a game, and in "The Jewish Wife," where the actual conversation of husband and wife, which is so far from explicit, is preceded by a series of "unreal" speeches, namely, three telephone conversations and several interrupted monologues.

Brecht does not claim to have discovered the drama of the future* but to have tried out several types of Epic Theater, one of which is the *Lehrstück* or Didactic Play—*The Measures Taken* is an example—another of which is the Documentary Play, *The Private Life of the Master Race* being a prime instance of this type. These are not experimental plays in the sense in which the term was used twenty years ago. But they are experiments, made in the conviction that drama from Diderot to Ibsen is one completed epoch, and that now we have to go elsewhere, not merely on account of the exhaustion of a technique but also because of changes in society and in men. If we knew the exact nature of these changes we might

---

* See pages 343–44 below.

be able to chart the future of the drama. Guessing, Brecht writes Epic Theater for an audience different from that of Sophocles, which presumably gazed in awe at the workings of inexorable fate, and different from that of Diderot, which wept in sympathy for the unhappy lot of one's neighbor who was also oneself. Greek tragedy demands some pity, some terror, and much impotent contemplation; the older modern drama demands pity and surrender of the self to the current of excitement and suspense; both Greek and modern types confer a kind of catharsis and are, in plain terms, a laxative of the soul. Brecht foreshadows a drama with a different interest and a different result. He sees the dramatist making an analysis of society, not portraits of individuals. He sees the audience as active, inquisitive, noncontemplative, in the spirit of our pragmatic, nonmetaphysical age. A great philosopher of this spirit, William James, found words about music much like Brecht's on drama:

> Even the habit of excessive indulgence in music, for those who are neither performers themselves nor musically gifted enough to take it in a purely intellectual way, has probably a relaxing effect upon the character. One becomes filled with emotions which habitually pass without prompting to any deed, and so the inertly sentimental condition is kept up. The remedy would be, never to suffer oneself to have an emotion at a concert, without expressing it afterward in some active way.

But, besides audience and author, there are two other factors in drama without which there can be no production: acting and staging. The Brechtian theater has few technical demands to make. It needs neither naturalistic paraphernalia nor expressionistic hocus-pocus. Readers of *The Private Life* will see that aside from one extraordinary item—the panzer—the whole thing can be done with platforms, screens, and economical lighting. Nor can much be said of the director in Brechtian production: he must be an artist of intellect, taste, and active, social interests. All the emphasis in Brecht is on the actor, and from him a special technique is required in accordance with the principles of Epic Theater. Again the negative idea is the avoidance both of naturalism and of stylization: all real style is neither stylized nor natural. In a piece by Brecht the actors should be cool but not mannered, accomplished and subtle but not ostentatious and artificial. They should not squander all their art on the single trick of pretending to *be* the character they are portraying; nor, if they are actors at all, can they remain themselves in every role. Modern actors who have been trained in the school of *Einfühlung* will have to give most of their attention to the art of *Verfremdung*.

Such is the Brechtian theater. It has aroused a good deal of opposition among German critics. To Thomas Mann, who once described Brecht as "very gifted, unfortunately," the whole Brechtian world is distasteful. An anonymous writer (it was Hermann Kesten) in Thomas Mann's journal, *Mass und Wert*, raised six specific objections:

1. That Brecht's work is "propaganda for propaganda's sake."
2. That actually *Fear and Misery of the Third Reich* is defeatist.
3. That all Brecht's characters are the same. There is, says the critic, differentiation neither of personality nor of levels of consciousness. The Brechtian drama is flat.
4. "The Brechtian characters are without hate, without love, without ambition or desire for revenge. All Shakespearean passions cease to exist."
5. "His people have no memory either. They are the opposite of Ibsen characters. Everything happens without looking back to the past. There are no cracks through which the past presses in."
6. Brecht claims on the one hand to be scientific, objective, cool; on the other hand he argues for didacticism. The contradiction is complete.

The first two points cancel each other, and the truth behind them is that, while Brecht's drama embodies his own ethics, it does not, like most propagandist art, underestimate the enemy. The third objection is unjust. The characters of *The Private Life* are differentiated psychologically, socially, and—something the translation does not show—regionally. Objection four was perhaps true of Brecht's early plays with their quasi-vegetative, passive people and the atmosphere of dreamy bewilderment, but it has no application to *The Private Life,* as the most casual reader can attest. Objection five also is not quite true of *The Private Life* since many of the characters (see "The Box" and "The Man They Released") are and will be deeply affected by memories. In fact the memory of "the old days" before 1933 is a leitmotiv of the play.

Objection six merely reiterates the fact that Brecht is not Ibsen, Shakespeare, or Sophocles. Brecht is objective *and* didactic in the same way as a doctor. His works are diagnoses; but with the diagnosis come proposals for cure. Of course the objectivity of an artist is not the same as that of a scientist; but among artists Brecht can portray society with rare analytic power and detachment. Compare his Nazis with those of Hollywood. The political proposals of a poet do not have the status of a doctor's prescriptions, but we are surely beyond the stage where we regard concern with practice and politics as something incompatible with objectivity.

I have the impression that Brecht's critics are die-hard defenders of the Ibsen tradition against all comers, and/or that they think Brecht is trying to replace drama that is all *Einfühlung* with drama that is all *Verfremdung.* That is not so. Such a scene as "The Jewish Wife" immediately arouses sympathy and compassion; misinterpretation would arise only if an actress played the scene for these emotions alone. Then the fine balance and interplay between *Einfühlung* and *Verfremdung* that Brecht's theater aims at would be upset, and the result would be a touching but by no means extraordinary one-act play. Aristotle said: pity *and* terror. Brecht says: sympathy *and* distance, attraction *and* repulsion, tenderness *and* horror.

The tension of the two contrary impulsions is the tension—so different from that of suspense—of the Brechtian theater.

The article in *Mass und Wert* is called "The Limits of the Brechtian Theater." Fair enough. Brecht—like all modern artists of any integrity—is content to be limited. Unlike Shakespeare and Sophocles, but not unlike Mann, Rilke, Yeats, Kafka, and the rest, Brecht has his own small tract of territory and sticks to it. Why must one compare him with Shakespeare or even Ibsen? This is not an age of greatness and fulfillment. It is an age of crisis and therefore at best a seedtime, an age of premonition. Brecht's theater consists of hints and premonitions. They must remain hints and premonitions—perhaps even so they sound pretentious—until they can be tried out, rejected, modified, or developed in an environment that offers real opportunity to serious dramatists and serious actors. It is better that they should remain hints and premonitions until they make or break themselves in the theater itself.

No single work of Brecht's is more important than *Fear and Misery of the Third Reich,* of which *The Private Life of the Master Race* is the stage version. Both for its intrinsic merits and for its interest as a portrait and interpretation of Nazi Germany it will probably be his best-known piece. Already it has been published in French by the *Nouvelle Revue Française.* We hear of performances of "The Jewish Wife" before Red soldiers at Leningrad and of a projected movie version by Pudovkin. Yet the piece will be widely misunderstood unless it is interpreted as Epic Theater.

I have heard it said after productions of "The Jewish Wife" and "The Informer" that Brecht "has abandoned his early experimentalism and, like the Soviet dramatists, has returned to naturalism." This opinion is convincing enough to those who have seen these scenes as one-act plays (which they are not), presented out of their context, and acted in the naturalistic manner. But it is wrong. *The Private Life* is Epic Theater, but Epic is not a "pure" type, exclusive of naturalism, expressionism, and all other styles. On the contrary, Epic is of its nature impure and hybrid. The very name is a challenge—like calling drama undramatic. The point was that epic, dramatic, and lyric elements could *all* be used. So could all styles the dramatist needed. The dialogue of the scenes in *The Private Life* is naturalistic, but the play is not naturalism. Within the scenes are many nonnaturalistic devices, such as the "quotations" mentioned above. More important: the spectator cannot be carried along on the surfboard of suspense, since there is no continuous plot, no turning point, no centerpiece of any sort. He might as well sit back, self-possessed but emotionally and intellectually alert, to take note of the succession of historical documents that constitute the play. The framework, with its recitations, songs, and placards, is not meant to provide an illusion of unified structure. It is a system of interruptions that break up the play into the atomic elements of which it consists. Interruption is for Brecht a dramatic device of the first importance.

Brecht's audience must be intellectually alert, but the alertness is not that required by the untheatrical Poetic Theater, which an audience has to strain every nerve to follow. It is an alertness much commoner in everyone's experience than the sweaty, emotional indulgence of the sensationally dramatic. It is the alertness of everyday curiosity, discussion, and activity. The facts are such and such; if they are presented with a lively appreciation of contradiction and dialectic in the material, and a lively appreciation of the moral urgency of the problems, the audience may not be intoxicated—intoxication produces first irrational behavior and then sleep—but they will be awakened and enlivened. Perhaps Brechtian plays are propaganda, but they are very different from the "passionate indictments" that have had such a vogue in the theater of the past generation.

Drama with so much theory attached to it, drama with so strong a didactic flavor, drama so analytic, objective, circumstantial, so lacking in thrills and "human" sympathy—is it a bore? It is a bore to those who are so busy observing the lack of Ibsenite qualities that they cannot observe the Brechtian qualities. And since Brechtian qualities are frequently more authentically good theater than those that pass for such, one can but regret the fact that Brecht has to be given to the public only in book form with a long theoretical exegesis. A man laughs somewhere at the back of the theater, a grotesque, half-hysterical laugh. His neighbors, snatched out of their trance, look angrily round and hiss: "Sh!" But in a Brecht performance such a man is usually right. The scenes set up the strangest pressures. There is a constant pulling this way and that (read "In Search of Justice"), and the result may very well be grotesque laughter. Brecht's repudiation of the sentimental theater is not a repudiation of theater.

The reader of *The Private Life of the Master Race* should regard himself as the director of the play. Then he will interpret the Horst Wessel verses not as Brecht's poetry but as a Nazi song, the Woman's Voice not as declamation but as ballad, the verses of The Voice as dramatic commentary. In the theater of the mind, he will supply the rumbling of the panzer, the strange vision of the twelve soldiers, the many pictures of Misery and Fear. Without stylization the Brechtian drama seeks to give back to gestures something of the force they have lost through the "naturalness" of current fashion. Repeatedly a hand jumps half-clenched to the face, a head turns abruptly round: what is wrong? It is the Fear of the Third Reich. Repeatedly a figure stands limp and still: it is the Misery of the Third Reich. Some scenes are conceived almost entirely in plastic terms—"Physicists," for instance, in which the whole effect is that of nervous movement, sudden opening of doors, speaking so as not to be overheard, speaking so as to *be* overheard. This is pure theater in the best, though not in the Broadway, sense. So is that special invention of Brecht's—doubtless suggested by movies—the tiny but complete scene of five or six lines. Where did Dumas, or even Ibsen, show a finer economy of means than Brecht in "The Two Bakers"? The style is new, to many, puzzling at first, to some, flat as a text for reading. But the cumulative effect can be dramatically every bit as strong as the unilinear development of a well-made play.

The effect is one of sheer accumulation. In Part One we see workers shortly after the Nazis came to power: a worker betraying a comrade, a worker debating with an S.A. man, workers in a concentration camp, in a factory, at home. We see the strength of the Nazis, and in "Prisoners Mix Cement" we see their opponents united, but too late. In Part Two we see several segments of German bourgeois life: scientists, judges, doctors, teachers. The picture is dark, sustained in longer scenic units, a masterly sequence of analyses. Part Three recovers the swift tempo of Part One in a series of quick shots of Misery and Fear, extending the analysis of Germany from one cell in the social organism to another until, in the final scene, Hitler enters Vienna.

But this is not the adventurous story of the rise of a villain-hero. The story is framed, "distanced" by being presented in retrospect. The date is 1941. The rise of Hitler is now only a "story"; but in Hitler's first five years of power—depicted in the inset scenes—is the whole truth of his career. To tell this story rather than that of 1938 to 1941 is further evidence of Brecht's desire to present beginnings, causes, essentials, rather than ramifications, spectacular results. The play ends with the Nazis singing of failure to the tune of their victory hymn. What should one feel when the play is over? Not, certainly, "full of vague recollection and vaguer hope," but more critical, more aware, not as one is more critical and aware after reading a blue book but as one feels after a perusal of Goya's *Disasters of War.* Here is the record, with Goya's almost *demure* superscriptions, the record presented with the matter-of-factness of a genius who does not need to shout and of a subject that renders exaggeration unthinkable. I sometimes wonder if the French title of Brecht's work is not the best: *Scènes de la Vie Hitlérienne.*

From Strindberg to Brecht
1946

> ...misunderstood naturalism...believed that art con-
> sists in reproducing a piece of nature in a natural way.
> But...the greater naturalism...seeks out the points
> where great battles take place.
>
> —AUGUST STRINDBERG

I tried to work up the brief discussions of Lucullus *and* Master Race
*into general introductions to Brecht—not without evident strain. A bet-
ter occasion was provided by the context in my first book on drama,* The
Playwright as Thinker. *I saw two traditions in the whole twentieth-
century movement, the naturalistic and the antinaturalistic (romantic,
surreal, and so on). Strindberg was the fountainhead of both, and Brecht
was the very latest thing in the first of these traditions. The only nov-
elty, in these classifications, was the prominence given to Brecht. Reread-
ing this chapter recently, I was happiest about two features: the sharp
contrast drawn between Brecht and Erwin Piscator and, secondly, the
mention here (possibly the first in an English-language book) of* The
Last Days of Mankind *by Karl Kraus. Piscator said the passage about
him was a Steckbrief—an informer's letter, calculated to get him in trouble with the police. But this assertion proved to be bluster and gave way
to sweet talk as soon as I accepted Piscator's invitation to debate with him
at his workshop in New York. Kraus's works I had learned to know
through Viertel and his friend Heinrich Jalowetz: "Jalo" had brought all
Kraus's books with him from Nazi Germany, and we used to sit in his*

Black Mountain cottage studying Kraus Talmudically—word by diffi-cult word expounded to me by a "rabbi."

WHEN ONE OF THE BEST JUDGES of drama said that the more original playwrights of the twenties "start completely afresh," he listed only antirealists. The antirealists always get all the credit for originality. Actually the realists were just as much in revolt. In a sense they were twice as much in revolt, since they rejected not only the antirealistic styles—such as expressionism—but the es-tablished naturalistic styles of the 1890s. They wanted to be more naturalistic still.

Of all the attempts to bring onto the stage even more of life, even less embellished by histrionics, Epic Theater is probably the most far-reaching. And though the ideas of Epic Theater may be known in America, if at all, by way of certain productions of the Federal Theater, by way of the Living Newspapers in which Arthur Arent presented the current news by means of actors, by way of certain things in Marc Blitzstein, Paul Green, Thornton Wilder, it is still necessary to go back to some of the main sources of these phenomena, not just because they are sources but because they are the purest and often the best examples of the genre. It is necessary, in short, to investigate the work and habitat of Bertolt Brecht, the unacknowledged fountainhead of so much in the the-ater of the past twenty years. For even the best imitations of Brecht—such as the rather sketchy extravaganzas of W. H. Auden and Christopher Isherwood—are no index to the original.

The seedbed of Epic Theater was that strange, seething, pre-carious state of affairs—the culture of the Weimar Republic. Al-though Epic did not make such a noise in the world as did expressionism, it nevertheless began with the first flush of a new modernism immediately after the First World War. Even before that critics had spoken of the *Episierung des Dramas*—the making-over of drama into epic—when Gerhart Hauptmann wrote his episodic *Die Weber* (*The Weavers*). The naturalism of the 1890s was a first step toward Epic, for the general loosening of form brought many dramas into existence that were narrative rather than "well-made plays." The three-volume play *Die letzten Tage der Menschheit* (*The Last Days of Mankind*), written by the great Viennese satirist Karl Kraus during the First World War, is a giant Epic Drama of war and peace. When the early twenties are thoroughly chronicled, many kindred phenomena will be found.

One therefore takes with a pinch of salt the assumption made by Erwin Piscator in his book *Das politische Theater* (*The Political Theater*) that Epic Theater was invented by him. But I do not mean to belittle his services to the theater. His work illustrates better than anything else the "starting completely afresh" that the realistic theater, the theater of the outer world, undertook at the same time as the theater of the inner world. To comprehend just how far the repudiation of the play, the unified drama, could go in favor of Epic slices of life one must follow Mr. Piscator's own account.

According to *Das politische Theater*, the first Epic Drama was a production of Piscator's in 1924 at which he used (in addition to actors) films and placards. There is a record in the book of another 1924 production entitled *Revue Roter Rummel* (*The Rowdy Red Revue*), which Piscator composed and executed with the one Gasbarra, "whom," he writes, "the Party had sent me." An eyewitness account is provided:

> It was a pilgrimage for the masses. As we approached, hundreds were standing in the street and vainly trying to get in. Workers exchanged blows to get seats. In the hall everything full and jam-packed. The air enough to make you faint. But faces beamed—on fire for the start of the production. Music. The lights go out. Silence. In the audience two men are quarreling. People are shocked. The dispute continues in the gangway. The footlights are switched on and the disputants appear before the curtain.

> They are two workmen talking about their situation. A Gentleman in a top hat steps up. Bourgeois. He has his own *Weltanschauung* and invites the disputants to spend an evening with him. Up with the curtain! First scene. Now it goes snip-snap. Ackerstrasse—Kurfürstendamm. Tenements—cocktail bars. Porter resplendent in blue and gold—a begging war cripple. Fat paunch and thick watch chain. Match vendors and collectors of cigarette stubs. Swastika—Vehm murders—*Was machst du mit dem Knie—Heil dir im Siegerkranz* [popular song and patriotic anthem]. Between the scenes: Screen, movie, statistical figures, pictures! More scenes. The begging war veteran is thrown out by the porter. A crowd gathers in front of the place. Workmen rush in and destroy the cocktail bar. The audience cooperates. What a whistling, shouting, milling...unforgettable!

But there is method in Piscator's callowness. Let us look at the program of *Trotz Alledem* (*For All That*), 1925, when "the Communist Party told us to arrange a production in the Grosses Schauspielhaus on the Berlin Party Day." This production was a historical review in twenty-four scenes with films in between:

> Scene 1: Berlin expecting war. Potsdam Square.
> Scene 2: Meeting of the Social Democratic Section of the Reichstag, July 25, 1914.
> Scene 3: In the Kaiser's Castle, Berlin, August 1, 1914...

After the final scene comes "the rising of the proletariat: Liebknecht lives!" and a chorus in which the audience joins. Although the whole thing is more of a demonstration than a drama, the temper and the method of a new realism—narrative realism—is here suggested. This is one of Brecht's starting points. Others are indicated in Piscator's perhaps rather bumptious remarks, directed against both expressionism and its contrary: "Not man's relation to himself, not his relation to God, but his relation to society is the main issue." And again: "No longer the individual with his private, personal destiny, but the age itself, the destiny of the masses is the heroic factor of the new dramaturgy." Above all: "Authors must learn to grasp the material in all its factuality, the drama of the great simple phenomena of life. The theater demands naïve, direct, uncomplicated, unpsychological effects."

One should acknowledge that Piscator failed, as much as Reinhardt, to make headway beyond a certain point. He continued the unhappy tradition of making the director—himself—the central figure in the theater. While at one moment he pleads that this is because he cannot find any good dramatists, at another he registers a determination not to accept completed scripts but to hand out material to authors and have them dramatize it along with him in the theater. This sounds chummy, but it would be really mischievous if the dramatist happened to be good. Piscator's book closes with the avowal that the theater has to be remodeled in its outlook, its dramaturgy, its architecture, and its technique, but that this cannot be done before the revolution. The masses under capitalism evidently do not wish to pay for a Piscator theater, and he is on the rocks just as if he had frankly addressed himself to the intelligentsia.

Today Piscator's work is interesting as a prelude to Brecht. The root idea of Brecht's Epic Theater is expressed in the name. Of the three types of literature—epic, dramatic, and lyric—the first two are to be fused, and Brecht has no objection to admitting the lyrical element too. This is against all the laws of the elders. Most older critics insisted on keeping the three types separate, just as college-educated movie critics today believe that the movies should be epic and that the drama should be—dramatic. There have long been those who favor separation of the genres; there have also been those who favor mingling. (In all spheres racial purity and cross-fertilization are rival allegiances.) There have long been two types of dramatic structure too: the open, diffuse play that starts early in the narrative and proceeds through it in many scenes and, on the other hand, the closed, concentrated play that has a late point of attack and lets us look back on the story from its climax—which is the play. In modern times we have been so schooled to respect the latter method—the method of Scribe, Dumas, and Ibsen—that it is regarded as "dramatic method" *pur sang*. Teachers of playwriting teach it as such. Critics of the novel have it in mind when they write of the dramatic type of novel. Indeed when we hear people saying that it was impudent of Shakespeare not to adopt the method, it is time to call a halt. Shakespeare's predecessors shared the impudence, and if the Greeks used the late point of attack they certainly had little else of the "dramatic method," which is found in its entirety only in the modern "well-made play" and—perhaps—in French classical tragedy. Most dramatic masterpieces are, therefore, by this criterion, undramatic. The Greeks and the French use long Epic narrations. Shakespeare's open structure is copied by all his imitators from Goethe to Hugo. Brecht's Epic procedure is this open structure.

But Epic Theater is more than a particular style of architecture. It drops other features of the Ibsenite play. The latter was built around a center, a crisis. Its unfolding was a gathering of clouds, its climax a thunderclap. With this pattern goes identification of the spectator with a protagonist, which presupposes a high degree of *illusion* as to his reality and a high degree of *suspense* in the telling of the tale. We have seen* how the process of ever greater and greater concentration proceeded as far as Strindberg's *Creditors* and *Miss Julie,* of which latter Strindberg wrote that he had eliminated all act and scene divisions because "... I have come to fear that our decreasing capacity for illusion might be unfavorably affected by intermissions during which the spectator would have time to re-

---

* In *The Playwright as Thinker.*

flect and to get away from the suggestive influence of the author-hypnotist." This pattern has not been much affected by modern experiments prior to Brecht. Expressionism abandons natural appearances but attempts to elicit an even more compelling drive of sympathetic emotion. It is obvious that dream and nightmare plays intensify the emotional participation of the audience in the play. We can best see the contrast between Epic Theater and earlier experimentalism by keeping the theory of Epic in mind while reading Nicolas Evreinov's account of his monodrama, an experimental form often regarded as the furthest departure from orthodoxy. In monodrama there is only one character to a play:

> The task of monodrama is to carry the spectator to the very stage so that he will feel that he is acting himself...The "I," the acting character, is a bridge from the auditorium to the stage...The spectator must know from the program with whom the author invites him to have a common life, in whose image he himself must appear...Monodrama forces every one of the spectators to enter the situation of the acting character, to live his life, that is to say, to feel as he does and through illusion to think as he does...in the end it must be clear to the dramatist that if he wishes to represent the life of the spirit, he must deal not with external realities but with the internal reflections of the real objects, because for the psychology of a given person his subjective perception of the real object is important but not the object in a relation indifferent to him...

Evreinov's monodrama is the furthest possible reach of the drama of individual psychology, the spirit, the subjective element, and it is coupled with a higher degree of "identification" than had ever before been demanded. If this "theater of myself" is at one extreme, Brecht is at the other. The following chart, made by Brecht himself, lets us see this:

The "Dramatic" Theater:	*The Epic Theater:*
the stage embodies a sequence of events	the stage narrates the sequence
involves the spectator in an action and	makes him an observer but
uses up his energy, his will to action	awakes his energy
allows him feelings	demands decisions
communicates experiences	communicates pieces of knowledge
spectator is brought into an action	is placed in front of an action
is plied with suggestion	with arguments
sensations are preserved	till they become insights
man is given as a known quantity	man an object of investigation
man unalterable	alterable and altering
tense interest in the outcome	tense interest in what happens
one scene exists for another	each scene exists for itself
linear course of events	curved course of events
natura non facit saltus	*facit saltus*
the world is what it is	the world is what it is becoming
what man should	what man must
his instincts	his reasons
thought determines reality	social reality determines thought

The facts before us already are sufficient to indicate that Epic Theater is realistic in a broad sense and is also a radical departure from most familiar types of drama. If Wagnerism is behind the antirealistic dramaturgies, it is interesting to find that Brecht protests against the *Schmelzprozess* by which Wagner merges one art with another, thus forfeiting the individuality of each. Brecht demands singers who will act and narrate the piece and not pour forth their souls, "which," he says, "are a private matter." For Brechtian Epic Opera the orchestra will be small and disciplined. It is distinguished from Wagnerian opera as follows:

Wagnerism:	*Epic Opera:*
the music enlivens	the music communicates
music heightening the text	music expounding the text
music asserting the text	music taking the text for granted
music illustrating	music taking a stand
music painting the psychic situation	music indicating behavior

The fact that Brecht is not a Wagnerite does not make him a Zolaist. Zola had been known for his emphasis on determinism by heredity and environment and, secondarily, for a theory of presentation according to which everything onstage must seem real. Indeed dramatic critics often mean by the term *naturalism* nothing more than a staging in which everything possible is done to create the illusion that a play is not a play but a slice of life. Real furniture and real beer replaced canvas and empty glasses. On the stage actors imitated the speech and deportment of men in the street. Playwrights cooperated by eliminating soliloquies, asides, songs, and other "interruptions."

By these tests Brecht is not a naturalist at all. Epic staging and acting are not in the manner of Antoine. They seek to destroy precisely the *illusion* of actuality that was the latter's chief aim. The Epic stage is artificial: instead of assembling on the stage real rooms, buildings, and their furniture, it uses slides, charts, film projections, simultaneous scenes, and tableaux rolled across the stage on treadmills. Brechtian acting is anti-illusory. The actor must not pretend to *be* the character. He must play the role from the outside, not—as the expressionists demanded—in a stylized and unindividual manner, but with as much finesse as Stanislavsky himself could have wished. The playwright, for his part, brings back choric commentary by introducing narrators, songs, soliloquies, and other "interruptive" devices.

Brecht is not a naturalist; but he is a realist. He wishes to be as faithful as possible to objective facts. Precisely because he has abandoned the fourth wall theory of presentation, which contrary to the conscious intention of its upholders tended to make a dream world of reality, Brecht is able to be more, not less, of a realist than the Zola of *Thérèse Raquin*. Zola's naturalistic theater, dedicated to actuality, was a theater of illusion, phantasmagoria, and—it might even be maintained—escape. It differed from its ostensible opposite, neoromanticism, in that one escaped to an ugly not to a beautiful island. Now the "unrealistic" elements in Epic staging are all devoted to imparting a greater sense of the actual world. They say to the audience: "The actual world exists and it is our subject. But this play and this stage are not identical with it." Zolaism, by saying, "The action on the stage is not a play at all but real life," created what an Epic dramatist would consider a sophisticated form of illusion, unnaturalness, and theatricality.

Negatively in its repudiation of the realm of dream and subjectivity, positively in its primary concern with the external, social world and the forces that move it, Epic Theater, though not realistic, is in the broad tradition that I have called realism. If expressionism and neoromanticism were a rebound from the earlier naturalism, Epic Theater was a rebound from the new romanticism and expressionism. If the earlier naturalism came in with the discovery of the "true meaning of life" in Darwinist science, the later Epic Theater came in with the discovery of the "true meaning of life" in Marxist "science." "Today," says Brecht, "when the human being must be grasped as the totality of social relationships, only the Epic form can enable the dramatist to find a comprehensive image of the world. The individual, precisely the flesh and blood individual, can be understood only by way of the processes wherein and whereby he exists. The new dramaturgy must acquire a form which will not make use of throbbing suspense, but will have a suspense in the relationship of its scenes which will charge each other with tension. This form will therefore be anything but a stringing together of scenes such as we find in revues."

Only the Epic form will do! Like his opposite number, Cocteau, who says that "pure" theater should be the only kind, Brecht mars his highly interesting suggestions with dogmatism and oversimplification. His defense of the theater of objectivity, for instance, is as ingenuous as Piscator's. In one essay he goes so far as to complain of the fact that "until now the theater has been a medium for the self-expression of the artist"! Unlike the language of the scientist, he continues, "dramatic imagery has sought rather to construct an independent world of emotion—to organize subjective sensations." Brecht assumes that the drama of subjectivity is very easy to manage: "for this purpose neither accuracy nor responsibility is required." Luckily, after all these centuries of inaccuracy and irresponsibility, salvation is at hand:

> In recent decades, however, a new kind of theater has developed—one which sets itself the goal of an accurate picture of the world . . . The artist who belongs to this theater no longer attempts to create his world . . . His purpose is to create images informative of the [external] world rather than of himself . . . The artist must refashion his whole method to suit a new purpose.
>
> The visionary ignores discoveries made by others; the desire for experiment is not among the mental traits of the seer. Unlike the visionary and the seer, the artist in pursuit of a new goal finds no subliminal apparatus ready

> to serve him. The inner eye has never needed microscope
> or telescope. The outer eye needs both.

Brecht assumes here that the individual self is only a repulsive "subliminal apparatus," a source of foolish visions and dangerous illusions. Even if it were, that would be no reason for ignoring it; if the artist's mind is so strange a beast, it should be put under close observation. Obviously Brecht is either parroting the claptrap of scientism or giving vent to that hatred of the self that is the root of all too much of the altruism and social conscience of our time. Even more than Bernard Shaw, Brecht habitually overstates any proposition that is serviceable to his art. Such a passage as I have just quoted should in itself be proof that Epic theory cannot always be taken literally. It does not even square with Brecht's practice. He does not eliminate stage-illusion and suspense: he only reduces their importance. Sympathy and identification with the characters are not eliminated: they are counterpoised by deliberate distancing.

"The effect of genius," said Longinus, two thousand years ago, "is not to persuade or convince the audience, but rather to transport them out of themselves . . . The object of poetry is to enthrall." Brecht says: "I do not like plays to contain pathetic overtones, they must be convincing like court pleas. The main thing is to teach the spectator to reach a verdict." Well: it is legitimate that some of the purposes of poetry should change in two thousand years, but one doubts if they have really changed as much as Brecht suggests. The modern drama has been much more inclined to persuade and convince than has premodern drama; nor am I one of those who regret it. But, like Shaw's criticism of Shakespeare, Brecht's denunciation of pathetic overtones has more significance as an attack on contemporary sentimentalism than it has literal truth. It is not really necessary to pulverize Euripides, Shakespeare, and Racine—the masters of pathetic overtones—in order to scold Sudermann and Barrie.

The disproof of Brecht's theory is Brecht's practice. His art makes up for his criticism. In his art there is stage-illusion, suspense, sympathy, identification. The audience is enthralled and the highly personal genius of Brecht finds expression. The apparently "objective" presentation of facts is for Brecht, as it was for Zola, an opportunity for individual and "subjective" expression. I do not mean that Brecht and Zola are in the end as subjective as Sartre and Evreinov. I mean that no work of art is wholly "objective" or "subjective." It is a matter of emphasis. In his theoretic pronouncements Brecht carries the realistic emphasis to an extreme impossible in practice. It follows that his practice must be either a catalogue of failures or inconsistent with the theory. The latter is the truth. Brecht is a realist, but nonrealistic elements are of more and more importance as his art develops.

The dramatic art of Brecht has so far gone through four phases. In the first, his apprenticeship, he took up the problems of the theater where Strindberg and Wedekind left them, that is to say, he had to think through the whole question of form almost from scratch. To help himself in this task he studied, and made adaptations from, Chinese, Elizabethan, and Spanish plays; and before the end of the twenties he had written four outstanding original works. Two were plays in a style of highly personal realism, two were operettas equally idiosyncratic. Only the last of all these to be written—his version of *The Beggar's Opera*—is fully developed Epic Theater.

If the first phase is cynical and brilliant and very much of the twenties, the second is stark and solemn and very much of the thirties. If the works of the twenties permitted critics to dismiss Brecht as a cabaret wit, the works of the thirties permitted them to dismiss him as an "artist in uniform," a "minstrel of the GPU." Though Brecht's bleakest, most barren works belong to this second period, so also does his *Saint Joan of the Stockyards,* a rich satire and a kind of prelude to the third phase, the first years of exile from Germany, during which Brecht wrote two full-scale dramatic fantasies (*Round Heads, Peak Heads*—and *Arturo Ui*) about the Nazi movement. Two other works of the third phase are *Mother Courage* and *Fear and Misery of the Third Reich.* In the first, Brecht withdrew from the current struggle to compose another Epic play in verse and prose, in song and monosyllabic conversation, a sardonic and circumstantial record, suggested by the seventeenth-century writer Grimmelshausen, of the process of war. In *Fear and Misery,* Brecht and the Third Reich are for the first time face-to-face. The title is a parody of Balzac's *Glory and Misery of the Courtesans,* and the work itself—a portrait of one cell after another in the social organism—is a German and a twentieth-century *comédie humaine* in miniature. In a series of over twenty scenes, unconnected by characters or plot, connected only by theme, the people of Hitler's Germany are revealed. Between the scenes a choric voice is heard, and (in the shorter stage version) a group of Nazi soldiers sings Brecht's words to the tune of their party hymn at the beginning and end of each act.

Though the narrative structure, the interruptions, and many other technical devices are Epic, one of Brecht's most friendly critics has suggested that in general the play need not be taken as Epic but can be interpreted as good drama with no theoretical strings attached. Certainly the more mature experimentalism of this play is able to draw on established methods much more than could the severe Epic plays in which Brecht first tried out his ideas. Such a scene as "The Jewish Wife" is in the nineteenth-century tradition and would have been accepted by Antoine for the Théâtre Libre. *Fear and Misery* is the *fullest* of the plays of the thirties. Its new use of realism, of strong situation, tableau, innuendo, charade, should prove to those who feared the contrary that Brecht is willing not only to exclude established forms and ideas from his theater but also to bring them back again in new ways.

The two most interesting plays of Brecht's latest, fourth manner—*The Good Woman of Setzuan* and *The Caucasian Chalk Circle*—are moralities "showing what kind of things a man chooses or avoids." They are both parables in Eastern settings and somewhat in the manner of Chinese theater. Both are Epic in their dramaturgy: the main story is framed, in one play by a singer and a chorus who act as narrators, in the other by alternate scenes in which the gods discuss the action. From time to time characters talk directly to the audience. There is suspense, but it is minimized. Each scene is interesting for itself and not as preparation...

The Good Woman of Setzuan tells how three of the gods come down to earth to learn if there is any goodness in human beings. They begin by looking for someone hospitable enough to offer them a night's lodging, and find nobody but the little Chinese prostitute Shen Te. She proves indeed to be the only human being who is thoroughly good, and the rest of the story is that of her life after the gods set her up in a little store with money of her own.

Very soon Shen Te finds herself imposed upon by the unscrupulous poor. A family of eight dumps itself on her doorstep. She finds that the store is in a bad location, that the rent is too high, that the tradesmen swindle her. Who is to pay her bills? Shen Te is hustled by her housemates into inventing a cousin named Shui Ta who is to settle her debts. Our surprise when a Shui Ta arrives and does so is mitigated by the discovery (made by the audience only) that he is Shen Te wearing a mask. At first Shui Ta is intended to be only a temporary helper. When he arranges for the marriage of Shen Te to the wealthy barber Shu Fu it seems that his services can be dispensed with. But no. The young flier Yang Sun, too poor to pursue the art of flying, unable to get a job, is about to hang himself from a willow tree when Shen Te sees him and falls in love. They agree to marry. Although Shui Ta discovers that Yang is marrying chiefly for money, Shen Te does not seem able to resist him. Only at the last moment, when she is certain that Yang Sun will prevent her paying her debts in order to satisfy his ambitions with her money, does she draw back.

Returning to meet her monetary needs alone, and finding herself pregnant, Shen Te again calls upon Shui Ta, who rapidly becomes a Tobacco King, a successful capitalist paying starvation wages and overcrowding the living quarters of his workers. Beginning at the bottom, Yang Sun works his way up in Shui Ta's factory until he is a manager. Meanwhile Shen Te's time grows near. The waistline of Shui Ta is seen to expand. Yang Sun hears a woman's sobbing in Shui Ta's room and feels sure that Shen Te is imprisoned there. Shui Ta is brought before a court of justice to account for his cousin's disappearance.

In the final scene of the play the three gods act as Shui Ta's judges. Shen Te recognizes them. Asking for the court to be cleared, she removes her mask and confesses all. But the judges are not angry. They are glad to find their one good human being again:

> THE FIRST GOD: Say no more, unhappy woman! What are
>   we to think, we who are so glad to have found you again!
> SHEN TE: But I must tell you that I am the bad man whose
>   misdeeds have been reported to you by everybody here!
> THE FIRST GOD: The good man whose good deeds have
>   been reported by everybody!
> SHEN TE: No, the bad man too!

Shen Te is desperate. How is she to go on living? What about her baby? The gods are not worried. "Only be good and all will be well," is their parting counsel. Hymning the praises of the good woman of Setzuan, they ascend into heaven on a pink cloud.

In other words, it is impossible to be good, in the traditional sense of altruistic, gentle, loving, in a world that lives by egoism, rapacity, and hate. A Christian might argue: "You can't change the world. All you can do is to exercise the Christian virtues in your own small circle." Brecht replies: "This is topsy-turvy reasoning. Your small circle is no circle but a segment of a large circle. The segment has no independence. It can move only when the whole circle moves. *Only* by altering the world can goodness become practical." Shen Te wished to be kind. But on one occasion she finds herself allowing an old couple to be ruined because she does not pay her debt to them. On another occasion she will not help a poor man to find redress for an injury willfully inflicted by the barber Shu Fu because at the time she is trying to win Shu Fu's lucrative hand. In order to survive, the good girl needs the assistance of the brutal exploiter. And when she appeals to the gods she receives as answer: "Are we to confess that our laws are lethal? Are we to repudiate our laws? Never! Is the world to be changed? How? By whom? No: everything is all right."

The theme of *The Good Woman of Setzuan* is not hard to grasp. Clarity is the first requisite of didacticism. The surprising thing is the way Brecht makes his lessons into works of art. Obviously there were many ways of bungling the treatment of the Setzuan story. It could lose force through being too quaint and charming. It could fall short of art if the allegory were too earnest and ponderous or if the propaganda were too eager and importunate. Brecht manages to escape these pitfalls, and the result is something entirely new in didactic theater. Although the message is firm and sharp, it is not coaxed into us by pathos or thrown at us in anger. It is worked out by craftsmanship, that is, by Epic procedure and Brechtian characterization. The dialogue, delicate but not quaint, strong but not heavy, poetic but not decorative, is diversified with songs such as only the poet Brecht could write. The mock naïveté, the speeches to the audience, the witty exchanges, the Chinese conventions, go to make a rich texture and a rapid tempo. The big scenes in the grand manner—such as the wedding (which never takes place) of Shen Te and the final trial scene—give the piece a dignity and a spaciousness that Brecht has perhaps only once before achieved—in his biographical play *Galileo*.

The Caucasian Chalk Circle opens with a discussion of the rights to a piece of land between two groups of Russians who return to it after the Nazis have been driven out. The question is: upon what principle should the question be settled? The main action of the play is an answer to the question.

During a civil war the Governor's baby is abandoned by its mother (who is more interested in saving her fine clothes) and brought up by the servant girl Grusha. Like Shen Te, Grusha is driven into wrong actions by necessity. To guarantee the child a respectable home and a decent upbringing, above all to free the child from being thought her bastard, she consents to marry. After all, she can say to herself, the prospective husband is dying. Unfortunately the latter turns out to be very much alive, and when Grusha's sweetheart returns from the wars he finds her married and—apparently—a mother. Without giving her a chance to tell him the whole story he leaves in despair. Her "bad" marriage, entered upon with "good" motives, is having mixed results: bad for itself, bad for her lover, good for the child. There are five acts, and this is the end of the third.

The fourth act is the story of an eccentric low character named Azdak. The vicissitudes of civil war make this almost Shakespearean rogue into a judge. He passes the most unusual judgments—in a case of rape he holds the woman responsible on account of her alluring buttocks—but they always favor simple folk and not their exploiters. Act 5 is the comedy of Azdak in his capacity of judge under the rebel government. Later the original government is restored and, since Azdak has by chance saved the life of one of its high officials, he is reappointed judge under the restored regime. One of the cases before him is that of Grusha, charged with having stolen the late Governor's child. Azdak places the governor's wife and Grusha in a chalk circle with the child; they are both to take hold of it; the one who pulls hardest and gets the child out of the circle wins the lawsuit. The mother pulls violently and wins. Whereupon Azdak reverses the decision and gives the child to Grusha, who loves the child too much to do it harm. He also gives her a divorce so that she can marry her sweetheart and all can end happily. The chorus states the principle

> that what there is
> shall belong to those who are good for it, thus
> the children to the motherly that they prosper

the carts to good drivers that they are well driven
and the valley to the waterers that it bring forth
    fruit.

Henry James said: "When vigorous writers have reached maturity, we are at liberty to gather from their works some expression of a total view of the world they have been so actively observing. This is the most interesting thing their works offer us." And since some such assumption has underlain my investigation of our greatest modern playwrights—Ibsen, Shaw, and Strindberg—I think it applicable also to Brecht. The political Brecht is a socialist. Beneath the socialist is what we might call the Confucian—by which I mean that Brecht's economic interpretation of human life, his materialism, is at the service of a finely humane, ironic, salty appreciation of normal experience. When he defends the normal, the ordinary, and the common, he is not therefore championing vulgarity and mediocrity; he is championing human nature. It is this that makes the average socialist writing appear bourgeois by comparison.

It was complained against some of Brecht's early plays that the people in them were unheroic and unsaintly, unsatanic also and therefore "undramatic." Their life had none of the memories of the high purposes of life in Shakespeare or Ibsen. There may have been justice in the complaint, but the point is that Brecht does not find "vegetative" life, that is, common, happy-go-lucky experience, disgusting, as did the elegant critics of the Weimar Republic.

An meiner Wand hängt ein japanisches Holzwerk
Maske eines bösen Dämons, bemalt mit Goldlack.
Mitfühlend sehe ich
Die geschwollenen Stirnadern, andeutend
Wie anstrengend es ist, böse zu sein.

On my wall hangs a Japanese woodcarving
Mask of an evil demon, painted over with gold.

Pityingly I see
The swollen veins of his brow intimating
How great a strain it is to be evil.

It is hard to be bad, evil is a mask, it is natural to be good. Although in a world of injustice and error, it is not easy to be natural—in fact it is impossible, as we learn in *The Good Woman of Setzuan*—that is no disproof of the original proposition. Before we can be natural again, before we can be good, there will be much struggle, and we ourselves will have swollen veins; that is the political problem. Its presupposition is a Rousseauistic belief in the natural, an almost Chinese willingness to rejoice in vegetative life.

Not that satisfaction in the processes of life is enough. Brecht represents goodness also as dynamic. "Great is the temptation of goodness," sings the chorus in *The Chalk Circle* as Grusha makes up her mind to save the governor's child whatever the cost to herself. Temptation indeed! An almost futile temptation is a society where justice can be done only through flukes and eccentricities, only through the canny, queer horse sense of the wise fool Azdak. Yet despite the fact that "goodness is impossible" the Grushas and the Shen Tes exist and from time to time succumb to the fatal "temptation of goodness."

The real character of Brecht might be illuminated by comparison with Jean-Paul Sartre, a comparison of Epic Theater, the theater of the outer eye, with Existential Theater, the theater of the inner eye. There is a basis for comparison in that, of the plays analyzed here,[*] one by each playwright gives a picture of things as they are and should not be (*No Exit* and *The Good Woman of Setzuan*), and each playwright (*The Flies* and *The Caucasian Chalk Circle*) shows the working out of positive and right moral principles. The differences are obvious. The starting point is different, the atmosphere is dif-

---

[*] In *The Playwright as Thinker*.

ferent, the philosophical background is different, the style is different, the emphasis is different. Brecht, I imagine, might easily think of Sartre as—in Arthur Koestler's terminology—a yogi, a believer in change purely from within, and Sartre might easily think of Brecht as a commissar, a believer in change purely from without.

We have to hope that both would be wrong. Sartre's Zarathustrian exile is no escape. His Orestes is, on the contrary, utterly engagé, the self-fulfillment is for him a moral and social as well as a personal and spiritual thing. We can see too that Brecht does not always set up society as an abstraction against the individual. His aim is to change the world so that the goodness of a Shen Te can come into effective existence. His preoccupation is the amiable common humanity of a water carrier, the unsung heroism of a member of the underground who has to accept ostracism with a good grace after he returns from the concentration camp, the enlarging of the area of human knowledge and control at the hands of a Galileo.

"Neither the saint nor the revolutionary can save us," says Arthur Koestler in *The Yogi and the Commissar,* "only the synthesis of the two." If he means that both the inner and the outer eye are necessary to men, then nobody will disagree. Certainly these four plays of Sartre and Brecht call for some combination of the two. Let us hope Sartre is no yogi. The yogi is an exile without being engagé. He could say with the immature Orestes "what a superb absence is my soul." Let us hope Brecht is no commissar. The commissar wants to have the world changed—as in the end Shen Te does—but he has not Shen Te's kindness as his motive; he is no victim to the "temptation of goodness." Both Brecht and Sartre are attempting a synthesis of the individual and the social. They differ in coming at it from opposite directions. Brecht comes to the individual via the collectivity; Sartre comes to the collectivity via the individual.

They are rival revolutionaries. Brecht's revolution is Marx's. It is "from without," for man is not independent of "externals." Sartre's revolution is—shall we say, Nietzsche's? the Existentialists'?

Christ's? It is "from within," for man is not simply a piece of the landscape. Yet Sartre's "inner" revolution leads to the liberation of Argos, and Brecht's "outer" revolution would bring "inner" peace to Shen Te. Sartre's hell is personal, yet a vote of censure against a society is implied. Brecht's hell—Setzuan—is social, yet it is its meaning in individual lives that is measured. Perhaps Sartre's argument starts from a metaphysic, but its significance spreads out over the natural life of man. Perhaps Brecht's argument is simply socialism, but its significance is seen much more concretely, dramatically, poetically than in so-called proletarian literature...

If the ideas in these Epic and Existential plays are not incompatible, their dramaturgy makes one think that the realistic and antirealistic traditions may also be coming closer together. Sartre was appreciably closer to realism than were his French predecessors. Brecht, for his part, has learned more from the antirealist theater than perhaps any other playwright who aims at an accurate picture of the outer world. When, to secure a more faithful version of the external world, Brecht gave up more and more of the methods of stage realism in favor of Chinese and other conventions, he was using nonrealistic techniques for realistic ends. He was mixing the two primary elements of art—nature and convention—in a new way. When his plays took the form of operettas and fantasies, parables and moralities, he was approaching a synthesis of what the realists and their antagonists had intended.

"X," writes Frank Jones, "brings to his form of didacticism a creative and critical skill that has made ample use of the three most vitalizing tendencies in contemporary writing: the revolt against realism, the widening of the content of poetry, and the return to myth." X could be Sartre. It happens to be Brecht. The work of both encourages one to look forward.

The Stagecraft of Bertolt Brecht
1950

I began to be aware of Brecht's craft in theater art—am thinking now especially of the nonverbal arts—when he worked on the Master Race *production in New York (1945) and the* Galileo *production in Hollywood (1947). But America never offered him the resources he needed, so it was an eye-opener to me to see Brecht working in European settings—at the Zurich Schauspielhaus (1948) and then in East Berlin, from 1949 on. The following essay was written in the latter year, and so does not take in my most extended experience of Brecht in rehearsal (Munich, 1950). Even so it was the only piece of work of mine that ever found favor with the head of the Berlin Ensemble, Helene Weigel—Mrs. Bertolt Brecht—who had it translated into German and distributed to actors and students. It was my best attempt to date to define what is Brechtian (not merely to fit Brecht into established pigeonholes as I had done in* The Playwright as Thinker*). Talking with Caspar Neher and Teo Otto helped me at this time, particularly as both made light of Brecht's theories while making much of his talent and individuality. (Neher told me Brecht's rejection of colored light onstage was based on a historical accident: power shortage in the bankrupt Germany of 1920. Car headlights were used instead of the regular stage lights, and Brecht fell in love with them.) With the short piece cited in the footnote below, this is the only thing by me ever published in the German Democratic Republic, namely, in the second Brecht issue of their magazine* Sinn und Form, *which came out the year following Brecht's death.*

AFTER SEEING MY PRODUCTION of *The Caucasian Chalk Circle* in Philadelphia, Harold Clurman wrote of Brecht: "One has the feeling that he is unconcerned with settings, with the traditional trappings of the theater—that the spoken word is his only concern."

Was this really the impression that the production made on the audience?* It is not what Brecht intends. No poet was ever more interested in the whole visual and auditory range of theater. When Brecht prepares a play, he works steadily, with the composer at the piano, on the whole musical score. When the production is ready, he has hundreds of photographs taken of the action, so that he can sit down and examine at leisure all that passes so quickly before the eyes in a performance; this, I think, may be called one of the chief ways in which Brecht studies the theater art. He intends each play to be, among other things, a succession of perfectly composed visual images in which every detail counts. But this, it may be said, is what every real playwright intends. The question is: What kind of images and details? What theatrical style has Brecht achieved? And these questions can be answered only by reference to German theater: the German theater Brecht long ago rebelled against and has still to combat today, and also the German theater he and other like-minded artists have tried to create.

The style of productions in Germany before Brecht was (most notably at any rate) baroque. The name of Max Reinhardt springs to mind, and the Reinhardt era might have been the last era of baroque theater. But history provided a stranger, if not a more dis-

---

* It is true that our stage was too empty, too formal, and too abstract for Brecht; we were saving money; it would be a mistake to imagine that Brecht's ideas can be carried out inexpensively.

   The curious reader may check with a series of five pictures from this production published in the anthology *Theater der Welt: Ein Almanach*, ed. Herbert Ihering. (East Berlin: B. Henschel, 1949), 70–75.

   The text that goes with the pictures is a German translation (or rather, reduction) of the 1948 piece, "Brecht on the American Stage," cited in the second appendix to this book.

tinguished, final chapter: the baroque theater of the Nazi period. And this period is not yet completely at an end. The German theater today lives all too much on the vestiges of the Nazi years. Look over some photographs of German productions since 1945 and you will certainly not say: "How poverty-stricken!" All the resources of the black market were tapped to make sure that the theater should continue to be a magic palace of art. Thus, at a time when Shakespeare production might be the theater's road back to reality, most Shakespeare productions in Germany are, at best, decorative and charming. In Stuttgart last spring I saw a *Much Ado* that had been *reduced* to decoration and charm—a decimation of the play. In Berlin I saw a *Twelfth Night* directed by Boleslaw Barlog, who has made a big name for himself in the past four years. It was unbelievably fancy. Someone had been studying up on Illyria and finding that it was less Italian than Turkish. The whole play was given a Middle Eastern setting, and Sir Toby Belch looked like Harun al-Rashid: a production from which the real substance of Shakespeare, and of life, was missing.

Perhaps I didn't see enough of Barlog's work at the Schlosspark Theater to know what was characteristic of him, but repeated visits to the Hebbel Theater gave me a very fair idea of at least one Berlin ensemble. The Hebbel Theater seems still to live in a former age. I was anxious to see this ensemble play their patron, Hebbel, but when I saw *Gyges und sein Ring* I found the actors practicing that elevated, biblical style of speech that the Germans call Pathos—and not this style in its prime, of course, but gone soft. Thus rendered, a dramatic poet is helpless. He may write precisely, sharply, he may even be saying something, but the actor will smudge the sharp outline, will let the thoughts lose themselves in clouds of vague feeling: his quasi-religious tone suggests that what he is saying must be important and at the same time prevents us from knowing what it is. This sort of actor throws himself at his part, throws his feelings at the helpless poet's words, and drowns the play in a mess of irrelevant emotion.

At the Hebbel Theater I also saw Sartre's *Flies*. It would be unfair, I think, to blame all I saw on the director, Juergen Fehling, for since he did his work, the play has run a long time and changes have been made in the cast. But what was more unfortunate than the sloppiness of the performance was the style and spirit of the whole production. Here is a play in which Greek myth is material for French conversation. The legend is not, properly speaking, redramatized; it is taken for granted. It is the backdrop for a discussion in a Parisian café. The more one sees this play, the more one realizes how much Sartre the playwright owes to Giraudoux: his Zeus is no god; he is Louis Jouvet.

Since all this must have been evident to a man of Fehling's gifts, I can only assume that the German tradition—I mean one particular German tradition, that of the modern baroque—was too much for him. When *The Flies* is played ponderously, every fly an elephant, you realize that the play lives by the one quality such a production lacks: lightness of touch. Sartre's rhetoric, always on the verge of the false, is often redeemed by a kind of irony in which the audience is asked not to take the whole thing too seriously. In performance, as Fehling's production showed, this irony can be eliminated—and with it the effectiveness of the play. I saw a production of *Les Mains sales* in Stuttgart that had similar deficiencies: I realized how much the Paris production owed to François Périer, who played Hugo with bravura, rendering with lively realism the French gestures and grimaces that *are* the role.

I am citing typical, not exceptional cases and, at that, typical cases on the highest level: in smaller towns than Berlin and Stuttgart, where very minor Fehlings are in the saddle, the general truth of my analysis is appallingly confirmed. And one feature of the pattern that I noticed most of all in the small provincial theaters was what might be called the Hitlerite actor: the actor who sounds for all the world like the late Führer addressing a mass meeting.

A decadent style can be ousted only by a fresh style, and the one fresh style in German theater today is Brecht. Brecht is important not simply because he is the only first-class playwright in Germany but also because his kind of theater could be the corrective that is needed. He has called it Epic on the grounds that it is a narrative form as opposed to the degenerate "dramatic" theater of our era in which narrative or plot has lost its priority.

The word *Epic* had some polemical value for a while, in that it annoyed the official guardians of dramatic art, but it has sometimes been a nuisance, in that it places Brecht's work in the category of the eccentric, the deliberately unorthodox, the willfully experimental. Even an admirer like Mordecai Gorelik overstresses Brecht's iconoclasm, his love of machinery and scientific paraphernalia. "It is freely admitted," he writes in *New Theatres for Old,* "that there is no sharp dividing line between Epic drama and a demonstration in a surgical or chemical auditorium. Epic plays have made use of lantern slides, placards and radio loudspeakers." Nonetheless I would maintain that when Brecht's method differs from conventional theater, it differs along the lines of a mature commonsense theory of the stage. Before he wrote his book, Gorelik had himself found a good term for this method: Epic Realism. One could simplify the matter still further and say Narrative Realism.

As a method of staging, Narrative Realism stands midway between the two extreme methods of the modern theater, which we may call naturalism and symbolism. A naturalistic stage setting of a room is a literal reproduction of the room—or what looks like such a reproduction—except that the fourth wall is missing. A symbolistic setting presents a number of objects and forms that form a substitute for the room: a door, for instance, is represented by two vertical posts. In recent years Thornton Wilder has been the most famous exponent of symbolism. He has written plays in which the audience's chief interest is in the symbolic nature of the décor—*The Happy Journey,* for example, which keeps its audience in a constant tizzy as they watch the opening and shutting of doors that aren't there, the pouring of imaginary water, and so on. Directors of plays like this speak very contemptuously of David Belasco and maintain that the future of theater lies in a revolt against realism. Brecht does not agree. He sees in the antirealistic tendency the danger of artiness, of cuteness. To use chairs instead of an automobile may at first seem an admirable economy, both monetary and artistic. But it is not economical of the spectator's attention. The device attracts more attention than it deserves. It would actually be more straightforward to use a real car.

The Narrative Realist neither reassembles the whole room nor tries to substitute symbols for actualities. He tries to avoid the remoteness from actuality of symbolism by using real objects, and the laborious explicitness of naturalism by making a more fastidious selection from among the all too many objects that make up the real scene. In representing a room, he will use only things that actually make up a room, but he won't attempt to show the whole room: one part of it will suffice—a piece of wall, or a door, some pieces of furniture.

It may be said that the naturalists also present only a part of a room: three walls instead of four. But, psychologically speaking, this three-out-of-four is no selection, for even in real rooms one seldom sees four walls at once. There is a difference in principle between the naturalist's selectivity and that of the Narrative Realist. The naturalist aims at giving the completest illusion of the real thing. He will omit something from the picture only if the omission (as of the fourth wall) goes unnoticed. What the Narrative Realist does by way of omitting and selecting he intends the audience to be entirely aware of. The difference in principle here springs from a different view, not of reality, but of the theater.

The naturalist tends to think of theater and reality as opposites. He says: "The theater gives an illusion of reality," a statement that implies that the theater provides the illusion and that the world outside the theater provides reality—in other words, the theater is taken to be unreal. I have called Narrative Realism a commonsense approach because it asks: why not accept the reality of the theater, accept the stage as a stage, admit that *this* is a wooden floor and not a stone highway, admit that *that* is the back of the theater and not the sky? When we have asked these rhetorical questions, we have found another justification for the "selected" stage setting described above. Because only part of the room is presented, a good deal of the stage is left undisguised, is seen *as a stage*.

Involved in polemical disputes, Brecht has had to overstress the negative aspects of this sort of staging, the fact that it destroys the illusion of reality. And his critics, always eager to say that Epic Theater is a denial of the basic principles of Western drama, find here a big bone of contention. They are right, I think, when they observe that illusion is inherent in the art of acting and thus in all theater. They are wrong only if they assume that the Narrative Realist eliminates illusion altogether. Illusion is a matter of degree, and a lesser degree of it is not necessarily less dramatic than a higher degree of it. When Brecht reduces the amount of illusion that we find in stage settings, he is not simply taking something away from the theater, impoverishing the theater; rather, he sets up an interaction between the "real" object (chairs, tables, or whatever) and the "artificial" frame (the stage). The Epic stage designer is to be judged by the skill and imagination with which he balances the two elements. The reader can see the truth of this from the stage designs of Caspar Neher and Teo Otto.* He will note also that these stage designs are handsome, even beautiful. The *schema* of Epic stage design may have been arrived at by a nonaesthetic argument; but, each particular design is subject to aesthetic criteria. The Epic mixture of theatrical and real elements is not merely a didactic strategy, a way of communicating the truth; it is also an opportunity for designers to create a fresh kind of beauty. The theatrical and real elements have to "come together" either in direct harmony or in effective dissonance. The designer is a master of such harmony and such dissonance.

Because Brecht does not believe in an inner reality, a higher

---

* Plates 6, 7, and 8 in *In Search of Theater.*

reality, or a deeper reality, but simply in reality, he presents on the stage the solid things of this world in all their solidity and with all the appreciation of their corporeality that we find in certain painters. (Brueghel is the painter from whom Brecht has learned most.) This means that he is more interested in the beauty and vitality of things than are the naturalists. At the same time, his approach has its own difficulties. There are many things that a playwright may want to include that cannot actually be placed on the stage. You cannot place a sun or a moon on the stage, or even a winding highway. But Narrative Realism is not a dogma, is not exclusive. Where a symbolistic idea seems the most practical solution, the Narrative Realist can use it. Symbolism can be used whenever naturalism is impossible. Thus a disk can represent the sun. Yet if we use such a symbol, we must not fool ourselves into believing that it is not a symbol but the reality. We must not hang the disk on an invisible wire and ask our audience to believe that this is a photograph of the sun. We can hang it on a visible chain. If, as in Caspar Neher's setting of *The Threepenny Opera,* the stage becomes a veritable network of such chains, it will be the designer's job to see that they form a pattern and not a chaos; here again the functional and the aesthetic elements have to be fused.

Deciding what objects to place onstage is half the designer's job; the other half is deciding how to light these objects and the stage in general. Again, Brecht's position proceeds by a common-sense argument from his general attitude to life. Again, it is a moderate position between the extremes of naturalistic illusion and symbolistic stylization. The degree of illusion is reduced at the outset by bringing the sources of light out from their hiding places behind teasers and other masking devices. This may seem a small point, but actually nothing does more to convey the idea that the stage is hocus-pocus than the appearance and disappearance of light as if at the bidding of unseen gods. (Oddly enough, it is the modern, scientific, electrical system that has thus made of the stage a mystery. There was no mystery about candles or gas.)

The Narrative Realist, who admits that the stage is a stage, admits also that a lamp is a lamp.

If the naturalistic director is too busy concealing the theatrical source of his lights and making the audience think the stage has no electrical or mechanical apparatus at all, the symbolistic director boasts of the freedom and creativity of his lights and is as excited as a child playing with fireworks. Thus, nonrealistic productions are usually much too ostentatiously lit. The lighting changes too often, and the attention of the audience is distracted from the play being lit. The perfecting of electric lighting meant, among other things, the possibility of graduating the intensity of stage lights, which consequently became a steady source of temptation to the arty. The ruling passion of stage designers after Appia and Craig was for semidarkness, a fact that the historian would have to relate to the whole spirit of the Wagnerian epoch. It is a great pity that books on modern stage design consist to such an extent of pictures of almost nothing: a solid black rectangle with perhaps a grayish-white spot in the right-hand corner—Hamlet's face.

If a playwright's whole lifework is a nocturne (one thinks of Maeterlinck), the "modern" style of lighting will be what he needs. If reality is invisible, the less we see, the better. But if, on the other hand, a playwright, like Brecht, believes that—figuratively speaking—he can throw light on reality, and that reality is indeed *there* to be thrown light on, he will want to use plenty of stage light—literally speaking. Thus, Brecht is in favor of switching on the lights and leaving them switched on, a revealing flood of white light covering the whole stage. It seems a sensible enough notion; yet in the present-day theater it is a heresy. When I produced a Brecht play in an avant-garde theater, I found that they had not found it necessary even to possess enough light to simulate a sunny day. So far has the impression gone that the theater is exclusively concerned with magic and mystery.

To the notion, shared by most modern directors, that life, as at a children's party, becomes much more interesting when you turn the lights out, the Narrative Realist opposes the notion that a stage is, of its nature, a place of prominence, a place in which life is held up to the light. This means, of course, that the stage presentation of night is something of a problem. Complete night is complete darkness, which, visually speaking, is complete nothingness. Since theater is, among other things, a visual art, complete darkness cannot therefore be said to be theatrical, except, possibly, for a moment—that is, in sudden contrast to light. Even approximate darkness reduces the visual element of theater to such an extent that one should be very sparing, surely, in using it. We often hear of Shakespeare's wonderful evocations of night—in *Romeo*, in *Macbeth*—but we forget that on the Elizabethan stage these were verbal evocations, made in broad daylight. Today the opening scene of *Hamlet* is nearly always thrown away because, in almost total darkness, one cannot pay attention to the longer speeches; darkness suggests the mood of a thriller, which only the first few lines of the scene will fully support: this scene can be restored to the play only when a director has the courage to turn the lights on. Here a departure from naturalism is a practical necessity. Rather than ruin a scene by a literal presentation of darkness, it is reasonable to symbolize night by hanging a moon from a chain.

We have to learn to use lights for the central purposes of theater. This means neither limiting them to the simulation of natural appearances nor letting them run wild in an orgy of independence nor switching them off because one loves darkness. The center of dramatic performance is the actor, and the center of the actor is the actor's eyes. We need to see them. It may even be (I have the suggestion not from Brecht but from Charles Laughton) that the actor needs to see our eyes too. If so, we shall have to switch on the auditorium lights as well. The idea is worth thinking about. If we can see not only a spot of light on Hamlet's left temple but also his eyes, his face, his body, and his surroundings, and if, in turn, Hamlet can look straight at us when he asks: "To be, or not to be?" Shakespeare's play will be quite a different thing from what of late it has become. Perhaps it will step out into the open and take on a larger existence.

The question of lighting leads us to the larger question of the psychological distance between actor and spectator, stage and auditorium. The subject is full of paradoxes. In one respect, the illusionistic stage brings actor and spectator closer together than does the Epic stage. Illusion brings the spectator to identify himself with the people in the story, to feel his way into the story (empathy), to let himself be carried away by the story's suspense. Epic Theater, on the other hand, famously sets the spectator at a distance ("alienation"), asks him not to identify himself too strongly with the characters, not to feel his way too deeply into the story, not to be carried away. The illusionistic stage has a comprehensive system (of acting, stage design, theatrical architecture) to help it toward its ends. Stanislavsky's acting methods help the actor to identify himself with the role and so help the spectator to leave himself behind and live himself into the play. Naturalistic and symbolistic stage design have, equally, the effect of creating a complete and self-sufficient world on the stage. The kind of theater building still most in use has a proscenium arch, hidden lights, a stage that leads the audience *into* this magic world. Everything in Brecht's theater, on the other hand, seems calculated to drive a wedge between actor and spectator.

It is also true that Brecht is not at home with those who in recent years have aimed simply at greater "intimacy" between actor and audience. With the champions of central staging, for example. Physical closeness has its disadvantages. When one is very close to the actor, it is hard to sit back and really *look* at what is going on. The spectator is entitled to a certain detachment. He must be granted the right to call his soul his own. The old distance between stage and auditorium is entirely defensible. What will help the spectator is not being brought closer to the actor but, perhaps, being placed *above* the actor—as he was in the Greek arena with its auditorium rising up from the stage. A spectator who looks up at a stage is at a disadvantage. His position is undignified. He has to *gawk*. A spectator who looks down on a stage has the priority he is entitled to. He can relax. He can really *watch*.

There is a sense in which Narrative Realism comes closer to the audience than does the illusionistic theater. The latter leads him into the illusion and, at the end, lets him drop. The illusion was another world, whether of reality (naturalism) or fantasy (symbolism). The illusionistic stage with its natural or stylized settings and its proscenium and its actors who *are* their roles might be defined as a machine for the creation of such another world. Brecht's stage is frankly in the same building, in the same room, as the audience; it is made of the same wood as the auditorium and belongs to the same spiritual realm. Here the actor and the play he enacts are all along in the same world as the spectator, a fact with many philosophical and aesthetic implications. A theater that never carries the spectator away can never let him drop. It stays with him all the time. It might claim to be a superior strategy in that, precisely by effecting certain kinds of separation, it comes nearer to its audience in the end. "Alienation" is an instance of the principle: *reculer pour mieux sauter.*

Like the realism of Brecht's staging, the "alienation" that is a leading characteristic of his dramaturgy has been rather negatively interpreted, partly again because Brecht was so busy destroying the enemy. "Alienation" has usually been described in terms of its destruction of empathy, of suspense, of pathos as if it, too, were a taking away of something, the deliberate impoverishment of an art by a fanatical didacticist. Actually, like illusion in the stage settings, these things were not eliminated but limited—limited by being placed alongside their opposites. The total result is a positive enrichment of the drama, even an enrichment of the emotional content.

"Alienation" is very boldly practiced in *Mother Courage.* At the end of the play the old woman is still singing the song she sang at the beginning. It is an end that might easily be sentimental (*merely* pathetic). But as Brecht directs the play, the harsh din of martial pipes cuts across the music at this point. Brecht and Engel wanted to neutralize the pathos, and prevent the audience from (the word is apt) "dissolving" into tears. Brecht also succeeds in enriching the drama of the scene. It becomes more moving.

A more subtle instance from the same production is the cook's singing "A mighty fortress is our God" while Dumb Kate goes through the elaborate sad pantomime of secretly trying on a whore's gaudy hat and boots. This procedure operates first as a joke but gradually reinforces the pathos that it begins by checking.

Brecht writes: "A bold and beautiful verbal architecture alienates a text." Beauty itself, form itself, brings off the alienation effect: by making order out of chaos, it sets the chaos at a distance, where we can look at it. We have here a utilitarian vindication of literature. The theory is also a valid apologia. It explains why, being fundamentally didactic in intention, Brecht remains a poet in method. To the general "alienation" of life that is effected by form, he adds many particular "alienating" devices, more or less deliberate. One that must surely be very deliberate occurs in *The Caucasian Chalk Circle*. This is the scene in which Grusha feels the temptation of goodness: the temptation to pick up and save the abandoned baby. Grusha acts the whole scene out in pantomime while the Singer in the third person and the past tense relates what she is doing. In this the Singer is doing for Grusha exactly what Brecht, in his essay "A New Technique of Acting," suggests should be done to help an actor emancipate him from the Stanislavsky procedure. If an actor hears his role talked about in the third person and his deeds talked about in the past tense, he stands apart from the role and the deeds and renders them, not as self-expression, but as history. When he uses the device in *Chalk Circle*, Brecht of course is radically "alienating" Grusha's actions so that we do not lose ourselves in our compassion. He uses the third person, the past tense, the art of pantomime, and a refined language as massed alienation effects.

The whole passage is sung. Just as Brecht inserts spoken poems into his dialogue in order to alienate certain emotions, so he inserts music. The use of music as an alienation effect is, it will be noted, the direct opposite of the usual theatrical use of music—which is simply to back up the dialogue, to "heighten" the mood. Orthodox theatrical music duplicates the text. It is stormy in stormy scenes, quiet in quiet scenes. It adds *A* to *A*. In a Brecht play, the music is supposed to add *B* to *A*. Thus *A* is alienated, and the texture of the work is enriched. Music can of course provide the sheerest alienation-through-beauty, and on occasion the beauty can have a special, "alienating" point. In *Mother Courage* Paul Dessau composed his most delicate and lovely music for "The Song of Fraternization," which is what its title suggests, and is sung by a whore. The tune seems to embody the pure love that the text reports the fall of. Such music constitutes a kind of criticism of the text. The same could be said of all the music that Hanns Eisler has composed for Brecht plays; and Eisler has worked out a theory of film music on similar lines (in *Composing for the Films*).

Brecht is primarily a poet, and words are the backbone of his plays, but he has also worked out, in theory and practice, a kind of theater in which the nonverbal arts play an essential and considered part. It is interesting that the same critic who thought Brecht uninterested in the nonverbal arts summed up Narrative Realism as an attempt to "irritate the audience into thought." The summary is not exactly wrong: the methods of Brecht's theater—its use of interruption and "alienation," for example—do constitute a kind of irritation. Yet if this is all we say, the conclusion drawn by many will be that, in order to annoy everyone, Brecht destroys his plays by deliberate incongruities and impertinent interpolations. In plays like *Mother Courage, Puntila,* or *Chalk Circle,* the idea is not to annoy but to awaken, and this not by flying in the face of dramatic art but by the re-creation, the enrichment, of dramatic art.

What is dramatic? Everyone seems to know the answer to this question. The standard modern opinion seems to be that the highly specialized, simplified forms of the Racine-Ibsen tradition are the quintessence of drama. Even when this opinion is not on a par with movie advertisements about "this dramatic story of a woman's love," and so on, it is arbitrary. Thus, a novel is defined as "dramatic" when it conforms to the Racine-Ibsen pattern, but not when it is closer to the Elizabethan form in which Shakespeare wrote.

Nine students out of ten today, asked to name a dramatic painting, would name something like Géricault's *Raft of the Medusa*, not something like Brueghel's *Battle of Carnival and Lent*. Géricault's painting is dramatic in the popular sense: it presents a standard "exciting situation." It is also dramatic in the academic sense: it is simple rather than compound in construction; it has a single focus. Brueghel's painting is dramatic in neither of these senses. It offers no solace to the eye that seeks swift, strong sensation. It invites the eye to linger on this detail and that. The eye that accepts the invitation discovers one "drama" after another in the picture and even a total drama of the whole, dramatic way of looking at life.

The eye that can relax over a Brueghel painting and yet find it highly dramatic can relax over a Brecht play and yet find it dramatic. During a Brecht performance one can relax and look with pleasure at the various parts of the stage—the wardrobe of Peachum, or the kitchen utensils of Mother Courage. The eye is not glued to one spot. Because suspense has been reduced to a minimum, one is not always asking what will happen next. One is not interested in the next scene, one is interested in *this* scene. Drama students are taught that "dramatic method" means reducing their material to a single situation and a single group of characters, and in bringing them into focus together. But this is not Brueghel's way or Brecht's. In the work of these men the principle seems to be not to cut away everything until only a center is left but to start with a center and to add layer upon layer.

In the Notes to his *Threepenny Opera,* Brecht ridicules the accepted notion that a playwright must "embody" everything in the characters and the action. Why should not comment from the outside also be possible? The words of the songs are superadded comment; the music is a comment on these words. In *The Threepenny*

Opera, ironical titles are projected on screens; so are drawings by Georg Grosz, drawings of nothing specifically mentioned in the play. In *The Good Woman of Setzuan,* characters throw out comments in the shape of short asides in verse.

It is arbitrary to hold that drama as such is fast rather than slow, hot rather than cold, and concentrated rather than manifold. But to secure agreement for this proposition would be to revolutionize dramatic criticism, since at present "slow," "coldly intellectual," and "diffuse" (not Broadway) are standard terms of disapproval. Yet just as there is quiet music as well as loud, slow music as well as fast, so there may be slow and cool drama. Not that Brecht's plays are uniformly slow and cool. But when people find *Mother Courage* "dramatic in parts," what they mean is that they will confer the word *dramatic* on the fast and hot scenes.

Brecht's plays compel a broader notion of the dramatic, a notion that would surprise and displease our forefathers less than it does our contemporaries. Brecht's methods are very often a return to older traditions above the head of the modern drama. In his earlier theoretical writings, Brecht himself created misunderstanding by using the word *dramatic* pejoratively and by calling his own method "non-Aristotelian." As to the latter term, it is clear that Narrative Realism is out of line with Aristotle's theory of tragedy, since Brecht's outlook is utterly untragic. Whether it would be out of line with Aristotle's theory of comedy we cannot know, since the few remarks on comedy in the *Poetics* scarcely amount to a theory at all. Brecht's theory of theater *is* a theory of comedy. Something very like the dramaturgy described by Brecht was practiced by Aristophanes. Something very like the kind of acting described by Brecht was practiced (one is inclined to think) by the commedia dell'arte players.

Brecht's theoretical writings will not have an immediate effect on the German theater, but his plays will, and so will those productions of his plays in which he had a hand, such as the Brecht-Hirschfeld production of *Puntila* at Zurich and the Brecht-Engel production of *Mother Courage* in Berlin. One may even speak of Brecht actors: Helene Weigel, Therese Giehse, Leonard Steckel, and two astonishing newcomers (in Berlin and Munich, respectively), Angelica Hurwicz and Erni Wilhelmi. As Mother Courage in Berlin, Helene Weigel probably came as close to Brecht's idea of acting as anyone has yet come. (Brecht holds that the theory cannot be fully practiced until not only the actors, but also the audiences, have had a different training. We see truly "epic" performance only at moments, and these are less frequent in actual performance than in rehearsal.) To a degree, Miss Weigel stands outside the role and in a sense does not even look like Mother Courage. She is cool, relaxed, and ironical. Yet with great precision of movement and intonation she intimates what Mother Courage was like. The art and beauty of the performance bring home to us the awful sadness and relevance of Mother Courage's career more convincingly and more movingly than the Stanislavsky method would be likely to do. At the very least, Helene Weigel's performance is a lesson in the craft of acting that the German theater (for reasons I stated at the beginning) very much needs. One would like to see this actress in Shakespeare. She might cleanse and renew Shakespeare for the Germans, as Barrault has been cleansing and renewing him for the French.

If one is looking for a movement in German theater today—something that would parallel the movements of the twenties—one will not find it, but there is Brecht, and there are those who work with him, like Engel and Neher and Otto and Weigel. There are also artists who have independently taken a somewhat similar direction, such as Walter Felsenstein, whose productions of *Carmen* and Orff's *Die Kluge* I saw in Berlin. *Carmen* was a model production for our times. Far from imposing a newfangled interpretation on it, or making an adaptation of it, Felsenstein discovered that there was a highly interesting original version with spoken dialogue and without the ballet and other such concessions to the Parisian opera public. He used this version and revealed the original *Carmen* as a brilliant piece of realism in which the alternation of speech and song is most "experimentally" employed. Carl Orff's amusing little opera Felsenstein produced on a sort of slanting boxing ring placed on the stage. His production had all the lightness of touch that the productions of Fehling and Barlog lacked. At the Burgtheater in Vienna, Felsenstein produced Schiller's *Robbers.* The style, like that of his *Carmen,* was decidedly similar to Narrative Realism: a characteristic feature was a huge realistic tree held up on the stage by visible supports.

At the Burgtheater also are Joseph Gielen and Berthold Viertel. Viertel's production of *The Glass Menagerie* (which I missed) has been much talked of, because (I gather) Viertel had his actors speak and move like human beings instead of ranting puppets. Work like Viertel's—of training the new generation to forget the voice of the Führer—is even more difficult, though less spectacular, than that of an operatic director like Felsenstein.

Gielen obviously had an uphill task in producing *Julius Caesar.* Some of his famous stars (notably Ewald Balser as Brutus) acted very badly indeed and seemed in temperament and physique cut out to sing Siegfried at the Met, but the ensemble was so good that much of the play's meaning was disengaged for (in my experience) the first time. The importance of the Roman mob impressed itself on me, not only in the surefire scene of the funeral orations, but equally in scenes that, by accepted standards, are trivial or irrelevant, such as the opening scene of the play and the scene of Cinna the Poet.

Even small black-and-white reproductions of Caspar Neher's designs* give some notion how Shakespeare's Rome was rendered. Projected pictures of Roman buildings do not clutter the stage and deaden the spectator's responses as naturalistic scenery would do. They do not stylize and rarify the play out of existence, like the curtains and sparse pillars of yesterday's art theaters. They have a kind

---

* As provided in the *Kenyon Review* (Autumn 1949).

of clear, unbedevilled truth that seems highly appropriate to this play, and, as designed by Neher, they have a sharp, manly beauty— the beauty of old Rome, not the bogus dignity of nineteenth- and twentieth-century neo-Romanism.

Neher's name brings us back to Brecht's. One can hardly get away from it if one is looking for intellectual vitality in the German theater today. His significance is not merely a matter of his own plays. Neher's work on *Julius Caesar* (and, I gather, Engel's productions of *Coriolanus* and *The Tempest*) are in the Brecht ambience. It has even been suggested that Brecht will translate Shakespeare; perhaps he could not remake the German theater, as he wishes to do, *without* translating Shakespeare, who is, after all, the leading German dramatist. Up to now Shakespeare has been the dramatist of German romanticism, which means that he has become a somewhat academic figure, a Walter Scott of the stage. Brecht would give us a very modern Shakespeare, and the hope would be that the modern style would contain more of the original Elizabethan spirit than the romantic style did.

The theater of Narrative Realism has more in common with the great theater of the remoter past than with the theater of today and yesterday.

Seven Plays
1960

Those great poets, for example, men like Byron, Musset, Poe, Leopardi, Kleist, Gogol... are and must be men of the moment, sensual, absurd, fivefold, irresponsible, and sudden in mistrust and trust; with souls in which they must usually conceal some fracture; often taking revenge with their works for some inner contamination, often seeking with their high flights to escape into forgetfulness from an all-too-faithful memory; idealists from the vicinity of swamps...

—Nietzsche

Art, life, and politics are inseparable and at the same time in conflict.

—Blok

In 1948, I directed The Caucasian Chalk Circle *at Hedgerow Theater in Pennsylvania; in 1950,* The Exception and the Rule *with the University Theater in Padua, Italy. Larger directing plans were in the air: I was to do* Puntila *in Rome for Paolo Stoppa,* A Man's a Man *in London for Michel St. Denis,* Caucasian Chalk Circle *in New York for Howard Da Silva... and in 1956 I did direct* Good Woman *in New York with a cast that included Uta Hagen, Zero Mostel, Gene Saks, Jerry Stiller, and Ann Meara. (That was in the year—1956—of the most Brechtian of my own stage works: a libretto for Offenbach's* Orpheus, *produced by the New York City Opera Company. Leo Kerz, who directed it, had also commissioned me to translate* A Man's a Man *and* Happy End.*) Instead of settling down to directing, however, I returned to writing, not excluding translating and discussing Bertolt Brecht. He had no regular American publisher until Grove Press began issuing his plays in the sixties, starting with the collection* Seven Plays by Brecht. *In 1960 I was asked to preside over the Gauss Seminars in Princeton. Since the subject was Brecht, many expected that I would "get a book on Brecht" out of the experience. What I "got" instead was the following long essay, which served as the preface to* Seven Plays.

Preliminary

Brecht, 1960. A writer, as Aristotle might say, is either fashionable or unfashionable. Neither condition is desirable. To be fashionable is to be celebrated for the wrong reasons, and to be unfashionable is not to be celebrated at all.

In the past ten years, Bertolt Brecht has passed from the depths of unrecognition to the heights of a chic celebrity. Such a change is not without interest to the gossip columnist or even the social historian. To the serious reader—and to the serious theatergoer if he exists—it is a bore. And in the history of the drama it is just a bad thing: Brecht has died, and what we have chosen to inherit is a cult, an *ism.*

Is it so long since the same thing happened to Ibsen? For half a century, a foggy phenomenon called Ibsenism, and many plays distinguished only for their Ibsenism, have stood in the way of Henrik Ibsen. Only after many years was any favorable change discernible, and by 1960 it was possible for Raymond Williams to write: "Ibsenism is dead, and Ibsen is very much alive."

Alas, poor Brecht! He stands where Ibsen stood in 1910: he is dead, and Brechtism is very much alive. But history need not repeat itself. War can be waged on Brechtism in the name of Brecht.

More shrewdly: the cult of Brecht might be exploited to arouse a deeper interest in the work of Brecht. The coming of the cult has this to be said for it, that the old air of secrecy has gone. Brecht's works are at least there to be read. There is even such a thing as Brecht scholarship. And a real discussion of Brecht could and did begin when Martin Esslin and Ernest Borneman and others broke through the taboos by which the priests of the cult hoped to keep their idol holy, if unreal.

The errors that have been promoted by the cultists (and the dilettantes) will be exposed gradually as genuine criticism proceeds. But one error needs pointing out in advance, as it is shared by the enemies of the cultists. This is the notion that there are two Brechts, who correspond to the period before his conversion to Marxism (1928) and the period after. To Herbert Luethy, the early Brecht is a good thing, the later a bad, just as to many Communists and fellow travelers, the early Brecht is a bad thing, the later a good.

It would be strange indeed if a poet could cut his creative life so neatly in half. I believe that one can only get the impression that Brecht did so if one is blinded by political prejudice. If Brecht had a divided nature, it was—as the word *nature* implies—divided all his life long. Such a division is discernible in every major play. Otherwise, the lifework of Brecht has a most impressive unity: what is found in the late plays is found in the early ones, and vice versa. This is not to say that there is no development, nor is it to deny that Brecht *attempted* something like the total change that the doctrinaires on both sides attribute to him. One might say he providentially failed in this attempt. More probably, he surely if dimly knew what he was doing. Behind the attempt to change was the knowledge that one cannot—and a wily, conniving refusal to go to all lengths in attempting the impossible. This is speculation about the fact of unity in Brecht's work. About the fact itself there can be little doubt.

Necessary to the appreciation of this fact is the discovery or rediscovery of the early plays, particularly *Baal* and *In the Swamp*.

In the Swamp

Emotional dynamics. Brecht's later plays were so unconventionally constructed that the dramatic critics, being the men they are, were bound to think them badly constructed. *In the Swamp* is well constructed and, for all the absence of act divisions, is constructed in a fairly conventional way. Brecht's originality shows less in the overarching main structure than in the details of his rendering of the emotions and their dynamics.

The word *dynamics* may at first seem inapplicable because the subject is passivity. But human passivity has its own negative dynamics—as has a donkey that refuses to budge, a possum that pretends to be dead, or a poodle that begs to be whipped. It would be arbitrary to assume that there is less drama in cessation than in initiation, in refusal than acceptance, in surrender than resistance. Nor is the passive man consistently passive. He is passive so much that occasionally he has to be the opposite. He overcompensates for inaction by action that is rash, sudden, and extreme. No lack of dynamics here! Combining the negative dynamics of refusal with the insane lunges of passivity interrupted, the young Brecht makes a drama out of apparently undramatic materials. Very modern materials. Critics have not been slow to see the connection between the Brecht of 1920 and the plays of Beckett in the fifties. If only Beckett had a quarter of Brecht's constructive power! It seems to me that the later author, for all his true theatricality, could not find the emotional dynamics to animate a full-length play...

Speaking of the aggressions of the passive type of person, the works of Brecht embody aggressions of colossal proportions, and make a special appeal to persons who harbor such aggressions of their own. I have known many Brechtians intimately: one and all persons positively possessed by aggression. This is something to think about when you read some of the current French and British Brechtians, who can give their writing a coolness of tone that accords with the theories of the Meister. Those theories came into being to create such a rational coolness of tone—and conceal the heat and irrationality of the aggressive impulse.

The menagerie of Bertolt Brecht. Between the art of Bertolt Brecht and the discussion of that art, a great gulf has been fixed. Maybe it was Brecht who fixed it by becoming a Marxist and letting us know about his art, even his early art, only in Marxist terms. Hence, for example, if you read about Mackie the Knife in Brecht's Notes, you would expect anything but the Mackie the Knife of Brecht's own play. The Notes are about capitalism and the world around us. The play shows . . . well, what? If this type of figure must be characterized in one word, that word will have to be *grotesque.* Yes, a grotesque figure may *represent* capitalism and the world around us, but here we are changing the subject to the author's intentions. What has he *done?* He has created a group of grotesques. This creation in no way results from Marxism: it antedates Brecht's reading of Marx. What one should rather observe is the way in which Brecht, when he joins the left, brings his menagerie with him. All he has to do is rename his jackals Capitalists.

By this time (1960), there are many people who approve of Brecht on the ground that he was a Communist. But is that why they are attracted to his work? Rather, he is approved for one reason and enjoyed for another. Some of the enjoyment may indeed be rather improper, almost illicit. An unbeatable combination!

Amerika. The menagerie is all complete in *In the Swamp.* In Garga and Shlink we already hear the sentiments and accents of Peachum. Worm and Baboon are our first Brechtian henchmen. The nickelodeon plays "Ave Maria," a Salvation Army officer shoots himself after uttering the last words of Frederick the Great, and a lynch gang goes into action at the bidding of the police! It is the Amerika that was discovered not by C. C. but by B. B. It is the Amerika of *Mahagonny* and *The Seven Deadly Sins.*

Homosexuality. The modern subject *par excellence*? Yet still an unusual subject for a play when Brecht wrote *In the Swamp;* and it seems that people can read this play and miss it. They miss a lot. If homosexuality is not talked about, it is as fully implicit as in Genet's *Deathwatch.*

There is candor and candor. If homosexuality is now a standard subject of sentimental commercial literature, that literature can be trusted to impose its own limitations on the subject as it did on previous "daring" subjects. Broadway plays on the theme only permit us to *discover* that the hero is homosexual, just as older plays let us discover that the unmarried heroine was pregnant.

Homosexuality can appear in commercial culture only by way of pathetic romance. A homosexual disposition is accepted as there, and society is "arraigned" for its failure to see this. Here is a group of people who prefer strawberries to raspberries, and society has made the eating of strawberries illegal: pathos! Brecht on the other hand, while he doesn't tag characters with clinical labels, reaches what clinicians will recognize as big facts.

One reason the treatment of homosexuality seems not very explicit in *In the Swamp* is that the author clearly puts sex in its place—the place for this kind of sex being entitled Masochism. As in Genet, Eros is subordinated to the struggle for power; in which struggle Brecht's characters tend to wish to lose.

Nihilism: a query. Discussions of Brecht's philosophy—of this period *or later*—would gain from an understanding of his emotions and attitudes. His philosophy as of this period is always described as nihilism. But is nihilism a philosophy? Is it not rather an emotional attitude in a philosophically minded person? The philosophy is pessimistic, but pessimism becomes nihilist only when espoused with resentment and rage. Nihilists are destroyers, though to study particular nihilists is often to find that they were very passive men. Are they men who become active only in destruction?

And when they are converted to causes that make high moral claims, can their nihilism be discarded as a mere opinion?

A Man's a Man

A new Brecht. The protagonists of the earlier plays—Baal, Kragler, and Garga—were mouthpieces for Brecht's own yearnings and agonies. We are still not as far as he liked to think from the agonized-ecstatic dramas of the expressionists. With *A Man's a Man* emerges the Brecht the world knows. The transition is rather an abrupt one, and I wonder that more has not been made of it. Formally speaking, it could be taken as a switch from tragedy to comedy. Brecht's final attitude would be vehemently antitragic. The newfangled notion of Epic Theater can be construed as a synonym for traditional Comedy.

Influences. None, luckily, are as marked as those of Rimbaud and Büchner on *Baal* and *In the Swamp*. Yet surely Charlie Chaplin runs these pretty close. It would be hard to prove this, though Brecht's admiration of Chaplin is a matter of record, and the latter's influence is obvious enough in such later plays as *Puntila* and *Schweyk in World War II*. As far as *A Man's a Man* is concerned, one needn't stress Chaplin individually: I would judge the influence to be that of American silent-movie comedy in general. It was this influence (among others) that enabled Brecht to write, as he already wished to, much more impersonally. He was able to dispel the expressionistic penumbra and draw his own creatures on white paper, as it were, in hard black lines. Georg Grosz may have been as valuable to him as Chaplin.

Later revisions. Brecht succeeded so well that later he was able to believe that *A Man's a Man* was Marxist before the fact: all it needed was a few extra touches, and it would be the model anticapitalist and antiwar play. The extra touches involved the omission of the superb final scenes (10, 11), and hence the blurring of the crucial Bloody Five–Galy Gay relationship. It was perhaps the puritanism of his Communist friends that made Brecht omit the castration episode (as it certainly made him tone down or omit the racier jokes). Brecht's famous revisions were usually doctrinaire and were seldom improvements.

Structure. The first version of *A Man's a Man* has a very clear structure. The accident to Jip provides only the point of departure. At the center of the action is Uriah. It is Uriah who decides that, since men are all interchangeable, Jip can be replaced: it is just a matter of picking out Galy Gay, making sure that Jesse and Polly go along, and then keeping at it. While Uriah conducts his experiment on Galy Gay, Bloody Five conducts one on himself. What's in a name?—the phrase would make a good title for the play. Bloody Five changes into a civilian at the bidding of Widow Begbick. His humiliations in the role persuade him to change back again and cling to the name Bloody Five at any cost. "It is not important that I eat; it is important that I am Bloody Five." Well, Bloody is successful by his own standard, but Galy Gay is even more successful by drawing the opposite conclusion: one shouldn't make a "fuss about a name" and "it is very important that I eat." Final Curtain.

Pirandello. Within this clear structure, there are some less clear, but no less fascinating, things, such as the one piece of spoken verse in the play (scene 9, sixth number), in which Brecht goes far beyond a sociological statement and enters the depths of personal confusion. Indeed, the whole of the fourth and sixth numbers bears witness to a very intimate kind of distress concerning the lack of identity, and the vehicle that Brecht finds to carry the sense is singularly Pirandellian:

URIAH: Fire!
GALY GAY *falls in a faint.*

POLLY: Stop! He fell all by himself!
URIAH: Shoot! So he'll hear he's dead!
They shoot.

Is* A Man's a Man *topical? In some ways, not. As of 1960, our Galy Gays wouldn't be so easily persuaded that war is pleasant. In some ways, too, this play was old-fashioned even in 1925. The imperialism envisaged seems to be that of the nineties ("We're soldiers of the Queen, my lads"), of jingoism, and the days when swords still had glamour, and Orientals seemed to some a lesser breed without the law.

The play belongs to the era of Georg Kaiser's critique of the Machine Age—man dwarfed by his machinery and caught in it—whereas in 1960 Professor Galbraith tells us that the machine is on the decline and that in the Affluent Society persons will be important. This last argument, however, is not really damaging to *A Man's a Man,* for *in what way* are our new managers and executives important? As organization men—as interchangeable ciphers. In their world, Bertolt Brecht's message is still pertinent: a man is most definitely a man.

Martin Esslin has remarked that the play is a prophecy of brainwashing. A good point, but the fable of brainwashing is combined, at least in the first and best version, with one that contradicts it: a fable of a sorcerer's apprentice or Frankenstein's monster. Uriah's brainwashing of Galy Gay can hardly be deemed successful if then Galy Gay eats Uriah's rations! Perhaps the right conclusion is that Brecht's fable happily transcends the topical applications that will crop up from time to time. Of the latter, here is one from *The Nation,* June 11, 1960:

> [Nelson] Rockefeller, the most intellectual advocate of strong Civil Defense, detailed his argument in the April, 1960, issue of *Foreign Affairs*... Rockefeller's words harmonize with the ponderous theorizing of other *Foreign*

Affairs contributors who talk in terms of numbers and percentages instead of horror and anguish, as if war were a chess game...When we concentrate on numbers, survival, and victory, as Rockefeller does, and drive from our minds visions of writhing bodies and screaming flesh, then war becomes thinkable...

Cruelty. It would be hasty to imagine that, in finding his own genre, Brecht could change his emotional system. The emotional patterns of *In the Swamp* are found in the later plays in this or that disguise.

The Brechtian world revolves about an axis that has sadism and masochism as its north and south poles. In one play after another, Brecht saw the humaneness in human nature swamped out by inhumanity, by the cruelty of what he at first thought of as the universe and later as capitalist society. The standard ending of Brecht plays is the total victory of this cruelty. If, near the end of *Days of the Commune,* he indicates in a song that the workers may do better later on, the fact remains that he chose as his subject a classic defeat. *In Brecht's world, badness is active, while goodness is usually passive.* That antithesis is well rendered in *A Man's a Man* in Uriah and Galy Gay. It will be the making of the split good-and-bad ladies of *The Seven Deadly Sins* and *The Good Woman of Setzuan.* And the passivity is not simply good, it has its perverse aspect— Galy Gay relishes his humiliations.

At the end of *King Lear,* Kent sees the world as a rack on which human beings are stretched. That's Brechtian. People talk of the lack of emotion in his plays. Perhaps they mean in his theory of his plays, or perhaps they mean the lack of pleasant emotions. Being tortured is a violent emotional experience, and Brecht's characters, from the earliest plays on, live (it is his own metaphor, taken from Rimbaud) in an inferno. Shlink is lynched, Bloody Five castrates himself, Galy Gay is brainwashed...What of the later plays written (we are told) in the spirit of rationalistic positivism and permitting the audience to keep cool? Self-castration occurs again in *The Private Tutor*. *The Good Woman* is the story of the rending asunder, all but literally, of a young woman. In *Courage*, we watch a mother lose all three children by the deliberate brutality of men. In *Galileo* (as not in actual history), everything hinges on the threat of physical torture. Though torture cannot very well (*pace* Shakespeare) be shown onstage, Brecht devised scenes that suggest great physical violence without showing it and that push mental torment to the limits of the bearable.

Are we to take plays such as *A Man's a Man* and *Mahagonny* as forecasts of the Nazi regime or even as comment on the already active Nazi movement? If so, we shall have to characterize as "Nazis" certain characters in the very earliest Brecht plays. The fact is that if the Nazis had never existed, Brecht would have invented them.

The scene in which Mother Courage is asked to identify the corpse of her son is thought by some to derive straight from such incidents in recent history—one of which is shown directly by Brecht in "The Zinc Box" (*The Private Life of the Master Race*). But is not the essence of the matter already present in that scene in *A Man's a Man* where the corpse of Galy Gay is supposed to be in a crate and the actual (or former) Galy Gay makes a tormented speech about it?

Brecht the stage director was always insisting that the perpetrators of cruelty not be presented demonstratively. Instead of gesticulating and declaiming, they were to be businesslike, *sachlich*. The actors usually found the reason for this in "the Brecht style," "the alienation-effect and all that," but what Brecht chiefly wanted was to make the cruelty real instead of stagey. And he had in mind a different sort of cruelty from that which the average actor would tend to think of—the cruelty of men who live by cruelty and by little else, men who can order tortures as matter-of-factly as an actor orders a cocktail. Here Brecht pierces through into the pathological—the pathology of a Himmler or an Eichmann.

Whatever else is said of cruelty in Brecht's plays, the nature and quantity of it defeat any attempt on the spectator's part to remain detached in the manner recommended in Brecht's theoretical writings. Brecht's theater is a theater of *more than usually violent* emotion. It is a theater for sadists, masochists, sadomasochists, and all others with any slight tendency in these directions—certainly, then, a theater for everybody.

Saint Joan of the Stockyards

Here Bernard Shaw's Joan enters the menagerie of Bertolt Brecht, Chicago being its location in no less than three Brecht plays—*In the Swamp* and *Arturo Ui* are the others.

Parody. Parody is more important to the modern than to any previous school of comedy. Already in Shaw, parody had become very serious—a way of calling attention to dangerous fallacies.

It has been said that good parody parodies good authors and does not decrease your respect for them. The authors parodied in this play are Shakespeare, Goethe, and Schiller, and certainly they are not the target. One could begin to explain what the target is by mentioning that many supporters of Hitler could and did quote all three of these authors a great deal.

Toward Shaw, Bertolt Brecht's attitude was ambivalent. Already in a tribute he paid the older author in 1926, Brecht had said in passing that the most treasured possessions of Shaw characters were opinions. How contemptuously Brecht thought of the right to your own opinions had already been indicated in certain speeches of Shlink and Uriah. He is at pains to ensure that *his* Joan is entangled in circumstances, not besieged by epigrams.

Whether Brecht had understood Shaw is another matter. It is by circumstances—those of the capitalist system, as interpreted by a Marx or a Brecht—that Shaw's Major Barbara is trapped. Nor are the opinions of Brecht's Joan Dark held to be immaterial. It is to an opinion (atheism) that she is finally won over, and Brecht tips the audience the wink that, had she lived any longer, she would have accepted that last word in opinions: communism.

Now as to Brecht's use of works by Goethe and Schiller, Shakespeare and Shaw in this play, the first two had better be ignored by readers of an English translation, for even the reader who spots the allusions to *Faust II* and *The Maid of Orleans* is still in the dark.

The "light" is the reverent acceptance by the German philistine public of their classics, a reverence that precludes any positive critical interpretation. To the English-speaking audience, the Shakespearean blank verse should, on the other hand, have something to say. For we know the emptiness of our Anglo-Saxon acceptance of Shakespeare, and we can see how serious Brecht's verse has to be to express the utter falsity of the mode of life depicted. In the Brechtian parody, this falsity is quite the reverse of self-proclaimed. The speeches of Mauler and Cridle and the rest are a good deal more dignified, intelligent, plausible than many speeches in the Congressional Record.

Shavianism. As for Shaw, as I said, ambivalence reigns. He is parodied and he is plagiarized. The borrowings are less from *Saint Joan* than from *Major Barbara*. The essence of Brecht's tale, like Shaw's, is that a girl of superior caliber joins the Salvation Army but is later disenchanted by discovering that the Army is involved in "the contradictions of the capitalist system." (Shaw and Brecht were the only good "Marxist playwrights"—partly, no doubt, because they regarded the dialectic as dramatic and not just as valid.) More interesting still is the adoption by both playwrights, in their maturer vein, of fine young women with shining eyes, and a limited or nonexistent interest in men, as the bearers of the banner of the ideal.

Communism. On the Communist question this play is discreet but clear. The Communists are mentioned by name just two or three times—mentions that are at the same time genuflections.

Yet the Communist critic Schumacher observes that Brecht's treatment of the masses is "abstract"—for him a very dirty word.

The Communist critic Kurella observed that such bourgeois converts to leftism as Brecht were obsessed with the conversion of bourgeoisie to leftism. It was a Communist critic who shows no knowledge of Brecht's work, Christopher Caudwell, who wrote the classic denunciation of such converts in the last chapter of his *Illusion and Reality* (1937). Though some today are shocked to hear Brecht accused of "unconscious dishonesty," that formula was applied by Caudwell to the whole class that Brecht belonged to—bourgeois writers with Communist leanings.

Official, or semiofficial, Party writers never had much of a liking for Brecht's attempts to deal with working-class life. It is true that he got it all out of books, out of brief slumming expeditions, out of his imagination. *The menagerie would do very well as Capitalists, but how to render the Proletariat?* Generally, we get those incarnations of sterling simplicity that many believe in and few have met with—I paraphrase one of the few great proletarian artists, D. H. Lawrence. The mother in Brecht's adaptation of Gorky's novel is an example. Another tack is that of agitprop: treat the workers as a group and present them onstage as a singing or verse-speaking choir. *Saint Joan of the Stockyards* belongs to Brecht's agitprop phase.

Galileo

History. The historical understanding played no part in the writing of *Galileo,* nor did Brecht pay his respects to historical accuracy except in the broad outline and in certain details. Not a great deal is known, but one can be sure that the historical Galileo was nothing like this; nor were his problems of this type; nor did his opponents resemble those whom Brecht invents for him.

Galileo is not a Marxist play either. What Marxist historian would accept the unhistorical major premise: namely, that if an Italian scientist had refused to renounce Copernicus in 1633 "an age of reason would have begun," and our age of unreason would have been avoided? What Marxist historian could accept the notion that a Catholic scientist of the seventeenth century, whose best friends were priests, who placed both his daughters in a convent as young girls, was halfway a Marxist, resented convents and church-going, doubted the existence of God, and regarded his tenets in physics as socially revolutionary?

But it is one of the open secrets of dramatic criticism that historical plays are unhistorical. They depend for their life on relevance to the playwright's own time—and, if he is lucky, all future times—not on their historicity.

It might, of course, be asked why a playwright would choose historical material at all, and pretend to be limited by it. There are reasons. For one, he relies on the public's ignorance of the secrets, closed or open, of dramatic criticism. Audiences assume that most of what they see in a history play did happen, and it may be that most of the "history" in the popular mind comes from such sources. By popular, I don't mean proletarian. I met a Hollywood director at the première of *Galileo* and asked him what he thought of it. "As a play? I don't know," he answered, "but it is always thrilling to hear the truth, to see what actually happened!" Well, the joke was not on Brecht, and this incident helps to explain why historical plays are still written.

The character of Brecht's Galileo. It is a play—not fact but fiction—and one of the criteria by which playwrights are judged is their ability to create characters who can, as it were, "take up their bed and walk"—who can assume the frightening autonomy of the six who once stood in the path of Pirandello. This play lives, to a large extent, by the character of the protagonist, a character Brecht cut out of whole cloth—that is to say, created out of his own resources. What makes this Galileo a fascinating figure is that his goodness and badness, strength and weakness, have the same source: a big appetite and a Wildean disposition to give way to it. His appetite for knowledge is of a piece with his appetite for food, and so the same quality can appear, in different circumstances, as magnificent or as mean. I don't see how the theory of Epic Theater could do justice to the ambiguity here. It calls for a theory of tragedy. The problem is not social and conditioned but personal and inherent.

Whatever the theorist makes of it, that particular ambiguity is very satisfyingly presented—is perhaps the play's chief exhibit. There is another ambiguity, equally fascinating, if not equally well defined. In this work, the self-denunciatory impulse in Brecht—not to speak again of masochism—has a field day. His Galileo denounces himself twice, and the two denunciations are designed to be the twin pillars upon which the whole edifice rests. The first of them, the historic abjuration of Copernicanism, was, we may be sure, what suggested the play in the beginning. The second was Brecht's invention.

One can hardly hear either for the crackle of dialectics. The first is immediately condemned by Andrea ("Unhappy is the land that breeds no hero"), and defended in a very Brechtian proverb by Galileo ("Unhappy is the land that *needs* a hero"). Then Galileo changes his mind, and in the last scene (as performed), the argument is reversed. Andrea takes the line that the abjuration had been justified because "Science has only one commandment: contribution," Galileo having by now contributed the *Discorsi*. Thereupon Galileo whips himself up into a self-lacerating fury: "Any man who does what I have done must not be tolerated in the ranks of science!" He who had made the great False Confession, which according to Brecht destroyed him in the eyes of the good and just, now makes the great True Confession, *which is his destruction in his own eyes—and before the eyes of the only person in the story with whom he has an emotional relationship.*

It is theater on the grandest scale, and I call the conception fascinating because it is an attempt to bring together the most widely divided sections of Brecht's own divided nature: on the one hand, the hedonist and "coward," on the other, the "hero"—and masochist. It is hardly necessary to say that "no masochism was intended." Any element of masochism destroys, of course, the Marxist intention of this finale. But, once again, *Brecht is not Marxism.* Brecht is Brecht—and Galileo is *his,* not Marx's, prophet.

Here the conscious and the unconscious motives are so directly in conflict that complete clarity cannot result. What we get is an impression of improbability. We recognize that the final self-denunciation is all very moral, but we are not convinced that the old reprobate would actually make it. Such a person naturally believes, "Unhappy is the land that needs a hero." What changed his mind? There would be a drama in such a change, and one wouldn't like to miss it. When Brecht simply *announces* the change, Galileo seems only his master's voice—a very different thing from being, as he was till then, his master's embodiment.

The matter is even less clear than I make it out. It is almost possible to believe that Galileo is only scolding himself (for which we give him credit) and in general is the same man as before. In giving his manuscript to Andrea he pretends he is, as usual, giving way to weakness, succumbing to temptation. The incident, particularly in the 1938 to 1939 version, is very endearing. In this respect the man is true to character to the end, and one has to admit his character has its points. *It is possible, in the main, to stay pro-Galileo to the end.* A familiar Brechtian feature! Moral disapproval goes one way, but human sympathy goes the same way! Onstage the apparatus of alienation is called into action *as a fire brigade.* The whole effort of the Berlin Ensemble production is to counteract the natural flow of sympathy to Galileo. These actors know this particular job well. They have performed it for *Puntila;* as I write, they are performing it for a *Threepenny Opera* in which Mackie is not to be allowed any charm; and they try in vain to perform it for *Mother Courage.*

Galileo as a portrait of the artist. The term *portrait of the artist*—for novelists and dramatists at least—is a relative one. A character may be three-quarters self-portrait and one-quarter a portrait of someone else or sheer invention. The proportion of self-portrayal may indeed be anything from zero to a hundred percent. There is sense in speaking of a portrait of the artist only when the relation to the artist is very marked and of special significance. In the present case, it is.

As already noted, there is a lot of Brecht in Baal, Kragler, and Garga. Then Brecht did not sit to himself for a long time. Which presumably means that he split himself up into *all* his characters. He often put the idealistic part of himself inside one of the young ladies with the shining eyes. He was likely to let the nonidealistic part of himself into the rogue of any play...

Why Galileo Galilei? Auden says the poet cannot portray the poet, and points to Shaw's Marchbanks as an awful example. But the poet can portray the poet by pretending he is something else, such as an architect (Solness) or a philosopher (Jack Tanner)—or a scientist (Galileo). Marxism considers itself scientific, which is one reason why it appealed to Brecht. Then there is the matter of History again. Whether or not the playwright is scrupulous about the historical record, a historical play carries the Idea of Fact...

Getting rid of one's personality, Brecht had written at the time he gave himself to social causes, was an amusing business. If only the subjective did not exist! If only one *were* history! And science! And by the time one *is* history and science—in this play, *Galileo*— it is interesting that one still has the same human constitution as before: one is a genius, one would like to be committed to a cause, but one is a rogue.

Rogues and knaves. Rogues are different from knaves—at least in plays. Uriah is a knave. He is the Enemy, the Cruel World, Capitalism, and so on. So, I think, is Peachum. They are nothing if not active, while your rogue, though applying himself busily to this or that, is fundamentally passive. Widow Begbick is a rogue, and in a late version of the script she sings a song celebrating her passivity— she calls it not resisting the current of the river. Macheath is more rogue than knave, and it is passivity, in the form of "sexual submissiveness," that defeats him, as the story indicates and two long songs emphasize. Brecht in fact created a long line of rogues of whom Mother Courage and Puntila are only the most conspicuous. They differ from the knaves in being likable, even charming. Whatever disapproval we might feel is cancelled by the fact that their roguery is unsuccessful and was predestined to be so. Or it is successful in a very small and unimportant area. Brecht will make sure we understand that our hatred, if given primarily to them, is misdirected.

Or will he? The problem is complicated by the extent to which the rogue is always Brecht himself. His enjoyment of himself was qualified by an unusually large quota of self-hatred. The former would show itself in first drafts; the latter would be given full play in later revisions, not to mention notes and other outside comments. (The first drafts of *Puntila* and *Galileo* are particularly revealing.)

Heroism, martyrdom, masochism. It has been pointed out that the passive sufferers of Brechtian drama are offset by the heroic resisters. It has also been pointed out that what the heroes do is as passive as what the sufferers do: they obey, consent, submit. Galileo, then, is given his choice of two kinds of passivity: submit to fear or submit to torture. The passive characters of the early plays (Galy Gay, Shlink) had submitted to torture—masochistically. Galileo submits to fear and later denounces himself—most masochistically, as we have seen—before Andrea. Had he submitted to torture, that would have certified him a hero and therefore no masochist. Such would be Brecht's alibi. But he didn't use it. And it is not a valid alibi because writer and character are distinct in this: that the portrayal of nonmasochistic heroism can itself be a highly masochistic act.

In any event, it is not really heroism, but martyrdom, that is in question, and it is well known that only a thin line divides masochistic submission from true martyrdom. If Galileo were tortured, you wouldn't get a tragedy, but, from Brecht's viewpoint, a happy ending, with Galileo a martyr of science. Here, however, we use the term *martyr* in a debased way. In Brecht's view, Galileo should have been willing to die because the news of his refusal to recant could have been exploited by the right side. This is the kind of thing we have in mind in modern politics when we say, "Let's not ruin such and such a man or we'll provide our opponents with a martyr." Anything further from the original idea of martyrdom could hardly be imagined.

Gluttony: a deadly sin. The most famous line Brecht wrote is, "Erst kommt das Fressen, dann kommt die Moral"—eating comes first; morality, second. It is one of his passive and charming rogues speaking (or rather, singing): Macheath. The sentiment is one that the passive and charming Brecht would endorse, but that the active and activ*ist* Brecht would denounce. He denounces it in *Puntila* where a tale is told, in tones of awe, of a young man named Athi whose heroic deed it was to starve rather than eat food that came from his capitalist foe. In this context—again it is the context of Brecht's own mind and work that matters—Galileo's love of food takes on more meaning. I rather think Laughton got the part because Brecht had seen the ravenous eating he did in the *Henry VIII* film. (In *Galileo*, Laughton tore a goose apart in exactly the same way.) Galy Gay's superiority to Bloody Five in *A Man's a Man* consists in his knowing that "it is very important that I eat," and his transformation in the final scene is shown mainly in his wolfing the rations of the three others. *In the Swamp* culminates in a conclusion written in a similar form of words, though containing no reference to food. "It is not important," says this particular passive protagonist (Garga), "to be the stronger one, but to be the living one." He is providing the reason for all that gluttony—as well as the provocation for Athi's hunger strike. Such, by the way, are the kinds of details through which the unity of Brecht's work is discovered.

It will be recalled that Brecht's word both for commercial entertainment and for the sensuous, thought-inhibiting, action-inhibiting high art of our era was *culinary.*

The Good Woman of Setzuan

Anna-Anna. Already in *The Seven Deadly Sins,* Brecht had made of his usual antithesis—kind versus cruel, humane versus inhumane, natural versus unnatural, idealistic versus realistic—a division within the same person. The world being bad, the good person requires a bad "half" if he is to survive. In this proposition, there is no contradiction between Brecht's natural constitution and Marxism, provided the negative side be identified with capitalism. Even the key role of the economic motive was something Brecht had worked out on his own: in *A Man's a Man,* written before the conversion to Marxism, we find Uriah only able to hold on to Galy Gay by the lure of a "deal."

Drama schematic and abstract. Brecht did not like the word *abstract.* He made a personal motto of the phrase "truth is concrete." And in this, most of the literary world, on both sides of the Iron Curtain, agrees with him. But what are they all agreeing to? The word *concrete* is an abstraction, and all art is abstracted from life, with considerable subtraction and distortion along the way—just think of the Brecht menagerie!

But I would not try to empty the antithesis concrete/abstract of all meaning. It makes sense to say *The Three Sisters* presents life more concretely than does the *Oresteia;* and it is a fact that writers today emulate this concreteness rather than that abstractness. Even so, most nonmodern drama was more abstract, and modern drama continually reverts to relative abstractness. After Ibsen (concrete), expressionism (abstract).

Brecht believed that he reinstated the concrete. But did he? On the contrary, beginning with *A Man's a Man,* he created a dramaturgy as schematic and abstract as any workable dramaturgy well could be. With its numbering, its blackboard demonstrations, its many unashamedly two-dimensional characters, it is surely the abstractest thing in drama since the Spanish *autos* of the seventeenth century. Nor am I speaking merely of the *Lehrstücke.* Beginning with *A Man's a Man,* and not least in *The Good Woman of Setzuan,* Brecht's drama is all schematic and abstract—more so perhaps than is acceptable to the larger theater public of many countries today.

A Man's a Man has the form of a scientific demonstration. One draft actually ends with the words "Quod erat demonstrandum." *The Good Woman* is similar. As in the earlier play, the first sequence of action presents a premise or hypothesis. Then comes the action, which is divided into clearly demarcated sections, each proving its own point. As Shen Te puts it at the end, she had only tried

1. to help her neighbor,
2. to love her lover, and
3. to keep her little son from want.

These are the three main sections and "actions" of the play. When Shen Te has failed in all three respects, even with increased help each time from her alter ego Shui Ta, she makes her appeal to the gods. There is nothing they can do. Q.E.D.

It sounds dismal! And what could have been a worse fate for the theater than the theories and "schemes" of Brecht without his talent, which so often works, not hand in hand with the theories and "schemes," but at daggers drawn with them? This much must be conceded to those who abhor the schematic and the abstract: the schematic and the abstract never amount to theater, drama, literature, art, *by themselves.* Yet, if what is added is not the "concrete" characterization and milieu that we are used to, what is it? In other words:

What is Epic Theater, actually? In the first instance, a misnomer. And this Brecht, in effect, has admitted. The word *epic* suggests too many things or the wrong things. In England and America, there is the added trouble that our schools don't make much use of the old triple division of literature: epic, lyric, dramatic. There is a lot to be said for *not* using it, as the dramatic is not a separate genre running parallel to the others without touching them. The dramatic has traditionally embraced epic and lyric elements.

But *epic* does make a good antithesis to *lyric*. In *Illusion and Reality*, Caudwell makes them so different it would be hard to conceive of the same person excelling at both, harder still to find him combining the two in one work. Caudwell's theory, oversimplified, is that the lyric writer writes himself while the epic writer writes the world. Even my oversimplification helps in explaining Brecht, who was originally a "lyric" poet, but who, when he discovered the world, tried to do without the self altogether and create a wholly "epic" drama.

Brecht never really succeeded in writing a novel—that is, never became a fully epic writer. He remained the Poet as Playwright, and if we speak not of intentions but attainments, we should call his theater a lyric theater. The name would certainly bring out his qualities, rather than his defects.

There are defects—or perhaps *deficiencies* would be the word— in the area where the novelist or epic writer excels, namely, in the full presentation of individual character. Brecht would show at his worst in a comparison with Ibsen. But Ibsen—the "modern" Ibsen, that is—would show at his worst in a comparison with Brecht: for he has cut out the lyric element by the roots.

Lyric theater would also prove a misleading term. There would be confusion with opera—or with decorative drama written in verse like, say, Christopher Fry's plays. Caudwell's formula guides us to a deeper interpretation of the lyric: the writer's relation to all of life is always at stake in it. The "lyricism" of *The Good Woman of Setzuan* is not isolated in the songs or bits of spoken verse. Rather, these are emanations of the spirit in which the whole play is composed. The prose, too, is poetry—not decorative, but of the essence.

Epic theater is lyric theater. The twentieth century has seen a series of attempts to reinstate poetry in the theater. Brecht made the most successful of these attempts. How? If it was not because he was a better poet—and one can scarcely maintain that he was a better poet than Yeats or Eliot—why was it? Cocteau's phrase "poetry of the theater" as distinct from "poetry *in* the theater" helps us toward the answer. As early as 1920, Eliot had completely debunked the kind of drama that is poetic chiefly in consisting of mellifluous or even exquisite lines. Nonetheless, his own interest continued to be in the poetic line and the way it was written: the free verse of *The Cocktail Party* is offered as an alternative to the blank verse and stanzas of the Victorians. Now, though Brecht too had his alternative forms of dialogue to offer, they are but a part of a Grand Design to replace the Victorian drama in all departments. And it is the design as a whole that provides the answer to the question: what kind of lyric theater? The poetry *of* the theater is not a poetry of dialogue alone, but of stage design, of lighting, of acting, and of directing. Nor is it enough that these be "imaginative"—to use Robert Edmond Jones's word for his vision of a poetry of the theater—they must also be called to order, subordinated to the statement being made. For this theater is no fireworks display. It is not there to show off the theater arts, together or individually, but to show off the world around us and the world within us—to make a statement about that world. Hence, while Jones's designs often look better in a book than on the stage, photographs of the Brechtian stage, thrilling as they are, fall short of doing justice to the phenomenon itself. There is this difference too. Jones was adding his own vision to that of an author: two inevitably somewhat disparate contributions were made toward what would be at best a happy combination. In the Brecht theater, though others made contributions, he himself laid the foundation in every department: he was the stage designer, the composer, and the director. The production as a whole, not just the words, was the poem. It was in essence, and often in detail, *his* poem.

Collaboration. It has not escaped attention that, following the title page of a Brecht play, there is a page headed *Mitarbeiter*—Collaborators. It has only escaped attention that these names are in small type and do not appear on the title page of the book or, presumably, on the publisher's royalty statements.

All the collaborators, and many who have witnessed the work of collaboration, have testified to Brecht's penchant for collaborating. We learn that at one period he didn't like to write alone and seated but only pacing the floor and talking with several "collaborators." We hear of his willingness to snap up a phrase or notion supplied by an onlooker.

Yet Brecht had no talent at all for collaboration if the word carries any connotation of equality, of give and take. His talent was for domination and exploitation, though the ethics of the procedure were in this sense satisfactory, that his collaborators were always people who wanted and needed to be dominated and exploited. That this should be true of friends and mistresses who never wrote anything notable of their own goes without saying. It is true also of the Big Names, including the biggest name of all—that of Kurt Weill. Weill has no more enthusiastic and enthralled listener than myself: the glory of his music for *Mahagonny* and the other Brecht works is not in question. But how was that success achieved? Brecht sometimes intimated that he himself contributed some or all of the tunes of *The Threepenny Opera*. For years I considered this a boast. Later I came to believe it. For I saw the way Brecht worked with composers, and I listened to the music Weill wrote before and after his collaboration with Brecht. Weill took on the artistic personality of any writer he happened to work with. He had no (artistic) personality of his own. For a theatrical composer this is conceivably an advantage. I am not arguing that point. I would only mention in passing that what is true of Weill is true of Eisler. The music of both is parasitic. When parasitic upon Brecht, it is nearly always superb. Parasitic upon second-raters, it is second-rate. And when they attempt music that is not parasitic at all, music that is bolstered by no writer, music that is not imitative of any composer, or even music that is not in some sense serious or flippant, a parody of other music, they court disaster.

What kind of stage designs has Caspar Neher made for other playwrights? Often, very good ones, but in what way? Either in his Brecht style or in some established mode that would not mark off his work from that of any other eminent modernist. The "originality" of Neher is concentrated in the work he did for Brecht. Since that work was inspired *by* Brecht, it is clear that the word *originality* is in need of redefinition.

Brecht dominated not only the collaborators who were present in the flesh but also the dead or absent writers whose works he adapted. *The Threepenny Opera* is not a "steal" but a new work and just as "original" as John Gay's *Beggar's Opera.* In no case can the success or the character of a Brecht work be attributed to the writer or writers whom he drew upon. Though you might, for example, believe that Brecht "ruined" *The Private Tutor,* by that very token you can hardly attribute the proven effectiveness of the new play to Lenz.

What is interesting is not the legal issue of plagiarism—a hare started by Alfred Kerr long ago—but a critical problem: how was it that Brecht arrived at his results in this particular way? Perhaps the burden of proof is on those who regard the opposite procedure as normal, since it is only in recent times that "life" and not literature has come to be regarded as the usual source for a dramatist's plots and characters. The most "original" playwright of all, Shakespeare, is also the one who keeps scholars busiest studying his literary sources. Molière said he took his material wherever he found it—and the place he meant was literature or the theater, not "life." Why did Brecht return to the earlier method? The question can hardly be answered en passant, but one thing is clear: that in exploring the whole range of dramatic art Brecht rediscovered the many-sided significance of collaboration.

The heart of the matter is that the individual artist contributes less to his art than is commonly supposed. A large contribution is always made by collaborators, visible and invisible. Drama, being narrative in a concentrated form, relies even more on the collaboration of others than does fiction. The dramatist draws on more "conventions" as a welcome shortcut—conventions being unwritten agreements with the audience. He is inclined to use not the raw material of life, but material that has already been "worked" by another artist. It takes all sorts of collaboration to make dramatic art, the final collaborative act being that which unites performer and spectator.

The book from which most comments on this last subject are—directly or indirectly—taken is *The Crowd* by Gustave LeBon. There is a fatal equivocation in it. LeBon fails to distinguish between the crowd in the concrete (say, one thousand people of any kind in a theater) and the crowd in the abstract (the proletariat, the masses, and so on). Slurring over this simple difference, he enjoys himself reaching unwarranted conclusions.

In English we would call the first phenomenon the *audience* and the second the *public;* and it occurs to me that English is unusual in having these two words. In French the audience is called *le public;* in German, *das Publikum.* Language seems to put English-speaking persons in immediate possession of a useful distinction.

We have heard much, too much, of the contribution the audience makes to a show. The audience laughs or cries, is attentive or fidgety, creates an atmosphere, sets up a current of psychic electricity between itself and the players . . . All of which is to speak of the problems that arise at the end of the whole process of writing and rehearsing. No essential problem can be solved at that late point, as has a hundred times been shown in the history of American out-of-town tryouts, without anyone's learning the lesson.

The audience's collaboration is one thing, the public's is another. There comes to mind Synge's historic statement that all art is a collaboration between the artist and his people. Synge correctly observed that something had gone terribly wrong in modern times. In my terms: the problem of the modern theater is the problem, not of the audience only, but of the public.

One sign of this is that your audience problem can often be solved, while the problem of the public remains where it was. The problem of the audience has been that it has lacked homogeneity, common purpose, warmth. You can get these things by picking an audience of people united in a common faith. I would say T. S. Eliot solved the audience problem when he put on *Murder in the Cathedral* in the cathedral at Canterbury. Here is a theatrical "experiment" that succeeded. But that audience did not help Mr. Eliot to write his play. The public was not only not collaborating, it was absent, indifferent, even hostile.

Bertolt Brecht's radical reconsideration of theater and drama includes a reconsideration of both audience and public. The trade unions and other large groups who would buy out the house once a week in the Germany of the twenties obviously represented a new audience and might also suggest the idea of a new public that corresponds to a new working-class culture. Seen in this connection, Brecht's communism will not appear as implausible as it does to many of his readers in America today. Such readers would do well to remember that an artist will accept almost anything if it seems to offer a future for his art.* Brecht accepted communism as Pascal advised accepting supernatural religion: as a bet according to which you have everything to gain and very little to lose. Concerned for the integrity of the theater art, Brecht looked to proletarianism as the only way in which the artist could regain the kind of collaboration that Synge in 1900 thought was barely available anymore.

Now, in his estimates of power and political success, Brecht showed shrewdness. At a time when the Soviet Union was considered weak, and the huge social-democratic movement in Western Europe tended to be anti-Communist, Brecht put his money on Moscow. There is little need, in 1960, to explain what a sound investment that was—if political success is the criterion. What if we apply other criteria—especially the very simple one of an audience and a public for Brecht?

---

* "Only by crawling on his belly can an unpopular and troublesome man get a job that leaves him enough free time." Thus spake (Brecht's) Galileo.

As far as the public goes, one normally considers it as collaborating with the artist while he is planning and writing. Brecht, however, believed that he belonged with the public of the future. Only socialism could give his works a home. He once told me in so many words that if world socialism did not come about he did not expect his works to have any future at all.

The Soviet Union gave Brecht the Stalin Peace Prize. East Germany gave him a place to live and a large subsidy for a theater. Does this amount to a public? Did Brecht's plays find their proper habitat? Did Epic Theater establish itself as the theater of the Communist countries?

There was a small production of *Threepenny Opera* in Russia some thirty years ago! Despite the visit of the Berlin Ensemble in 1957, the Russians are still (1960) not doing any Brecht plays. Nor are most of the East German theaters. The failure to find a public is total. On the other hand, Brecht has found an enthusiastic audience. But it consists of just the sort of people he ostensibly didn't want—chiefly the intelligentsia of "decadent" Paris and London.

As for what Brecht really wanted, we find the same ambivalence in this field as in others. When in America, he was brave about being ignored on Broadway. "Why expect them to pay for their own liquidation?" he once said to me. But he fretted about it too, and made a few stabs at crass commercial success. His attitude to the avant-garde theater was similar. The "so-called avant-garde" was not important, but, "under certain conditions," it would take up his plays. "What conditions?" I once asked him. "Well," he replied, "if I were a Frenchman—or if I became the rage in Paris." And to be the rage in Paris—"intellectual," "advanced," almost "revolutionary" Paris—is, as far as worldly success goes, the highest achievement of Brecht to date.

Even aside from politics, it is questionable whether Brecht could have had what he wanted. There comes to mind Georg Lukács's statement that, in the great ages, the drama flowed "naturally" from the existing theater, while, from Goethe on, the poet-dramatist rejects the theater, writes plays that are "too good for it," and then calls for the creation of the kind of theater that will be good enough for the plays. Brecht saw the weakness of the post-Goethe position—without being able to escape it. If there is any theater you cannot see a man's plays naturally flowing from, it is a theater that doesn't yet exist! If there is any public that is not a collaborator, it is a public that isn't yet there! We all applaud the work of the Berlin Ensemble, but that institution is not the product of a new proletarian society. Its audience is the bourgeois avant-garde. Its leaders—Herr Engel and Frau Weigel—are noble relics of the culture of the despised Weimar Republic. As for Bertolt Brecht, the point is not so much that he didn't succeed in getting any plays written about the doings in East Germany, as that, if he had, they would inescapably have been the product of the mind and sensibility that made *In the Swamp*. East German literary critics have been happier with Thomas Mann, who made no bones about being bourgeois, than with this uncomfortable Bavarian rogue.

Has **The Good Woman of Setzuan** *dated?* This query is not as easy as it sounds, because all plays "date" in many respects, even though some go on being played and read forever. In this case, the question is, does the play belong irretrievably to the Depression era? It does presuppose general unemployment on the one hand, and, on the other, slave-driver capitalists, like those of the factory system in the classic era of capitalism as described by Marx and Engels. An audience that does not presuppose these things will not cry "How true!" as often as the author would like. Today's audience knows, for example, that the composer who in the thirties predicted the swift demise of American capitalism in *The Cradle Will Rock* is today writing another revolutionary opera with the help of money from Henry Ford.

But such changes in background are negative factors: they only explain why a play will not receive an artificial "lift" from the audience. To the extent that *The Good Woman* is a good play and not absolutely confined in relevance to the Depression, it can command an audience. I see no reason, for that matter, to try to limit the interpretation of Brecht's plays to what is known to be his own understanding of them. As Shaw would put it, he was only the author. He was neither the audience nor the arbiter. During the Stalinist era, *The Good Woman* presented a good picture of current tendencies in Soviet society, with Shui Ta as the necessary "realistic" correction of the earlier idealism, and Yang Sun as, eventually, a high Party functionary, rising by the path of Stakhanovism. More permanently, the two sides of Shen Te, as they arise from the divided nature of Brecht, express such a division for all of us—and the tendency thereto that exists *in* all of us.

Mother Courage

Beyond place and time. It would be rash to expect this play to be any more historical than *Galileo* is. The vein of cynicism in which Mother Courage sings and speaks of war is the tone of the twentieth century, more particularly of Bertolt Brecht, and not that of seventeenth-century peasant women. Like Brecht's Galileo, she has all the negative side of Marxism under her belt, lacking only the positive belief in social progress.

Indications of place mean no more than indications of time. You can tell that from the way Brecht would change both. "The Song of the Great Souls" in *Mother Courage* (Sweden, Germany, and so on, in the seventeenth century) is taken bodily from *The Threepenny Opera* (England in the nineteenth to twentieth centuries). The "Song of the Fishwife and the Soldier" seems, from its setting in *Mother Courage,* to tell a German tale. The omission of the one word *Volga* conceals the fact that an earlier rendering had set it in Russia. An action can be transported thousands of miles by the changing of a single word! In short, there is no concrete locality in Brecht's drama. Place, like time, is abstract. This feature represents an inheritance from expressionism. Brecht's work is continuous with that of the expressionists to the extent that he tried to construct abstract models of his subject. *Mahagonny* and *The Threepenny Opera* provide, not a socialist-realist report on capitalism, but the Platonic idea of it.

But Brecht sank his roots much deeper in human history than the expressionists did—and in the history of the abstract in drama. Obsessed with religion—a subject he could not keep away from for more than a few pages at a time—he often thought in terms of traditional religious abstractions. He wrote a *Seven Deadly Sins* and sketched a *Dance of Death.* His first and best book of poems had the form of a manual of piety. Converted to communism, his mind ran, not forward to some Artwork of the Future, but back to the cantata and the oratorio. His "invention," the *Lehrstück,* is a sort of Catholic morality play revised by a Marxist reader of Luther's Bible.

The Deadly Sins and the Christian Virtues. *The Good Woman* is a schematic and abstract study of the three parts of Shen Te's goodness: love of her neighbor, love of her man, and love of her offspring. *Mother Courage* is equally schematic, and is also tripartite. The action divides into three sections at the end of each of which a child is killed. Each child represents one of the virtues. Eilif is called the Brave Son. Swiss Cheese is called the Honest Son. Kattrin is characterized by kindness in the little charade of the black cross. In that charade, the whole action is seen in advance. In the "Song of the Great Souls," near the end, it is summed up retrospectively and abstractly in terms of the virtues themselves. Caesar, too, was brave and got killed. Socrates was honest and got killed. Saint Martin was kind and died of cold. As it was demonstrated in *The Seven Deadly Sins* that natural and healthy impulses become "sins" that society will not tolerate, so it is demonstrated in *Mother Courage* that the cardinal virtues are not for this world. In other words, *Mother Courage* is quite close, in what it says, to *The Good Woman.* For that matter, it is close to *The Threepenny Opera,* where also the "Song of the Great Souls"— under the name of the "Song of Solomon"—can be taken as a summary of the whole play. Brecht is one of those artists—Ibsen and Conrad are others—who do not really change their subject from one work to the next but, all their life long, worry the same point.

Such an artist soon becomes a bore unless that point is of great moment and unless he can present it in various aspects. How can the principle of variety be applied to the notion of the Virtues? One way is by irony. Eilif's bravery turns out in the end to be only what is wrongly called bravery: like Galy Gay he is transformed into a foolhardy bandit. Another way to variety is by parallelism and contrast in character and narrative. Not only is one brother offset by a second, the daughter is offset by another kind of daughter (a daughter of joy). Yvette's career yields the one success story in the play. This has its own irony. Yvette's success is doubly ambiguous: it is accompanied by physical and moral deterioration, and it is exhibited with (the author's) disapproval. Kattrin, by contrast, is a failure at the start and becomes more of a failure all the time. But just as Brecht (in the full text) had drawn an analogy between Swiss Cheese and Christ, so he makes of Kattrin his own type of hero—the activist—and confers upon her a kind of glory.

The Positive Hero. At this point, the virtue which Kattrin represents comes within range of the virtue of the Positive Hero in Soviet literature. But that was not the kind of abstractness to which Brecht was naturally drawn. He is careful not to make Kattrin an idealist. It is not for an idea that she dies but, on the contrary, because, on the subject of children, she is not rational: she is a *Kindernarr,* crazy for little ones. If Brecht moves toward the abstract in this characterization, the abstraction is not Philanthropy but Mother Love, an instinct celebrated in a whole series of his plays. Another touch that belongs very much to this poet, rather than to a school of thought, is that Kattrin cannot speak. In the world here depicted, Virtue has no voice, or at least, if she has, even the poet cannot find it. And yet there is rebellion. "The stones begin to speak," says the scene heading. And Mother Courage had called

Kattrin "a stone in Dalarna." (Symbolism with a vengeance! Though *symbolism*, in Brecht circles, was as nasty a word as *abstraction*, like abstraction it will prove a necessary word to true critics of Brecht.)

Brecht chose to be the voice of the voiceless. Such was the positive side of his impulse toward radicalism, a side sometimes obscured by his readiness to excuse Stalinist brutality.

> Und die Einen sind im Dunkeln
> Und die Anderen sind im Licht.
> Und man siehet die im Lichte
> Die im Dunkeln sieht man nicht.
>
> Some are children of the darkness
> Some are children of the sun.
> You can see the sons of sunshine
> Sons of dark are seen by none.

To bring light into this darkness was the mission of Bertolt Brecht, who had all the makings of a popular, though not of a proletarian, poet.

The "drum" scene is possibly the most powerful scene, emotionally, in twentieth-century drama. Any actress playing Courage might be hard put to it to hold her own, and, if one "sovietized" the play, Kattrin would be the protagonist. To put her mother center stage was to invite the complaint that the play was not truly Communist but pacifist, defeatist, and bourgeois. But Brecht did put her mother center stage, and did not entitle his play *Dumb Kattrin*.

That Brecht should have proved the leading Communist writer of the Stalin era is perhaps the most striking of all the Brechtian contradictions. The Positive Hero is one of the few ideas that Stalin and Zhdanov contributed to literary discussion, and Brecht stood for nothing if not the opposite. His protagonists from Baal through Azdak are nothing if not *negative* heroes. Brecht got angry when actresses made Courage noble and even—supreme error!—

courageous. For this writer's first weapon—and here again he stands in direct contrast to Stalin's writers—is irony. Nicknamed Courage by a fluke, as she readily explains, the lady represents, in the first instance, the diametric opposite of courage, namely, cowardice, and the diametric opposite of active virtue, namely, passivity. That she keeps herself busy—works her hands to the bone—is an added irony. Such are the "ridiculous superhuman efforts" that Brecht's Galileo attributes to the peasantry in general: they are passive in the class struggle, which is to say, in history. As in her previous incarnation as Widow Begbick, Mother Courage is content to flow with the tide—even though her own song (of the Fishwife) tells where the tide inexorably leads: to death.

Critics of *Mother Courage* could hardly fail to observe that people in it die, but they don't seem to have noticed that dying is implicit in the play from the first scene on—a scene that begins with the song, "Let your men drink before they die!" and ends with the prophecy of the death of all three children. The vision of death, the prospect of death, is what is most vivid about the play. The spirit it is shot through with is that of the death-wishing Brecht of the early plays: Mother Courage is a new spokesman for the old disenchantment. If Brecht put some of himself into Kattrin and she sums up Brecht the activist and lover of mankind, he put even more into his passive and negative heroine, Mother Courage the coward.

The final touch—which I think only one critic (Esslin) has spotted—is that, in the last instance, Mother Courage does have courage: not the kind that Brecht officially favored, not the kind he could have admitted to be there at all, but the kind he must have covertly respected since he makes it command respect in the play. This is, to borrow a phrase from Brecht's friend Paul Tillich,* "the courage to be"—the courage to exist in the face of a world that so powerfully recommends nonexistence.

---

* I do not know how much of a friend, but I first met Dr. Tillich in the Brecht-Berlau apartment at 124 East Fifty-seventh Street, New York.

Critics who confront *Mother Courage* may need to speak not only of the abstract and symbolic but of the tragic. But this we have already found to be true of *Galileo*. We shall find it true of *The Caucasian Chalk Circle* as well.

Why the Thirty Years' War? Because in German history it is the locus classicus of death—the death, not of individuals, but of cities and populations. Brecht had seen World War I, and could *fore*see World War II. Even if the play did not find a permanent place in the repertoire, it would always remain a great literary document of our age of world wars, as Grimmelshausen's *Simplicissimus* is a great literary document of the seventeenth century.

To some extent Grimmelshausen was the inspirer of *Mother Courage*. His work certainly brought to Brecht a sense of death, decay, and disaster, corresponding rather closely to his own, yet insofar as the sources—or provocations—of the play are literary, there is an author who has an even better claim to be considered the main source. If the Thirty Years' War had been lived through by Grimmelshausen, it had been seen in perspective by a much better-known German writer who also happens to be Germany's most widely admired dramatist, Friedrich Schiller.

The left-wing intelligentsia of the twenties had it in for Schiller. Piscator deglamorized *The Robbers* by making it a picture of the class struggle à la Marx. Brecht was strongly anti-Schiller. There were times when he seemed to see himself as *the* Anti-Schiller, a sort of German equivalent of the Antichrist. If Schiller gave the heroic view of the war—classical in its dignity, romantic in its presentation of women—Brecht would give the antiheroic, anticlassical, antiromantic worm's-eye view. *Mother Courage* stands to *Wallenstein* as *Saint Joan of the Stockyards* to *The Maid of Orleans*. This is a two-sided statement, for Brecht did not merely parody the classics. His procedure in his *Saint Joan* contrasts with that of those modernizers who take an old theme and vulgarize it. No work of Brecht's is so resolutely stately. He was trying to find an equivalent for Schiller's sublimity. As for *Mother Courage,* it might well have been suggested by the first part of the *Wallenstein* trilogy.

The Caucasian Chalk Circle

Charm and naïveté. How is this play built? The incident of the chalk circle takes up only one scene. What is the rest of the play there for? So that we can get to know the Judge? But he doesn't appear till the second half. What is the first half of the play there for? It would be hard to find a satisfying reason in the doctrinaire terms in which Brecht and his colleagues discussed plays. Why couldn't a reason be found along traditional artistic lines? Not all the play is didactic. Was not Brecht capable of relaxing a little, telling a touching story, and filling it out with a poem and a song?

He was. Not the least of the many disservices of his theorizing to his cause was to obscure the presence in his work of the primary attributes of good theater. Take such a thing as *charm.* The word has been preempted, latterly, by advertisers of clothing and cosmetics. That isn't the word's fault. Only the most egregious art snob or the blindest art theorist can overlook the role of charm in art. In the theater, which directs itself to the eyes and ears, it is primary. Goethe himself speaks of going to the theater to gaze at beautiful bodies. What beauty is to the body, charm is to the word, to the person. How vacuous to discuss the "thought patterns" in *As You Like It* and not allow for the charm of Rosalind's personality! How portentous to deal with Shaw as Marxist, Wagnerian, vegetarian, antivivisectionist, and pass over the fact that his characters woo us and win us—not with their philosophy but with their charm! Another of the open secrets of Brecht was that, while he attacked other forms of charm, he had his own. Being a dramatist, he passed it on to his characters, particularly to those with whom he was strongly identified—Galy Gay, Macheath, Galileo, Mother Courage, Azdak.

Something similar needs to be said of *naïveté*. The word has been used more and more in our century because more and more people have come to regard themselves as *not* naïve—as subtle fellows. It is now the usual word with which to strike down an argument you cannot answer, an opponent whose weak spot you cannot find. It is pleasant, therefore, to find Brecht, in his last years, saying a good word for naïveté. He described it as a sort of ultimate goal for any stylist.

In question is not the kind of simplicity an artist starts out with at the age of nineteen; his style may well be at its most "complex" at that age. In question is the simplicity that is achieved when much complexity has been worked through and worn down. To the truly naïve reader such not-really-naïve art is "deceptively" simple. The late lyrics of Brecht are a case in point. They are cryptic. The sense is between the lines. It is doubtful if Brecht is simpler than poets who parade their difficulty.

Of the charm of *The Caucasian Chalk Circle* there is no doubt. As to whether the presentation is naïve, that is a matter of definition. In any case, naïveté of style would be no guarantee of unambiguousness of import. Like many another wily Bavarian peasant, Bertolt Brecht could be devious in very simple words. I hasten to add that what we call deviousness in behavior becomes, in literature of genius, richness of texture and fullness of significance.

Chinese boxes. Friedrich Luft has said that while the younger Brecht wished to use theater to alter the world, the later Brecht took a step back when he said the theater should only show the world to be alterable. I'm not so sure that even the earlier Brecht theater had such direct designs on the world as had the theater of Piscator or Odets, but I agree that some sort of withdrawal took place later. I would place it in the late thirties. The explanation is simple: Brecht was forced by Hitler into a withdrawal from political life in his own country. Living among foreigners who did not know him or his language, he could not be the kind of writer he had recently decided to become: the Party activist. He was forced into that very withdrawal that most artists crave—and that the activist seeks to avoid. Those of us who knew Brecht in exile can testify to the extent of the withdrawal. It is to Hitler, then, that we owe the big plays of these years, plays which were more deeply meditated, drawn from sources deeper inside as well as more remote in time, than those of the preceding years.

I mean chiefly *Galileo, Mother Courage,* and *The Caucasian Chalk Circle,* the last of which marks an end point. In most of what Brecht is known to have written afterwards, I find him taking no new steps—only retracing old ones. In the sense here suggested, *The Caucasian Chalk Circle* is his last play. It is certainly the play of deepest withdrawal. The form, puzzling at first, can be seen as Chinese boxes, one inside the other, Azdak's story being a box within the Grusha story, the innermost box being the narrative of Azdak's two big songs.

The first of these songs is a description from the time of Azdak's grandfather of the miserable state of the people and the appalling conduct of the ruling caste. The second of the songs describes a popular revolution. It is based on an ancient document that Brecht had already quoted in his essay on five ways of telling the truth. The further back we go in time the closer we come to what Brecht regards as present and future. The flashback is used in order to flash forward. The urgent and the ultimate are presented in a dream within a dream, a memory within a memory. Azdak "disappeared and was never seen again," and his time became a legend of a "brief golden age."

The prologue. We are not surprised when we read that West German theaters put the play on as a "charming fantasy," or that the dialecticians of the East rise up in wrath to explain the prologue. The prologue is not set in prehistoric times but at a date later than the year when Brecht started work on the play. If the rest of the play, without the prologue, might be taken to be "unreal," the prologue is set in what for a Communist is the most real of all real places, Soviet Russia. It might also be assumed that, once the prologue is played, you can't forget it, and so everything that happens all evening is seen in relation to it.

Now it seems to me quite likely that this was what Brecht intended, and certainly the prologue was not added after Brecht got to East Berlin—it was present in the first manuscript I saw of the play (1946). The question is whether we can take the will for the deed. If the little prologue cannot function as some of Brecht's Marxist friends would wish it to, it is not for lack of good intentions but for lack of weight. It does not, in fact, stay in the mind and compel us to refer back to it later. To the *Intendanten* of the West who omitted it, I would say: put it back in and relax, it will make no difference.

Everything of course depends on the political views you bring to the play—which is to say that the play exerts persuasive power on none. The prologue itself, in the eyes of all except the converted, presents yet another fantasy: the non-Russian Stalinist's view of Stalin's Russia. One can see that this fantasy was meant to be the largest of all the Chinese boxes—and was not meant to be a fantasy. For that matter, set in Georgia, the play is without doubt intended as a bouquet to the most stalwart Georgian of them all, Joseph Stalin, from a future winner of the Stalin Peace Prize. The quotation in the prologue from Mayakovsky, Stalin's favorite poet, is "a word to the wise . . ."

Brecht and tragedy. The last time I saw Bertolt Brecht (June 1956) we spoke of Ernst Busch's performance as Azdak, and Brecht said the actor had missed the "whole tragic side of the role." I think the comment has the highest interest for Brecht criticism because Brecht usually talked *against* tragedy, and those who have found "a tragic side" in his work have assumed that he was unconscious of it. What *is* tragic about Azdak? On the surface, the part is all racy and ironic comedy, but, aside from anything he says, Azdak performs an action near the beginning of his part of the play that casts a good deal of light on the whole: *having let the Grand Duke escape, he denounces himself to the authorities for doing so.* It is a very bizarre incident, in itself hard to believe, and, as acted by Busch, flatly incredible. What is its moral and psychological content? First, self-denunciation, as often in Brecht and Communist culture generally, is seen as good. Azdak is doing what Galileo abysmally failed to do: taking his punishment. Second, the "goodness" is cancelled by the fact that the authorities surrendered to are bad. The tragedy of Azdak, as found in this incident, is that his effort at heroism is reduced to absurdity by the circumstances. "Doch die Verhältnisse, sie sind nicht so," to quote Mr. Peachum, "that isn't how things are." *The tragedy of Azdak is that his life is a comedy.*

The incident has a third aspect. It carries a note of personal poignancy to the degree—the very considerable degree—that Azdak represents his author. There is nothing tragic in Brecht's willingness to denounce himself. What is tragic is his suspicion that the authorities he might denounce himself to were no better than those he had rebelled against. If *The Caucasian Chalk Circle* is implicitly dedicated to Stalin, also implicit is the question, "What if Stalin should prove a Grand Duke—or a mad Czar?" One can hardly forget that *Galileo* and *The Caucasian Chalk Circle* followed in the wake of the self-denunciations of Radek and Bukharin.

I am not concerned here with manuscripts that have been coming to light showing that, in the fifties, Brecht was more than worried about communism in East Germany. My point is rather that this more-than-worry—this haunting suspicion—antedates "East Germany." Disenchantment was burnt deep into Brecht's personality, and it would be naïve to think that it affected only his thoughts about capitalism. Stalin's pact with Hitler in 1939 was a baffling blow, and Brecht (as he once told me) had not been able to say, with Nexö and others, "Well, Hitler is a socialist too." He was full of doubt, dread, and guilt, as some of his poems testify—and as some of his conversation testified. And what makes most credible Wolfgang Harich's claim in 1956 that Brecht belonged to the anti-Ulbricht, anti-Stalin "rebellion" is that Brecht had for a long time kept ajar that door to non-Stalinist thoughts that better Communists kept tightly shut. I have heard him defend Silone in company that was horrified, and in June 1956 the book I saw open on his desk in East Berlin was the American edition of Koestler's *Invisible Writing...* The dark lining to Azdak's comic coat of many colors is the tragedy of the disenchanted revolutionary.

Azdak, oddly enough, has much in common with Brecht's Galileo. Not only are they both of them rogues in the sense defined above, they both embody the same contradictions: for instance, of talking, particularly about sex, like men about town but behaving more like hermits. They are essentially solitary. Azdak comes out of solitude and returns to it. Galileo is progressively detached from the world and his friends. Both characters reflect the isolation of Brecht.

I recall exchanging letters with Brecht about certain rather elementary and even banal problems of communism and literature. I was brought up sharp by his remarking that *I was the only person with whom he discussed such things.*[*] Now I was not a member of what was regarded as his circle of intimates. As a non-Communist, I was, in a sense, not even persona grata. I suddenly realized that Bertolt Brecht, surrounded by disciples and "comrades," lived, in-

---

[*] Letter from Bertolt Brecht to Eric Bentley, dated November 12, 1949. The first part of the letter contains a defense of Brecht's interpretation of *Hamlet* against what I had called "inaccuracies" in it. The next topic is his play *Days of the Commune.* I had said one had to be a Marxist to accept it. Brecht comments: "[That] is probably correct. But, to take a classical example, must one not accept the viewpoints of Montaigne or Bacon before one can accept *Hamlet* or *Troilus and Cressida*?" It is after adding that his play offered no deliberate parallel between the Paris of the Commune and the Berlin of the days of the airlift that Brecht made the statement paraphrased in my text.

tellectually at least, in a state of total isolation. Behind that Iron Curtain it is not only the Pasternaks who have lived alone! Nor was it only behind the Iron Curtain that Brecht lived lonely amid the crowd. Things were quite similar in California, where *The Caucasian Chalk Circle* was written.

Why labor a commonplace? However antitragic a poet's philosophy, if he is truly a poet, the tragedy of his life will find some echoes in his work. To the question, "Was this what Brecht meant when he spoke of the tragic side of Azdak?" one must answer, in the first place, "Obviously not," but, in the second place, "Yes."

"Theater ist einfältig, wenn es nicht vielfältig ist." This punning dictum of Brecht's can be freely translated: theater is simpleminded unless it is open-minded, or the dramatic poet has a one-track mind unless his mind runs on several tracks. One sometimes has to quarrel with Brecht's "contradictions," but *to quarrel with* can be *to pay homage to.* In any event, there are authors who *must* be quarrelled with—not because (or not only because) they are wrong and you are right, but because this is the only way they can be encountered. Was anyone ever able to read Nietzsche without fighting him? There are philosophers whose views you just memorize: Nietzsche makes you fight. He is "wrong"—but he is hard to answer! He is "wrong"—but, unlike those who are right, he is hard to ignore or forget! What is a philosopher for, finally? And even if you decide that a philosopher is there to provide you with correct opinions, is that what an artist is for? There is another view: that the artist is there to experience and express the contradictions, whether or not he can resolve them. If this view is valid, a critic is not captious when he points out what those contradictions are. Nor is he accusing the artist of stupidity or deceit if he remarks that some contradictions were less conscious than others. The criticism that is unworthy of Brecht is the criticism that ignores or denies the contradictions. Such criticism is either disingenuous or simpleminded—and makes Brecht so.

If there is a tendency now, in Paris or East Berlin, to put Brecht on a pedestal, one should recall that the older German poets are already on such pedestals, and that Bertolt Brecht spent quite a lot of energy trying to pull them down.

A Man's a Man
1962

In 1962 two off-Broadway productions of A Man's a Man *opened—on successive nights. Two different adaptations were used: one was mine. I wrote a long piece for—was it a magazine called* Show?—*but they rejected it and not without reason. My nerves were frayed by the infighting of the competitors, and much of what I wrote was intemperate, even petulant. I later extracted from the piece what seemed to me worth keeping, and used it as preface to* A Man's a Man *in the Grove paperback: this is the piece that follows here. A piece of sixties thinking? Well, it may be of some interest to those who have come along later to learn that, until the sixties, Brecht never caught on in America. It was Vietnam that made the difference. What we call* Vietnam *had not happened in 1962, but the era had opened. The Cuban missile crisis occurred while our show was running. One of our managers proposed that we shut down and flee to Westchester, and our Widow Begbick wept un-Brechtian tears onstage when she had to sing of soldiers going to their death like cattle: "None on the list/Are ever missed."*

THERE IS BRECHT THE FAD, AND there is Brecht the living presence. What manner of man, of artist, is the Brecht who is a living presence in America today?

Not a Communist. Nor is American youth afraid of communism, as their seniors were ten years ago. They take it coolly. In talking to students, I notice how much more excited I am likely to get on this subject than they are. It shocks them at all that Brecht was a sympathizer with communism, though few of them sympathize with it themselves.

A group of them are what some time ago we would have called Fellow Travelers. It would be more accurate to call them *fidelistas*, for Castro is their hero, not Mao nor Khrushchev, let alone the late Joseph Stalin. And Bertolt Brecht is their hero, too, if they are at all interested in theater, poetry, or drama. If there is to be an American cult of Brecht with more life to it than we find among the Brechtians of the New York theater world, then it would be from the young of the New Left that it would come.

The New Left in America has this in common with the old left in America: it gives an impression of far greater strength than it really possesses. To hear people talk now, you'd think we who were in college in the thirties were either Red or lived surrounded by Reds. We weren't. We didn't. May there be no myth in the future to the effect that the students of 1962 were "New Leftists"! If one must generalize, and if one must pretend that the largest homogeneous minority is really a majority, then 1962 is the time, not of Leftism and Castro, but of Pacifism and Erich Fromm and Norman Thomas and H. Stuart Hughes. And this is extremely interesting in relation to Bertolt Brecht, since war had provided the experience that determined his outlook, and opposition to war was his most consistently held stance. True, in 1928 he was converted to Marxism, and he stuck by the policies of Stalin until death came in 1956—except possibly in the privacy of works that have not even yet been published. Even so, there were ambiguities in Brecht's communism, as the Communists were the first to point out. If communism was the solution, it was a desperate solution, accepted in the spirit of Pascal's wager. In his last years Brecht is said to have called the West an old whore and the East a young one—preferable only because she was pregnant. Now, Brecht called on no such cynicism—or, if you like, historicism—to justify his *pacifist* convictions.

These were solid as a rock. At times they even conflicted with his loyalty to the Communists: he put on his antimilitarist play *Trumpets and Drums* at a time when East Germany, as well as West, was rearming. It was not the only time he unmistakably called on both the Germanies NOT TO GO AND DO IT AGAIN. In "To My Countrymen" he wrote:

> You who live on in towns that passed away
> Now show yourselves some mercy, I implore.
> Do not go marching into some new war
> As if the old wars had not had their day
> But show yourselves some mercy, I implore.
>
> You men, reach for the trowel, not the knife.
> Today you'd have a roof above your head
> Had you not gambled on the knife instead
> And with a roof you have a better life.
> You men, reach for the trowel, not the knife.
>
> You children, that you all may stay alive
> Your fathers and your mothers you must waken
> And if in ruins you would not survive
> Tell them you will not take what they have taken
> You children, that you all may stay alive.
>
> You mothers, from whom all men take their breath
> A war is yours to give or not to give.
> I beg you mothers, let your children live.
> Let them owe you their birth but not their death.
> I beg you mothers, let your children live.

When I speak of Brecht the pacifist, I am not implying that he ever espoused nonviolent Gandhiism, but neither is his pacifism limited to mere protestation against wars. It led, rather, to a profound study of humanity in wartime. *Mother Courage* is a panoramic war play with at least one feature that must be unique in this class of drama: it contains no battle scenes. It is a play of everyday life at a time like the present—when war is an everyday fact, and war stands condemned in it not for its atrocities, but for being itself the supreme atrocity: a condition of life that should not, must not, be tolerated.

In Brecht's world, war is not an isolated iniquity but the extreme instance of a universal abuse, the rule of force. Even those plays of his that stand at the furthest extreme from communism do not stand at such an extreme from pacifism, because they are studies in force, in the domination of man by man.

> Force in the hands of another exercises over the soul the same tyranny that extreme hunger does; for it possesses, and *in perpetuo,* the power of life and death. Its rule, moreover, is as cold and hard as the rule of inert matter. The man who knows himself weaker than another is more alone in the heart of a city than a man lost in the desert.

This is not Bertolt Brecht speaking, but one of the great religious thinkers of our time, Simone Weil. She comes closer, however, to describing the world of Brecht than most of his critics have done. "The man who knows himself weaker than another is more alone in the heart of a city than a man lost in the desert." Brecht's very earliest plays convey just this sense of aloneness in the heart of the city—that city that Simone Weil calls a desert and that Brecht called thicket, jungle, and swamp.

In one of Brecht's early plays, *In the Swamp,* a man is, in effect, raped by another man. In a play written a little later, a man is, in a social sense, raped by a group of men: this is *A Man's a Man. In the Swamp,* we blithely say, is about homosexuality; *A Man's a Man* is a social play, an antiwar play; but, in Brecht, the two things are one. This has even been proved recently by the posthumous publication of a poem from which we learn that the raped man in the two plays was for Brecht the same person. A Freudian critic might fairly say that the social rape of the later play is a symbol of sexual rape, while a Marxian critic might with equal justice say that the sexual rape of *In the Swamp* prefigures the social rape of *A Man's a Man*. The Marxian point is more interesting, partly because all Brecht's mature plays tend to present social rape, the rape of the innocent individual by a cruel society, partly because for Brecht sex is less a psychic than a social phenomenon (even loneliness is a matter of feeling "weaker than another"). The reason many people don't readily recognize that *In the Swamp* is about homosexuality is that they are still not accustomed (despite Genet) to seeing sex in terms of a power struggle. In Brecht's "swamp," Garga is the man who "knows himself weaker than another." The play presents the "tyranny" exercised over the soul of Garga by Shlink—and eventually, vice versa. What Brecht calls a boxing match might just as well be called a tug of war.

A Man's a Man only narrowly escapes being another play about homosexual rape. It, too, presents a struggle for supremacy between two men, Galy Gay and Bloody Five, and the latter declares in one scene that he'll be raping the former if he isn't given speedy satisfaction by prostitutes—clinically speaking, a classic homosexual pattern of action and fantasy. But the directly sexual material is here pushed even farther into the background. In the foreground is the question of coercion and domination. At the close of *In the Swamp*, we find the dominator dominated—and dead: the plot hinges upon this simple reversal. The tables are similarly turned in *A Man's a Man*. Here, too, the stronger man, the rapist, is in the end discomfited by the weaker, whom he has "raped." In both plays Brecht worries the question, "Who after all *is* stronger, who weaker?" His answer in both cases is that the strong man with an emotional weakness (a weakness for certain emotional "outlets") is less likely to win than the weak man who is willing to deny himself emotional "outlets." Brechtians will recognize here the pattern of some better-known Brecht works, such as *The Seven Deadly Sins* and *The Good Woman of Setzuan*. It was in *A Man's a Man* that Brecht first split characters into contrasting halves. There is Bloody Five, the disciplined soldier, whose discipline disintegrates when he feels sexual passion, and there is Galy Gay who manages to turn from being soft and good to being hard and bad, and so to be the victor in this hard, bad world of ours.

Underlying the literary and ideological games is the archetypal modern problem: the problem of individual identity. For, though there is nothing modern in the question *who am I?* characteristically modern is the lack of *sense* of identity, the feeling of *I am no one*—of which the feeling *I am more than one person* is a variant. "I am someone, no one, and a hundred thousand people," as one of Pirandello's titles (almost) reads.

For Brecht pacifism and the problem of identity are connected, and the connection is found in *A Man's a Man*. The protagonist, Galy Gay, brought by the cruel society he lives in to doubt if he has a real identity, accepts a false identity—an identification with the cruelty that is being exerted upon him, with the power that is overpowering him. From a cynical viewpoint, then, he may be said to be effecting a homeopathic self-cure—finding the answer to power in power, which is surely what those are doing who find the answer to hydrogen bombs in more hydrogen bombs. I find myself quoted in the press as saying *A Man's a Man* is about Madison Avenue. In a sense, it is. Another critic had said the play was about brainwashing. That also, in a sense, is true. But the brainwashing it gives a sense of is that of "Madison Avenue." (Also of "bipartisan foreign policy"—the idea behind which is to make anyone who dissents feel like a traitor.) Even so one must not *blame* Madison Avenue. Its bullets could not strike home if we were not vulnerable, and the vulnerability consists in our weak sense of identity. Madison Avenue offers a false identity *to those who feel the need of one.*

This interpretation of *A Man's a Man* covers more ground than the avenue between Fifth and Park: it reaches as far as the White House. Power, superpower, atomic power is today offering to fill the terrible void in lives that have no true identity; but this it can never do, since power is itself a void, the supreme void.

Total material destruction would be the perfect symbol of our spiritual plight and its most logical consequence. It is silly to talk as if the holocaust, if it occurred, would be an accident. It is silly to talk as if it were happening because we haven't managed to find a way out. What we confront today is a lack of will to find a way out or even a will *not* to find the way out: we tend to wish to be destroyed. But, of course, the various statesmen present this cosmic crisis to their respective peoples as a vulgar melodramatic conflict between their own High Ideals and the Low Ideals of their antagonists, and this, to the universal disaster, adds a touch of the ridiculous and the obscene.

All of which brings it about that Bertolt Brecht is a living presence among the American young. I don't say that American youth, as a whole, is of a mind to picket the White House. Such large groups as "American youth" have no mind. Nonetheless, there is widespread unrest. It reaches many who neither concur with Castro nor resist the police on Times Square. It is not "pacifist" in the narrower sense of a definite program, such as unilateral disarmament, but it *is* pacifist in the sense of meaning business in the antiwar movement, and accusing the governments of both Russia and America of not always meaning business in their alleged concern for arms control.

Certainly, the unrest I am speaking of is only a vague, unfocused discontent, grounded in a shrewd suspicion that we are all getting swindled, and that the swindle is leading to universal disaster. Such an attitude is itself quite vulnerable, and I might go on to criticize it, were I attempting more than to explain the rapport between young Americans and Bertolt Brecht. This rapport is all the more powerful because somewhat irrational. It is all the more powerful because it is not just a matter of communism. (Parisian Brechtians, whose real wish is for communism, will end up espousing communism and dropping Brecht—or explaining with how many reservations they accept him.) It is precisely the Brecht the Communists condemn that young Americans are attracted by— which explains why New York has recently seen *In the Swamp, Threepenny Opera,* and *A Man's a Man,* and not the later plays. Brecht has become, and will remain, a symbol of malaise and rejection here. But I come back to pacifism because the American Brecht is not *merely* cynical and, in the popular sense, anarchistic. He is anarchistic in a sense closer to the spirit of the great Anarchists. His negatives imply positives. All this hate means love. All this conflict means conciliation. All this war means peace. If we are beginning to conceive, and to build, any alternatives to domination and coercion, it is with the help of Bertolt Brecht.

What Is a Zonk?
1962

As Charles Eliot Norton Professor of Poetry at Harvard in 1960, the least I could do was to study Brecht as Poet. My method, wherever possible, was to find music that his lyrics were set to, sing the songs in German and then, as translator, seek singable words for the same music in English. A graduate student asked if he could tape-record me. This was James Lyon, later to be the author of Bertolt Brecht in America *(1980). Thus emboldened to sing for an audience of one, I went on to sing to audiences somewhat larger than that—as well as to cut discs for Riverside Records, Spoken Arts, and, above all, Folkways. The piece that follows grew out of a class of Stanley Burnshaw's at New York University and was published by Stanley in his book* Varieties of Literary Experience *(1962) under the title "The Songs in* Mother Courage.*" Part of it reappeared in a music journal called* Listen, *in the March–April 1964 issue, under the title "Brecht und der Zonk."*

THE GERMAN FOR *SONG* IS *LIED.* Therefore we need a word for the sung parts of Brecht's plays which he called in the German text *Die Songs.* There being none, I propose that we simply take what the Germans say and spell it phonetically: *Zonks.* You are no Brechtian after all till you can bandy phrases like Brecht's Zonks, die Zonks *der Sreepenny Ohperah,* "dair Barbarah-Zonk."

The Zonk does not resemble the English folk song—or the Irish one as Sean O'Casey liked to introduce it into his plays. It does not resemble the songs in *The Beggar's Opera*. There Gay's idea was to set new words to old tunes of any kind. It was also his conception that the dialogue could be interrupted at any time by these musical quotations, however brief. One could even jump straight from one quotation to another. All of which is a far cry from the songs of *The Threepenny Opera*, which are almost never musical quotations and never mere snatches. The first thing we notice is that the Brecht Zonk is an individual item, clearly marked off from its context, like an individual number in vaudeville.

The song, then, is a sheer interruption of dialogue, but it would perhaps be less misleading to say that in Brecht's plays the dialogue is an interruption of the Zonks—in other words, that the Zonks are the heart of the matter.

In my preface to *Seven Plays by Brecht* and elsewhere, I have taken the position that "epic theater is lyric theater," and an intelligent Marxist critic has accused me of unclarity. What I meant, however, is very clear indeed: that the lyrics are the core of the play.

There have been dramas based on lyrics before. The *Peribáñez* and *The Knight from Olmedo* of Lope de Vega are probably based on the little ballads contained within them. But this is a matter of plot and character. The lyrics from which Brecht's plays spring, or on which they rest, do not contain his plots and characters. They expound his themes. This is the most surprising thing about a Brecht play: that the songs, which we expect to be at once frivolous and peripheral, are dead serious and central, all appearances to the contrary notwithstanding.

A shrewd Catholic critic, Henri Gouhier, has written of *The Threepenny Opera:* "The intimate collaboration of Bertolt Brecht and Kurt Weill rejuvenates the formula of musical comedy in entrusting to the part that is sung the expression of whatever goes beyond mere incidents..." This is the other end of my own statement: musical theater is redeemed from banality and mere intrigue by Zonks, which reinforce incident with interpretation.

A comparison of *The Little Mahagonny* with the full-length opera indicates the process at its simplest. *Mahagonny* begins as but a group of lyrics in *Die Hauspostille*. From the beginning they have tunes—apparently of Brecht's own invention, and certainly not by Kurt Weill. Then comes *The Little Mahagonny* of Brecht and Weill, still not too much more than a setting of some songs. But drama is bursting out all over, and the end product is one of the (in every sense) big works of our day.

The versatility of Brecht gave an impression, for a while, of lack of continuity. He would set each play in a different place and time, and establish a completely different style of dialogue. The songs would represent continuity. The places and times of Brecht's plots are such that they can all be equally hospitable to the same songs. The "Song of Solomon" occurs in both *The Threepenny Opera* and *Mother Courage*. Why? Because the same themes come up in both, and especially the theme of this song: the futility of the virtues. *Mother Courage* also contains a song that goes all the way back to *Die Hauspostille*, "The Fishwife and the Soldier." Brecht's thoughts about the military life are neither a "cliché of the nineteen-thirties" nor simply derivative from his Marxism. They represent a constant preoccupation from one end of his work to the other.

If Brecht puts his themes into the songs, he puts his theatrical genius into them too. As Gouhier puts it, in speaking of *The Three-penny Opera*, Brecht and Weill impose on the part that is sung a "rhythm such as cannot be sung without being acted." So true is this that many Brecht songs can, so to speak, be acted without being sung. Lotte Lenya acts songs. This fact can be appreciated even by listeners to her recordings: her voice acts the songs. Conversely, it can be fatal to give a Brecht lyric to a singer: the histrionic values tend to be swallowed up in the musical ones. I was present when Brecht fired a singer who was doing the "Song of Shelter" in *Mother Courage*. "*Far* too beautiful," was his only comment. He knew that one had no sense of a serving maid in a kitchen singing at her work: one was transported to a concert hall where singing *is* the work.

As a model of that Brecht singing that is really acting, I would suggest not only Lotte Lenya but also Trude Hesterberg—Frau Peachum on the Columbia recording of the complete *Threepenny Opera.* Her rendering of the "Ballad of Sexual Submissiveness" is one of the great things in the Brecht repertoire.

Frau Hesterberg, whom I met in 1949, told me she ran a night-club in Munich in the early twenties. One day a strange young man came to be auditioned, small, dark, owlish, reserved. She was sure he was coming to the wrong address. Then he sang to the guitar in a thin, piercing voice. "There's something very unusual about your material," she said, "where did you pick up these songs?" He said: "They're my own." It was Bertolt Brecht, and the kind of thing he wrote in those days is preserved in *Die Hauspostille,* complete with the tunes he used. I do not know if he composed these tunes. The book attributes them to no one. But to learn these songs—words and music—is the best possible introduction not only to the poetry but to the theater of Brecht.

In *Mother Courage* there are seven full-dress songs and two fragments. The songs are

1. Song of Mother Courage;
2. The Fishwife and the Soldier;
3. Camp Follower's Song (Fraternization);
4. Song of the Hours;
5. The Great Capitulation;
6. Song of the Wise and Good; and
7. Song of Shelter.

We might take the last one first as showing how singing functions dramatically in Brecht's plays. The "Song of Shelter" is the entire written content of a scene (number 10), yet the content of the song would not give you the scene. The scene consists of a gesture or, rather, a posture: Kattrin and her mother are pulling the wagon themselves now. Exhausted, they stop. A voice is heard from inside a farmhouse. The drama of the scene is in the relationship of the voice to the two listeners. The singer has shelter; the listeners do not. That is the upshot of the song. The conception is distanced and decorated by a preceding stanza celebrating the singer's participation in the less utilitarian, more lovely things. But Brecht used to point out to actors the error of singing the song chiefly for its charm—with chiefly the roses in mind. The voice must sing not only joy in the garden's beauty but complacency in possession of the garden and the house.

This scene, which needs no dialogue, also needs no movement. It is a tableau, an image. Movement is left entirely to the music—handled by an unseen singer.

No dialogue. The scene belongs to a girl who cannot speak: Kattrin, who will be killed in the next scene.

We have to ask ourselves how many dramatists can do so much with a pause in the action, filled only by an offstage singing voice.

Some are indoors "in the warm"; others outside in the cold. Brecht tends to divide mankind that way. Class struggle. Class antagonism without struggle. And the word *class* has some misleading connotations. *The Threepenny Film* has it:

> Und die Einen sind im Dunkeln
> Und die Andern sind im Licht—
>
> Some there are who live in darkness,
> some there are who live in light.

Brecht's poetry is one long defense of those who live in the darkness—like Kattrin.

The little song tends to universalize the statement the play is making. Zonks generally have this tendency. Sometimes they have it supremely. The preceding Zonk—"Of the Wise and Good"—is an instance. It presents, like the "Song of Shelter," one of Brecht's leading conceptions. It also sums up *Mother Courage.*

The play tells the story of the killing of Courage's three children: the Honest Son, the Brave Son, and the Kind Daughter. The song takes an instance of honesty (Socrates), of bravery (Caesar), and of kindness (Saint Martin) and shows how all are killed. The singers (the Cook and Courage herself) do not forget their own position. They are identified with Solomon, whose wisdom was knowing the futility of wisdom, and with those who have obeyed the Ten Commandments to no effect.

The summing up is appropriately placed just before the final catastrophe of the story: the shooting of Kattrin. Such placing is obvious enough. Something that might escape attention is the relation of this song to "The Great Capitulation" (scene 4), which comes just after the first catastrophe: the shooting of Swiss Cheese. These two songs are two pillars supporting the play as a whole. They make complementary statements. The first speaks of the necessity of defeatism, of going down on your knees "to God Almighty if you please!" The second records what the fruits of such piety are.

Everything runs downhill in this play—in the action and in the thinking—but if you read it backward it is optimistic. The fruits of the piety wouldn't be there but for the piety. The piety wouldn't be there but for the capitulation. Moral: don't capitulate—an optimistic injunction, if ever there was one! If the play doesn't quite back it up, it would like to, as witness the enormous sympathy for the one who does not capitulate: Kattrin. No absence of empathy and identification there!

"The Great Capitulation" is the second "Song of Mother Courage" herself, and it contains her story. The "Song of Fraternization" contains Yvette's story. The simplest alternative to capitulating is fraternizing—if you can't lick 'em, join 'em. And it seems preferable.

The stories of failure that this play otherwise consists of are offset by the success story of Yvette. She comes up in the world while all the others come down or stay down. "It pays to fraternize." I find myself speaking ironically because the whole episode is ironical. As usual, a Zonk contains the essence. The one positive and really "successful" thing in Yvette's life is over before our tale begins: she has once been in love.

Directors will have to take care, when casting an Yvette, to pick an actress who can not only suggest what she is and becomes but what she once was and felt.

Songs two and three contain the story of Eilif and Swiss Cheese, respectively, but with various indirections or effects of distance. "The Fishwife and the Soldier" is actually sung by Eilif, but he takes no responsibility for the contents. It is something his mother taught him, and he had learnt it by rote. He identifies himself, not with the song, but with the soldier in it who cries, "The life of a hero for me!" Heaven knows how the little incident would end if his mother did not chance to be eavesdropping! She gives the song an ending Eilif would scarcely care to confront. And she knows what she is singing.

But there is no indication that, even now, Eilif has got the point. For him it was just a nice war song.

The total effect of this little song resembles that of the charade of the black cross in the previous scene. The end of the play is prefigured in the beginning. Brecht uses the pattern of oracle and fulfillment with considerable emphasis in this play, if with some humor and irony. Some may think it too fatalistic a pattern for a "social" playwright, but his point is that fatality rules where people will not rule, where they have capitulated and are on their knees.

Courage's partial unawareness, coupled with Eilif's total unawareness of the meaning and relevance of the song, gives us irony within irony. It is Brecht's way to make his Zonks flash significance this way and that. When Helene Weigel sings "Your heroic deeds won't warm me!" her inflection, coupled with a plural form of "your" that we don't have in English, makes the line refer to all the Nazis and potential Nazis in the audience.

How bold and unabashed Brecht is in resorting to artifice! It is not at all likely that mother and son would meet in this way, let alone that a song could just happen to be divided between them in this way. Yet in the theater, that natural home of the unnatural, it all passes off with an air of spontaneity.

In 1949 I attended a meeting of the Communist Youth in East Berlin at which Brecht was questioned by the young about the new production of his play. One of the boys questioned the whole mode of Eilif's performance in this song, and asked why he performed a weird sword dance between the stanzas. Brecht stuck his cigar in his mouth to gain time—as he had done when questioned by the Un-American Committee in Washington two years before. Then he mildly said: "There are two answers to that. One is: people do perform such dances. The other is: why not?"

Perhaps the boldest example of Brechtian theater in *Mother Courage* is the Chaplain's singing the story of the death of Jesus just before Swiss Cheese is shot. This "Song of the Hours" is often omitted from German productions, and was omitted from the principal printings of my own rendering of the play. I now think it should always be included—in performance and in reading. However, I don't think the reason for the omission was ever the fear of offending anyone's religious susceptibilities. These would be much more offended by other things that never were omitted. What seems to faze producers is the difficulty of adding so weighty an item to an already very weighty scene. But surely the sheer audacity would carry it: it is the extreme case of universalizing the meaning of a scene in the lyrics. Though the analogy of Swiss Cheese and Christ may at first seem flippant, in the actual treatment it turns out not to be. Gottfried von Einem, the composer, has subsequently had no trouble at all making an independent choral work from this song. Brecht's Christ is—inevitably—the good boy in a world that crucifies goodness. Since it is stupid to be good under such conditions, this is a stupid Christ, however sweetly amiable. But beneath Brecht's recognition of stupidity is his compassion.

The "Song" of Mother-Courage-the-character is also the "Song" of Mother-Courage-the-play. The sound of the song, and the sight of Mother Courage singing it on or beside her wagon—

these began as a stunning theatrical "effect" and have become symbols of the play as a whole, its grandeur and its meaning for many people in many countries.

This Zonk has a double action. Its words, from beginning to end, are bottomlessly cynical, blackly pessimistic. Yet people come away from the play in general, and this Zonk in particular, saying, "I doubt that any other play has paid such homage to mankind's greatest virtue, its heroic determination to somehow, almost anyhow keep on pulling the wagon further on . . ." This is Tennessee Williams speaking, and it is possible that ignorance of German has led him to be guided too exclusively by the music and by visual images. Yet what he says is neither pointless nor wholly wrong. The words of this song are, in a sense, cancelled by the act of singing them. One may be a pessimist, but to sing one's pessimism is to transcend it. To sing one's pessimism humorously adds another twist. Humor also has a double action. It contains an admission of defeat: nothing to be done. But, like song, it is itself a kind of victory. You exorcise these dreadful thoughts by uttering them humorously. Mother Courage is always saying cynical things but not for one moment do we take her for a cynic, unless all cynics are doing the same thing: overcoming despair by humorous indulgence in it.

To achieve real despair in this Zonk, Brecht had to take it away from Mother Courage and write, without humor, a final stanza for soldiers' chorus:

> Dangers, surprises, devastations—
> 　　The war takes hold and will not quit.
> But though it last three generations
> 　　We shall get nothing out of it.
> Starvation, filth, and cold enslave us.
> 　　The army robs us of our pay.
> Only a miracle can save us
> 　　And miracles have had their day.

Thornton Wilder and director Max Reinhardt going over the script of *The Merchant of Yonkers,* New York, 1938.

Twelfth Night in the garden of Exeter College, Oxford, 1937. In the lead, Robertson Davies (later the eminent Canadian novelist), then Eric Bentley as Sir Toby Belch, Alexis France as Maria, and a student Fabian.

Eric Bentley with Richard Ellmann, future biographer of
Oscar Wilde. Florida, 1940.

STANDING *(left to
right):* Eric Bentley,
Clark Foreman.
SEATED: The
historian Charles
A. Beard, Franziska
De Graaff. North
Carolina, 1943.

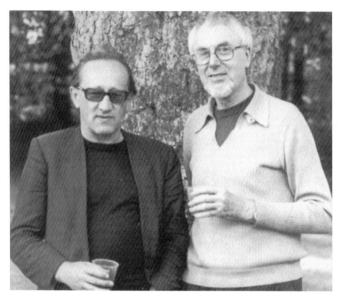

Heiner Müller and Eric Bentley—parricides both? Bertolt
Brecht's daughter Barbara has described Müller as *"der Vatermörder."* When Müller was introduced to Eric Bentley, he exclaimed: "Der andere Vatermörder!"

Eric Bentley circa 1990.

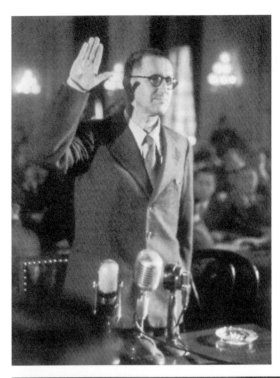

Brecht before the
Un-American
Activities
Committee, 1947.

Lion Feuchtwanger, Stalin, and B. M. Tal, editor of *Pravda*. In Brecht's circle, only Feuchtwanger seems to have got into the actual presence of Stalin. This was because he had been chosen to make the official retort to André Gide on the subject of freedom in the U.S.S.R. Viking Press published the result in the book *Moscow 1937*.

Elisabeth Hauptmann, 1950.

Brecht and Ruth Berlau, 1944–45. Taken with Brecht's
Leica, probably by Charles Laughton.

Brecht and his wife Helene Weigel (later to play Mother Courage)
around the time he finished writing the play. From a painting by Ernst
van Leyden (now lost).

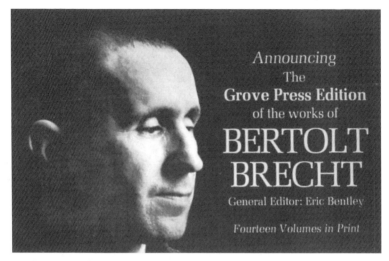

In the sixties, Grove Press published fourteen volumes of Brecht
with Eric Bentley as general editor.

Hobby Hollywood

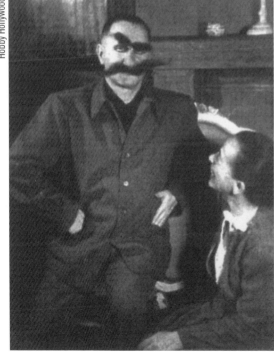

Helene Weigel
smiles while
Brecht poses as
Stalin, 1943.

Surabaya Johnny

Words by Bertolt Brecht
Music by Kurt Weill
English words by Eric Bentley

I was young, my God, on-ly six-teen When you came up from Bur-ma to us,_____ And you told me that I should go with you, You would fix things and make no fuss._____ I asked_____ a-bout your oc-cu-pa-tion, And as sure as I stand here you said to me:_____ You had some-thing to do with the

From *Happy End*, music by Weill.

Woodcut by Ilse Schreiber, 1996.

Brecht, 1938.

Bentley, 1988.

Theatre Arts cover,
1962.

After Eisler's death, Paul Dessau was East Germany's leading composer.

When he met Brecht, Eric Bentley was pre-occupied with Stefan George, here drawn by B. F. Dolbin.

W. H. Auden

Peter Lorre

Christopher
Isherwood

(Left to right) Hanns Eisler, the director Harry Buckwitz, and Teo Otto.
Eric Bentley arranged for Buckwitz to direct *Chalk Circle* in Dallas, Texas.

Brecht with Charles Laughton; Hollywood, 1947.

Berthold Viertel drawn by
B. F. Dolbin.

Lotte Lenya

Bertolt Brecht with the actor (and Brecht's collaborator on *Life of Galileo*) Charles Laughton and the artist Georg Grosz; New York, 1946.

Caspar Neher

Thornton Wilder invited Eric Bentley to lunch and talked of Brecht a bit disparagingly.

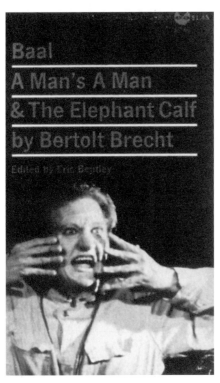

Paperback cover for Brecht's *Baal, A Man's a Man, and The Elephant Calf,* with John Heffernan as Galy Gay.

Photograph for *A Man's a Man,* from *Life* magazine, New York, February 8, 1963, with John Heffernan as Galy Gay.

Olympia Dukakis as Widow Begbick in John Hancock's production of *A Man's a Man;* New York, 1962.

"SEE THIS ONE" — Kerr, Her. Trib.

"THE BETTER OF THE TWO" — Taubman, Times

"INFINITELY SUPERIOR" — McClain, Journal Amer.

"MARVELOUSLY EXCITING" — Time Mag

BERTOLT BRECHT'S

A MAN'S A MAN

a comedy with music

adapted by
ERIC BENTLEY

MASQUE THEATRE 442 WEST 42nd ST.
CH 4-1350

Poster, New York, 1962, when two productions of *A Man's a Man* ran at the same time.

A Man's a Man poster at Harvard, 1961, with Clifton James pictured.

Bentley and Brecht outside the
Schauspielhaus; Zurich, 1948.
Photographs by Ruth Berlau.

Song Of Mother Courage

From Darius Milhaud's piano-vocal score of *Mother Courage*.

Ilse Schreiber's woodcut for the 1997 *Mother Courage.* Jean Cocteau Rep, New York.

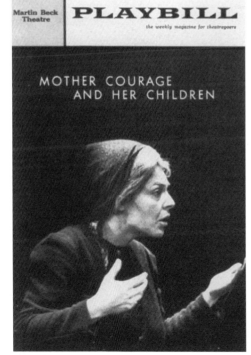

Anne Bancroft as Mother Courage, 1963.

The Exception and the Rule, Italy 1950, directed by Eric Bentley for the Bologna Festival.

COMPAGNIA STABILE
DEL TEATRO DELL'UNIVERSITÀ DI PADOVA

L'ECCEZIONE
E LA REGOLA
DI BERTOLT BRECHT

A Brecht-Hughes double bill at the Greenwich Mews Theatre; New York, 1964.

The Exception and the Rule, New York, 1965. With Paul Richards, Joseph Chaikin, and Richard Hamilton. Directed by Isaiah Sheffer.

Album cover for Folkways recording of *The Exception and the Rule,* Greenwich Mews Theatre. Première: May 20, 1965.

The Good Woman of Setzuan; London, 1956. At left, Peggy Ashcroft.

The Good Woman of Setzuan, New York, 1956. Center Stage: Jerry Stiller and Uta Hagen. Other faces that stand out: Ann Meara *(right)* and at left, Zero Mostel, Nancy Marchand, Albert Salmi, and Jane Hoffman.

January 1942. This American magazine cover (caricature by Arthur Szyk) suggested to Brecht how he should portray the Nazi leaders in his *Schweyk*.

The Caucasian Chalk Circle, Sunday *Times,* March 20, 1966. Illustration by Al Hirschfeld.

At Joe Papp's Public Theater, New York, 1974.

Eric Bentley sings at the Edinburgh Festival, 1985.

Albert Salmi, Uta Hagen, Zero Mostel, and Jane Hoffman in *The Good Woman of Setzuan,* a production adapted and directed by Eric Bentley at the Phoenix Theatre, Second Avenue and Twelfth Street. (From the *New York Times,* December 16, 1956.) Albert Salmi subsequently killed his wife and himself.

Milton

Shulman

AT THE

THEATRE

PEGGY ASHCROFT — girl with a big heart, and a jaunty cad.

Super-colossal Brecht—but it still leaves us wondering

Two views of a production of *The Good Woman of Setzuan* in London at the Royal Court in 1956. Neither Brecht nor Bentley nor Peggy Ashcroft got rave reviews. (*Top*, from the *Evening Standard*, Thursday, November 4, 1956. The caption reads: "PEGGY ASHCROFT—girl with a big heart, and a jaunty cad." *Bottom*, from *Punch*, November 7.)

Baal
1963

Another thing about the sixties: American audiences were ready for Brecht's early plays. The late plays had reached them first. The colleges had per-formed Good Woman *and* Chalk Circle *down through the fifties. For a while, those two plays—plus the watered-down version of* Threepenny Opera *devised by Marc Blitzstein—were Brecht.* A Man's a Man *was the borderline case. It led forward to the social, the Marxist plays, but just as evidently it led backward to the "anarchic," "individualistic" plays of Brecht's youth:* Baal, Drums in the Night, Edward II. *I had some sense of this possibility when I brought out a translation of* Baal *in the Grove edi-tion in 1963. By 1965, off Broadway was ready to launch the play. The pro-duction was glorious for James Earl Jones's bizarre-grandiose performance as Ekart, inglorious for the fact that the producer, Theodore Mann, had to be taken to court for nonpayment of royalties. (A more amusing incident of the time was that Brecht's play asking for the unionization of labor,* The Exception and the Rule, *was itself picketed when produced off Broadway in 1965—by the press agents' union. I was told that the pickets left their lim-ousines on the next block so as not to compromise their proletarian status.)*

THE FAME OF BRECHT'S LATER PLAYS has been bad for the repu-tation of his earlier ones, and in combating this phenomenon one is combating some powerful preconceptions. It is assumed that a major writer steadily improves. Early works are placed in such categories as "juvenilia" and "apprenticeship." Also, the earlier work is judged by criteria suggested by the later. Brecht himself judged his early work by criteria suggested by the later, which compounded the problem and created the cliché. The cliché reads as follows: "The later Brecht was a great man who had found himself in finding a great philosophy. The early Brecht was a confused and misguided young fellow who would never have come to any good had he not found the great philosophy and, through it, his greater self. In other words, the early work represents the sin from which Marxism redeemed him. The early Brecht is the unregenerate Saul; the late Brecht, the Sainted Paul." This cliché is the more important because it is taken over—with a little rewording—by many non-Marxists. It can be taken over without misgivings by anyone who is prepared to assume that to go from despair and pessimism to some sort of "positive" philosophy is necessarily to become a finer artist.

To protest this cliché should not be to reverse it. An artist is not confronted with the alternative: progress or regress. More normal is simply development—with ups and down. And that is what the career of Brecht has to show. This much, however, must be said on behalf of his early work: that had he died immediately after writing it, he would, in time, have been classed with other such youths of amazing poetic genius as Büchner and Rimbaud.

In time. His work, like theirs, could not be assimilated by the contemporary public. It was too original. In any case, the broader public takes up "unpopular" work only on the basis of some misunderstanding. Brecht himself was to become popular through misunderstanding when the German bourgeoisie would take *The Threepenny Opera* to its big clammy bosom in the belief that the philosophy of the piece was summed up in, "Erst kommt das Fressen, dann kommt die Moral." If an author cannot be understood, it is important, for his bankbook at least, that he be misunderstood, but *Baal*—Brecht's first play except for high-school juvenilia—did not get across in either way. It was intelligible, in the 1920s, only to persons who themselves had unusual insight into our life and times. In a prologue that Hofmannsthal wrote for the Viennese première in 1926, the older poet put his finger on the very pulse of the play: "... all the ominous events of Europe," says one of his spokesmen, "which we have witnessed these last twelve years are nothing but a long drawn-out way of laying the weary concept of the European individual in the grave..." Oscar Homolka, who played Baal, receives this speech from Hofmannsthal: "We are anonymous forces. Psychological possibilities. Individuality is one of the fantastic embellishments which we have stripped from us. You'll see how I'm going to play Baal."

We are taught in school about "the end of heroism" in the drama of the eighteenth and nineteenth centuries. The hero of tragedy was replaced by the individual of the nineteenth-century novel and play. Ibsen's work is par excellence the drama of that individual. Yet even here, where the dramatis personae are most individual, individuality is seen as threatened. Failing to be a hero, Master Builder Solness manages to be an individual—but only just, for the threat of complete disintegration is ever-present. In the dream plays of Strindberg the individual is dissolving in mist and mysticism. Here, instead of personalities, there are memories, bits of experience, cross-references, images, names, momentary encounters. In Pirandello's plays of around 1920 the nonexistence of the individual is proclaimed, but to sustain the form of a play Pirandello reverts to the traditional types, a little dressed up in Ibsenish "biography." So there is an element of contradiction between the *theory* that there is no such thing as continuity in character and the presentation, in practice, of people who *are* continuous and of a piece. Yet Pirandello does more than state the idea of discontinuity. He also projects the state of soul of those who believe in this idea, those who feel discontinuous with themselves, the disoriented, the metaphysically as well as neurotically lost: men of the twentieth century.

Baal is neither a Strindbergian dream play nor a Pirandellian "play in the making." What was in part a theory for the older men is here wholly a practice, a state of being, a fact of life. Few of us did see how Homolka played Baal, yet the script itself suggests vividly enough the truth of his remarks. Baal is a "stripped" character—is man stripped of character. There is a paradox about the Victorian Man of Character, the Independent Individual of the age of individualism, which is that he was formed by that age and belonged utterly to that society. The rejection of the individual that comes with the twentieth century, and especially after World War I, is a rejection of the society around him, and even of society as such. Baal is the asocial man.

It would be natural enough to call him amoral, and his actions stamp him as what Freud called polymorphous perverse: sensuality is acceptable to him in itself, and he does not limit himself to the "outlets" of which society approves. However, if this were the beginning and end of Baal, the play that bears his name would simply be a tract favoring the noble savage, a return to an innocent paganism. Nothing could be further from the text before us. The image of an innocent paganism is present in it, but is by no means the image of the play as a whole. Baal beholds the innocence, the amorality, of Nature all around us, but from a distance and with longing and envy. The *sky* would be an ideal mistress indeed, but how far off it is, how unreachable! Between us and primal innocence stands the world, which includes that very society of men that one would reject.

"Screw the world!" Those three syllables sum up a whole school of modern art and thought. Lautréamont had given the idea sodomitic form even earlier: "Oh that the universe were an immense celestial anus! I would plunge my penis past its bloody sphincter, rending apart, with my impetuous motion, the very bones of the pelvis."

The prologue to *Baal* reads:

> And that girl the world who gives herself and giggles
> If you only let her crush you with her thighs
> Shared with Baal, who loved it, orgiastic wriggles
> But he did not die. He looked her in the eyes.

No innocent enjoyment of beautiful Nature here! If Lautréamont is sadistic, Brecht is coolly defiant. He looks "that girl" in the eyes. How much lies behind such a look! How much pain and despair, how much living!

Though all drama tends to be about guilt, one might expect that a drama without individuals, without respect for society—a drama without ego or superego—would be an exception, would be "beyond guilt." One has read that to give up the individual is to give up the whole notion of responsibility, but it is not so unless one is uttering a tautology: to give up the individual is to give up *individual* responsibility. Responsibility and guilt remain, and only seem the more unwieldy, the more oppressive, for not being neatly tied to this person and that action.

Brecht does make Baal seem cut off from the meaning of his own actions: from his killing of Ekart and his virtual killing of Johanna Reiher. Only with difficulty, looking back on the play, can one say to oneself: *It is a play about a murderer.* And yet by any humane standard, murder is only one among Baal's several offenses and amid his consistent offensiveness. The immediate reason for this difficulty is to be found in Brecht's special perspective. He lends Baal a quality of innocence, but it is an innocence on the other side of guilt. Our minds, which are used to thinking here of a duality (guilt-innocence), have to stretch themselves a little to think in terms of three instead of two: innocence (1), guilt, and innocence (2). This innocence (2) is the subject of much of Brecht's writing in this period. It could even be said that around 1919 to 1921 his favorite subject was the innocence that can accrue to extremely vicious, even extremely criminal, people. It is as if one were to speak of regained innocence in an old whore.

Dostoevsky does speak of such innocence. It is even inherent in Christianity and was written out once and for all in the New Testament story of Mary Magdalene, but Brecht's second innocence has no such authority behind it. It has no one's blessing except his own. It carries no fringe benefits in this world or the next. It is not a state of beatitude that endures or that presages endurance. It is no more than a poet's feeling, an inspired hunch, a momentary dream, "just a thought"; hence its peculiar pathos. If it holds out a hope, it is a hope neither of utopia here nor heaven there; it says merely that a life could—at moments—be conceived of that is not quite so bad:

> träumt er gelegentlich von einer kleinen Wiese
> mit blauem Himmel drüber und sonst nichts.

> He dreams at times about a little meadow
> A patch of blue in the sky and nothing more.

There *is* a dream of celestial bliss in Brecht's early work, but it has the character of an ephemeral image, something that crosses the line of spiritual vision and is gone, a small loveliness sandwiched in between huge horrors. (Thus too, in a not so early work, the fragile lyric "Die Liebenden" is inserted in the story of *Mahagonny* between copulations that are paid for.) Insofar as Dostoevsky managed to believe in a real heaven, he could see it as transcending and swallowing up all that is unheavenly, even as eternity swallows up time. In Brecht it is hell—hell on earth—that is eternal, heaven that is swallowed up. The pathos of unbelief is pervasive in Brecht's lifework. It is his personal pathos, but cogent and significant because it is the characteristic pathos of the whole epoch.

For in the modern era, from Kierkegaard to Graham Greene, even the believers are not sure they really believe; they are sure only that they should. They are able only—like Brecht when later he came to "believe" in communism—to "commit" themselves to a belief—that is, to take the consequences of joining the ranks of the faithful even though their faith is not really felt.

Baal is solid and firm where the Brecht plays that affirm communism are, in that affirmation, rather shaky and hollow. *Baal* conveys the actual *Weltgefühl* of Bertolt Brecht throughout his career. A play like *The Mother* articulates the weltanschauung that he agreed to commit himself to in the hope that a better *Welt* might come out of it, after which the original *Weltgefühl* would change by itself. Even if this plan had all worked out, it would not make *The Mother* a better piece of art than *Baal;* just the contrary. If all Brecht's later plays had been patterned on *The Mother,* his later works would simply have proved inferior to the earlier.

Brecht's "heaven" is momentary, and does not redeem. The guilt remains, and the guilt is all the greater for not being only a guilt for specific offenses. When the individual disappears, what is left is the race. And the race is seen by Brecht as burdened with a primal curse—that which caused the Greeks to repeat that "not to be born is the best for man" and the Christians to formulate a doctrine of "original sin." If at moments we think that Brecht takes Baal's crimes too lightly—murder, after all, is murder—we quickly realize that in saying "Baal is no worse than the rest of us" he is not taking a high view of Baal but a low view of the rest of us. He is saying we are ourselves no better than murderers. We may even be worse than Baal, in that we may have missed the romance with the sky, and the dream of the little meadow. We may be Baal minus the poetry.

And—what is partly the same thing—minus the pleasure. For though Baal's pleasures are finally poisoned by guilt and ended by aggression, they were not impure at the source. On the contrary, the search for pleasure is the one truly affirmative element in the play, and the reason why the poetry of the play retains a directly and even ingenuously romantic aura. Baal really was seeking

Immer das Land wo es besser zu leben ist.

Ever the country where there's a better life.

More than thirty years later, Brecht was to take a look back at this play and speak of the love of pleasure, the search for happiness, as its subject. The comment is to be taken the more seriously in that

Baal is, in all other respects, so unacceptable to the later Brecht; but the human longing for happiness "which cannot be killed" (as he put it) was a theme he was ready to pursue at all times. He reports that he tried to pick up the thread of *Baal* twenty years afterward in an opera-libretto about a Chinese god of happiness.

True, he had come by then to believe that Russia was "the country where there's a better life" and that "happiness is—communism." With the early Brecht, it is as if he was striving to break through to a hedonism as radical as that of Herbert Marcuse or Norman O. Brown. That guilt and anxiety blocked this path may, in one respect, however, have been fortunate: he was a dramatist—conflict was his raw material.

In the fact that Baal is respected by Brecht as pleasure-seeker (though some readers may come to the play with an unfortunate puritanic prejudice) lies part of the reason that he is not pure villain. Walter Sokel has written of him eloquently as a parody of those expressionistic heroes whose life was a sacred mission, but since Brecht considered the expressionist missions spurious, he makes Baal's mission genuine. Baal is an ambiguous, ambivalent figure: part monster but partly, too, the martyr of a poetic hedonism. And the positive element is more prominent than the negative because it is Baal's special contribution—his monstrousness he has in common with a monstrous world.

Later, the peculiar acidity of *The Threepenny Opera* would come from the implied proposition: "We onstage may be little crooks; but many of you out front are big ones."

Yet if in the figure of Baal the more sympathetic element prevails over the less, in the play of *Baal* the poetry of life is overwhelmed by the prose, the beauty by the horror. If, as I tend to believe, a good play amounts finally to a particular vision of life seen as a whole, then this play is a vision of life as an inferno, and the occasional faint gleam of beauty only makes the ugliness look more intensely black. Baal will let no one persuade him he has lost all chance of pleasure, but self is something he lost so long ago its discovery is never in the cards. One might better put it that he never had a self. Whereas in Ibsen the self is threatened, and in Pirandello it is *said* not to exist, in Brecht both the Ibsenite self and the Pirandellian discussion are so far in the past they are forgotten. There remains the horror: Lowell's "horror of the lost self," and this horror belongs even more to the play than to the protagonist.

"We possess nothing in the world—a mere chance can strip us of everything—except the power to say *I*." So said Simone Weil. What then can a poet say for whom there is no *I* to affirm? "Nada y pues nada y nada y pues nada. Our nada, who art in nada, nada be thy name..." From Hemingway, in this famous passage published in 1933, to Samuel Beckett in the 1950s, with his "nothing is more real than nothing," contemporary poets and poet-novelists and poet-dramatists have found themselves confronted and surrounded by nothingness. Brecht found himself in this situation in 1918 at the frighteningly youthful age of nineteen or twenty. "Das Schönste ist das Nichts." ("The most beautiful thing is nothing.") Googoo says this in the thirteenth scene of *Baal*. Brecht says it in every scene of *Baal*. Man, here, is alienated from the others and from himself, to the degree that both others and self may be said to nonexist, to be nothing. This idea—better: this sentiment, this lacerating conviction—gives a new poignancy to the old "ashes to ashes, dust to dust." If death is, on the one hand, an ironic ending to pleasure and beauty, it is, on the other, a direct, unironic continuation of the universal nothingness, the omnipresent death-in-life.

Baal is about nothingness. By that token it is also about death. Brecht might well have taken yet another idea from the playwright who most influenced him, Büchner, and called his play *Baal's Death*. The mythic Baal was a fertility god, a god of life. This mythological (unpsychological) drama presents the archetypal battle of life and death, Eros and Thanatos. Traditionally, such a story would follow the pattern of rebirth: death followed by resurrection. Brecht who was always to parody the traditional patterns is doing so already in his first play where death is followed by... death.

Some readers have found the play formless. What it finally achieves in the way of organic form must perhaps remain a matter of opinion, but analysis will demonstrate at least that there is some very deliberate patterning here. *Baal* is the play in which the protagonist dies three times—in three ways that are poetically diversified. First, he dies as "Teddy" and speaks his own funeral oration (as Galy Gay is to do in *A Man's a Man*). Second, he relates his own death in the poem "Death in the Forest." Third, there is his actual death scene, with which the play ends. The identity of the three deaths is clearly established by the identical forest setting and the identical cruel attitude of the dying one's fellowmen. ("The coldness of the forests will be with me to my dying day," Brecht said in a famous poem; and he could have said the same of the coldness of those who are in attendance at the dying day—one thinks forward to the death of Swiss Cheese and, for that matter, the death of Brecht's Jesus in his "Song of the Hours.") Perhaps the whole play was planned as a kind of air and variations on the theme of dying. The drowning of Johanna is less an action than a leitmotiv.

A word on the Baal myth and Brecht's attitude to it. A writer from Augsburg, Brecht's native town, describes the poet's room at the time that he wrote *Baal:*

> ...over the bed [was] a lifesize picture of his idol Baal, that Semitic-Phoenician deity of insatiability which Christianity had declared the principle of evil...Caspar Neher had drawn it in the then current style of Masereel after Brecht's model, a male vamp named K. from Pfersee near Augsburg.

And this is probably to place the emphasis correctly: what would interest Brecht is that Baal was the enemy of the Christian-Judaic, puritanic, ascetic tradition. Perhaps he knew, too, that in the Canaanite *Poem of Baal* this god had an enemy, Môt, "the god," as Theodore Gaster says, "of all that lacks life and vitality." The very name Môt means death. Standing for fertility, Baal was also the god of rainfall, and the association of fertility with rain is something Brecht would remember when he created his comic fertility god—the Bloody Five of *A Man's a Man.*

Gaster's book *Thespis* reports many things that it is tempting to connect with Brecht's play, such as that the god Baal copulated with a calf, and that "Baal's enveloping robe is . . . identified with the sky," and that, at his death, Baal "fell into the earth." In relation to the recurrent image of a corpse floating down a river, it is startling to read in Gaster that the motif is common in the folklore of Brecht's part of the world:

> In many of the seasonal mummeries representing the rout of the Dragon, or the expulsion of Death, Blight, or Winter, he is *flung into the water.* Thus, at Nuremberg, the traditional song specified that "we bear Death into the water." . . . At Tabor, Bohemia, it was said that "Death floats down the stream" . . . and at Bielsk, Podlachia, the effigy was drowned in a marsh or pond . . . In Chrudim, Bohemia, Death was flung into the water on "Black Sunday." [One of Brecht's early poems refers to Black Saturday.] . . . In Silesia, children used to throw the effigy of Death into the river . . . while at Leipzig this was done by the local prostitutes and bastards . . .

There is enough here to guarantee that Brecht's *Baal* will sooner or later be interpreted wholly in terms of myth and ritual. Such interpretations will be unbalanced—but surely less unbalanced than those that try to make sense of *Baal* on the lines of what was conventional drama in 1918.

Historians have shown that, in *Baal,* Brecht was mocking the expressionists. He sought to debunk Hanns Johst's image of the poet as ecstatic visionary amid the wicked materialism of the surrounding world. In effect, though, the young Brecht had taken on a much larger antagonist than any expressionist playwright. He had made a tabula rasa of the modern drama as a whole and on that bare surface had erected a primitive and already sturdy structure of his own. For better or for worse, a new era in dramatic art dates from this play.

A New Aestheticism
1964

In 1964 the Times Literary Supplement *asked me to review Brecht's theoretical writings. Seven volumes of them had just been issued in German, and one volume,* Brecht on Theatre, *edited by John Willett, had been issued in English. I used most of my space to argue with the editors, German and British. What I want to preserve by reprint here is the rest of my space: devoted to Brecht himself. The title I submitted to the* TLS *was "Brecht on Brecht, or Art at All Costs." They (December 3) used only the first and less interesting half of that. Here I use a new title that, I hope, makes my point better.*

JOHN WILLETT'S NEW BOOK BEARS the subtitle "The Development of an Aesthetic," and the attempt to demonstrate such a development gives the volume excitement and unity. Of the result, it can be said at best: almost thou persuadest me. It *is* of interest to trace the mind of Brecht through the radical skepticism of his early years to the theory of Epic Theater in its first, narrow form, and thence to the broadening of this theory and its tentative replacement by Dialectical Theater. Given his intention, Mr. Willett's choice of material is a wise one, and the notes that follow each item provide continuity. At the same time Mr. Willett's treatment may be said to subject the aesthetics of Brecht to a scrutiny they cannot well survive and were probably never meant to encounter. Aesthetics? Do we have an aesthetician here whose work can stand beside that of the chief philosophers in the field, or their more adept pupils and expositors, or even beside the playwrights who have also been outstanding theorists, such as Schiller and Hebbel? Brecht himself anticipated the question with characteristic shrewdness: "My whole theory is much more naïve than people think, or than my way of putting it allows them to suppose." Now if Brecht's way of putting his theory actually makes it impossible for people to see what the theory is like, it would seem to be a mistake to reprint his theoretical writings at all, let alone to try to show that "an aesthetic" is developing in them year by year, and article by article. Possibly Brecht did not intend us to take his disclaimer any more seriously than the disclaimer takes his claims, but then how seriously can the critic take the whole tale of claims, disclaimer, and possible disclaimer of the disclaimer?

The story that unfolds in Mr. Willett's very readable volume is less interesting as aesthetics than as part of the Brecht biography. This is not because the writings might be classed as "polemic rather than philosophy," for some of the best philosophy has come out of polemical disputes. It is because neither of the two systems or quasi systems that Brecht works out—the Epic Theater of 1930 nor the Dialectical Theater of the 1950s—constitutes a really notable aesthetic. Epic Theater does suffer from the limitation noted by the later Brecht: it reduces the role of pleasure in art to a ridiculous degree. But if Epic Theater represents a puritanic extreme, what Brecht then "developed" as an alternative "aesthetic" was nothing more remarkable than what most people already believe: that pleasure, in some definition or other (and Brecht has nothing special to offer in definitions either), is the main end of art. Worried wellwishers find *relief* in this kind of "development." They are glad their friend has "mellowed." But there is no *philosophic* interest in it.

The only features of the later "aesthetic" that the philosophic reader might possibly find startling he will also find puerile. For it is puerile to see the history of art as progressive. What is to be thought of a "philosopher" who, in the lifetime of Stalin, cited no trace of barbarism in Soviet Russia but whose principal comment on Sophocles and Shakespeare reads: "Human sacrifices all round! Barbaric delights! We know the barbarians have their art. Let us create another"? Aside from the moral issue, such a philosopher is a poor historian and a poorer critic. Even Brecht's facts are often wrong. He thinks the Greeks had circuses, and that Robert Louis Stevenson was an American. He is more anxious that his remarks should have a Marxian ring than that they should be true, as witness this kind of stuff: "Anyone can see the colonial adventures of the Second Empire looming behind Delacroix's paintings and Rimbaud's 'Bateau Ivre.'" Now whether or not those adventures "loom behind" the "Bateau Ivre," they certainly are not something "anyone" can see there: are they visible even to a critical genius? As for Delacroix (1799–1863), his style was fully formed, obviously, before the Second Empire even came into being. The sentence just quoted is preceded by this one: "The linking of particular emotions with particular interests is not unduly difficult so long as one simply looks for the interests corresponding to the emotional effects of works of art." To which one can only retort that nothing is "unduly difficult" to a thinker who so glibly manipulates facts to match formulas.

Perhaps what Mr. Willett has done had to be done if only to show that it cannot be done—or at least that it cannot redound to the Meister's credit. But what an ungrateful task! Some of those who have read all of Brecht in German will end wishing Mr. Willett had adopted just the opposite principle of choice: had picked, not items in which an "aesthetic" seems to be developing, but items in which a poet addresses his poet's imagination and wit to the registration of immediate impressions and such conclusions therefrom as stay within the realm of personal preference, individual vision. Granted that some other people consider such items comparatively trivial. Granted, too, that Mr. Willett has Brecht's own backing in trying to make it seem that the theatrical opinions are grounded on universal principles: in this way those opinions could, it was hoped, become the laws of the Medes and Persians, or at any rate, the Germans and the Russians. However, Mr. Willett's own volume provides the proof that the theatrical opinions of Brecht do not derive from Marxist philosophy, since they were in Brecht's mind—in essence—before he was a Marxist.

It is not enough to state that the material is less interesting as aesthetics than as biography unless it be added that Brecht biography is itself a large and legitimate subject. What specifically *does* the critical writing contribute to it?

Brecht was one of those artists—Berlioz and Shaw were others—who took on the task of putting their art across and were their own agents, promoters, propagandists. It is doubtful if anything else in life except this task—and the art it promoted—really interested him. It is true he told the Committee on Un-American Activities that he had set everything else aside to help in the fight against Hitler: the stance suggests that of writers like Ralph Fox who gave up the pen for the sword. Fox was killed; Brecht on the other hand was a Schweykian, Keunerian, Galileist master of the art of survival. Hitler deflected him neither from writing nor from one kind of writing to another. Hitler provided perfectly Brechtian material for his writing. And how little the writing about Hitler contributed to the downfall of Hitler can be judged by the history and character of the plays about Hitler, *Round Heads* and *Arturo Ui*. Neither from stages nor in book form did they reach any sizable public, and they are far too indirect and elaborate and literary to make good popular propaganda. On the other hand, though not among his finest plays, they meant for Brecht the maintenance of a perfect continuity with what he was already doing. Not only did he carry on: it is positively amazing what obstacles to such continuity he managed to remove from his path. The Hitlers and the Mussolinis came and went, but what Bertolt Brecht had to show for those gory years (1933 to 1945) was a list of masterworks.

If, in a sense, plays like *Round Heads* and *Arturo Ui* misfired, the writings on theater never got into the gun. Many of them did not even reach a tiny public, since they were not published at all. All the more impressive, then, is the fact that they got written: it is further tribute to Brecht's *undiscourageability,* to his utter concentration on his own writing. As a preface writer he will be compared with Shaw. But the comparison is not really apropos. Shaw's prefaces cover a wide range of subject matter: education, politics, sex, prisons, religion . . . Brecht's really are "on theater," that is to say, they really are about the Brechtian theater: they are Brecht on Brecht. If Shaw play-acted egoism, it is Brecht who is truly ego-centered. And that is his strength. His attitude could hardly be called Marxian: it is diametrically opposed to the kind of thing the Communists admire. Art for art's sake? Say, rather: *art at all costs.* His *Galileo* is about this, with science substituted for art. In the final version speeches have been inserted to please Brecht's Communist friends, rejecting "science at all costs." But the play was originally written to defend just that.

Why Has Broadway Rejected Bertolt Brecht?

1965

In 1965 Seymour Peck of the New York Times *asked me why Brecht had always failed on Broadway, so I told him. I also made the mistake of adding a pep talk for theater people (here omitted) assuring them all might yet be well on the Great White Way or not too far from it, and so on and so on. The* Times *called my article "What Ever Became of Bertolt Brecht?" (January 17) but I had called it "Why Has Broadway Rejected Bertolt Brecht?"*

IT IS NEARLY HALF A CENTURY SINCE Bertolt Brecht started writing plays, and it is about fifteen years since he wrote his last notable play. In all these years, the Broadway record is meager indeed. *The Threepenny Opera* was produced at the Empire in 1933 and had only twelve performances. *Galileo* was to be seen at the Maxine Elliott in 1947. After reading the mixed reviews, Charles Laughton, the star, was no longer interested in trying to make a long run of what had, in any case, been scheduled for a single week in an experimental series. If there were fourteen years between *Threepenny* and *Galileo,* there were sixteen between *Galileo* and the next Brecht on Broadway. This was the Jerome Robbins–Cheryl Crawford pro-

duction of my own *Mother Courage* adaptation. It had fifty-two performances. A few months later came the David Merrick production of *Arturo Ui*, directed by Tony Richardson. It closed "on
Saturday night." That was 1963. In 1964 the name Brecht was spoken on Broadway only in whispers. Why—the *New York Times*
asked me—has he failed?

To be sent to hell is to be in very good company. To be excluded
from Broadway—likewise. Excluded from regular production—
staged in the hope of a long run—are most of the great plays of the
world from those of Aeschylus on. Even the greatest playwright in
our own language, Shakespeare, is now very seldom launched for an
unlimited run in the regular way of show business. How then should
we expect to see lesser Shakespeares or foreign ones on Broadway?

Well, it may be retorted, Brecht is a modern playwright, and
Broadway does not differ from the theater of past ages in offering
chiefly contemporary works. To this, one can only rejoin: it offers
contemporary works, but which? Was it offering Ibsen in 1880 or
even in 1910? Or Strindberg? Was it offering Wedekind and Hauptmann in 1920? How much has Broadway seen of Synge or O'Casey?
Of Gorky or Mayakovsky? Of García Lorca or Ugo Betti?

Of the leading foreign playwrights of the past hundred years,
which has Broadway seen much of? Shaw? Yes. But Shaw was
also often unsuccessful, was launched by an organization that
today would be designated "off Broadway" (the Theatre Guild as
of the twenties), and finally only had a smashing success after his
death—with *My Fair Lady*, which you could also say isn't Shaw.
Pirandello? Yes: Brock Pemberton introduced him successfully in
the early twenties with *Six Characters*. The Shuberts had a success
with *As You Desire Me* in the early thirties. These were modest
successes compared with the smash hits of that period or this.
Chekhov? He is known on Broadway. The 1943 *Three Sisters* is
still spoken of, as the 1964 one will be ten years from now. But the
latter was a limited run, and there are a lot of years between 1943
and 1964. Giraudoux? As I recall, he had but one success, chez

nous, in his lifetime—the Lunts in *Amphitryon 38.* Then came the success-with-difficulty of *Madwoman,* the failure of *The Enchanted,* the limited run of *Ondine*...

There is just one successful foreign playwright on Broadway today: Jean Anouilh. And even he isn't surefire, as Hal Prince and Donald Pleasance, after *Poor Bitos,* will ruefully concede.

So Bertolt Brecht is not exactly being discriminated against. Not one German playwright has ever had even the semisuccess on Broadway of a Shaw, a Pirandello, or a Chekhov. Shouldn't we really be asking why a Broadway success was ever expected for Brecht? Why did David Merrick pay ten thousand dollars as an advance for the right to produce a flop? How was it that four hundred thousand dollars could be raised among American "capitalists" for the privilege of putting on *Mother Courage* and *Arturo Ui* unsuccessfully?

But I do not mean to imply that there are no specific barriers between Bertolt Brecht in particular and the Broadway public. There are many. Let me specify two: first, communism, and second, irony. When I say communism is a barrier I am not thinking of the fact that many Broadway ticket-buyers are against communism. That Governor Rockefeller is against communism doesn't stop him buying pictures by the Communist painter Picasso. Nor is the theater public of 1964 *shocked* at the fact that a playwright was a Communist (or sympathizer). The reason that communism is a barrier is that it represents an unfamiliar world of thought and feeling. At performances of *Mother Courage* in New York I had the impression that even the jokes were funny only to those who had a somewhat left-wing background. Anne Bancroft told me she sometimes felt she was playing to two distinct audiences, one in the orchestra, one in the balcony, and only the latter thought the jokes were funny. Incidentally, the balcony was usually full, whereas the orchestra usually wasn't, but (so said the producer's voice in my ear) "unless we can fill the orchestra too, we can't keep this show going." In other words, a Broadway public need not be all that large: it need only be all that rich.

Second, irony. Anyone can be ironical, of course, even a politician; and the Jewish humor that is acceptable everywhere in America, even on Broadway, is thoroughly ironical. There is irony and irony. And one kind that has always had hard going in the New York theater is the black, European irony. Some European playwrights—Wedekind, Sternheim—have hardly been heard from at all in New York because this irony is their method and their language. If Brecht can be said to have been heard from in the seven-year run of his *Threepenny Opera* off Broadway, it is also of interest that the black, European irony was removed by the adapter and the director of that script.

Edward II
1965

Brecht is not the poet of Gay Liberation. In his later years, this poet did not want to hear about the abundant overt homosexuality in his early works. A friend who wrote a book-length memoir of Brecht's youth explicitly refused to discuss with me the possible basis that this preoccupation might have had in real life: real life, I was given to understand, was off limits to us students of realism. But Edward II *is on the record. Sexuality, which remained marginal in the Marlowe play it is based on, is here central and pervasive. Not, however, positive. Sex, here, is a "power trip." It seems doubtful that Brecht knew the difference between homosexuality and sadomasochism, nor can homosexual devotees of S and M take comfort thereby: the cruelty here is ugly and serious ... The same young director who had introduced* A Man's a Man *at the Loeb Theater, Harvard, in 1961, brilliantly introduced* Edward II *to an American audience at the Actors' Workshop, San Francisco, in 1965: John Hancock.*

IF BRECHT'S EARLY WORKS HAVE been neglected and underrated, *Edward II* must surely be the most neglected and underrated of them all. I was told by several persons that they assumed the play would not turn up at all in an English-language edition of Brecht's works, "since it is a translation from the English, and who wants to have Marlowe translated back from the German?" My reply is that the same point was made, earlier, about *The Threepenny Opera,* with as little justification. Brecht was uninterested in translation and probably incapable of it. Anything he touched became inalienably his own. It is true that he was prepared to lift many lines from other authors, not to mention incidents, but even lines and incidents reproduced by Brecht without change are always utterly changed by their new context. The work of other authors was infinitely suggestive for Brecht, but *what* it suggested was entirely his own affair, and would have surprised those other authors very much indeed.

Even when people are told that Brecht's treatment of Marlowe's *Edward II* is "free," what they expect is Marlowe cut and edited, as by an expert stage director or scholarly popularizer who aims at providing the "essence of Marlowe." Possibly Brecht uses almost as much of Marlowe's plot as that kind of adapter, and quotes almost as many of the lines, yet his aim—to realize which he has to write in many lines of his own, and invent new incidents—is diametrically opposite. Telling a tale that is only outwardly, and not at all points even outwardly, the same, he tells it about quite different people to the end of embodying quite a different theme and communicating quite a different vision of life. The remarkable thing is how much of the original can be absorbed in what is essentially a brand-new play. An aspect of Brecht's genius for which he has not yet been given full credit is his gift of assimilation. How many fruits he sucked dry! This is not to say it was a matter of indifference what fruit came his way. To speak less metaphorically, the material must be transformable, but must also, in its as yet untransformed state, have something substantial to offer. And Brecht had an uncanny way of finding what offered him most, whether it was a particular Japanese Noh or a play by Marlowe that few Germans had even heard of, which is yet another aspect of his genius.

What was it that Marlowe's play did offer him? Many things, a number of which will emerge as we proceed. What first comes to mind is the subject—a Brechtian one—of a homosexual relation-ship seen as a fatal infatuation, seen, moreover, as masochistic in relation to the male principal and as sadistic in relation to women. Secondly, the form. The form of an Elizabethan chronicle play of-fered Brecht that distance from immediate experience that later he would bring under the heading of *Verfremdung*, or alienation. En-gland in the Middle Ages is another of his exotic-grotesque pseudomilieus. Marlowe's *Edward II* has a remarkably expressive pattern of action that can be taken over and perhaps in some re-spects improved upon. According to this pattern, the hero be-comes a more sympathetic person as his fortunes grow worse, while his chief antagonist becomes more and more repellant as he has more and more success.

If that—plus a lot of usable incidents and lines—is what Mar-lowe had to offer Brecht, in what did the Brechtian transformation consist? Anyone interested in the technique of playmaking—the carpentry of it—might learn much from watching the young Brecht reduce the number of characters from about forty to about twenty and simplify the incidents to match this reduction. In one who was only just starting out as a playwright, the technical achievement alone was one to mark him as a dramatic genius; but little of this simplifying was done for its own sake. Brecht had no objection to a bewildering complexity, as his other plays of this pe-riod show. The point—as with his more famous transformations of later years—was to turn things around, to write a counterplay, to *re*write Marlowe, to correct him, to stand him on his feet.

A reader of Marlowe who starts to read the Brecht is surprised and perhaps disappointed very early on by Brecht's omission of the most famous purple patch in the play, Gaveston's speech about the fun he and Edward will have together:

> I must have wanton poets, pleasant wits,
> Musicians, that with touching of a string
> May draw the pliant king which way I please:

Music and poetry is his delight,
Therefore I'll have Italian masks by night,
Sweet speeches, comedies, and pleasing shows,
And in the day, when he shall walk abroad,
Like sylvan nymphs my pages shall be clad;
My men, like satyrs grazing on the lawns,
Shall with their goat-feet dance an antic hay;
Sometime a lovely boy, in Dian's shape,
With hair that gilds the water as it glides,
Crownets of pearl about his naked arms
And in his sportful hands an olive tree,
To hide those parts which men delight to see,
Shall bathe him in a spring . . .

If the topic is homosexuality, would not such a passage seem relevant? Reading on, one finds that it is not relevant—is not
possible—to the experience Brecht depicts, the world he creates. A
whole dimension of the poet Marlowe is not usable, and it may
well be the dimension that most of his English-language readers
find the most attractive: Renaissance sensuousness finding expression in luxurious words and sinuous rhythms.

Brecht's refusal of the Marlovian line is not motivated by mod-
esty. The Brechtian "counterplay" is always a sort of serious parody,
converting the sublime to the grotesque. In Marlowe the steady
roll of the blank verse has an effect comparable in solemnity to the
rhymed Alexandrines of French classical tragedy. The Brecht version intersperses iambic pentameter with shorter lines—and sometimes with longer ones—that break the pattern and shatter the
icon. As with the form, so with the content. The homosexuality in
Marlowe is at once aesthetic and ambiguous. Sometimes seeming
conscious, physical, and even animal, it seems at other times but the
Elizabethan cult of poeticized friendship. When the Elder Mortimer says Edward will get over it soon, we aren't compelled to disbelieve him. As for Brecht, some readers have had the impression

that he wanted to be "shockingly frank" and sensational in the modern manner. That is not the point. It is not even true. Whereas Marlowe's Gaveston is seen not just as bedfellow but even more as royal "favorite," and a marriage we need not regard as phony is being arranged for him with a princess, Brecht's Gaveston is a sexual partner first and last. The word *whore* is bound to recur, as it does, if, as we do, we keep hearing what his enemies think of him.

A reader who looked at the end of the play first, even though there is no sex in it, would receive the same jolt from Brecht's changes as the reader who looks at the opening scenes. When Marlowe's Edward has to give up not only Gaveston but this world, what he is left with is the Christian religion—the hope of a next world. His friend Baldock provides the cue:

> Make for a new life, man: throw up thy eyes,
> And heart and hand to heaven's immortal throne...

And so the lyric afflatus prompted in the beginning by sex is sustained in the end by religious sentiment:

> Yet stay a while, forbear thy bloody hand,
> And let me see the stroke before it comes
> That even then when I shall lose my life
> My mind may be more steadfast on my God...

And:

> I am too weak and feeble to resist.
> Assist me, sweet God, and receive my soul.

Now, though Brecht's Edward also ends up as a metaphysician, the metaphysics is a travesty of Christianity (close in its wording to an acknowledged parody Brecht wrote on the subject, the "Great Thanksgiving Hymn"):

> Therefore
> Who is dark, let him stay dark,
> Who is unclean, let him stay unclean.
> Praise deficiency, praise cruelty, praise
> The darkness.

And we find, in this ending, an instance of the same words coming to mean the opposite when used by Brecht. I refer to Mortimer's summing up, his speech about the wheel of fortune. In Marlowe's play this Elizabethan commonplace concerning the fate of "magistrates" is not felt to be contradicted by an affirmative treatment of young Edward's accession to the throne: by a turn of fortune's wheel Mortimer gets his deserts, but the accession of Edward III is an improvement and a purification. Brecht on the other hand, through Mortimer, turns the argument against the new King, as much as to say, "Your turn will come." Here, the wheel of fortune is an image of a philosophy that hovers over the whole play: history goes meaninglessly round and round.

Luckily, it is not the only philosophy in the play, or it would reduce all the characters to mere pawns on a historical chessboard. No one could see or read Brecht's *Edward II* and feel that this is what they are. Brecht's Edward is far less passive than Marlowe's. This is indeed Brecht's most decisive divergence from his source, and it is in looking further into it that we begin to discover what Brecht put into the play to make up for the Marlovian elements he so drastically cut. Whether he came out with a play which is better or worse than Marlowe's is, I think, a question not to be asked: their plays are, finally, so different as to be incommensurable. But, like many another great play, Marlowe's has shortcomings, and Brecht sometimes found solutions where his predecessor had found none. This much by way of explanation, if what follows gives the impression that I consider Brecht's a better play.

Marlowe's eloquence has rightly been praised, yet there is something about his eloquent *Edward II* that is dramatically unsatisfying.

"Edward sings too many arias," one tends to say: yet the fact that he does so serves to conceal a dramatic weakness, which derives from Edward's passivity. Thinking about the shortcomings of Marlowe's play, one recalls W. B. Yeats's rejection of passive suffering as a dramatic subject. Whether or not it should be rejected out of hand, passive suffering certainly presents problems that are seldom solved. Looking at this particular narrative, one finds two nodal points in it: the point where Edward gives Gaveston up and the point where he gives the crown up. Both are actions that are not actions. "That's Edward," Marlowe might have said. It is a proposition that is reversed by Brecht, whose Edward refuses to give up either Gaveston or the crown. He loses them anyway, so, from a cynical point of view, there's no difference between the two Edwards. There is all the difference in the world from a tragic point of view—and is not *Edward II* the one play of Brecht's that can be called a tragedy in any accepted sense?

However this may be, we are confronted here with opposite characters in opposite stories. One play is about a weak man who, under pressure, gives up his friend first and his crown later, and interests us only in his very human weakness and by virtue of the faint halo that is cast around it by all the grace and poeticizing. The other is a play about an infatuated man, made palatable to us in the beginning by no poetry or charm, but earning our admiration, gradually and with difficulty, by a surprising loyalty both to his friend and to his idea of himself as king. Marlowe's play, for all its magnificent rhetoric, is a little monotonous because Edward for so long stays the same, repeating himself not only in words but in action (or rather in inaction). Though the young Brecht is often spoken of as mainly a lyric poet, nothing marks him more unmistakably as a dramatic genius than the way in which he was able to make Edward change not just at the end but throughout the play. We see a different Edward in the middle of the play already when we find him toughened by a soldier's life in the open. That is the outward form and result of a toughness that, Brecht makes us re-

alize, must always have been there. It is not out of a clear sky that
Edward, when facing his worst and final sufferings, proves then
most strong and most serene:

> ...such water hardens my limbs which are now
> Like cedar wood
> The stench of excrement gives me boundless
>   greatness!
> And the good sound of drums keeps me awake,
> Though weak, so death won't find me fainting but
> Waking.

Now, if one had to illustrate Marlowe's gift of character creation
from *Edward II,* one could not say very much about any character
save Edward himself. If Brecht eliminated about twenty of Marlowe's figures, he did so in order to develop more fully the four
leading personae, who, after Edward, are Gaveston, the Queen,
and Mortimer. I have already tried to suggest what he made of
Gaveston. It should be added that Gaveston is here given further
touches of reality that belong to the situation of a young man who
has not so much worked hard to get a Great Personage's attention
as he has had this attention forced upon him:

> I...do not know
> What it was about me of too much or little
> That made this Edward, now the King,
> Unable to leave me alone
> For my own mother found nothing in me
> Any different from the extremely
> Usual, no goiter, no white skin...

Because Edward is really infatuated, Gaveston does not have to
be a seducer or even a schemer, and the pattern is more human,
more typical, and, finally, more dramatic this way. The downfall of

Gaveston has the more poignancy because it is so much more than he "asked for."

If Gaveston, in the Brecht, is less the standard wastrel, the Queen is far less shadowy. It is remarkable how skillfully the young Brecht was able to mark the stages in this character's development. Whereas in Marlowe the Queen's liaison is suddenly there, and mentioned, in the Brecht we see it happen step-by-step, and feel the inexorable logic of it. The drama in the material is found by underlining her reluctance, on the one hand, and Edward's aggressive misogyny, on the other. (Are the dynamics of sexuality—hence its drama—always better seen in the sadistic and masochistic components than in the romance?) Again, there is great technical accomplishment in the modern play; but, again, that is subordinate to a larger human matter: in this case, the Queen's gradual loss of all sense of herself and, therewith, of reality generally. Nowhere is Brecht's audacity more marked or, to my mind, more triumphant than in the scene entitled "The emptiness of the world makes the Queen laugh." No topic has been more often dilated upon by modern writers than this "emptiness of the world." Credit is due to Brecht not for taking the subject up but for showing in a succession of dramatic encounters how the Queen *discovers* the void.

In Marlowe, Edward has but one partner and foil: Gaveston. In Brecht, he has three: Gaveston, the Queen, and Mortimer. The contrast is a strong one between the infatuated, stubborn king and the lost, embarrassed, not stupid, fundamentally rather innocent boyfriend. The contrast is strong, too, between Edward and his queen. Though this Edward has been able to become a father, everything else we know of him seems homoerotic. Gaveston is not the whole story. Even in his isolation, later, Edward is the man's man, finding strength on horseback and in the tent, an aging Hippolytus. And even the asexuality of his final phase is part of the complex. The Queen, on the other hand, is "all woman." She will be loyal to her man as long as she is allowed to be, but when this loyalty is mocked and forbidden, she will drift to another man.

There is a convincing morbidity in this drift as Brecht shows it, since it is a drift to her former man's principal enemy and opposite.

Principal enemy and opposite: that is why Mortimer is the principal partner among Edward's three. And therein lies another achievement of Brecht's. Marlowe's play suffers because his Edward has no adequate partner once Gaveston drops out in the middle. In Brecht's play, Gaveston is less important from the start than Mortimer, and so is the more expendable: if all four characters are mostly Brecht's own inventions, Mortimer is 99 percent so. Marlowe's young Mortimer is a barbaric young man who is capable of having at Gaveston with his sword to cap an argument. We feel he takes over the Queen only because that's what barbarians do. It is Brecht's idea that Mortimer was a scholar and has to be won from his books before he enters the political arena at all. More original still, his meditations have already led him to Solomon's conclusion: all is vanity. What for the Queen is a destination was for him a point of departure. The absolute "nullity of human things and deeds": what a premise for political action! The conception permits Brecht to create, in the first instance, an effectively tragicomic scoundrel and, in the second, to define the perfect antithesis to Edward: Edward is the man of feeling, Mortimer of reason. But so long as the contrast remains so general it has little human interest or dramatic force. These it derives from an "action" that gives it concrete expression and by further "interpretation" of what reason and feeling, in this context, signify. Mortimer remarks that Edward "Antaeus-like...draws strength from the soil." Antaeus was the son of the Earth Mother, and Edward himself says:

> Dull-eyed, you Mortimers do arithmetic, and
> Burrow in books like worms.
> But in books there is nothing about Edward who
> Reads nothing, does not do arithmetic,
> Knows nothing and has intimate ties with Nature.
> He's nourished by quite different food.

One thinks of poems, novels, or plays in which Nature and Reason confront each other and are both benign. Nature can imply a utopia of noble savages; Reason can be the law of a God who is all-wise and all-good. In the world of the young Brecht, such benignities have all been replaced by horrors of disenchantment. Some bizarre but solid paradoxes result. The "Nature" of Edward is precisely what for the world at large passes for *un*natural:

> Oh, Spencer, since words are rough
> And only part us heart from heart
> And understanding is not granted to us
> Amid the deafness nothing remains except
> Bodily contact between men.

The "Reason" of Mortimer is hardly that of the optimistic Rationalist. At best it is that of some of the French existentialists who see the whole universe as hostile and Reason as the element that, if you're lucky, reduces the hostility to temporarily manageable proportions. The final paradox is a certain fundamental agreement between Edward and Mortimer. Both see the world as impossible but suggest the hope that it may at times become "possible" if we appeal to what is most human in us. What they disagree about is the character of our humanity, Mortimer finding it in reason, Edward in feeling, which—in Brecht's context—makes of the former a Machiavellian or even fascistic politician, and of the latter...a homosexual. Obviously, from the point of view of almost any modern theater public, this whole story is "beyond good and evil."

A minor character in Marlowe's play compares Gaveston to Helen of Troy:

> Monster of men,
> That, like the Greekish strumpet, train'd to arms
> And bloody wars so many valiant knights...

Brecht, who at any point can take what one Marlowe character says and give it to some other character, not only gives this comparison to Mortimer, but also makes of it the longest and perhaps most important speech of the play: a sort of centerpiece for the whole drama. From it we learn that such a relationship as that of Helen and Paris or Gaveston and Edward is the source of human trouble, but not because society considers it immoral. It makes no difference to Mortimer "whether Helen was a whore / Or had a score of healthy grandchildren." It is simply that "the ear of reason had ... been stopped up." Mortimer offers himself and his own philosophy as the nearest the world can come to any solution. His opposite, Edward, represents the worst that the world can know: infatuation, surrender to pure feeling.

At bottom, Mortimer's philosophy is less paradoxical than contradictory, for if we believe him when he tells us the world is nothing, we are hardly disposed to take him up on it when he offers to save that world from passion. The poet is able to indicate by the tone of Mortimer's speeches that they can scarcely be accepted at face value:

> Because a few hats are off and on the ground
> Before a son of a bitch, the English people
> Push their Island over the precipice.

Well, any tears Mortimer sheds over this prospect are crocodile tears, since disaster is for him normal and natural and inevitable, and, in the play, we know this without even going through the logical reasoning, since Mortimer, though not the usual villain, is still the villain.

Edward, though not the usual hero, is still a hero. This story is, if you like, yet another of those modern defenses of the sensitive homosexual destroyed by a cruelly hostile world and can be confidently recommended to the broad public such stories apparently command. If at bottom Mortimer's philosophy is contradictory, if his rationalism is finally irrational and his reason unreasonable, Edward's antirational view, the world being what it is, is rational.

> Amid the deafness nothing remains except
> Bodily contact between men.

If the Trojan War was as mad and meaningless as, say, World War I, then isn't it possible that what Paris and Helen did in bed was the only part of the whole transaction that had any human value or even much human substance? Whatever you and I, in the context of our own lives, make of this question, isn't it cogent for Edward, in the context of Brecht's play, to answer the comparable question in the positive: the relationship between Edward and Gaveston—not seen "poetically" as by Marlowe but in all its physicality—provided something to hold on to, which is more than could be said for anything else that transpires in the play, with a single exception I shall revert to in a moment.

Brecht's brilliant, complicated dialectic is seen in the endings to which Mortimer and Edward come, which are "the same" but also "the opposite." Both men end quietly, accept their end philosophically. There is something stoical, and hence traditionally tragic, about both endings. Mortimer's is the more ostentatiously so (he has two big speeches, the bull speech and the wheel-of-fortune speech), and the ostentation "gives the show away"—that is, gives away that he *is* putting on a show. He enacts the very parody of a hero's death. That he is really *un*heroic is clear in that he closes with a taunt toward the young king. Edward's heroism is genuine, and his power to endure is that other "something to hold on to" that I just mentioned.

Heroic courage is the tragic virtue, and Edward has it. Mortimer's courage, if we take it to exist at all, is unheroic because it needs to be propped by hatred and cynicism: it is easier to die if you are spitting hatred against others all the while and if you truly find all living worthless anyway. (Hence the abundant unheroic

courage of modern militarists.) Not the least interesting feature of
Brecht's Mortimer is that he has known this all along:

> ... frightened like one burned to death
> I wrap myself in the skin of another man:
> This butcher's son.

Here, quite early in the action, Mortimer thinks of the skin of
Gaveston as a cloak in which he can hide. Our strong man is weak.
Our courageous man is unheroic.

I have indicated that what makes a hero out of Edward in
Brecht's play is that, unlike Marlowe's protagonist, he *can* say no.
His two refusals, spaced out in the way they are, do much to give
the play its grand and cogent structure. Edward can say no because
he possesses the primordial, Promethean tragic virtue of sheer endurance. The effect and meaning of this are much heightened by
Brecht, because he gives Edward much more to endure. Less ethe-
really poetic, the Brecht play is far more brutal than the Marlowe.
If some of the more external barbarities (like bringing on Mortimer's head) are discarded, far more real torture is inflicted. At
times the story itself is changed to this end. It is Brecht's doing that
Edward had the chance to save Gaveston and missed it, giving
Mortimer his chance to turn his knife in the psychological wound:

> had you
> Not drowned their words out with your drums,
> Had not, that is, too little confidence
> And too much passion, too swift anger
> Troubled your eye, your favorite Gaveston
> Would be still alive.

As for the sequence where Edward is asked to abdicate, Brecht not
only changes the action to a refusal to abdicate, but also makes it
essentially a contest between Edward and Mortimer. (In Marlowe's

abdication scene, Mortimer is not even present.) This contest has the character of a cat-and-mouse game. While the cruder tortures of the Gurneys are mostly kept offstage, the pressure inflicted by Mortimer upon Edward's spirit—Mortimer's attempt to brainwash him—is all presented and is of the very essence of this play.

If the tale of Edward's imprisonment and death is mostly taken from Marlowe, who had mostly taken it from Holinshed, Brecht's changes are still considerable, and underline both Edward's final victory and the horror of the conditions that failed to defeat him.

> This dungeon where they keep me is the sink
> Wherein the filth of all the castle falls . . .
> And there in mire and puddle have I stood . . .

That is Marlowe. Holinshed had spoken of "a chamber over a foul filthy dungeon full of dead carrion," but Brecht paints a picture that is not only more revolting than Marlowe and Holinshed but belongs to a different pattern and intention. Where his Edward stands is nothing more nor less than the cloaca, and we see him there actually steeped in excrement and presumably continuing to be shat and pissed on before our eyes. So ends Edward the playboy. The Baalian quester for pleasures, for anal pleasures, ends in the sewer. It would be a mistake to consider the young Brecht merely fascinated by filth, though he may *also* have been fascinated by it. There is dramatic appropriateness and irony in Edward's final condition. For one thing it is very close to the primal condition, the situation of the human being born *inter faeces et urinas,* and it is not just that Edward finds himself there, but that there he achieves strength, and even serenity.

In its own Schopenhauerian way, Brecht's *Edward II* is a heroic tragedy, and as such is unique in the lifework of Brecht, for while he would often portray courageous action and the self-sacrifice it entails—as with his Kattrin in *Mother Courage,* the son in *The Mother,* the revolutionaries in *Days of the Commune*—the context of the later heroism is imposed by the author's optimistic progressivism, which negates tragedy as traditionally accepted. Edward's heroism belongs to the category of the traditionally tragic in that it is not utilitarian but serves only (only!) to demonstrate that man is not a worm.

For Brecht personally, there is a continuing thread from this early hero of his to the truly "positive heroes" found here and there in his later works. It is to be found in that ability to say no that for Brecht had such very urgent importance. For this there are clear historical reasons, notably the inability of his own people, the Germans, to say no to the Mortimers of the Nazi Party. "Will none of you say NO?" cries the chorus before the last scene of Brecht's chronicle of life under the Nazis, while the scene itself ends on the decision to issue an anti-Nazi pamphlet consisting of the one word *no*. Conversely (the word is needed often in expounding the works of this great dramatic dialectician), the person who cannot say no is a constantly recurring figure of the Brecht oeuvre. He is depicted most flat-footedly in the poem "On Giving This World One's Endorsement," which depicts and denounces the average fellow traveler of Nazism:

> I'm not unjust but I am not courageous
> They pointed out their world to me today
> I saw the hand that pointed: it was bloody
> I like your world, I hurried on to say
>
> I saw the murderers and I saw the victims
> It was just courage not compassion that I lacked
> I saw the murderers picking out their victims
> And cried aloud that I endorsed this fact...

He receives his classical definition in Galy Gay of *A Man's a Man,* and he gets subtle, two-sided, definitely dialectical, and possibly ambiguous treatment in Herr Keuner, Mother Courage, Schweyk, Galileo, and Azdak.

Edward II should make us rethink the whole topic of Brecht's development. The early plays are lumped together as negative in spirit, and in them the men who can't say no are spotted and reported on by the critics. But for all the despair that floats free in these plays, they frequently bear witness to a kind of human strength. In the introduction to his excellent translation of *Drums in the Night,* Frank Jones makes us aware that Kragler is one of Brecht's strong men. If we had not noticed it, it is because we take his abandonment of the revolution as irreclaimably "negative." No doubt the later Brecht wanted the Kraglers of this world to be disapproved of, but the Brecht who wrote *Drums in the Night* presented Kragler's achieving of independence as positive.

It is interesting that in Brecht's plays the men of sheer action are generally bad, whereas good actions tend to come, if at all, from people who have hitherto been markedly passive. Whereas the men of action in *Mother Courage* keep busy slaughtering people, good actions get performed after long preparation by persons who were so gentle they seemed till then quite inactive, such as Swiss Cheese and Kattrin. If the passive people of the early plays never become doers-of-good, the principal ones do shake themselves out of their passivity: Kragler, for example, at the end of *Drums,* and Garga at the end of *In the Swamp.* Baal is characterized, on the one hand, by an extreme passivity, yet, on the other, is a sort of nonspiritual Don Quixote in quest of happiness. Only *A Man's a Man* is a study of complete inability to say no, and even there the joke, in the original version, is that once Galy Gay is reconstructed he becomes a Leader: he has moved from the camp of the amiably passive to that of the brutally active.

When the young Bertolt Brecht chose Marlowe's *Edward II* as the basis for a play, one could only have supposed that he chose it as one of the classic studies of passivity and weakness, and one could only have expected he was himself interested in presenting to the world a man who couldn't say no. That he presented a man who *could* say no, and this long before he heard any talk about "positive heroes" or even studied Marxism, should give us pause.

Close to all the other early plays, *Edward II* is especially close to *In the Swamp* and *A Man's a Man*. All three dramatize a contrast between two men, depict a struggle between two men, and in similar terms. It is a question of the actual or virtual rape of one by the other, and it is a question of the masochistic pleasure that the raped one takes in the rape. "It was the best time," as Garga succinctly puts it, after being seduced and taken over by Shlink. In *A Man's a Man,* Galy Gay is "raped" by the British army in the form of a machine-gun unit, but the character-contrast is with Bloody Five upon whose quest to identify him *as* Galy Gay, not Jeraiah Jip, the story is built; and by a very suggestive quirk Bloody Five speaks at one point of the possibility of raping Galy Gay. However, the contrast is almost wholly in terms of the active/passive elements, rather than hetero/homo.

In Marlowe's *Edward II* one could believe that the King was seduced by Gaveston. What we notice first about Brecht's rendering is that the responsibility rests more with the King, who is infatuated, while Gaveston preserves a degree of detachment. But the Brechtian "rape" is no more directly sexual in this play than in *A Man's a Man.* It is again a military rape. The rapist is neither the King nor Gaveston but Mortimer, and Brecht reworks the plot to give the King's part in this relationship a decisive and unmistakable masochism. Where, in Marlowe, Mortimer simply escapes, in Brecht he is released by the King for no clear reason. The reason is *made* clear by the subsequent action and, more specifically, by the King when questioned about it later:

> I spared Mortimer for the wicked pleasure
> It gave me to do just that.

Sparing Mortimer gave pleasure for its sheer arbitrariness: the King did it for "the hell of it," "for kicks." But what hell, and what was it that kicked? Surely the part of Edward that wanted his enemy to win, the part of Edward that wanted to lose. To the sad logic of the old tragic tale from Holinshed and the old tragic drama of Marlowe, Brecht adds a further kind of doom: a psycho-logic. It entails transferring the homosexuality to Mortimer, for not only is Mortimer drawn very dynamically into a close relation with Edward, he desires Edward's wife, a fact that, in this context, must be taken as homosexual girl-sharing. *Edward II* is close to *Baal*.

Brecht's tragedy has a puritanic aspect. His hero has been a heterosexual before the play opens; becomes a homosexual later; and, later still, withdraws, through friendship, and, even more, through friendship betrayed, into heroic solitude. At the end he is almost a saint. The role of Mortimer has a precisely contrary movement. He begins in bookish isolation and then plunges headlong into Edward's world. When he takes over the Queen he is experiencing Edward's hetero- and homosexual phases at the same time, and this fact is presented in an Elizabethan rather than a Brechtian vein: as morally heinous. Yet, if such puritanism seems a far cry from the pansexuality propagated by the character Baal, the play of *Baal* also bears witness to much sexual nausea, to much hatred of sex and therefore much fear of sex, and what is perhaps the finest lyric in the play proposes a romantic, asexual purity as an alternative:

> He dreams at times about a little meadow
> A patch of blue in the sky and nothing more.

While a first impression of Brecht's *Edward II* may make us say how much "more sex" there is in it than in Marlowe's play, the point of the sex is not sex itself. A vulgarized Freudianism, which finds sex hidden at the bottom of everything, would be the worst of all critical philosophies to bring to a play in which the surface itself is all sex and at the bottom is . . . what? My metaphor itself smacks too much of popular Freudianism. Literary subject matter cannot always be neatly split into manifest and latent. In *Edward II* it is less a question of sex concealing something else than of being part of a larger whole, part of a human fate that is a sexual fate but not exclusively so. While Edward's relation with Gaveston is more blatantly sexual than it had been for Marlowe, that does not prevent the poet Brecht from finding in it an image of a fate that is not just sexual:

> Against the hour when the corpse is found
> Prepare a worthy grave. And yet
> Don't hunt for him!
> He's like the man who walks into the woods
> And the bushes grow up thickly behind him and
> The plants shoot up again and
> The thicket's got him.

One cannot ask that a theater audience should have read Brecht's "Ballad of Friendship," his "Ballad of Cortez's Men," and his "Fort Donald Railroad Gang," in order to feel more at home with such a treatment of the theme. Perhaps indeed the passage just quoted is more powerful if it comes as an astonishment. Of a sudden we then see Gaveston as part of that vast organism, Nature, to which Edward acknowledged so close a relation. A self-devouring organism: Gaveston was part of it and is swallowed up by it. Specifically by a *thicket*. The word is the same as in the title of *Im Dickicht der Städte* (*In the Thicket of the Cities*). And for all the jungle beasts, tigers, wolves, or wild bulls, that haunt *Edward II*, a *Dickicht* is, incidentally, not a jungle: only density of vegetation is implied, not the presence of wild animals. Edward pictures a Gaveston not torn to pieces by beasts but stifled by the under- and overgrowth. And it is soon as if he had never been: what flourish are the grasses, the plants, and the trees. The image is cosmic rather than clinical.

Even Edward's final triumph over sex should not be taken as the farthest reach of the poet's imagination in this play. This heroism is more than a newfound chastity. The chastity is itself but an aspect of something else: independence. Edward had not been able to do without Gaveston. He had not been able to do without the

Queen even when he insulted and rejected her: a contradiction she spotted and taunted him with. He could not do without his last loyal retainers until the chief one proved *dis*loyal and betrayed him. (The Baldock episode is another brilliant innovation of Brecht's.) It is only when he *is* without all these people he "could not do without" that Edward finds he not only can do without them, but also that he is now a man, he is now himself, for the first time. It's like a hypochondriac cripple who does not discover he can stand upright and walk without assistance until his crutches have been brutally torn from him.

It has been remarked—it could hardly not be—that *Brecht's plays present victimization,* and many have got the impression that his early plays show and represent a mere wallowing in it, but this is to see what one might call the primary movement of the action and not the countermovement that ensues and for the sake of which the play was written. *Each of these plays is actually a cry of "Don't fence me in!"* Baal may be cruelly left to perish, but he has lived, and under the open sky: he didn't let them fence him in. Kragler wouldn't be fenced in even by an ideology that the author of *Drums in the Night* would—much later—accept. (That is, of course, not all he wouldn't be fenced in by.) *In the Swamp* ends as Garga breaks loose from Chicago itself, the cage in which the whole action had been enclosed. The paradox of Edward's final posture is that he is physically fenced in but spiritually liberated. There is nothing more they can do to him, and this in two senses: he cannot suffer worse humiliations, and his fearlessness is an iron barrier they cannot cross: he has fenced *them* in. In each case, Brecht shows a man giving way to pressure and exhibiting human weakness; but in each case there comes the countermovement: the worm turns, the weak man shows strength, and the ending is in some sense a victory. Even Galy Gay, in the original conception, not the Marxized version, is getting his own back at the end. "He'll have our heads yet," say those who once had called him "a man who can't say no." These endings are not pious, renewing our faith in human goodness, while the sun comes up at the back, and soft music plays. That kind of ending stands rebuked by the young Brecht. But so does a kind of ending he was more likely to have had in mind: the ending of the typical naturalistic play in which life is simply too much for pathetic little *homo sapiens*, and someone jumps in a lake at the bottom of the garden or shoots himself in the next room.

Mother Courage
1965

Mother Courage *clambered onto the English-speaking stage rather clumsily. In Britain, Joan Littlewood, Eithne Dunne, and Flora Robson all tried the part early on. I think Beatrice Manley must have been the first American Courage at the Actors' Workshop, San Francisco, 1956. Jerome Robbins directed the play on Broadway in 1963 with a cast that included Anne Bancroft, Gene Wilder, Mike Kellin, Zohra Lampert, and Barbara Harris. The following piece was written for the National Theatre's production, London, 1965.*

THE ROLE OF MOTHER COURAGE is hard to play and is always being miscast. Why? "Because middle-aged actresses are such ladies and lack earthiness." But who has succeeded in the role? Outstandingly, Helene Weigel. Is she very earthy, is she notably proletarian? On the contrary—there is nothing proletarian about her except her opinions. Then what is it those other women lack that Helene Weigel has? Among other things, an appreciation of the role, an understanding of what is in it, and above all the ability to portray contradictions. For whenever anyone says, "Mother Courage is essentially X," it is equally reasonable for someone to retort: "Mother Courage is essentially the opposite of X."

Mother Courage is essentially courageous. That is well known, isn't it? Tennessee Williams has written of the final moment of Brecht's play as one of the inspiring moments in all theater—inspiring because of the woman's indomitability. On she marches with her wagon after all that has happened, a symbol of the way humanity itself goes on its way after all that has happened, *if* it can find the courage. And after all we don't have to wait for the final scene to learn that we have to deal with a woman of considerable toughness and resilience. This is not the first time she has shown that she can pick up the pieces and continue. One might even find courage in the very first scene, where we learn that she has not been content to cower in some corner of Bamberg but has boldly come to meet the war. A troublemaker, we might say on first meeting the lady, but the reverse of a coward.

Yet it is impossible to continue on this tack for long without requiring an *on the other hand*, beginning with the reason why she is nicknamed Courage in the first place.

> They call me Mother Courage because I was afraid I'd be
> ruined, so I drove through the bombardment of Riga like
> a madwoman with fifty loaves of bread in my cart. They
> were going moldy, what else could I do?

Did those who gave her the name intend a joke against an obvious coward? Or did they think she was driven by heroic valor when in fact she was impelled by sheer necessity? Either way her act is utterly devoid of the moral quality imputed. Whether in cowardice or in down-to-earth realism, her stance is Falstaffian. What is courage? A word.

Somewhere hovering over this play is the image of a preeminently courageous mother who courageously tries to hold on to her young. More than one actress, offering herself for the role, has seen this image and nothing else. Yet valor is conspicuously absent at those times when Mother Courage (however unwittingly) seals the fate of her children. At moments when, in heroic melodrama, the protagonist would be riding to the rescue, come hell or high water, Mother Courage is in the back room concluding a little deal. For her, it is emphatically not "a time for greatness." *She is essentially cowardly.*

A basic contradiction, then, which the actress in the role must play both sides of, or the play will become the flat and simple thing that not a few journalistic commentators have declared it to be. An actress may be said to be beginning to play Mother Courage when she is putting both courage and cowardice into the role with equal conviction and equal effect. She is still only beginning to play it, though; for, as she proceeds with her interpretation, she will find that, in this play, courage and cowardice are not inherent and invariable qualities but by-products.

Of what? We can hunt for the answer by looking further into particular sequences of action. It is not really from cowardice that Mother Courage is in the back room concluding a little deal when her children are claimed by the war. It is from preoccupation with "business." Although *Mother Courage* is spoken of as a war play, it is actually a business play, in the sense that the incidents in it, one and all, are business transactions—from the deal with the belt in scene 1, through the deal with the capon in scene 2, the deal with the wagon in scene 3, the deals with bullets and shirts in scene 5, through to the economical funeral arrangements of the final scene. And since these transactions (except for the last) are what Courage supports her children by, they are "necessary." Those who condemn her have to face the question: What alternative had she? Of what use would it have been to save the life of Swiss Cheese if she lacked the wherewithal to *keep* him alive? The severe judge will answer that she could take a chance on this, provided she does save his life. But this is exactly Mother Courage's own position. She is fully prepared to take the chance if she has to. It is in determining whether she has to that her boy's life slips through her fingers: life or death is a matter of timing.

To say that Swiss Cheese is a victim of circumstances, not of Courage's character, will not, however, be of much use to the actress interpreting this character. If cowardice is *less* important here than at first appears, what is *more* important? Surely it is a failure in understanding, rather than in virtue. Let me elaborate.

Though only one of Brecht's completed plays is about anyone that a university would recognize as a philosopher, several of his plays present what one might call philosophers in disguise, such as Schweyk, the philosopher of a pub in Prague, and Azdak, the philosopher of a Georgian village. To my mind, *Mother Courage is above all a philosopher,* defining the philosopher along Socratic lines as a person who likes to talk all the time and explain everything to everybody. (A simple trait in itself, one would think, yet there have been actresses and directors who wish to have all Courage's speeches shortened into mere remarks. Your philosopher never makes remarks; he always speechifies; such abridgment enforces a radical misinterpretation of character.) I do not mean at all that Courage is an idle or armchair philosopher whose teachings make no contact with life. On the contrary, her ideas are nothing if not a scheme of life by which, she hopes, her family is to do pretty well in a world that is doing pretty badly.

Here one sees the danger of thinking of Mother Courage as the average person. Rather, she resembles the thoughtfully ambitious modern mother of the lower-middle or better-paid working class who wants her children to win scholarships and end up in the Labour Cabinet. (Minister of Education: Kattrin. Chancellor of the Exchequer: Swiss Cheese. Minister of War: Eilif.) Has it escaped attention that if one of her children turns out a cutthroat, this is blamed on circumstances ("Otherwise, I'd have starved, smarty"), while *the other two are outright heroes*? Anyone who considers this an average family takes a far higher view of the average than is implicit in the works of Bertolt Brecht.

What is the philosophy of this philosopher? Reduced to a single proposition, it is that if you concede defeat on the larger issue, you can achieve some nice victories in smaller ways. The larger issue is whether the world can be changed. It can't. But brandy is still drunk, and can be sold. One can survive, and one can help one's children to survive by teaching each to make appropriate use of the qualities God gave him. The proposition I have just mentioned will apply to this upbringing. A child endowed with a particular talent or virtue should not pursue it to its logical end: defeat on such projects should be conceded at the outset. The child should cunningly exploit his characteristic talent for its incidental uses along the way. In this fashion the unselfishness of a Swiss Cheese or a Kattrin can be harnessed to selfishness. The result, if the philosophy works, is that while the world may shoot itself to blazes, the little Courage family, one and all, will live out its days in moderate wealth and moderate happiness. The scheme is not utopian. Just the opposite: the hope is to make optimism rational by reducing human demands to size.

The main reason it doesn't work is that the little world that Mother Courage's wisdom tries to regulate is dependent upon the big world that she has given up as a bad job. Small business is part of the big war, which is part of the big business of ownership of *all* the means of production and distribution. No more than the small businessman can live in a separate economic system from the big can the small philosopher live in a separate philosophic system from the big. *Mother Courage,* one can conclude, exposes the perennial illusions of the petit bourgeois scheme of things. This has often been done before in modern literature. But usually only the idealism has been exposed. Mother Courage, on the other hand, could claim to be a cynic. She has the theater audience laughing most of the time on the score of this cynicism—by which *she* deflates illusions. Cynicism is nothing, after all, if not "realistic." What a cynical remark lays bare *has* to be the truth. Brecht makes the truth of his play the more poignant through the fact that the cynicism in it ultimately favors illusion. Mother Courage had gone to all lengths to trim her sails to the wind but even then the ship wouldn't move. So there is irony within irony (as, in Brecht's work, there usually is). Courage's cynicism can cut down the windy moralizing of the Chaplain easily enough, but only to be itself cut down by a world that cannot be comprehended even by this drastically skeptical thinking.

What alternative did Mother Courage have? The only alternatives shown in the play are, on the one hand, the total brutalization of men like the Swedish Commander (and, for that matter, her own son Eilif) and, on the other hand, the martyrdom achieved by Swiss Cheese and Kattrin. Presumably, to the degree that the playwright criticizes her, he is pushing her toward the second alternative. Yet, not only would such a destiny be out of character, within the terms of the play itself it is not shown to be preferable. Rather, the fruitlessness of both deaths is underlined. Why add a third?

Given her character, Mother Courage had no alternative to what she thought—or, for that matter, to the various "bad" things she did. In this case, can she be condemned? Logically, obviously not; but was Brecht logical? The printed editions of the play indicate that he made changes in his script to render Mother Courage less sympathetic. After having made her thoroughly sympathetic in his first version, Brecht later wanted her less so. One can see the sense of the changes in polemical terms: he did not wish to seem to condone behavior that is to be deplored. But to make this point, is it necessary to make Mother Courage a less good person? Personally I would think not, and I should like to see *Courage* played sometime in the urtext of 1940 and without the later "improvements." But one should not minimize the complexity of the problem. Like many other playwrights, Brecht wanted to show a kind of inevitability combined with a degree of free will, and if it doesn't matter whether Courage is less good or more, because she is trapped by circumstances, then the play is fatalistic. I tend to think it *is* fatalistic, as far as the movement of history is concerned, and that the element of hope in it springs only from Brecht's rendering of human character. Brecht himself is not satisfied with this and made changes in the hope of suggesting that things might have been different had Mother Courage acted otherwise. (What would she have done? Established socialism in seventeenth-century Germany?)

Brecht has stressed, in his Notes, that Mother Courage never sees the light, never realizes what has happened, is incapable of learning. As usual, Brecht's opinions, as stated in outside comments, are more doctrinaire than those to be found embodied in the plays. It may be true that Mother Courage never sees that "small business" is a hopeless case, though to prove even this Brecht had to manufacture the evidence by inserting, later, the line at the end: "I must get back into business." She does see through her own philosophy of education. The "Song of Solomon" in scene 9 concedes that the program announced in scene 1 has failed. The manipulation of the virtues has not worked: "A man is better off without." The song is more symbolic, as well as more schematic, than most Brechtians wish Brecht to be, for there is a verse about each of her children under the form of famous men (Eilif is Caesar, Swiss Cheese is Socrates, Kattrin is Saint Martin), but more important is that this is the "Song of Solomon" (from *The Threepenny Opera*) and that Solomon is Courage herself:

> King Solomon was very wise
> So what's his history?
> He came to view this world with scorn
> Yes, he came to regret he ever had been born
> Declaring: all is vanity.
> King Solomon was very wise
> But long before the day was out
> The consequence was clear, alas:
> It was his wisdom brought him to this pass.
> A man is better off without.

I have heard the question asked whether this conclusion was not already reached in the "Song of the Great Capitulation" in scene 4. Both songs are songs of defeat (Brecht's great subject) but of two different defeats. The second is defeat total and final: Courage has staked everything on wisdom, and wisdom has ruined her and her family. The first is the setback of "capitulation," that is, of disenchantment. When Yvette was only seventeen she was in love, and love was heaven. Soon afterward she had learned to "fraternize behind the trees": she had capitulated. It is perhaps hard to imagine Courage as a younger and different person from the woman we meet in the play, but in the "Song of the Great Capitulation" we are definitely invited to imagine her as a young woman who thought she could storm the heavens, whose faith seemed able to move mountains.

Scene 4 is one of several in this play that one can regard as the whole play in miniature. For Brecht is not finished when he has set forth the character of Mother Courage as one who has passed from youthful idealism to cynical realism. For many a playwright, that would no doubt be that, but Courage's exchange with the angry young soldier leads to other things. We discover that Mother Courage is not a happy Machiavellian, boasting of her realism. She is deeply ashamed. We discover in Courage the mother of those two roaring idealists (not to say again, martyrs), Swiss Cheese and Kattrin. "Kiss my ass," says the soldier, and why? His bad language had not hitherto been directed at her. But she has been kind to him only to be cruel. If she has not broken his spirit, she has done something equally galling: she has made clear to him how easily his spirit can be broken. When you convert a man to the philosophy of "You can't win," you can hardly expect to earn his gratitude at the same time.

In the way Courage puts matters to the soldier we see how close she came to being a truly wise woman. We also discover in this scene that, despite the confident tone of her cynical lingo, Courage is not really sure of herself and her little philosophy. She teaches the soldier that it is futile to protest, but she apparently does not know this herself until she reminds herself of it, for she has come here to protest. Here we learn to recognize in Courage not only contradiction but conflict. She knows what she has thought. She is not sure what to think.

And this is communicated by Brecht in a very bold—or just poetic—manner. For while Courage does not give herself to despair until the end (and not even then for those who can take at face value her "I must get back into business"), she had correctly foreseen the end from the beginning: the despair she gives herself to had been there from the moment of capitulation. At times it would strike her between the eyes: she is very responsive and has worked out the Marxist interpretation of religion for herself. Scene 2 contains a song she had taught Eilif as a boy: it predicts the manner of his death. In scene 1 she predicts doom for the whole family in her pantomime of fortune-telling. It could be said that everything is there from the start, for the first thing Mother Courage does is to try and sell things by announcing an early death for her prospective customers. The famous "Song of Mother Courage" is the most extraordinary parody of the kind of song any real *vivandière* might try to attract customers with. Mother Courage's "Come and buy!" is nothing other than "Come and die!" In that respect, her fortune-telling is on the level, and her wisdom is valid.

Scene 4, I have been saying, is one of several in this play that one can regard as the whole play in miniature. The main purpose of the play, for Brecht, was, I think, to generate anger over what it shows. Yet Brecht realizes how pointless angry plays have been—and angry speeches outside the drama. It is said that Clifford Odets's *Waiting for Lefty* made millionaires angry for as long as it took them to get from their seats to where their chauffeurs tactfully waited for them at the end of the block. Such is the anger of the social drama in general.

There is the anger of a sudden fit, which boils up and over and is gone. And there is the anger that informs the work of long years of change. *Why* can't the world be changed? For Mother Courage, it is not from any inherent unchangeability in the world. It is because our wish to change it is not strong enough. Nor is this weakness innate. It is simply that our objection to the present world isn't as strong as it once was. What is outrageous does not outrage us as it once did. It only arouses the "short rage" of Brecht's soldier—and of Courage herself—not the long one that is required. Because we—they—have capitulated.

Capitulation is not an idea but a feeling, an agony, and is located not just in the scene of the Great Capitulation but in the whole play of *Mother Courage*. Everything that happens is related to it, above all the things that are furthest away from it: the deaths of Swiss Cheese and Kattrin. If these children are what their mother made them, then their refusal to capitulate stems from her, is her own youth, her own original nature.

The ultimate achievement of an actress playing this role would be that she made us sense to what an extent Courage's children are truly hers.

The Caucasian Chalk Circle (I)
1966

The best headnote to the essay on Chalk Circle *is a piece I wrote for the* New York Times *on the occasion of the play's production at Lincoln Center, "The Magic Circle of Bertolt Brecht" (printed under another title,* NYT, *March 20, 1966).*

Friends old and new! We ask tonight
Who owns a child and by what right?
There is a bit of Chinese lore
About a circle chalked on a floor . . .
Two different women claim one child
Their quarrel drives the neighbors wild,
So they betake them to the King.
He with some chalk describes a ring
Around the infant where he stands.
"Take him," the King says, "by the hands
And pull! She who can get him out
Must be his mother without a doubt!"
One woman briskly goes to work
And yanks the child out with a jerk.
The other doesn't have the heart
For fear she'll tear the babe apart.

"Which," quoth the King, "proves that this other
Who would not harm him is his mother."
The logic's bad. Only the blind
Could hold that mothers all are kind.
And yet one hopes the King's surmise
Chanced to be right, for otherwise
What a disturbing situation:
The mother an abomination
While the false claimant is a love!
This crisis won't bear thinking of.
Who owns a child? And who says so?
We find such questions à propos
Like: who owns Natchez and Birmingham?
Santo Domingo? Or Vietnam?
The crisis spared the Chinese King
We'll try to face this evening
Telling a touched-up tale in which
The actual mother is a bitch.
Even the circle chalked on the floor
Will not be what it was before.

These lines of mine constitute a possible prologue to Brecht's *Caucasian Chalk Circle* as it finally reaches Manhattan this Thursday. They won't be used in the show but they may serve to introduce the subject here. I haven't the space to explain just how Brecht "touched up" the Chinese tale, and besides I want people to find that out in the theater. The charm of this work is a highly theatrical thing, and it has *more* charm than any other work of its author. Let me tell here a less august story, that of the adventures of Brecht's *Caucasian Chalk Circle* in the United States.

Some twenty-two years ago, Samuel French, Inc., of New York, arranged for their client Bertolt Brecht to write a play for production here. And for a particular actress, though there seems to be some difference of opinion as to which one. Luise Rainer has been quoted as saying the play was written for her. Elisabeth Bergner has also been mentioned, and one sees the logic of that, since the play was to be a revision of one she had appeared in, under Max Reinhardt's direction, in 1925: *The Circle of Chalk*. This 1925 *Circle of Chalk* was itself a revision. The ultimate source was a Chinese classic dating from about A.D. 1300.

It is now 1966, and neither Miss Rainer nor Miss Bergner has yet appeared in the Brecht play, but it was finished by 1945, and has had a strange, eventful history. Its world première came in 1948. One of my graduate students (today a UCLA professor) staged it with his own pupils at Carleton College, Northfield, Minnesota. I still remember the performance in the overcrowded little improvised theater, with specially composed music a bit on the sugary side, agreeably naïve, enthusiastic acting by most, and a distinctly professional black actor as Azdak who alone, among that cast, found easy access to the Brechtian irony. I used this actor, Alvis Tinnin, when I myself staged the first professional production of the play at the Hedgerow Theater near Philadelphia later in the same year.

The Hedgerow production was probably the most Brechtian of American Brecht efforts up to that time. It even attracted a little attention. John Houseman and T. Edward Hambleton came down to look at it. Harold Clurman came down and reviewed it. A businessman wrote me he would like to produce the play in New York. It was a delightful work, he said, and could even make the big time if rewritten by . . . himself. Bertolt Brecht enjoyed hearing about this; but the businessman never heard from Bertolt Brecht.

But, as they say west of the Hudson, New York is not America, and *The Caucasian Chalk Circle* has, I believe, been produced in most of the fifty states, if, most often, in rather modest circumstances. A production in Chicago some fifteen years ago came to Brecht's attention and mine only after it was already on the boards. We applauded the spirit of enterprise in the Chicagoans and asked for royalties. The management expressed surprise at the request but agreed that they had shown enterprise and suggested we come out and see the show at our own expense. I think they did come through with fifty dollars or so after about twice that had been spent on telegrams and phone calls. The group was the Playwright's Theater Club and included Mike Nichols and, I seem to recall, Barbara Harris.

Meanwhile, where *The Caucasian Chalk Circle* was not acted, it was read. Those who think of plays in terms of performance easily overlook the fact that any play that lives is read by at least a thousand persons for every one that sees it in a theater. Bertolt Brecht has countless readers in the United States who have never seen a Brecht play on a stage. Then again, the McCarthy era, while it discouraged performance of plays like *The Caucasian Chalk Circle,* did not stop people from drawing the blinds, locking all doors and windows, and curling up on the sofa with the works of Bertolt Brecht.

Once McCarthy was finished, America breathed more freely. The new generation was enthusiastically Brechtian. Snobbery and modishness were involved. They always are. Bertolt Brecht had become a World Figure. It was not, one can be sure, his Stalin Peace Prize (1955) that turned the trick here in the West. It was, rather, the triumph of his Berlin Ensemble at the Théâtre des Nations in Paris, in 1954 to 1955.

In the IRT subway in 1945, Brecht had remarked to me that if only he were a Frenchman, Broadway producers would be doing his plays. He added that, since this couldn't be arranged, the next best thing would be to be applauded by Frenchmen, to have his plays successfully performed in Paris. Nine years later he had had his wish.

Whereupon *The Threepenny Opera,* which opened to mixed reviews in New York in 1954, gathered momentum and ran till 1961. Some say that particular success was Kurt Weill's or Marc Blitzstein's. In any case, by the 1960s, although Bertolt Brecht remained a cipher for TV, for Hollywood, and one could even say for Broadway, his name was a byword everywhere else: off Broadway in New York, in the community and resident theaters all around the country, above all in that "university world" that now, whether you like it or not, dominates American culture. As a publisher put it to me recently, "What do I care about 'Broadway flops' if the books are selling like hot cakes in every college bookstore in the land?"

It was not just a matter of books. Samuel French, Inc., was back in the picture, not, this time, with Broadway contracts, but with college productions, community and resident theater productions, year in, year out, in the fifty states.

Brecht is now a known quantity. *The Caucasian Chalk Circle* is a known, even a beloved, play. Here is something unusual, perhaps altogether new: that a play should not start out in New York and owe everything to New York (including a substantial percentage to the New York purchaser of subsidiary rights) but should come to New York at the end of a twenty-year "national tour." I don't say it couldn't have been otherwise. Five years ago André Gregory offered me a ten thousand dollar advance on a Broadway production of the play. He also seemed to be offering me Zero Mostel as Azdak and Paul Robeson as the narrator, but at the time I was too busy quarreling with the Brecht estate (or they were too busy quarreling with me) to be interested in mere money or mere theater. "You need time," as *The Caucasian Chalk Circle* says, "for a good quarrel." I (we) needed till 1965, by which time the Vivian Beaumont Theater was ready for me (us, it).

I suppose the three leading resident theaters in this country are the Arena Stage, Washington; the Minnesota Theater Company, Minneapolis; and the Actors' Workshop, San Francisco. All three put on *The Caucasian Chalk Circle* in the 1960s, and all three had a high degree of success with it, which brings this little chronicle to the threshold of the present. In 1965, the directors of the Actors' Workshop moved from California, where Brecht wrote his *Caucasian Chalk Circle,* to New York, where it was commissioned. *Full* circle! A play that began in the Samuel French office on West Forty-fifth Street had traveled the twenty blocks up to Lincoln Square by a roundabout route indeed.

The Caucasian Chalk Circle (II)
1966

IN THE PROLOGUE TO *The Caucasian Chalk Circle,* the people of two collective farms in Georgia debate their respective titles to the ownership of a piece of land. Up to now it has belonged to one farm, but now the other claims to be able to make better use of it. Who should own *anything?* Should possession be nine-tenths of the law? Or should law and possession be open to review? That is the question Brecht raises. In the first draft of the play, the date of this bit of action was the 1930s. Later, Brecht shifted it to 1945 for two reasons: so that the land can be approached as a new problem, in that the farmers on it had all been ordered east at the approach of Hitler's armies; and so that the farmers newly claiming it can have partially earned it by having fought as partisans against the invader.

The prologue is a bit of a shock for American audiences. Here are all these Communists—Russians at that—calling each other comrades, and so on. That is why, until recently, the prologue was always omitted from American productions. In 1965, however, it was included in the Minnesota Theater Company's production without untoward incidents or, so far as I know, outraged comment. With the years the prologue had not changed, but the world had. America had. The existence of the U.S.S.R. is now conceded in the United States. That Communists do use the title *comrades* is taken in stride. There is even understanding for the fact that the play-wright Bertolt Brecht sympathized with communism in those days, more consistently than Jean-Paul Sartre and Peter Weiss do today.

However, disapproval of the prologue is not caused merely by the labels. A deeper malaise is caused by the *mode* of the dispute over the land. Land has always been fought over, often with guns. The expectation that some individual should pull a gun, or threaten to, is part of our stock response to the situation; but in the prologue, this expectation receives a calculated disappoint-ment. The conflict is, or has been, real, but a new way of resolving it has been found, a new attitude to antagonists has been found. Not to mention the new solution: the land goes to the interlopers, the impostors, because they offer convincing evidence that they will be able to make better use of it. Both the conclusion and the road by which it is reached imply a reversal of the values by which our civilization has been living.

And Soviet civilization? Were we to visit Georgia, should we witness such decisions being made, and being arrived at in Brecht's way? It is open to doubt, even in 1966, while, in 1945, nothing could have been more misleading than Brecht's prologue, if it was in-tended to give an accurate picture of Stalin's Russia. We hear that Soviet citizens have themselves complained that, quite apart from the political point, they find nothing recognizably Russian in this German scene.

Is it thereby invalidated? "The home of the Soviet people shall also be the home of Reason!" That is certainly a key line in the prologue, but the verb is "shall be," not "is." That Brecht aligned himself with socialism, and saw the Soviet Union as the chief champion of socialism, is clear, yet that is only to say that he saw Russia as on the right path, not by any means as having arrived at the goal. Let the worried reader of the prologue to *The Caucasian Chalk Circle* also read Brecht's poem "Are the People Infallible?" in which the poet speaks in this vein of the death in 1939 of the So-viet playwright Tretyakov:

1

My teacher
Who was great, who was kind
Has been shot, sentenced by a People's Court.
As a spy. His name has been condemned.
His books have been annihilated. Conversation
    about him
Is suspect and has subsided.
Suppose he is innocent?

2

The sons of the people have found him guilty.
The collective farms and factories of the workers
The most heroic institutions in the world
Have found in him an enemy.
No voice was raised on his behalf.
Suppose he is innocent?

3

The people have many enemies.
In the highest positions
Sit enemies. In the most useful laboratories
Sit enemies. They build
Canals and dams for the good of whole continents
    and the canals
Clog up and the dams
Collapse. The man in charge must be shot.
Suppose he is innocent?

4

The enemy walks in disguise.
He draws a worker's cap down over his face. His
    friends
Know him for a zealous worker. His wife

Displays the holes in his shoes:
He went through his shoes in the service of the
  people.
And yet he is an enemy. Was my teacher such a
  man?
Suppose he is innocent?

5

To speak about the enemies who may be sitting in
  the courts of the people
Is dangerous. For the courts have to be respected.
To demand papers with the proofs of guilt on them
  in black and white
Is senseless. For there need not be any such papers.
Criminals hold proofs of their innocence in their
  hands.
The innocent often have no proofs.
Is it best, then, to be silent?
Suppose he is innocent?

6

What 5000 have built, one man can destroy.
Among 50 who are sentenced
One may be innocent.
Suppose he is innocent?

7

On the supposition that he is innocent
What will he be thinking as he goes to his death?

In any case, to prove Brecht wrong about Russia would not necessarily be to prove him wrong about socialism.

A socialist play: is this play for socialists only? That is for
nonsocialists to decide. From Brecht's viewpoint, a lot of people

are potential socialists who might—at this time, in this place—be surprised to hear it. It is a play for all who are not identified with those it shows to be the common enemy, and it may turn out to be a play even for some of those who *are* identified with the enemy, since they may not recognize the identification, preferring a life-illusion. French aristocrats applauded *Figaro*. *The Threepenny Opera* must have been enjoyed by many who, very shortly afterward, voted for Hitler.

The prologue shows a country (forget it is Russia, if that offends you) where Reason has made inroads upon Unreason. Unreason, in *The Caucasian Chalk Circle,* takes the form of private property, and the laws that guarantee it. "Property is theft," and, by paradox, a private person who steals another private person's property, infringing the law, only reenacts the original rape of the earth, and confirms the law—of private property. The characters in *Chalk Circle* who most firmly believe in private property are most actively engaged in fighting over private property—whether to cling to it or to grab it.

Where is private property's most sensitive spot? One learns the answer when a businessman announces that his son will be taking over the business or when a spokesman for all things holy comes to his favorite theme of mother and child.

> ... [O]f all ties, the ties of blood are strongest. Mother and child, is there a more intimate relationship? Can one tear a child from its mother? High Court of Justice, she has conceived it in the holy ecstasies of love, she has carried it in her womb, she has fed it with her blood, she has borne it with pain...

This is the voice of one of the spokesmen for all things holy in *The Caucasian Chalk Circle,* and so, when the possession of a child has been in dispute, whether at the court of Solomon in Israel or before a Chinese magistrate in the year A.D. 1000, the question asked has been only: Which womb did it come out of? Which loins begat it? The ultimate *locus* of private property is in the private parts.

Plato had other plans. He knew that a given parent may be the worst person to bring up his or her child. Our concern, he assumes, should be to produce the best human beings, the best society, not to sacrifice these ends to an, after all, arbitrary notion of "natural" right. The point about an umbilical cord is that it has to be cut. Children should be assigned to those best qualified to bring them up ... Plato's Republic *is* "the home of Reason."

The Georgia of *The Caucasian Chalk Circle* is not. After a prologue that provides a hint of what it would mean to begin to create a home for Reason on this earth, the play transports us to a world that, for all its exotic externals, is nothing other than the world we live in, *our* world, the world of Unreason, of Disorder, of Injustice. Those who are upset by the idealizations of the prologue, by its "utopianism," need not fret. The play itself provides an image of life in its customary mode—soiled, stinking, cruel, outrageous.

Even in a jungle, lovely flowers will spring up here and there, such being the fecundity of nature, and however badly our pastors and masters run our society, however much they pull to pieces that which they claim to be keeping intact, nature remains fecund, human beings are born with human traits, sometimes human strength outweighs human weakness, and human grace shows itself amid human ugliness. "In the bloodiest times," as our play has it, "there are kind people." Their kindness is arbitrary. No sociologist could deduce it from the historical process. Just the contrary. It represents the brute refusal of nature to be submerged in history and therefore, arguably (and this *is* Brecht's argument), the possibility that the creature should, at some future point, subdue history.

For the present, though—a present that has spread itself out through the whole course of historical time—the sociologists win, and man is not the master but the slave of society. History is the history of power struggles conducted (behind the moralistic rhetoric familiar to us all from the mass media) with minimum scrupulousness and maximum violence. To give way to the promptings of nature, to natural sympathy, to the natural love of the Good, is to be a Sucker. America invented that expressive word, and America's most articulate comedian, W. C. Fields, called one of his films *Never Give a Sucker an Even Break*. This is the credo of Western civilization as depicted in the works of Bertolt Brecht.

In *The Caucasian Chalk Circle* a sucker gets an even break. That seems contradictory, and in the contradiction lies the whole interest of the story, or rather of its second part. In the first part, we see the inevitable working itself out. The sucker—the good girl who gives way to her goodness—is not given any breaks at all. She is punished for her nonsin, her antisin. She loses everything, both the child she has saved and adopted, and the soldier-fiancé whom she has loyally loved and waited for. She is abandoned, isolated, stripped, torn apart, like other people in Brecht's plays and our world who persist in the practice of active goodness.

> The Ironshirts took the child, the beloved child.
> The unhappy girl followed them to the city, the
>   dreaded city.
> She who had borne him demanded the child.
> She who had raised him faced trial.

So ends Part One: a complete Brecht play in itself. In Part Two Brecht was determined to put the question: Suppose the inevitable did not continue to work itself out? Now how could he do this? By having a socialist revolution destroy private property and establish the rule of Reason? That is what he would have done, had he been as narrow and doctrinaire as some readers of his prologue assume. But what is in the prologue is not in the play itself. For the second half of his play, Brecht invented a new version of the Chalk Circle legend, which is also a new version of another idea from literary tradition, the idea that the powers that be can sometimes be temporarily overthrown and a brief Golden Age ensue.

Who will decide the case?
To whom will the child be assigned?
Who will the judge be? A good judge? A bad?
The city was in flames.
In the judge's seat sat—Azdak.

Inevitably, necessarily, a judge in the society depicted in *The Caucasian Chalk Circle* must assign a child to its actual mother. In that proposition, the law of private property seems to receive the sanction of Mother Nature herself—that is to say, the owners of private property are able to appeal to nature without conscious irony. Such an event, however, would give Brecht at best a brief epilogue to Part One. What gives him a second part to his play, and one which enables him in the end to pick up the loose ends left by the prologue, is that the judge is Azdak, and that Azdak is a mock king, an Abbot of Unreason, a Lord of Misrule, who introduces "a brief Golden Age, almost an age of justice."

The reign of Zeus [says F. M. Cornford in *The Origin of Attic Comedy*] stood in the Greek mind for the existing moral and social order; its overthrow, which is the theme of so many of the comedies, might be taken to symbolize ... the breaking up of all ordinary restraints, or again ... the restoration of the Golden Age of Justice and Lovingkindness, that Age of Kronos which lingered in the imagination of poets, like the afterglow of a sun that had set below the horizon of the Age of Iron. The seasonal festivals of a Saturnalian character celebrated the return, for a brief interregnum, of a primitive innocence that knew not shame, and a liberty that at any other time would have been licentious. Social ranks were inverted, the slave exercising authority over the master. At Rome each household became a miniature republic, the slaves being invested with the dignities of office. A mock king was chosen to bear rule during the festival, like the medieval Abbot of Unreason or Lord of Misrule.

In this case, how is the play any different from the prologue, except in the temporariness of Azdak's project? Its temporariness is of a piece with its precariousness, its freakishness, its skittishness, its semiaccidental character. Only with a touch of irony can one say that Azdak establishes a Golden Age or even that he is a good judge. The age remains far from golden, and his judging is often outrageous enough. But his *extra*ordinary outrages call our attention to the ordinary outrages of ordinary times—to the fact that outrage *is* ordinary, is the usual thing, and that we are shocked, not by injustice *per se,* but only by injustice that favors the poor and the weak. Azdak did not rebuild a society, nor even start a movement that had such an end in view. He only provided Georgia with something to think about and us with a legend, a memory, an image.

So much for the ideological schema. The play would be too rigidly schematic if Brecht had just brought together the Good Girl with the Appropriate Judge, using both characters simply as mouthpieces for a position. But there is more to both of them than that.

Discussing the role of the Ironical Man in ancient comedy, F. M. Cornford remarks that "the special kind of irony" he practices is

feigned stupidity. The word Ironist itself in the fifth century appears to mean "cunning" or (more exactly) "sly." Especially it meant the man who masks his batteries of deceit behind a show of ordinary good nature or indulges a secret pride and conceit of wisdom, while he affects ignorance and self-depreciation, but lets you see all the while that he could enlighten you if he chose, and so makes a mock of you. It was for putting on these airs that Socrates was accused of "irony" by his enemies.

This passage sets forth what I take to be the preliminary design of Azdak's character, but then Brecht complicates the design. Azdak is not simply an embodiment of an ironical viewpoint, he is a person with a particular history, who needs irony for a particular reason—and not all the time. It is through the chinks in the ironical armor that we descry the man. *Azdak is not being ironical when he tells us he wanted to denounce himself for letting the Grand Duke escape.* He supposed that, while the Grand Duke and his Governors were busy fighting the Princes, the carpet weavers had brought off a popular revolution, and, as a revolutionary, he wished to denounce himself for a counterrevolutionary act.

What kind of revolutionary was he? A very modern kind: a disenchanted one. Those who like to compare Azdak the judge to Robin Hood should not fail to compare Azdak the Politician to Arthur Koestler. Before the present revolt of the carpet weavers, decades earlier, there had been another popular uprising. Azdak maintains, or pretends, that this was in his grandfather's time, forty years ago, and not in Georgia, but in Persia. His two songs—which lie at the very heart of our play—tell both of the conditions that produced the uprising and of the uprising itself.* The pretense is that revolution represents disorder, and the suppression of revolutions order, and that Azdak is appealing to the Generals to restore order. This last item is not a hollow pretense or a single irony, for

---

* Azdak's "Song of Chaos" is adapted from a translation of an ancient Egyptian lament, brought to notice in 1903 but dating back to about 2500 B.C. The document describes a state of social disintegration and revolt and appeals to the King and other authorities to take action. Brecht reverses the point of view, as his custom is, but since he does so ironically, he is able to stay close to such words of the original as the following:

> Nay, but the highborn are full of lamentations, and the
>   poor are full of joy. Every town saith: "Let us drive out
>   the powerful from our midst."
> Nay, but the son of the highborn man is no longer to be
>   recognized. The child of his lady is become [no more
>   than] the son of his handmaid.

Azdak has not championed revolt. He has withdrawn into his shell. His job as a "village scrivener" is the outward token of the fact. In a note, Brecht advises the actor of the role not to imagine that Azdak's rags directly indicate his character. He wears them, Brecht says, as a Shakespearean clown wears the motley of a fool. Azdak is not lacking in wisdom. Only it is the bitter wisdom of the disillusioned intellectual, and, in Brecht's view, a partly false wisdom prompted not alone by objective facts but quite as much by the "wise" man's own limitations.

Azdak has the characteristic limitation of the Brechtian rogue: cowardice. Or at any rate: courage insufficient to the occasion. He is Brecht's Herr Keuner saying no to tyranny only after the tyrant is safely dead. At least, this is how Azdak is, if left to himself. Yet, like other human beings, he is not a fixed quantity but influenceable by the flow of things, and especially by the people he meets. A passive sort of fellow, he acts less than he *re*acts. Our play describes his reaction to a new and unforeseen situation and especially, in the end, to a single person: Grusha. This gives the last section of the play its organic movement.

Azdak needs drawing out, and what Brecht does is expose him to a series of persons and situations that do draw him out. (That he also brings with him into the Golden Age his unregenerate self creates the comic contradictions. It is hard, through all the little trial

---

Nay, but the boxes of ebony are broken up. Precious sesnem [*sic*] wood is cut in pieces for beds.

Nay, but the public offices are opened and their lists [of serfs] are taken away. Serfs become lords of serfs.

Behold, ladies lie on cushions [in lieu of beds] and magistrates in the storehouse. He that could not sleep upon walls now possesseth a bed.

Behold, he that never built for himself a boat now possesseth ships. He that possessed the same looketh at them, but they are no longer his.

(Translated from the Egyptian by A. M. Blackman and published in *The Literature of the Ancient Egyptians*, by Adolf Erman [London, 1927].)

scenes, to tell where selfishness leaves off and generosity begins: this is a source of amusement and also enables Brecht to question accepted assumptions on the relation of social and antisocial impulses.) The Test of the Chalk Circle with which the action culminates does not follow automatically from the philosophy of Azdak but is a product of a dramatic development. At the outset he is in no mood to be so good or so wise. He has just been mercilessly beaten; but then he reacts in his especially sensitive way to all that ensues, and above all to the big speech in which Grusha denounces him:

AZDAK: Fined twenty piasters!

GRUSHA: Even if it was thirty, I'd tell you what I think of your justice, you drunken onion! How dare you talk to me like the cracked Isaiah on the church window? As if you were somebody. You weren't born to this. You weren't born to rap your own mother on the knuckles if she swipes a little bowl of salt someplace. Aren't you ashamed when you see how I tremble before you? You've made yourself their servant so they won't get their houses stolen out from under them—houses they themselves stole! Since when did a house belong to its bedbugs? But you're their watchdog, or how would they get our men into their wars? Bribe taker! I don't respect you. No more than a thief or a bandit with a knife. Do what you like. You can all do what you like, a hundred against one, but do you know who should be chosen for a profession like yours? Extortioners! Men who rape children! Let it be their punishment to sit in judgment on their fellowmen! Which is worse than to hang from the gallows.

AZDAK: Now it is thirty.

She could hardly know how she got under his skin. Her denunciation, quite guileless and spontaneous, happens to be couched in just the terms that come home to him. For she is representing him as a traitor to his class. Who does he think he is, who is now setting himself up as a lord over his own people? Well, in his own view, Azdak *was* something of a traitor to his class, but he has been busy for a year or two trying to make it up to them, and now Grusha is providing him with the happiest of all occasions to prove this. His decision to give her the child grows out of his sense of guilt and out of his delight in opportunities to make good.

One could say, too, that his earlier confrontation with Granny Grusinia prepares the way for the later one with Grusha. Here, too, he has to be drawn out, partly by threats, but even more by finding again his original identification with the cause of the people. Between them, Granny Grusinia and Grusha are the Marxian, Brechtian version of the "eternal feminine" whom our blundering, uncourageous Faust needs, if he is to move "onward and upward." Hence, although the Chalk Circle incident occupies only a minute or two at the end of a long play, it is rightly used for the title of the whole.

The incident not only clarifies the meaning of Azdak, it also brings together the various thematic threads of the play. In the first instance, there is the stated conclusion:

> Take note what men of old concluded:
> That what there is shall go to those who are good
>   for it, thus:
> Children to the motherly, that they prosper,
> Carts to good drivers, that they be driven well,
> The valley to the waterers, that it yield fruit.

But this was never in doubt. Any spectator who has spent the evening hoping for a surprise at the end courted disappointment. He should have been warned by the prologue. In an early draft Brecht planned to let the decision on the collective farms wait till the Chalk Circle story has been told. That, however, is politically ludicrous, if it means, as it would have to, that Soviet planners depend on folksingers in the way that some other leaders depend upon astrologers. And an infringement of a main principle of Brechtian drama would have occurred. In this type of play there should be no doubt as to what is going to happen, only as to how and why.

The valley is assigned to the waterers already in the prologue, and already in the first scenes that follow we see that Michael has had a bad mother but has been befriended by a better one. What remains to be said? On what grounds can we be asked to stay another couple of hours in the theater? One sufficient reason would be to see Grusha *become* the mother. This is not Plato's Republic, and Grusha is no trained educator in a Platonic crèche. In the first phase of the action her purpose is only to rescue the child, not keep it: she is going to leave it on a peasant's doorstep and return home. We see the child becoming hers by stages, so that when Azdak reaches his verdict in the final scene, he is not having a brainstorm ("Grusha would be a splendid mother for this child") but recognizing an accomplished fact ("She *is* the mother of this child"). Another paradox: in this play that says possession is not nine-tenths of the law we learn that (in another sense) possession is ten-tenths of the law.

In the end, the child becomes Simon Shashava's too:

> GRUSHA: You like him?
>
> SIMON: With my respects, I like him.
>
> GRUSHA: Now I can tell you: I took him because on that Easter Sunday I got engaged to you. So he's a child of love.

Michael had been a child of the lovelessness of his actual mother and the lifelessness of his actual father, but now it turns out that he will have a father who has been spared death in war and is very much alive and a mother who did not love him at his conception, nor yet at his delivery, but who loves him *now*. The term *love child* is applied to bastards, and Michael, who was legitimate in the legal sense, however illegitimate humanly and morally, will now become a bastard in a sense that the story . . . legitimizes.

> Your father is a bandit
> A harlot the mother who bore you
> Yet honorable men
> Shall kneel down before you.

> Food to the baby horses
> The tiger's son will take.
> The mothers will get milk
> From the son of the snake.

Brecht's play broadens out into myth, and we hear many echoes—from the Bible, from Pirandello—but it is more relevant to see the phenomenon the other way around: not that Brecht lets his story spread outward toward other stories but that he uses other stories, and mythical patterns, and pulls them in, brings them, as we say, "down to earth," in concrete, modern meanings. Most important, in this regard, is Brecht's use of what a Shakespearean scholar has called festive comedy. *The Caucasian Chalk Circle* is not an *inquiry* into the dispute over ownership presented in the prologue but a *celebration* of the assignment of the land to "those who are good for it."

A main preoccupation of this oldest form of comedy in Western tradition was with Impostors. The point of comedy was and has remained to expose the imposture. *The Caucasian Chalk Circle* does this, for what could be a more gross imposture than the claims to either rulership or parenthood of the Abashwili couple? But Brecht does not leave the ancient patterns alone. Even as he turns around the old tale of the Chalk Circle, so also he plays his ironic, dialectical game with the patterns. *For Azdak and Grusha are impostors too.* That is what makes them brother and sister under the skin. In the impostor-mother, the impostor-judge recognizes his own.

> As if it was stolen goods she picked it up.
> As if she was a thief she sneaked away.

Thus the Singer, describing how Grusha got the baby. He is too generous. Legally, she *is* a thief; the child *is* stolen goods; and Azdak has "stolen" the judgeship, though, characteristically, not on his own initiative: he is a receiver of stolen goods. The special pleasure for Azdak in his Chalk Circle verdict is that, at the moment when he will return his own "stolen" goods to their "rightful" owners, he is able to give Grusha and Simon "their" child in (what they can hope is) perpetuity.

I have called the irony a game, for art is a game, but this is not to say that Brecht's playfulness is capricious. In the inversion lies the meaning, and it is simply our good fortune that there is fun in such things, that, potentially at least, there is fun in *all* human contradictions and oppositions. The old patterns have, indeed, no meaning for Brecht *until* they are inverted. For instance, this important pattern: the return to the Age of Gold. We, the modern audience, Russian or American, *return* to the Age of Gold when we see Azdak inverting our rules and laws. Azdak *returns* to an Age of Gold when he nostalgically recalls the popular revolt of a former generation. On the other hand, the Age of Azdak is not, literally, an Age of Gold at all. It is an age of war and internecine strife in which just a little justice can, by a fluke, be done. Nor is the traditional image of a Golden Age anything like a revolutionary's happy memories of days on the barricades: just the reverse. Finally, Brecht repudiates our hankering after past Ages of Gold altogether. That revolutions, for Azdak, are identified with the past is precisely what is wrong with him. In *The Caucasian Chalk Circle* we move back in order to move forward. The era of Azdak has the transitory character of the Saturnalia and so is properly identified with it. After the interregnum is over, the mock king goes back into anonymity, like Azdak. But the prologue suggests a *regnum* that is not accidental and short-lived but deliberate and perhaps not *inter.* And then there is the ultimate inversion: that the Golden Age should be envisaged not in the past but in the future, and not in fairyland or heaven, but in Georgia.

The Russian Georgia. But the American Georgia is included, at least in the sense that the play is about our twentieth-century world, and in a specific way. As Brecht saw things, this century came in on a wave of democratic hope. A new age was dawning, or seemed to be. So universally was this felt that the most powerful of counterrevolutionary movements, the Hitler movement, had to represent itself as socialist and announce, in its turn, the dawn of a new age. It could bring in no dawn of its own, of course, but in Germany it certainly prevented the arrival of the dawn that had seemed imminent.

This grouping of forces is what we have in *The Caucasian Chalk Circle.* A true dawn is promised by the rebellious carpet weavers. It never arrives, because the Ironshirts are paid to cut the weavers to pieces. At this point, when a triumphant Fat Prince enters, very much in the likeness of Marshal Goering, Azdak points at him with the comment: "There's your new age all right!" The thought of the new age, the longing for a new age, hovers over *The Caucasian Chalk Circle* from beginning to end, and any good production should seem haunted by it.

The prologue will say different things to different people as to what has already been achieved and where, but to all it conveys Brecht's belief that the new age is possible. What his audience is to be haunted by is not a memory, a fantasy, or a dream, but a possibility.

Galileo (I)
1966

Words—on a planet that is no longer in the center!

More pages of this book are devoted to Galileo *than to any other play.
That is not a value judgment; only a personal accident. Brecht's houseguest in Santa Monica at the time* Galileo *was being staged by him and
Joseph Losey, I became therewith a house guest of the Brechtian theater.
That's the positive side. It is also true that this play has always irked me.
That must be why I "go on" so long about it in the piece that follows. It
is a work that goads me into talking back. Ultimately a critical essay is
not the place to do that. One has to tackle the playwright on his own
ground, which I had the temerity to do in a play of my own,* The Recantation of Galileo Galilei, *begun in the fifties, finished in the sixties,
produced and published in the seventies.*

BRECHT WAS ALL WRONG ABOUT the seventeenth century in
general and about Galileo Galilei in particular. His main assumption is that the new cosmology gave man only a peripheral
importance, where the old cosmology had given him a central
one. Actually, this argument is not found in the works or conversation of Galileo, or of his friends, or of his enemies, or of anyone
in his time. Discussing the point in his *Great Chain of Being,* the
historian Arthur O. Lovejoy observes that the center was not

212

held to be the place of honor anyway: prestige was out beyond the periphery, where God lived.

So much for the universe. As for the new scientific attitude, for Brecht it apparently is summed up in the pebble his Galileo likes to drop from one hand to the other to remind himself that pebbles do not fly but fall. In short, the scientist notices, in a down-to-earth way, what actually goes on: he accepts the evidence of his senses. In this he is contrasted with the theologian, who uses imagination and reasoning. This is all very well, except that the little parable of the pebble does not characterize the stage to which physical science was brought by Galileo. It does cover his initial use of the telescope. That was a matter of looking through lenses and believing your own eyes. However, no startling conclusions could be reached, and above all nothing could be proved, without doing a great deal more. What actually happened to physics in the seventeenth century is that it became mathematical. This meant that it became, not more concrete, but just the opposite. After all, the evidence of one's senses is that the sun goes round the earth. That the earth should go round the sun is directly counter to that evidence. The average man today accepts the latter idea on pure faith. So far as he knows, it could be wholly untrue. For the demonstration lies in the realm of the abstract and the abstruse.

Brecht is no nearer to the kind of truth that interests a biographer than he is to the kind that interests a historian of science. A good deal is known about the historical Galileo Galilei. For example, he had a mistress who bore him three children. The most human document of his biography is his correspondence with one of the daughters. The love between these two may well have been the greatest love of his life, as it certainly was of hers. But Brecht is interested in none of this, nor can it be retorted that the details of Galileo's professional life preoccupied him. Much is known of the trial of Galileo, and the material has the highest human and dramatic quality, on which various biographers have capitalized. But Brecht passes by the trial "scenes" too. Even the character of his

Galileo seems only in part to have been suggested by the personality of the great scientist. The historical Galileo was a proud, possibly a vain, man. This makes him the villain of Arthur Koestler's book *The Sleepwalkers*, and, to be sure, it contributes to the villainous element in Brecht's Galileo, though Brecht is less concerned than Koestler to nag him, and more concerned to show that there are social reasons why excessive self-reliance fails to get results. Yet Galileo's self-reliance *would* have got results—as Brecht tells the story—but for a quality that Brecht has to invent or reinvent for him: cowardice. The axis of Brecht's story is passivity–activity, cowardice–courage, slyness–boldness. To make his story into a play, Brecht exploited whatever ready-made material came to hand but must himself take full responsibility for the final product.

Would Brecht himself have admitted this, or would he have claimed that he was writing history? If I may draw on my memory of Brecht's conversation on the point, I'd say he had a variable attitude. Sometimes he talked as if he had indeed taken everything from the historical record; other times (and this is true in the printed Notes too) he would admit to changes but maintain that they didn't distort history; at other times still, he would talk as if he had an entirely free hand (as when, in 1945 to 1946, he changed Galileo's big speech in his last scene).

Whatever Brecht thought he was doing, what good playwrights always do was perceived by Aristotle and confirmed by Lessing. When Aristotle observed that tragedy was more philosophical than history, he was noting that drama had a different logic from that of fact. History can be (or appear to be) chaotic and meaningless; drama cannot. Truth may be stranger than fiction; but it is not as orderly. Or as Pirandello stated the matter: the truth doesn't have to be plausible but fiction does. The facts of Jeanne d'Arc's life, as the historical record supplies them, did not seem to Bernard Shaw to have either plausibility or interest, for the historical Jeanne was the victim of the machinations of a vulgar politician (the historical Cauchon). The story becomes plausible and interesting by the replacement of this Cauchon with an invented one who can oppose Jeanne on principle. Now the antagonists of Brecht's Galileo would be inconceivable had Shaw not created Warwick, Cauchon, and the Inquisitor, and, equally, Brecht's Barberini and Inquisitor could not get into his play except by replacing the Barberini and the Inquisitor of history. The historical Barberini seems to have made himself a personal enemy of Galileo, and the Inquisitor (Firenzuola) seems to have intrigued most mercilessly against him. But Brecht follows Shaw in having his protagonist's foes proceed solely from the logic of their situation. In this way the central situations of both *Saint Joan* and *Galileo* take on form and meaning. It is a paradox. The historical truth, rejected for its implausibility, has the air of an artifact, whereas the actual artifact, the play, has an air of truth. The villains of history seemed too melodramatic to both authors. The truth offended their sense of truth, and out of the less dramatic they made the more dramatic.

If what playwrights are after is fiction, why do they purport to offer us history plays at all? A teasing question, not, perhaps, to be answered without a little beating around the bush. People who ask this question generally have in mind the whole expanse of human history and envisage it all as available to the playwright. Yet a glance at history plays that have had success of any sort will reveal that they are not about the great figures of history taken indiscriminately but only about those few, like Julius Caesar, Joan of Arc, and Napoleon, whose names have become bywords. Another paradox: only when a figure has become *legendary* is he or she a good subject for a *history* play.

Are such figures as Shakespeare's Henry IV or Strindberg's Eric XIV exceptions? Not really. Within Britain, at least, the kings were legends: certainly Henry V was, as a great deal of ballad lore attests, and Henry IV is a preparation for Henry V. Something similar is true of Strindberg's histories: Swedish history was suitable for plays insofar as it was the folklore of nationalism. Because the historical dramatist is concerned with the bits of history that have stuck in people's imagination, he may well find himself handling bits of pseudohistory that are the very *product* of people's imagination. Is it likely that William Tell actually shot an apple off his son's head? What is certain is that Schiller would never have written a play about him had that story not existed.

Again, why do playwrights purport to put history onstage? Is it because the events of a history at least *seem* more real, since many spectators will assume that such a play *is* all true? After all, very much of our "knowledge" of the past is based on fiction. Did not Churchill himself claim to have learned English history from Shakespeare? Was Shakespeare's distortion of the Anglo-French quarrel just Providence's way of preparing Churchill for the Battle of Britain? So should we be prepared to see a modern, Marxist playwright distorting history in order to prepare young Communists for some future Battle of Russia? The proposition is not as remote from Bertolt Brecht's *Galileo* as it may sound. The question is whether the factual distortions have to be accepted at face value. It seems to me that even for spectators who know that a history play is bad history, such a play might still seem to have some sort of special relevancy, a more urgent truth.

Writing on Schiller's *Don Carlos*, Georg Lukács has suggested that while playwrights and novelists depart from the *facts* of history, they still present the larger *forces* of history. But the forces of what period in history, that of the ostensible action, or that of the playwright? To me it seems that the claim of the chronicle play to be close to history is valid only if it is contemporary history that is in question. *Don Carlos* belongs to the eighteenth century, not the sixteenth; Shakespeare's histories belong to the sixteenth century, not the fifteenth. Now obviously there is also an inevitable departure from the facts of the dramatist's own time. It is not even *possible* to stay close to these facts, since nothing overtly contemporary is there at all. What is it that the historical dramatist finds in the earlier period? In Brecht's terminology, it is an alienation of the subject. The familiar subject is placed in a "strange" setting, so that one can sit back and look and be amazed. What kind of strangeness? It is a matter of what strangeness will throw the subject into highest relief, and of what strangeness a particular writer's gift can re-create. But the strangeness is, anyhow, *only* a setting, and within the setting there must be a situation, a grouping of events, an Action, which provide a little model of what the playwright believes is going on in the present. Dramatists may spend decades looking for such settings and such Actions, or hoping to stumble on them.

Sometimes a sudden irruption of the past into the present will call the dramatist's attention to the new relevance of some old event. The canonization of Jeanne d'Arc in 1920 was such an irruption. It prompted the writing of a play that seemed to be about the age that burned Joan yet that was actually about the age that canonized her—though it would burn her if she returned. Like *Saint Joan* and all other good history plays, *Galileo* is about the playwright's own time.

Like many of Brecht's works, it exists in a number of different drafts, but it is unusual among them in taking two broadly different forms. There are two *Galileo* plays here, both of which exist in their entirety: the version of 1938 and the version of 1947. Partial analogies to the changes exist in other Brecht plays. For Brecht, it was no unique thing to create a winning rogue and then later decide to make the audience dislike him. The revisions of both *Mother Courage* and *Puntila* show this. But in *Galileo* the change was more radical.

Brecht became interested in the historical Galileo at a time when he was preoccupied with friends and comrades who remained in Germany and somehow managed to continue to work. Prominent in his thoughts was the underground political worker plotting to subvert the Hitler regime. He himself was not a "worker," he was a poet, but a poet in love with the idea of science, a poet who believed that his own philosophy was scientific: what then brings Galileo to mind?

What the mention of Galileo brings to mind is a single anecdote (incidentally, not found before 1757):

> The moment he [Galileo] was set at liberty, he looked up
> to the sky and down to the ground, and, stamping with
> his foot, in a contemplative mood, said, *Eppur si move*
> [*sic*]; that is, still it moves, meaning the earth.*

His study was the universe, and its laws are what they are, irrespective of ecclesiastical pronouncement. "Still it moves!" And Galileo can now write a new, epoch-making work and smuggle it out of the country with these words:

> Take care when you travel through Germany with the
> truth under your coat!

This sentence from the first version of Brecht's *Galileo* puts in a nutshell the most striking analogy between that version of the play and the time when it was written, the 1930s, in which, indeed, truth in Germany had to be hidden under coats. It was the time when Wilhelm Reich had copies of his writings on the orgasm bound and inscribed to look like prayer books and in that form mailed from abroad to Germany. It was the time when Brecht himself wrote the essay "Writing the Truth: Five Difficulties." The fifth of these difficulties, and the one to which Brecht gave most attention, was the need of "cunning" in disseminating the truth. Although Galileo is not included in the essay's list of heroes who showed such cunning, the whole passage is quite close to the thought and frame of mind reflected in the first version of the Galileo play. Even the special perspective that caused Brecht's friend Walter Benjamin to say its hero was not Galileo but the people is found in such sen-

---

* For further details, see *Discoveries and Opinions of Galileo,* trans. Stillman Drake
(Garden City, N.Y.: Doubleday Anchor, 1957), 292.

tences as "Propaganda that stimulates thinking, in no matter what field, is useful to the cause of the oppressed." The early version of *Galileo* is nothing if not propaganda *for* thinking.

The later version of *Galileo* is also about the playwright's own time, but this was now, not the 1930s, but the mid-1940s. Brecht has himself recorded what the motive force of the new *Galileo* was:

> The atomic age made its debut at Hiroshima in the middle of our work. Overnight the biography of the founder of the new system of physics read differently.

To a historian it would seem bizarre to suggest that he should reverse a judgment he had made on something in the seventeenth century on account of something that had just happened in the twentieth. To a dramatist, however, the question would mainly be whether a subject that had suggested itself because it resembled something in the twentieth century would still be usable when asked to resemble something quite different in the twentieth century.

In the 1930s what commended the subject of Galileo to Brecht was the analogy between the seventeenth-century scientist's underground activities and those of twentieth-century left-wingers in Hitler Germany. But that is not all that Brecht, even in the early version, made of the exemplum. The abjuration was defined as an act of cowardice, and the act of cowardice was then deplored for a precise reason, namely, that more than certain notions about astronomy were at stake—at stake was the liberty to advance these and any other notions:

> ANDREA: ... [M]any on all sides followed you with their
> eyes and ears, believing that you stood, not only for a
> particular view of the movement of the stars, but even
> more for the liberty of teaching—in all fields. Not then
> for any particular thoughts, but for the right to think at
> all. Which is in dispute. When these people heard

what you had said *abjured,* it seemed to them not only that certain thoughts about the movements of the stars had been discredited, but that thinking itself, which is regarded as unholy when it operates with reasons and proofs, had been discredited.

VIRGINIA: But it is not true that the authorities have forbidden the sciences, as just stated. Father Philip says the Church will include my father's great inventions and discoveries in the textbooks. Only theology, which is quite a different science—there he should not take issue with their views.

GALILEO: In free hours, of which I have many, I have wondered how my conduct must look to that scientific community to which I of course no longer belong, even though I am still acquainted with some of its modes of thought. (*Speaking as on an academic occasion, his hands folded over his belly:*) It will have to ponder whether it can be satisfied that its members deliver to it a certain number of propositions, let us say about the tendencies of falling bodies or the movement of certain stars. I have shut myself off, as was said, from the scientific way of thought, but I assume that, faced with the danger of annihilation, science will hardly be in a position to release its members from all further obligations. For example, the obligation to contribute to its own continuance as science. Even a wool merchant, aside from buying cheap and delivering decent wool, can also be concerned that trading in wool is permitted at all and is able to proceed. Accordingly, then, a member of the scientific community cannot logically just point to his possible merits as a researcher if he has neglected to honor his profession as such and to defend it against coercion of every kind. But this is a business of some scope. For science demands that facts not be subordinated to opinions but that opinions be subordinated to facts. It is not in a position to limit these propositions and apply them to "some" opinions and "such and such" facts. To be certain that these propositions can always and without limitation be acted on, science must do battle to ensure that they are respected in all fields.

After Hiroshima, Brecht deleted these speeches, in order to substitute another idea. The point was no longer to demand from the authorities liberty to teach all things but to demand from the scientists themselves a sense of social responsibility, a sense of identification with the destiny, not of other scientists only, but of people at large. The point was now to dissent from those who see scientific advance as "an end in itself," thus playing into the hands of those who happen to be in power, and to advance the alternate, utilitarian conception of science:

> GALILEO: ... I take it that the intent of science is to ease human existence. If you give way to coercion, science can be crippled, and your new machines may simply suggest new drudgeries. Should you, then, in time, discover all there is to be discovered, your progress must become a progress away from the bulk of humanity. The gulf might even grow so wide that the sound of your cheering at some new achievement would be echoed by a universal howl of horror.

In this respect, *Galileo I* is a "liberal" defense of freedom against tyranny, while *Galileo II** is a Marxist defense of a social conception of science against the "liberal" view that truth is an end in itself.

---

* These are perhaps the handiest terms to describe the two broadly different texts of the play. It is *Galileo II* that is found in the collected plays as published by Suhrkamp Verlag.

If this philosophic change is large enough, it is accompanied by an even larger change in the dramatic action. In *Galileo I,* a balance is struck between two opposing motifs. On the one hand, Galileo is admired for his slyness and cunning, while on the other he is condemned for his cowardice. The admiration is never entirely swallowed up in the disapproval. On the contrary, we give Galileo a good mark for conceding his own weakness. Then, too, Brecht brings about a partial rehabilitation of his hero in two distinct ways: first, by stressing the admirable cunning of the underground worker who can write a new masterpiece under these conditions and arrange to smuggle it out to freer lands; second, by defining his hero's lapse as a limited one, thus:

> ANDREA: ... [I]t is as if a very high tower which had been thought indestructible should fall to the ground. The noise of its collapse was far louder than the din of the builders and the machines had been during the whole period of its construction. And the pillar of dust which the collapse occasioned rose higher than the tower had ever done. But possibly it turns out, when the dust clears, that, while twelve top floors have fallen, thirty floors below are still standing. Is that what you mean? There is this to be said for it: the two things that are wrong in this science of ours are out in the open ... The difficulty may be the greater; but the necessity has also become greater.

And indeed there is something good about the new book's having a disgraced author. It must now make its way on its own, and not by authority, which will be a gain for science and the scientific community. And dramatically it means a lot that *Galileo I* ends with the emphasis on the renewal of friendship between Galileo and Andrea. The old scientist is after all able to hand his work on, as to a son.

Revising the play after Hiroshima, Brecht decided to condemn Galileo far more strongly, and not only to render an unqualified verdict of guilty, but also to picture a shipwrecked, a totally corrupted human being. The sense of the earlier text is: I should not have let my fear of death make me overlook the fact that I had something more to defend than a theory in pure astronomy. The sense of the later text is: to be a coward in those circumstances entailed something worse than cowardice itself, it entailed treachery. In the early text, Brecht alludes to the Church's belief that Galileo risked damnation for squandering the gift of intellect. In the later text, it is clear that Galileo sees himself as already in Hell for having actually squandered (betrayed) the gift of intellect. And so what we see in the penultimate scene of the later text is a portrait of a "collaborator," a renegade. And Brecht's Notes* stress that Galileo should register a malign, misanthropic contempt for Federzoni, as well as shouting in sheer self-hatred to Andrea:

> Welcome to my gutter, dear colleague in science and brother in treason: I sold out, you are a buyer . . . Blessed be our bargaining, whitewashing, death-fearing community!

Which version is better? There can be no doubt that many small improvements were made throughout the play by which the later version benefited, but as far as this penultimate scene is concerned, it is not clear that, in making it more ambitious, Brecht also improved it. To show the foulness of Galileo's crime, he has to try to plumb deeper depths. The question is whether this befouled, denatured Galileo can be believed to be the same man we have seen up

---

* Some of Brecht's Notes on *Galileo* are provided in the Suhrkamp and Methuen editions of the play. Others are given in *Aufbau einer Rolle: Galilei,* the three-volume presentation of the play published by Henschelverlag in East Berlin (1958). Suhrkamp has also published a separate volume of Notes on *Galileo* that are not limited to either of these two previous sources (*Materialien zu Brechts "Leben des Galilei,"* 1963).

to then. The impression is, rather, of someone Brecht arbitrarily declares bad at this stage in order to make a point, which would be of a piece with Communist treatment of the betrayal theme generally. One moment, a Tito is a Jesus, and the next, a Judas. There is an intrusion of unfelt Communist clichés about traitors and renegades in the later *Galileo*. One cannot find, within the boundaries of the play itself, a full justification for the virulence of the final condemnation.

If the crime of Galileo, in the earlier text, being less cataclysmic in its results and less anguished in its style, at first seems less dramatic, it is actually rendered *more* dramatic by the tragicomic relationship in which it stands to Galileo's Schweykian cunning. I find the ambiguity of the earlier ending more human and more richly dramatic, as well as more Brechtian and more consistent with the rest of the play.

Sidelights are provided by performances of the play, and their background. It seems to me that even Ernst Busch, the Galileo of the Berlin Ensemble production, could not make real the image of a corrupted Galileo. Busch was very much the Old Communist. The danger was that he might have been just that and never Galileo Galilei. He never seemed the sinner in Hell, but, rather, the Party Member who had strayed and was now practicing Self-Criticism. Charles Laughton would seem a likelier casting. Brecht said Laughton felt guilty for having stayed in Hollywood during World War II instead of returning to fight for Britain, and this sense of guilt, he said, was what would come in useful in *Galileo*. Laughton did indeed have subtly personal ways of making guilt seem real that would have delighted Stanislavsky himself. When he made his entrance after the abjuration, he seemed, as Brecht said, a little boy who had wet his pants, but, in his last scene, when Brecht wanted the audience to reject Galileo in horror, Laughton made sure they accepted him in pity—while loving him at the same time for the way he outwitted the Inquisition. In other words, the actor put something of *Galileo I* back into *Galileo II*. Perhaps it is hard not to. The *action* (Galileo smuggling his new book out) is apt, in a theater, to speak louder than mere *words* of denunciation, but then again the way in which Laughton "stood out" from his part was not exactly what the Brechtian theory bargains for. For it was through an actorish narcissism that he kept aloof; and this limited his power to communicate the content of the play. It also made the sinister and self-defeating pride of the scientist dwindle into a movie star's showy and nervous vanity. Laughton had a unique equipment for this role. It is unlikely that anyone again will combine as he did every appearance of intellectual brilliance with every appearance of physical self-indulgence. But actorish vanity allowed him to let the brilliance slide over into drawing-room-comedy smartness. Narcissism prevented him from even trying to enter those somewhat Dostoevskian depths into which Brecht invites the actor of the penultimate scene, version two.

Brecht added a detail in the later text that might help a great deal to define that "tragedy of pride" that is certainly a part of this drama. Galileo is offered a conceivable way of escape—the patronage of the iron founder Matti. But he is not an astute enough politician to get the point and prefers to believe not only in the authorities themselves but in his own ability to go it alone. Laughton, by not seeming to take in what Matti was saying, threw this little scene away. The effect was not of arrogant overconfidence but merely of lack of rapport or maybe—again—trivial vanity. (Perhaps Brecht learned from this. The Suhrkamp-Methuen text gives a yet later version of the scene, in which the iron founder, now an industrialist called Vanni, explicitly offers himself as an alternative to the Inquisition and is explicitly turned down.)

It was also through Charles Laughton that the notion was first spread around that *Galileo* not only touches on the atom bomb but is essentially concerned with it. Here is Brecht himself in this vein:

> Galileo's crime can be regarded as the original sin of modern physical science ... The atom bomb, both as a technical and as a social phenomenon, is the classical end product of his contribution to science and his failure to society.

But such a meaning does not emerge from the story as told either by historians or by Brecht. Had those who wished to stop Galileo and scientific advance had their way, there would be no atom bomb. Conversely, if we accept the Brechtian premise that Galileo could have changed history by making an opposite decision, then he would have changed history by joining hands with Matti-Vanni the industrialist, and the atom bomb might have been invented a little earlier—say, by Wernher von Braun.

In East Berlin, 1965, Heinar Kipphardt's play about J. Robert Oppenheimer began in the setting left onstage from Brecht's *Galileo,* and the newer play "shows what society exacts from its individuals, what it needs from them," as Brecht said his *Galileo* did. However, one is struck by the extreme difference between the two main dramatic situations—that in which it is Reaction that suppresses discovery and that in which it was inhumane to push *for* science and the *making* of a discovery.

One American production of Brecht's *Galileo,* at my suggestion, posted up the following words for the audience to read after the abjuration scene:

> I was not in a policy-making position at Los Alamos.
> I would have done anything that I was asked to do.
> —J. ROBERT OPPENHEIMER

But I now think there is sensationalism in this idea, for Galileo has not offered to do "anything" he might be "asked to do" at all. And dramatically it makes a big difference that he is not being asked to do something but asked not to do something. He is being asked not to pursue his researches. Then he goes and pursues them anyway, muttering, "Eppur si muove."

The story to which the Oppenheimer dossier leads, when interpreted by a Marxist, is told, not in Brecht's *Galileo,* but in Haakon Chevalier's novel *The Man Who Would Be God.* Here the faith the protagonist stands for is obviously Marxism. He betrays it and his best friend (who is also his best comrade) in order to become the man who can make Reaction a gift of the atom bomb. The ending resembles *Galileo II* to the extent that both protagonists are shown as burnt-out ruins of their former selves; but Chevalier's man does not practice Self-Criticism.

Chevalier makes it clear he thinks the Action of his story describes a curve like that of Greek tragedy; and this curve may suggest, too, the Action of Brecht's play. The rhythm of both, we might at first think, is from battle to defeat, loyalty to betrayal, commitment to alienation. But to write religious tracts for a cardinal, as Galileo did, is not to devise a monstrous weapon, as Oppenheimer did. For one thing, while it is quite credible that devising a monstrous weapon would give a man delusions of satanic grandeur, thus corrupting him, Galileo's obligation to turn out a little conformist journalism is merely a boring chore.

It is true that *Galileo II* touches, or almost touches, on many of the problems that were created or augmented by the atomic bomb—and this has legitimately been stressed by the judicious H. E. Rank in defending Brecht against a charge of unseriousness made by Nigel Dennis.* Still, even *Galileo II* is based not on Oppenheimer folklore but on Galileo folklore and a preoccupation with the similarities, by blinding critics to the enormous differences, is, in my view, a disservice to Brecht the dramatist. It prevents the Action as a whole from being perceived. If we begin by assuming that the play is about the atomic scientists, we shall end by complaining that Brecht doesn't get to the point till very near the end.

If *Galileo* is not "all about the atom bomb," is it a tragedy of pride? One might begin to answer this question with the observation that no tragedy of pride would end in its hero's lacking, not only pride, but even self-respect. At the end, supremely, the true hero reveals his true heroism, and if lack of self-respect has been in question, as in Conrad's *Lord Jim*, then what he will do with his

---

* Dennis's piece is in *Encounter* (October 1960), Rank's in *Stand* V, 1 (n.d.).

self-respect at the end is precisely to regain it. *Galileo* (*I* or *II*) is more of a tragedy of *lack* of pride; but that, to be sure, is no tragedy at all. Brecht himself, speaking of his play in terms of a commitment abandoned and betrayed, indicates that he has nothing against writers like Copernicus, who never made a commitment. Copernicus simply left his book for men to make of it what they would after his death. Galileo embarked on a campaign to change the world, then quit. Brecht shows the trend of his own thinking about the play by the use of words like *opportunism, collaboration, betrayal.* To these one must add the equally Brechtian term *capitulation.* To begin full of fighting spirit, to end capitulating ignominiously: this is the rhythm of life as Brecht so often depicted it, and so deeply felt it. In *Mother Courage,* the "great" capitulation—Courage's own—is over before the first curtain rises. We find it only in certain speeches and a retrospective song. In *Galileo,* on the other hand, it is the hinge of the whole Action. The play is a tragicomedy of heroic combat followed by unheroic capitulation, and the ending of the later version is of the harrowing sort common in tragicomedy when it achieves greatness: no noble contrition, no belated rebellion even, but savage, misanthropic self-hatred. This Galileo is the victim of his own curse upon Mucius.* Received "into the ranks of the faithful," he is exiled from the ranks of mankind, *and that by his own decree.*

---

* The reference is to a page or so of scene 9 in the published German text that is not in the Laughton version (scene 8). Mucius is a scientist who, after studying mathematics with Galileo, sides with the Church against him. The brief confrontation ends thus:

> GALILEO: And don't talk about problems! I didn't permit the plague to stop me continuing my research.
> MUCIUS: Mr. Galilei, the plague is not the worst.
> GALILEO: Let me tell you this. A man who doesn't know the truth is just an idiot, but a man who knows the truth and calls it a lie is a crook. Get out of here!
> MUCIUS (*in a toneless voice*): You are right. (*Exit.*)

That the horror of the self-denunciation scene did not fully
emerge in the 1947 production Brecht was inclined to blame on
Laughton. It was one of the few passages, he says in his Notes, which
the actor had difficulties with. He did not seem, Brecht continues,
to grasp the playwright's plea that a condemnation of the oppor-
tunist must be inherent in the condemnation of those who accept
the fruits of the opportunism. Not using the squint-eyed, worried
grin he had worn in the abjuration scene, Laughton here robbed the
opening of the big speech on science of its superciliousness:

> It did not entirely emerge that you are on the lowest rung
> of the ladder of teaching when you deride the ignorant
> and that it is a hateful light which a man emits just to have
> his own light shine . . .

Laughton failed to make his audiences feel that "that man sits in a
Hell worse than Dante's where the gift of intellect has been gam-
bled away."

But could not Laughton be partly excused for not playing what
Brecht calls the low point of the Action on the grounds that this low
point is hardly reached in the writing? When we ask this we are
asking a question not only about the dialogue of the penultimate
scene but also about the scene that sets it up: the abjuration scene.
This scene represents an extreme instance of Brechtian method.
Brecht well knew that the obvious way to write this scene was to
confront Galileo with his enemies. Some playwrights would make
you sit there three hours for the sole pleasure of seeing this happen
at the end.* Brecht's reason for doing otherwise is clear: the people

---

* Not a mere speculation. The only Galileo play I have read that precedes Brecht's
is by the nineteenth-century French dramatist François Ponsard. Ponsard's final
curtain line is "Et pourtant elle tourne!" I doubt very much that Brecht had read
Ponsard, but, if he had, one would be able to say he took the older work and
stood it on its head (or feet) in his usual fashion. Ponsard gives us a wholly noble
Galileo and is at pains to free the scientist from the *possible* charge of cowardice.

he wishes to confront Galileo with are—his friends. In the theater, it is a truly marvelous scene, with its offstage action, its two groups waiting onstage (the friends and the daughter), the climactic, anticlimactic entrance of Galileo Galilei, the collapse of Andrea, and the laconic, meaning-packed summing up of Galileo's retort to him: "Unhappy is the land that *needs* a hero!" This line has a partly new meaning in *Galileo II,* being now far more ironical, yet it contains a direct, unironic truth still, expressing, as Brecht says, the scientist's wish to deprive Nature of her privilege of making life tragic and heroism necessary. Yet the scene is perhaps a shade *too* oblique. One senses the presence of an intention that is not entirely achieved: to avoid the hackneyed, overprepared climax of conventional drama in the big, long trial scene by bringing down the hero with a flick of the wrist. The abjuration is there before one is ready for it. Our man collapses without a fight. Something is gained. There is a special interest in collapse being so prompt, so sudden, so actionless, after all the overconfidence that had gone before. The Brechtian avoidance of psychology does pay off here in shock. But I wonder if it doesn't force the playwright to omit something we need at once for continuity of narrative and later for our understanding of Galileo's descent into hatred of himself and contempt for others?

To condemn Galileo for his abjuration, one must believe, first, that he had a real alternative and, second, that this alternative was worth all the trouble. Thirdly, his enemies must be as convincing in their way as he is in his, or the whole conflict lacks the magnitude it could have. Now, to take the last point first, the enemy figures in *Galileo,* though done with adroitness, are markedly less impressive than those they are roughly modeled on—the enemies

---

He confronts Galileo with a tragic choice between Science and Family: as a noble hero, he must of course choose the latter. The Family is represented by his daughter; and so concern for his daughter's welfare becomes the high cause for which he suffers. How tempting to conclude that Brecht did read Ponsard and decided on the spot to have his Galileo ride roughshod over his daughter's happiness! And so on.

in *Saint Joan*. As to Galileo's alternative, the trouble is not that we may feel asked to believe that the *historical* Galileo had such an alternative, the trouble is that, unless we can see all history and society in these terms of progressives and reactionaries, we shall not respond as Brecht would like us to. Faced with this kind of objection, Brecht used to say that *all* plays require agreement with the author's philosophy. But do they? Don't they require, rather, only a suspension of disbelief, a temporary willingness to see things through the playwright's spectacles? And is that the issue, here, anyway? Could not the terms of this conflict be objected to on the grounds of the very philosophy Brecht did accept—Marxism? It seems to me that a Marxist should object that the dialectic of history and society is here excessively attenuated. The result is a melodramatic simplification. And the fact that this story cannot be thought of as actually taking place in the seventeenth century does become a dramatic defect *by being called attention to*. In this it resembles the story of Mother Courage, who is condemned for what she did, though what she ought to have done instead (help to destroy the system) was not in the seventeenth-century cards. There is something absurd, then, in condemning her, and there is something absurd in asking Galileo Galilei to strike a blow for the philosophy of Bertolt Brecht. If Cardinal and Inquisitor are abstract and simplistic, so is the play's rendering of the alternative to them, as shown in the character of Federzoni, the idealized worker. *Federzoni is made of wood*, and so, even more obviously, are various smaller characters, introduced to make points, like Mucius the Renegade and Matti-Vanni the Businessman. Before Galileo is arrested, Brecht offers him through Matti-Vanni the alternative of working for the rising bourgeoisie. The point is made, but only by being mentioned, as it might be mentioned in an essay. It does not register as drama, because Matti exercises no pull on Galileo: he is a mere mouthpiece.

These weaknesses would be cruelly displayed by any director who labored under the misapprehension that this was a Shaw play. *Galileo* can suffer by being compared to *Saint Joan* in that Shaw puts much more thought into drama and finds much more drama in thought. *Saint Joan,* on the other hand, might suffer a little by comparison with *Galileo* if what one was after was not thinking but poetry—whether the poetry of the word or the poetry of stagecraft.

"The hero is the people." Walter Benjamin's hyperbole applies, not to the prosaically imposed "vulgar" Marxism of the Federzoni figure, but to the impact of Galileo's life upon the commonalty, a topic to which two whole scenes are devoted—the carnival scene and the last scene of the play, in which Andrea is seen leaving Italy. The people are the hero in that the final interest is not in Galileo himself but in what he did, and what he failed to do, *for* the people. And here objections on historical grounds—that the seventeenth-century populace did not react in this way, that Galileo wrote in Italian instead of Latin, not to reach the people, who couldn't read, but to reach the middle class—cannot be upheld, because the poet has created a vision that transcends literal reportage. The carnival scene usually goes over better with an audience than any other scene in the play. Cynics may say this because it is a creation of the director and composer. The design remains Brecht's own. The little scene gives us an image that resembles the image of Azdak in *The Caucasian Chalk Circle.* In each case, the common folk, in their long night of slavery, are given a brief glimpse of a possible dawn, and Brecht is able to convey this, not discursively, but in direct, poetic-dramatic vision.

And it is a matter, not just of a scene, but of the whole play. As we work our way back from the last scene, through the scene of abjuration, to the long preparation for the abjuration scene, we can discern the curve of the whole Action. One might find the key to this Action in the phrase "the New Age." It is a favorite Brechtian topic, and Brecht explains in his Notes to *Galileo* that the phrase "the New Age" brought to his mind the Workers' Movement as of the beginning of the twentieth century:

... [N]o other line from a song so powerfully inspired the workers as the line, "Now a new age is dawning": old and young marched to it...

This is the theme that is sounded in the very first scene of *Galileo,* and again I wish to make a more than parenthetic allusion to Charles Laughton, since here Laughton the adapter conspired with Laughton the actor to evade an important issue. The actor found the speech about the New Age far too long, so the adapter cut most of it out, and had the remainder rebuked by an Andrea who says: "You're off again, Mr. Galilei." But it was Mr. Brecht who was off again, and a really long speech is needed here, a veritable paean to the idea of a New Age, or we cannot grasp the importance of the conception or the sentiment in the main design. The paean is a poem, though in prose:

GALILEO: Walls and crystal spheres and immobility! For two thousand years mankind believed that the sun and all the stars of heaven turned around them. The Pope, the cardinals, the princes, scholars, captains, merchants, fishwives, and schoolchildren thought they were sitting, stationary, in this crystal globe. But now we're emerging from it, Andrea.

For the old age is through, and a new age is upon us. During hundreds of years it has been as if mankind awaited something.

The cities are narrow, and so are brains. Superstitions and plague. But now the word is: since it is so, it does not remain so. For everything moves, my friend.

On our old continent a rumor has arisen: there are new continents. And since our ships have sailed to them, the saying circulates on the laughing continents: the great, much-dreaded ocean is just a puddle.

And men have come to take great pleasure in searching out the causes of all things: why the stone falls when it is dropped, and how it rises when it is thrown into the air.

Every day something is found. Even the centenarians have the young shout in their ears what new thing has been discovered. Much has been found already, but more can be found in the future. And so there is still much for new generations to do. The old teachings, believed for a thousand years, are on the point of collapsing. There is less wood in the beams of these structures than in the supports which are supposed to hold them up. But the new knowledge is a new building of which only the scaffolding is there. Even the teaching of the great Copernicus is not yet proved. But mankind will soon be properly informed as to its dwelling place, the heavenly body where it has its home. What is written in the old books does not satisfy mankind anymore.

For where Belief has sat for a thousand years, there today sits Doubt. All the world says: yes, that is written in the books, but now let us see for ourselves.

The most celebrated truths are tapped on the shoulder. What never was doubted is doubted now.

And thereby a wind has arisen which blows up the gold-brocaded cloaks of princes and prelates, so that fat or skinny legs are seen beneath, legs like our legs.

The skies, it has turned out, are empty. Men laugh merrily at that.

But the water of the earth drives the new distaffs, and five hundred hands are busy in the rope and sail shops at the dockyards making a New Order.

Even the sons of fishwives go to school. In the markets, the new stars are talked about.

It was always said that the stars were fastened to a crystal vault so that they could not fall. Now we have taken heart and let them float in the air, without support, and they are embarked on a great voyage—like us, who are also without support and embarked on a great voyage.

But the universe lost its center overnight, and in the morning it had a countless number of centers. So that now each one can be regarded as a center and none can. For there is a lot of room suddenly.

Our ships sail on far seas, our stars move in far space. In chess the rooks can now be moved right across the board.

So that the poet says: "O early dawn of the beginning! O breath of the wind that comes from new-found shores!"*

This speech creates a sense of that Enchantment that will later, as the very climax of the Action, turn to Disenchantment (ambiguously in one version, unequivocally in the other). In *The Caucasian Chalk Circle,* we learn how much too early the carpet weavers tried to establish a people's regime, and for how short a time Azdak's people's regime can eke out its fluky existence. In *Galileo,* the point is that the coming of such a regime is actually postponed by the protagonist's principal act. And though we cannot take this as history (of the seventeenth century), we can certainly make sense of it as politics (of the twentieth century).

It has become customary to cut the last scene, but this is because directors insist on believing that Galileo is the hero. If the people are the hero, the last scene is a needed conclusion and a needed correction of the carnival scene. The people will not emerge into the dawn in the sudden ecstasy of Carnival. The journey out of night is long and slow, all the slower because of Galileo's abjuration and all analogous capitulations. At the end, the play

---

* *Galileo I.* The sentence about the rooks seems to be based on the erroneous belief that in former times the rooks could move only one square at a time.

abuts upon the Marxist realization that the people must learn not to rely on the Great Men of the bourgeoisie for their salvation: they will have to save themselves. But discreetly enough, this is not spelled out. Brecht speaks here through image and action.

In *Galileo II* the smuggling out of the new book has a meaning somewhat different from what it had in *Galileo I*. It is less of a triumph for Galileo, but it does take up the theme of *eppur si muove* and partially redeem it from the cynicism that, especially in this version, it must carry. The earth continues to revolve, and even the bad man can continue to contribute good science. Or, on a more literal plane: though a social setback is recorded, science marches ahead—in which contrast, that between a rotten society and a flourishing science, we again glimpse the twentieth century.

A further comment is perhaps needed on the protagonist of Brecht's play. What does this Galileo—as against the Galileo of the historians—finally amount to? The topic can conveniently be approached through the following passage from Isaac Deutscher's life of Trotsky:

> He [Brecht] had been in some sympathy with Trotskyism and was shaken by the purges; but he could not bring himself to break with Stalinism. He surrendered to it with a load of doubt on his mind, as the capitulators in Russia had done; and he expressed artistically his and their predicament in *Galileo Galilei*. It was through the prism of the Bolshevik experience that he saw Galileo going down on his knees before the Inquisition and doing this from a "historic necessity," because of the people's political and spiritual immaturity. The Galileo of his drama is Zinoviev or Bukharin or Rakovsky dressed up in historical costume. He is haunted by the "fruitless" martyrdom of Giordano Bruno; that terrible example causes him to surrender to the Inquisition, just as Trotsky's fate caused so many communists to surrender to Stalin. And Brecht's famous duo-

logue: "Happy is the country that produces such a hero"
and "Unhappy is the people that needs such a hero" epit-
omizes clearly enough the problem of Trotsky and Stalinist Russia rather than Galileo's quandary in Renaissance
Italy. (Brecht wrote the original version of *Galileo Galilei*
in 1937–38, at the height of the Great Purges.)

Unless Mr. Deutscher has his hands on some version of *Galileo*
not known by the rest of us to exist, he can't read straight. *Galileo
II cannot* be taken the way he proposes, since the capitulation,
there, is denounced as loudly as he could wish. If we assume, as
perhaps we must, that it is *Galileo I* he is talking about, then how
could he take the Church (Stalinism) to be something Galileo
"could not bring himself to break with," in view of the fact that his
Galileo cheats and outwits the Church triumphantly? Maybe Mr.
Deutscher never got to the penultimate scene. Brecht's Galileo is
not haunted by the martyrdom of Bruno, either, and if Bruno is
Trotsky, then Trotsky hardly comes within the purview of the play
at all. And does Mr. Deutscher take "Happy is the country that
produces such a hero" to be about Trotsky? If so, inaccuracy has
again tripped him up, as the line actually reads: "Unhappy is the
land that breeds no hero!" and the reference is to Galileo's failure
to be heroic.

But Mr. Deutscher's incursion into dramatic criticism raises
the question whether he claims to describe Brecht's conscious
thoughts or things that crept in, in the author's despite. If the
former, then the Deutscher thesis is highly implausible. Brecht
may have been troubled by inner doubts,* but on the whole he
seems to have given his approval to the Moscow trials, much in
the spirit of his close friend Feuchtwanger, whose ardently Stalinist book *Moscow, 1937* is mentioned by Mr. Deutscher. Besides,

---

* A poem published in 1964 could be cited in evidence. The title is "Are the People Infallible?" My translation appears on pages 197–98 above.

the abjuration in *Galileo I* is in part a means to an end, which is to go on writing subversive things. Though reprehensible, it is also a neat trick, and no occasion for Slavic breast-beating. That Brecht would knowingly have depicted Stalin as the enemy is, on the evidence available so far, improbable.

Yet it may well be true that not only the Nazi but the Bolshevik experience found their way into the play, especially into its later version, which Mr. Deutscher doesn't seem to have read. The Communist idea of self-criticism, going to all possible lengths of self-denunciation and a demand for punishment, undoubtedly exerted considerable sway over Brecht. In 1943 to 1945, he is using it in *The Caucasian Chalk Circle*, in a passage so "Russian" that Western audiences have trouble following the argument. If we are now guessing at unconscious motives, instead of just noting the provable ones, we might guess that the self-denunciation of the new version of *Galileo*, written in 1945 or so, was put there to correct and place in proper perspective the famous self-denunciation before the Inquisition, around which the story is built. The abjuration is a spurious piece of self-denunciation. It cries out, Brecht might well have felt, for a real one. And the real one, by all means, suggests the world of Zinoviev, Bukharin, and Rakovsky. However, if this interpretation is valid, Brecht's unconscious made, surely, the same identification as his conscious mind, namely with Stalin, not with his enemies, who are felt to be guilty as charged.

But wasn't the Nazi experience far more important to the play than the Bolshevik one? The real complaint against Galileo is that he did not rise up like Georgi Dimitrov at the Reichstag trial in Leipzig and denounce his judges. The real complaint is against German physicists who announced that there was such a thing as Aryan physics as distinct from Jewish physics. The real complaint is against the conspiracy of silence in which most German scholars and writers took part in those years. Brecht's poetry of the 1930s reverts again and again to this subject.

Aber man wird nicht sagen: Die Zeiten waren finster
Sondern: Warum haben ihre Dichter geschwiegen?

But men won't say: The times were dark,
But: Why were their poets silent?

And Brecht's personal relation to this subject? He was by no
means silent, but he knew how to take care of himself. He did not
volunteer in Spain. He did not go to Moscow to risk his neck at
the headquarters of Revolution. And undoubtedly such guilt as
was felt (if any was) by Charles Laughton at not taking part in the
Battle of Britain was felt by Brecht a thousand times over at not
taking more than a literary part in *any* of the battles of his lifetime. This guilt, one can readily believe, is concentrated in the protagonist in whose footsteps some people think Brecht trod when
before the Un-American Activities Committee he cried, "No, no,
no, no, no, never," at the question: "Have you ever made application to join the Communist Party?"

"The sick inmost being of a poet," Jean Paul has it, "betrays itself nowhere more than in his hero, whom he never fails to stain
with the secret weaknesses of his own nature." Brecht felt in himself a natural affinity with the shirker and the "quitter." In that respect *Galileo,* a late play, looks all the way back to the earliest plays,
and especially to *Drums in the Night.* A whole row of Brecht protagonists belongs to this species in one way or another (Baal, Galy
Gay, Macheath, Mother Courage, Schweyk, Azdak...),* and what

---

* To this list, except that he is not the protagonist of a play, belongs Herr Keuner.
And interestingly enough, Brecht introduced into *Galileo I* a complete "Keuner
story," thus:

Into the home of the Cretan philosopher Keunos, who was beloved
among the Cretans for his love of liberty, came one day, during the time
of tyranny, a certain agent, who presented a pass that had been issued by
those who ruled the city. It said that any home he set foot in belonged to
him; likewise, any food he demanded; likewise, any man should serve

gives these figures dramatic tension is that their natural passivity has either to be redeemed by the addition of some other quality (as with Schweyk's intuitive shrewdness and humanity) or worked up into something much worse that can be roundly denounced. This working up took Brecht a little time, as we know from the revisions of *Mother Courage* and *Puntila*. It was a quarter of a century before Brecht made it clear that Kragler, of *Drums in the Night,* was to be utterly rejected. And, of course, the wholehearted rejection of Galileo's "crime" took Brecht some eight years to make—eight years and two atom bombs. Brecht, one might put it, was a moralist on second thought, and, however moralist-critics may judge him as a man, they can hardly deny that this "contradiction" in him was dramatically dynamic and productive.

Galileo is a self-portrait in respect of incarnating the main contradiction of Brecht's own personality. That can hardly fail to have interest for students of his work. But it can hardly be the main point of *Galileo,* if we judge *Galileo* to be a good play, since good plays are not, in the first or last instance, personal outpourings. A writer writes himself, but a playwright has written a play only when he has written more than, or other than, himself. Even should his material stem from himself, the test is whether he can

---

him that he set eyes on. The agent sat down, demanded food, washed, lay down, and asked, with his face to the wall, before he fell asleep: "Will you serve me?" Keunos covered him with a blanket, drove the flies away, watched over his sleep, and obeyed him for seven years just as on this day. But whatever he did for him, he certainly kept from doing one thing, and that was to utter a single word. When the seven years were up, and the agent had grown fat from much eating, sleeping, and commanding, the agent died. Keunos then wrapped him in the beat-up old blanket, dragged him out of the house, washed the bed, whitewashed the walls, took a deep breath, and answered: "No."

The speech is given to Galileo in scene 8, and Brecht is able thereby to differentiate Galileo from Andrea, in preparation for later scenes:

(*The pupils laugh. Only Andrea shakes his head.*)
ANDREA: I don't like the story, Mr. Galilei.

get it outside himself and make it not-himself. He has to let him-self be strewn about like dragon's teeth so that other men may spring up, armed. In *Galileo,* a contradiction that had once merely been Brecht's own—had been, then, merely a character trait—is translated into action, into an Action, and this action, reciprocally, attaches itself to someone who is neither Bertolt Brecht nor the Galileo Galilei of history. Though he bears the latter's name, he is a *creation* of the former, and surely a very notable one. It is not just that Brecht's Galileo is contradictory. Such a contradiction would count for comparatively little if the *man* who is contradictory were not both deeply, complexly human and—great. Nor is greatness, in plays, taken on trust or proved by citation of the evidence. Rather, it must be there as a visible halo, and felt as an actual charisma. As the man speaks, moves, or merely stands there, his greatness must, for his audience in the theater, be beyond cavil. In this play, Brecht proves himself to be, with Shaw, one of the very few modern play-wrights who can compel belief in the greatness of their great ones.

It would be a pity if we were so busy arguing the *Problematik* of science and authority that we overlooked an achievement of this sort. Playwrights, after all, should be allowed their limitations in the stratosphere of science and philosophy, since their main job is down on earth, giving life to characters. The role that, however mis-leadingly, goes by the name of Galileo Galilei is not only notable in itself, and functions well in the Action, as I have tried to show, it also solves a very real problem posed by Brecht's subject. Our world is no longer in the center of the universe, *ergo* man has lost his cen-tral importance in the scheme of things. If this proposition is not of the seventeenth century, it is very much of the twentieth, and it has always been important to Bertolt Brecht. He places it at the heart of Garga's nihilism in *In the Swamp,* and of Uriah Shelley's in one of the versions of *A Man's a Man.* Man is absolutely nothing is Uriah's premise and conclusion. And yet Galileo Galilei, who (al-legedly) made this discovery, is something? Is this the ultimate con-tradiction about him? Actually, he is assigned his share in worthlessness and nihilism (if nothingness is divisible), particularly in the later text. But the main point is in the contrast between this discovery of nothingness and the something-ness, the greatness, of the discoverer. God, as Brecht's Galileo puts it, will be found, from now on, "in ourselves or nowhere." Man will be great, not by the role assigned to him by Another, nor yet by his position in space, but by his own inherent qualities. If *Galileo II* verges on being merely a repudiation of its protagonist, then, as I have already intimated, it carries Brecht's vision of things less completely than *Galileo I*. But even in *Galileo I* the "crime" must be taken very seriously, because it is an abdication of what the protagonist alone has to offer (human greatness), and if human greatness were wiped from the record, then the "discovery" that "man is nothing" would be the truth.

Or are the sterling, but more modest, merits of Andrea and Federzoni sufficient to justify existence? In the terms imposed by the play, it is not clear that they are. That these two men disapprove of the abjuration tells us nothing to the purpose. They were never put to such a test. Nor could they be, since, not possessing greatness, they could never have had as much to lose as Galileo had. "The hero is the people." I have conceded that there is much truth in Benjamin's dictum, but the thought in the play is "dialectical," many-sided, ironic, and the individual greatness of the protagonist is essential to the scheme. In the final crisis, he is an antihero, and that is bad (or, in the first version, partly bad). What I am stressing is that he is also a hero, the hero as great man, human greatness being what offsets the Copernican blow to human narcissism.

> It was . . . a time which called for giants and produced giants—giants in power of thought, passion, and character, in universality and learning. The men who founded the modern rule of the bourgeoisie had anything but bourgeois limitations. On the contrary the adventurous character of the time inspired them to a greater or less degree . . . But

what is especially characteristic of them is that they almost
all pursue their lives and activities in the midst of the contemporary movements, in the practical struggle; they take
sides and join in the fight ... Hence the fullness and force
of character that makes them complete men.

I don't know if this passage from Engels's *Dialectics of Nature* suggested the theme of Galileo Galilei to Brecht. It *is* cited in the
Berlin Ensemble program of his play. Reading it, one reflects that
Galileo, according to Brecht, was one who at a crucial moment was
disloyal to his "side" in "the fight." That can hardly be unimportant. The character will stand, as Brecht intended, as an examplar
of a certain kind of weakness. But will it stand, even more impres-
sively, as the exemplar of human greatness, a proof that greatness
is possible to humankind? For that matter, would the weakness be
even interesting if it were not that of a great (which is to say: in
many ways, a strong) man?

Galileo (II)
1967

The name of Brecht is at the center of any discussion of political theater. Each of his plays strives toward a condition of urgency. Sometimes the day's headlines—edicts of the muse of history—provide the perfect occasion. Yet that occasion can be missed, that opportunity muffed, as the following report indicates. It would be well to elaborate on the reference to Hannah Arendt in this piece. I arranged for her to write on Brecht in the Kenyon Review *in 1948. At that time she seemed full of enthusiasm both for Brecht and for my Brecht translations. Later she had second thoughts, it would seem, on both topics. In 1967 Herbert Blau had intended to have me write on* Galileo *in the Lincoln Center program. When he was driven out, I was replaced in this small role by Ms. Arendt . . . All rather boring gossip to be hearing later, but the episode brought me this far-from-boring message handwritten on a postcard:*

> *Dear Eric, Your piece on Galileo much needed saying. (Too bad you had to be so brief on Hannah!)*
>
> *In my opinion there* is *a deeper criticism of BB, not relevant in the present context. He seemed to have a need (a kind of spite) to deny excellence—a refusal to lose himself in God's wonders.* This *is why the scientific debates are not inward. This goes, in my opinion, with a mistaken theory of revolution. But thanks. Paul Goodman.*

IN 1947 HAROLD CLURMAN SAW Joseph Losey's production of *Galileo* and my production of *The Caucasian Chalk Circle* and reported in the *New Republic* that we in America had not yet learned how to present Brecht's plays. He was right. And, on the evidence of *Galileo* at the Vivian Beaumont Theater today, one could only conclude that, even now, the lesson has not been learned.

Not that the new show doesn't have its points. One understands how the directing of John Hirsch gets to be praised for firmness. His show is what it is, and one is not left in doubt. One is tempted to describe it as highly *audible* except that, if you sit at the side, the actors' voices reverberate as in a cathedral every time they turn away from you (which is often, since the play is done on an apron stage). That one does not readily think of warmer epithets than *audible* has its reasons.

Not flawless, by any means; as Galileo, Charles Laughton brought far more to the role than Anthony Quayle ever will. First, he could effortlessly portray a self-indulgent guzzler; second, he was able to seem an intellectual, and even a genius. The *combination* of physical grossness with intellectual finesse was theatrical in itself and of the essence of Brecht's drama. In regard to playing the intellectual, this too should be said. It is not done by playing intellect itself. It is done by making the characteristic attitudes of the intellectual live—emotionally. Laughton would always bristle when he talked with bureaucrats or businessmen: his Galileo was allergic to them. Conversely, when talking to his students he made it clear how much he got from their admiration of him: the classroom was his element. Mr. Quayle, on the other hand, treats everyone else onstage as a stranger and even likes to have them at a distance so he can address them as a public meeting. The question why a British actor had to be hired for the role is all the more relevant since the British way of reducing people to their voices is highly inappropriate to this German representation of a great Italian. Mr. Quayle is convincing neither as the guzzler nor as the thinker. For the first he substitutes extrovert heartiness; for the second, schoolmasterishness. In the final scene he consents to play emotion, but it is the comparatively uninteresting emotion of self-pity that comes through. He sobs. This time his isolation from others is to the point. But self-pity is only self-pity.

One comment on the show has been that what the ecclesiastics argue with Galileo about is treated somewhat pedantically. This is partly the fault of Mr. Quayle and the production, but probably Bertolt Brecht shares the blame. The debating scenes are not in the class of those in *Saint Joan*—what debating scenes are?—and, in depicting a lecturer, Brecht becomes a lecturer himself to an undue extent. Still, to leave the matter there and conclude that the *play* is a lecture is to miss the most interesting—and dramatic—things in it.

The replacement of Ptolemaic by Copernican theories of the universe is described in the play but is not the subject of the play. All credit to the playwright—and in this case to Mr. Quayle too—that they lend to the description a certain poetry that produces, at moments, a quickening of the spectator's pulse. However, the emphasis given to this aspect by Mr. Quayle and the director threw the drama as a whole badly off. The struggle of ideologies is the background or, at most, the premise. The drama itself has to do with the human confrontation of this struggle and—in the version presented at Lincoln Center—with human inadequacy to it.

In a play, it is true, sheer inadequacy is none too interesting, but this inadequacy is not sheer. It is the inadequacy of a man from whom we would have expected better things. It is the inadequacy of a man who is also great and who has been shown to us *exclusively*—up to the point where he caves in—as a great man. The moral would (at the very least) be: "What good is it to have great qualities *A, B,* and *C,* if at the testing time, you fail, like any little poltroon?" But Brecht was after bigger game than even that. His subject might even be called tragic, since he makes the bad not just a contrast with the good but the complement of it—its shadow. His Galileo is a "slave of his passions," as one of his antagonists puts it; but even his love of science was an addiction, like his love of wine and good food. This man felt, like Oscar Wilde, that there was nothing to do with temptation but give way to it. One thing that tempted him was the Copernican theory: he succumbed, hook, line, and sinker. He *always* acted spontaneously, did what he felt like doing. And what he felt like doing when he was shown the instruments of torture by the Inquisition was—saying whatever was necessary to avoid being tortured. So he said that the sun went round the earth, though it was his own unique contribution to human history to prove that the earth went round the sun.

At this point, however, something snapped inside him. Giving way to temptation suddenly ceased to be an unalloyed pleasure. Why? Because he sensed what less hedonistic souls also sense: that the Inquisition's demand called for some other response. Galileo's favorite pupil formulated it thus: "Unhappy is the land that breeds no hero." The scientist takes that in, is obviously "hit," but manages to find a formulation to strike back with. It is this: "Unhappy is the land that *needs* a hero." I think the author of *A Man for All Seasons* took this formula to be Brecht's summing up: his own play seems intended as a riposte. The riposte, however, is in Brecht's own play already, but it is provided in Brecht's own way, not in that of the conventional theater.

First we have to concede that a land that needs heroes *is* unhappy. The good society will not make such demands on its citizens, and Brecht's Galileo feels this the more keenly because he suffers for it: after all he is a man who has always tried to shun suffering and have fun. That ever *he* was born to put it right! On the other hand, given that the land *is* unhappy, one must not, as Galileo had done, blithely ignore the fact, but proceed to ask what follows? And what follows is the pupil's conclusion: Unhappy is the land that breeds no hero.

This Galileo, in the enforced seclusion of house arrest, recognizes readily enough. Defect of intelligence was hardly his problem: on the contrary. It was the assumption that he could blithely ignore social reality that he had to give up, even if it meant that he would come to loathe himself in the process. He who had been such a plucky and confident fellow in so many a tight spot proved a coward on the day of reckoning.

That this sounds rather vague and general—*universal* is the word in academic circles—is what seemed to permit John Hirsch to present the main action of this play so blandly. It is all a little too obvious to be interesting. So the boaster is a coward, eh? But isn't that usually so? Perhaps it is, yet this is not where Bertolt Brecht rested his case. *Cowardice* is not, ultimately, the right word. *Passivity* would come closer, or *submissiveness.* All Germans who think about Germany become somewhat preoccupied with submissiveness—for evident reasons. Very many Brecht characters are studies in submissiveness, and they are perhaps the most interesting characters in all his work: Schweyk and Mother Courage, Macheath and Azdak and Galy Gay . . . In Galileo's case, submissiveness has a kind of tragic inevitability, as I have hinted, because it is bound up with his very virtues, his receptivity to all impulses, his great gift for acceptance and enjoyment. How *could* such a man suddenly stop embracing the world—and hit out at it?

He doesn't. But because Brecht then seems to make the demand that he should have, and that future Galileos *must*, we are less convinced than distressed by the conclusion—the conclusion, that is, as presented at Lincoln Center. Actually, Brecht added another scene that modifies the main thesis. In this scene the onus for hitting out at the world is shifted from Galileo, the individual genius, to his principal pupil, and hence to helpers and servers generally, to "the people."

Mr. Hirsch is not the only director who has omitted the scene, but the others (those I know about, anyway) had spotted that its thematic content is present in an earlier scene that is never cut, the carnival scene. Alas, this is being presented at Lincoln Center amateurishly, frantically, all hither and thither, all buzz and blur. Mr. Hirsch seems to have thought it was the comic—or maybe spectacular?—relief, whereas in fact it is the poetic and thematic center. Its main feature is a long and splendid ballad by Brecht and Eisler, much of which is cut in Mr. Hirsch's production and the rest of which is rendered unintelligible by busy romping and stomping. Since the climactic lines are thrown away by being given to the mob to sing, let me tell those who are seeing the show what they should also be hearing:

> Good people who have trouble here below
> In serving cruel lords and gentle Jesus
> Who bids you turn the other cheek like so [*gesture*]
> While they prepare to strike the second blow:
> OBEDIENCE WILL NEVER CURE YOUR WOE...

Speaking with the wisdom of the folk tradition, the balladeer who sings these lines has just been praising the rebelliousness of Galileo. The people will need to share it, if they're going to get anywhere. Now at this time Galileo has not recanted. When he does, what will the ballad come to mean? That we, the people, cannot hide behind our great men. They may let us down. If disobedience is to be learned, it will have to be learned by us.

This (arguably) is the main idea of Bertolt Brecht's *Galileo,* and it would readily emerge as such if the last scene were *not* omitted. It is (certainly) the idea that has most life and pertinence in the United States today. We have here a play written to urge not Galileo but us—us!—to disobedience, civil and less civil. The week it opened in New York, Martin Luther King also opened up a drama—with his demand for conscientious objection to the war in Vietnam.

Brecht's plays naturally attach themselves to such issues, and Brecht himself always was concerned that the attachment should be firm and visible. His is a theater of commitment, and his plays seldom get across unless they carry some of the appropriate activist fervor. Well, "get across" is a loose phrase. Brecht's plays could be said to "get across" in some fashion as objets d'art, as instances of avant-garde theater, as formal experiments. Only, if that is what they are, I for one would begin to believe that his detractors are right and that after all "there isn't very much to him." The Hirsch production is handsome and carefully designed, but even if it were handsomer, even if the design were brilliant as well as careful, the result would still be insufficient to convince an audience that it is face-to-face with a major playwright.

The Lincoln Center production does hint at a certain grandeur. The story is lucidly enacted; the lines are, for the most part, clearly read; Brecht and his translators are permitted to make an impact. But the grandeur fans out into grandiosity. If not dull, the show is a little formal and inert. And the reason—beyond the reasons already given, such as the limitations of Mr. Quayle's acting (and he is the best of the actors)—is a complete lack of urgency. The show has nothing to say because Mr. Hirsch assumed that what Mr. Brecht had to say was that the earth goes round the sun or that a scientist's life is picturesque (model: Don Ameche as Alexander Bell).

What goes on at Lincoln Center? Last year people were complaining that Herbert Blau made propaganda—and from a radical viewpoint—in flamboyant press releases and programs. *Galileo* was chosen as a play for him to direct; he leaves; and the play is done as if its issues belonged to the seventeenth century or the Hollywood view thereof. As for poor BB, he is handed over, in the program, to the tender mercies of Hannah Arendt. And she, who has so successfully disposed of so many, has little trouble disposing of *him*. Oh, she loves his poetry, but as to his point of view she finds it in sore need of correction—by her. So Brecht is set right in the program to his own show. No use to say, I suppose, that the fishmonger does not cry stinking fish. No fishmongers, we: since the departure of Mr. Blau we are—well, what?—aesthetes? Students of Hannah Arendt? Whatever the answer, an author who is apologized for, if not positively debunked, in the program, is also presented evasively onstage. But as it happens, that is not an artistic gain. To vindicate this author as an artist, you have to present his point of view sympathetically, passionately, aggressively. Only then will the lines begin to crackle, the characters to light up, and the themes to burn.

Ibsen, Shaw, Brecht
1969

The occasion for many of my comments on Brecht has been theatrical. For some—as for the comments here—academic. David Daiches was editing a multivolume history of letters, The Literature of the Western World. *For me the opportunity was to present Brecht in a broad context and specifically to relate him to two great predecessors, Ibsen and Shaw.*

MATTHEW ARNOLD EXPECTED FROM poets in general a "criticism of life," and many today would not only agree but would add that this criticism should be a social one. Some will even argue that it *must* be a social one, because literature, in their view, is by nature social. Society, that is, can be regarded as providing both the source and the substance of literature. It can also be maintained that to communicate a thought to another person—even more, to a group of other persons—is to socialize it.

As for the drama, it has often been regarded as, in several senses, yet more social than other kinds of literature. In sense one, the theater appeals most strongly and helpfully *to* society:

> The theater is the most potent and direct means of strengthening human reason and enlightening the whole nation.[1]

In sense two, the theater has an especially close connection with the social conditions of the moment:

> No portion of literature is connected by closer or more numerous ties with the present condition of society than the drama.[2]

In sense three, drama is preeminently the genre in which what is currently the characteristic type of relation of man to man is represented:

> Thus investigation as to which type of man is suited to dramatic art coincides with the investigation of the problem of man's relation to other men.[3]

Finally, drama since Ibsen has frequently been regarded as even more social than earlier drama, as peculiarly concerned with social problems: a thesis that can best be documented in the lives of the three dramatists to be commented on here.

Although Henrik Ibsen would seem to us today to have been concerned with modern social problems from the very beginning, he did not seem so in his early works to the leading Scandinavian critic of the time, George Brandes, who criticized *Brand* (1865) as reactionary and read the playwright (as well as the rest of the world) this lesson:

> What keeps a literature alive in our day is that it submits problems for debate. Thus, for example, George Sand debates the problem of the relations between the sexes, Byron and Feuerbach religion, John Stuart Mill and Proudhon property, Turgenev, Spielhagen, and Emile Augier social conditions...[4]

To which Ibsen replied, "...[Y]our work is a great, shattering, and emancipating outbreak of genius," and, "[W]hat cannot withstand the ideas of the times must succumb." Undoubtedly Brandes's writings, which, as Ibsen said, disturbed his sleep, also led him toward his great "modern period." Some fifteen years after Brandes's Inaugural Lecture, Ibsen's plays disturbed the sleep of George Bernard Shaw and led him to modernism and to the theater. In 1886 he took the part of Krogstad in a reading of *A Doll's House* (1879) staged by Karl Marx's daughter Eleanor. In 1890 he gave a Fabian lecture about that play. In the next year appeared the first book on Ibsen in English: Shaw's *Quintessence of Ibsenism.* One year later Shaw's first play, *Widowers' Houses,* was ready. "It deals," Shaw said in a preface, "with a burning social question, and is deliberately intended to induce people to vote on the Progressive side at the next County Council election in London." It will be noted that Shaw is pushing the idea of problem literature further than Brandes had. Not debate now, but political pressure, though on a local, municipal scale. The scale would be enlarged later. In May 1895, a magazine called *The Humanitarian* asked a number of public men to answer the question, "Should social problems be freely dealt with in the drama?" Shaw answered:

> We are...witnessing a steady intensification in the hold of social questions on the larger poetic imagination...If people are rotting and starving in all directions and nobody else has the heart or brains to make a disturbance about it, the great writers must. In short, what is forcing our poets to follow Shelley in becoming political and social agitators, and to turn the theater into a platform for propaganda and an arena for discussion, is that whilst social questions are being thrown up for solution almost daily by the fierce rapidity with which industrial processes change and supersede one another...the political machinery by which alone our institutions can be kept abreast of these changes is so old-fashioned...that social questions never get solved until the pressure becomes so

desperate that even governments recognize the necessity
for moving. And to bring the pressure to this point, the
poets must lend a hand...

Shaw pushed the idea of problem drama further than Ibsen, but
Bertolt Brecht pushed it further than Shaw. The changes correspond, of course, to stages of history—and of disillusionment. In
1871 there still seemed time for debate. In the 1890s it still seemed
worthwhile to put pressure on governments, local and national. All
Brecht's playwriting came after the definitive collapse of nineteenth-
century civilization in World War I. By that token, it also came
after a crucial attempt to build a new civilization by means other
than parliamentary debate and propagandist pressure, namely, by
revolution. The question that arose now was whether the theater
could be of any use at all. Could the modern world even be portrayed in it? Brecht answered that it could, if it was portrayed as alterable. And for him, to portray it as alterable was to help to alter
it, beginning with an alteration of the means of portrayal, an alteration of the theater itself:

> [H]alf a century's experiments... had won the theater
> brand new fields of subject matter and types of problem,
> and made it a factor of marked social importance. At the
> same time they had brought the theater to a point where
> any further development of the intellectual, social (politi-
> cal) experience must wreck the artistic experience.[5]

> ... *The Mother* is a piece of antimetaphysical, materialistic,
> non-Aristotelian drama. This makes nothing like such a
> free use as the Aristotelian theater does of the passive em-
> pathy of the spectator; it also relates differently to certain
> psychological effects, such as catharsis. Just as it refrains
> from handing its hero over to the world as if it were his in-
> escapable fate, so it would not dream of handing over the

spectator to an inspiring theatrical experience. Anxious to teach the spectator a quite different practical attitude, directed toward changing the world, it must begin by making him adopt in the theater a quite different attitude from what he is used to.[6]

By means of a new kind of theater, Brecht would work on audiences in a new way and, by changing them, would help to change the world.

So far, so good. These quotations from our three authors are unequivocal, and suggest accurately enough three clear phases of recent history. What they hardly begin to suggest is the actual tenor of the three writers' creative work. I have only been citing, really, the official stance of each man: the quotations are all from theoretical works, not from plays. If one wanted to document from actual theater what has been cited here as principle, it would be easier to document the Brandes-Ibsen position from plays by Alexander Dumas *fils;* the Shaw position from plays by Eugène Brieux; and the Brecht position either from Erwin Piscator's production experiments or from Brecht plays that most critics would regard as his weakest efforts. Here, for example, are the first and last speeches of Brieux's *Les avariés* (*Damaged Goods,* 1901) cited in the translation (1909) for which Shaw wrote a preface:

I. Before the play begins, the manager appears upon the stage and says:

Ladies and Gentlemen, I beg leave to inform you, on behalf of the author and of the management, that the object of this play is a study of the disease of syphilis in its bearing on marriage.

II. DOCTOR: This poor girl is typical. The whole problem is summed up in her: she is at once the product and the cause. We set the ball rolling, others keep it up, and it runs

back to bruise our own shins. I have nothing more to say.
(*He shakes hands with Loches as he conducts him to the door,*
and adds in a lighter tone) But if you give a thought or two
to what you have just seen when you are sitting in the
Chamber [of Deputies], we shall not have wasted our time.

These passages correspond exactly to the young Shaw's belief that
drama should put pressure on the people's parliamentary representatives. The significant thing is that no such passages occur in any
play by Shaw. Even if they did, we could be sure that they would
have an entirely different tone. Even where the theoretical remarks
of our three authors are consistent with their respective practice,
they really give no idea what that practice is. Were the plays to disappear and the prefatory remarks to survive, posterity would receive a wholly misleading impression of what the plays had been
like. This ought not to amaze us: an author's official positions are
one thing; his creative achievements are another. It is minor authors who make movements and are content to exemplify their
principles. Major authors may start movements or join them, but
they do not become submerged in them. To read Zola's proclama-
tions, you would gather that novel writing was a science and that
once you had mastered the latest teaching on heredity and environment you could put a novel together. Perhaps. But it would not
be a Zola novel, which is a remarkably "unscientific" work, compounded of Gothic imagination, great human warmth, and even a
macabre sense of humor...

It need not be argued that Ibsen, Shaw, and Brecht are *not* social dramatists, only that the definition of the word *social* may need
enlargement if it is to fit them, and that, in any case, each must be
regarded not as a member of a school or as an example of a trend,
but as an individual genius, making his own peculiar and wondrous
explorations. Although all three have had imitators, the results do
not show that any of the qualities for which we value them are im-
itable. Their criticisms of social phenomena may not be unique in

the form in which we can abstract them from the work, but they *are* unique in the emphasis and color given to them in the setting of the work. Which is why it is to that setting that we must pursue them.

"The object of this play is a study of the disease of syphilis in its bearing on marriage." Nine out of ten students, questioned about this sentence, would guess that it referred to Ibsen's *Ghosts* (1881). Captain Alving had syphilis, and as a result his son Oswald becomes an idiot in front of our eyes. Brieux would use this story as a pretext for urging us to take all possible measures to combat venereal disease. We get no hint as to whether Ibsen would urge anything of this kind. What is *his* interest in the story? To be sure, Oswald's collapse is the central happening. But what does Ibsen do with it?

The question can be answered only in terms of the whole play, a fact that is in itself significant and, as it turns out, a tribute to Ibsen's genius. Oswald is an Orestes for whom the Furies (Erinyes) do not turn into Wellwishers (Eumenides) in accord with a poet's desire to affirm life and, by implication, the phase of life that his culture is passing through. He is irreclaimably doomed by "ghosts." Ibsen generally knew what he was doing, and never more so than in his choice of title for this play. Not *The House of Alving*, not *Mrs. Alving*, not *Oswald*, although any of these titles would have been in the classical tradition. Rather, he chose a title in the tradition of *The Eumenides* and *The Bacchae*. In ancient literature these are unusual titles because they stress extrahuman forces normally left in the background. Such forces come into the foreground at certain crises of history: Aeschylus celebrated the creation of the democratic city-state; Euripides pronounced a doom upon the whole Hellenic experiment. (I leave aside the question of how far back in history the accepted titles of Greek plays go. Suffice it here that they *are* accepted titles.) Ibsen is a Euripidean playwright dramatizing the crisis of middle-class culture in his own day and somewhat beyond. Accordingly, his "ghosts" are neither furies nor bacchantes. What they *are* is very precisely, though complexly, worked out. To begin with, they are ghosts in the most ordinary sense, that of superstition. Overheard in the next room by Mrs. Alving, Oswald and Regina sound like the ghosts (*revenants,* returned spirits, spooks) of Captain Alving and Regina's mother. *Sound like*—the word *ghosts* is in the first instance a simile. In the second, it is a metaphor.

Captain Alving's legacy of disease: this is how syphilis enters into Ibsen's scheme of things. But it is not where he leaves his presentation of ghosts. They are more than superstition, and more than physiology. They are cultural and social: they are a matter of the characters' beliefs and attitudes, their decisive and therefore dramatic beliefs and attitudes.

When Mrs. Alving hears the "ghosts" in the next room, she is brought that much nearer to telling Oswald what she (at that point) believes to be the whole truth about his father. The simile drives her to explain the metaphor. And that would be where a conventional nineteenth-century play would have ended. But Ibsen's last and greatest act is still to come. In the process of telling this truth, Mrs. Alving finds that it is not the whole truth. Under the traumatic influence of those events or discoveries that are Ibsen's plot, she finds herself telling a different story and realizing a different truth: that not only Alving, but she herself, was responsible for the *debacle.* For she was a victim of the third kind of ghost, the ideological ghost. When she had tried, as a young wife, to flee from her husband to Parson Manders, who loved her, Manders had turned her away from the door, and she had consented to be turned away and to return to Alving. Not all the reading she then did in modern literature could erase the facts of her nonmodern actions. In her fantasy life, she wants liberation from bourgeois culture. In actuality, she cannot defy the marriage laws; cannot contemplate the incestuous union of her son with his half sister; cannot practice mercy killing.

Corresponding to this double twist whereby Mrs. Alving's narrative turns from husband-denunciation to self-discovery, there is duality, too, in the main narrative line. Oswald's collapse, it has been ventured, is the central happening. One could even say it is the *only* thing that happens on this stage, and that once it *has* happened the play is over—the play of the superstition simile and the physiological metaphor. But this is to overlook the happenings within the breast of Mrs. Alving. *Ghosts,* finally, is the story of Oswald *as witnessed by his mother.* The final effect is the effect upon her. She is the onstage audience: such has been her fate from the beginning. What she now does, or fails to do, with her son, she had previously done, or failed to do, with her husband: she reduces herself to the position of helpless, agonized onlooker. Oswald's paralysis—physical, unaccompanied by suffering, and exceptional—is as nothing to hers as she stands there holding the lethal pills and not using them: with a life still to live, in unbearable agony, and typical of a whole class of people, a whole phase of history. At this point we see how different from furies or bacchantes, and how much more modern, Ibsenian ghosts are. Pale as they are by comparison, they are far more negative because they have no possibility of being transformed into Eumenides. They are inertia, where what is needed is movement. They are regression, where what is called for is progress. They are imprisonment and death, where what is "desired" is liberation and life. (I put the word *desired* in quotation marks because the authenticity of the desire is in question.) In the situation depicted, hope is mere cultured fantasy and modish liberalism. Wherever the seeds of life are shown to be still faintly alive, as in Oswald's hankering after joy *and after his half sister,* they are precipitately, hysterically exterminated by Ibsen's enlightened abortionists.

It is tempting to call Ibsen the most ironical dramatist since Sophocles; for him, nothing that glitters is gold. Now such irony is not interesting if it merely has the impact of a trick or mannerism. It is interesting only (a) if it seems the author's authentic mode of vision, and (b) if it succeeds in redefining the author's subject for us. To establish that it is indeed Ibsen's authentic mode of vision, one can only refer people to his work. On the redefinition of subject, one might cite yet again the notion of ghosts. Those who have noticed that Ibsen's ghosts are not furies have perhaps not noticed that they are also not a curse rooted in real crimes (as in Greek drama and the mythology on which it is based), or in original sin (as in much Christian literature down to, say, T. S. Eliot's *Family Reunion,* based as it is on the Orestes legend). In *Ghosts,* there is a clear reference to the Old Testament idea of the sins of the fathers being visited upon the children, yet it would be disingenuous to cite this idea without noting that Ibsen exactly inverts it. The idea that emerges from *Ghosts* is that what Alving did was not sin after all, but was the unfortunate result of his legitimate joy in life. Can we conclude then that Mrs. Alving was the sinner? Not that either. What was wrong was that she *believed* that Alving had sinned. What was wrong was what gave her this belief: her education, her culture, her background, her epoch, and her class—in a word, her society.

Here we have the deeper sense in which Ibsen's drama may truly be called social. Not to harp too long on one string, it can equally well be illustrated from *Hedda Gabler* (1890). One need only cite the ending. Hedda shoots herself to avoid being in Judge Brack's power. But Brack himself indicated that she had alternatives. The relevant passage is worth quoting. Brack knows that Løvborg shot himself with Hedda's pistol.

> BRACK: No, the police have it.
>
> HEDDA: What will the police do with the pistol?
>
> BRACK: Search till they find the owner.
>
> HEDDA: Do you think they will succeed?
>
> BRACK [*bending over her and whispering*]: No, Hedda Gabler, not so long as I keep silent.
>
> HEDDA [*looking askance at him*]: And if you do not keep silent, what then?
>
> BRACK [*shrugging his shoulders*]: One could always declare the pistol was stolen.

HEDDA [*firmly*]: It would be better to die.

BRACK [*smiling*]: One says such things; one doesn't do them.

HEDDA [*without answering*]: And if the pistol were not stolen and the police find the owner, what then?

BRACK: Well, Hedda, then, think of the scandal.

HEDDA: The scandal?

BRACK: The scandal, yes, which you are terrified of. You'd naturally have to appear in court, both you and Mademoiselle Diana. She would have to explain how the thing happened, whether it was accident or murder. Did he threaten to shoot her, and did the pistol go off then, or did she grab the pistol, shoot him, afterward putting it back into his pocket? She might have done that, for she is a hefty woman, this— Mademoiselle Diana.

HEDDA: What have I to do with all this repulsive business?

BRACK: Nothing. But you will have to answer the question: why did you give Løvborg the pistol? And what conclusion will people draw from the fact that you did give it to him?

HEDDA [*dropping her head*]: That is true. I didn't think of that.

BRACK: Well, fortunately, there is no danger as long as I keep silent.

HEDDA [*looking up at him*]: That means you have me in your power...

BRACK [*whispering softly*]: Dearest Hedda, believe me, I shall not abuse the position.

HEDDA: In your power, all the same. At the mercy of your will and demands. And so a slave! [*Getting up impatiently*] No! I won't endure that thought, never!

BRACK [*looking at her half mockingly*]: People manage to get used to the inevitable.

Why could Hedda not tell the police the pistol had been stolen, as Brack suggested? In her own mind, the answer is that she could not tell such a lie. Why not, considering that she is quite a fluent liar? Because this lie would hurt her image of herself as an aristocrat. It would be petty. Hara-kiri would be indicated. Nonsense, says Brack, such suicides have been abolished by bourgeois respectability. In any event, Brack is toying with Hedda. He himself would no doubt publicly deny that the pistol was stolen. He moves on to his principal threat. Unless he keeps his peace, there will be a scandal. What is a scandal? It is not wrongdoing itself: Løvborg is not being accused of iniquity and, if Mademoiselle Diana shot him, it was in self-defense. Hedda's response is all the more ironic because *she* really is the sinner in this whole affair. It is not sin or wrongdoing that Hedda finds repellent, but talk about it, being talked about, having her "name dragged through the mud." True, she will be accused of a wrong, placing a pistol in the hands of an unbalanced man, but to most people the man would remain the responsible party. She will be just a dubious character who was implicated—an object of scandal. In short, she will have a bad reputation.

Reputation is the social value par excellence. It is the equivalent of credit in financial matters: if people think you have it, you have it, for it is only what people think that counts. If, therefore, "people"—that is, a given social system—are given a positive valuation by the dramatist, then reputation will also be seen positively. It will be seen as honor and, despite its basis in opinion, will be regarded as the rock on which civilization rests, as it is in the classic drama of Spain. Now Hedda, as a character, has some vestige of feeling for genuine honor. This is one component of her statement that rather than lie she would kill herself. And it is a component of her actual suicide. It is seen in a corrupted, sick form in her fantasies of a heroic death for Løvborg, and it is because *he* didn't "do it beautifully" that *she* has to do it beautifully. What, then, prevents her suicide from being truly beautiful? The fact that it is only a transcendence in one aspect while being mainly an evasion of responsibility, an enactment of defeat, the expression of a simple death wish. Hedda has vaguely wished for death from the outset and accordingly was shown toying with her pistols in the first scene. Now she finds the energy to use them in what had all along been the "logical" way. Prodded by fear: and not of God, but of scandal; not of wrong, but of talk about wrong and about her.

"One says such things; one doesn't do them." "People manage to get used to the inevitable." "People don't do such things." So says Judge Brack in the last couple of minutes of the play. The idea was stated earlier by Hedda herself, when Mrs. Elvsted spoke of the shadow of a woman standing between herself and Løvborg. (We sense that it is Hedda herself.)

> HEDDA: Has he told you anything about her?
> MRS. ELVSTED: He spoke of her once—vaguely.
> HEDDA: What did he say?
> MRS. ELVSTED: He said that when they parted she threatened to shoot him.
> HEDDA [*with cold composure*]: What nonsense! No one does that sort of thing here.

"Here" is bourgeois society, Brack's society. Brack's calculations are exactly as dependable as the social order itself. In this society, a woman will take an uncongenial lover, and even let a man have a blackmailer's power over her, rather than create a scandal. Brack does not misunderstand the social system, except in assuming that it has completely assimilated everyone. He is fooled by a vestige of aristocracy, however decadent, in Hedda. Adultery would have been all right. As for dishonor, if she had been Hedda Tesman through and through, even in this there would have been no problem. But she was Hedda Gabler, the general's daughter.

If the play had been written, not by Ibsen, but by Judge Brack, or even by an enemy of Brack who belonged to Brack's milieu—

that is, by someone who lived wholly within the bourgeois scheme of things—then it would have been social drama on a familiar pattern, and would have ended with Hedda as Brack's mistress and victim. The "social drama" of Ibsen gains another dimension from his own ending and all that goes with it. Because the values of his society are not the values of the play, but only the rejected values *in* the play, the vision of the whole is a much broader one. In other words, Ibsen presupposes alternatives to his society.

One need not be surprised that he has generally been regarded as a pessimist. Clearly, his spirit, like the spirit of tragic artists in the past, is shot through with a sense of *curse* and *doom*—a curse upon the life he sees around him, the doom of his fellowmen and the form of noncommunity they have wrought. That the Judge Bracks in his audience find him totally negative is entirely correct from where they sit, and not entirely incorrect from where anyone else sits, because Ibsen put down on paper what he saw, not what he would have liked to see. Nonetheless, what he would have liked to see is present as something more than a fantasy of the impossible. The "ghosts" that in fact doom Mrs. Alving, and the fear of scandal that in fact dooms Hedda Gabler, are not divine or diabolical, nor do they partake of any necessity other than the historical—which is to say, they are necessary only for a time. They have their day and cease to be. They become unnecessary.

Napoleon said: "Politics is fate." The view that permeates the modern epoch after Napoleon is that *history* is fate, and although history has been seen in various ways, there is one characteristically modern way: history as evolution. This implies a possible, if not an inevitable, progression. That Ibsen was captivated by this vision is very explicit in his letters and speeches, and was dramatized in an early play, *Emperor and Galilean* (1873), which as an older man he still made a point of endorsing (in an after-dinner speech in Stockholm, 1887). Now, because drama deals with collisions, it may be natural that what preoccupied the playwrights, when they were inspired by the modern historical outlook, was a single factor: the collision of two epochs. Friedrich Hebbel stressed this in the 1840s. Ibsen wrote of Brandes's Inaugural Lecture of 1871 (already cited):

> No more dangerous book could fall into the hands of a pregnant writer. It is one of those works which place a yawning gap between yesterday and today...What will be the outcome of this mortal combat between two epochs I do not know, but anything rather than the existing state of affairs, say I.

Emperor and Galilean presents the clash of the pagan and Christian epochs. Christianity wins, but it is not seen by the young (or old) Ibsen as the solution. As a guideline for such positive solutions as may be worked for, there hovers the vision of a Third Kingdom. So in the modern plays of Ibsen, there is a break with the past, but it is not a liberation from the past: for that we must wait long after the fall of the final curtain. Even some final curtains that at first seem optimistic prove not to be so under further examination. *Little Eyolf* (1894) is a clear instance, and *When We Dead Awaken* (1899) a more debatable one. Ibsen had no optimism about optimists: he depicts them as weaklings (Rosmer being the classic case) who fall headlong into pessimism. And *optimism* is probably not the best word to describe the positive conviction that underlies the critical thought and negative emotion of Ibsen himself. One can only say he withstands the luxury of pessimism; shows the evils depicted to be unnecessary; and therefore entitles us to retain an irreducible minimum of hope—not of Heaven, and not for oneself alone, but for human society, for civilization.

Ibsen made tragedy modern by infusing it with his sense that society is fate. In comedy, society has always been fate; and Ibsen can also be seen as fusing the tragic and comic traditions in his own essentially tragicomic vision. But the "society" of older comedy had been as immutable as the fate of older tragedy. Shaw and Brecht followed Ibsen in presenting an evolving, historical fate, of which the theatrical form might best be expressed in some words by Chekhov: "You live badly, my friends. It is shameful to live like that." For people do not have to live like that. It need not be necessary for people to live like that.

But how will it come about that they *won't* live like that? Shaw's simplest (but by no means only) answer is that he will talk them out of it. "I write plays with the deliberate object of converting the nation to my opinion..." (Preface to *Blanco Posnet*). And Shaw was also inclined to see Ibsen as engaged in that kind of effort. As he says in the same preface: "Every one of Ibsen's plays is a deliberate act of war on society as at present constituted... [Ibsen undertook] a task of no less magnitude than changing the mind of Europe with a view of changing its morals." Brecht once said that for Shaw a man's most precious possession was his opinions, and it should be added that part of Shaw remained ever hopeful of robbing people of their most precious possession, offering them his own by way of reparation. Behind Shaw's remarks in this vein is the Victorian liberal tradition that sees culture as the final locus of free trade. Presupposed are open ears and sympathetic souls. Not presupposed are conflicts of interest along class lines or "false consciousness" as a mode of intelligently deceiving oneself. Shaw himself learned to be highly critical of this liberalism, but it played a part in putting together his own conception of a drama in which all characters can genuinely claim to have something to offer. "They are all right from their several points of view; and their points of view are, for the dramatic moment, mine also. This may puzzle the people who believe there is such a thing as an absolutely right point of view... [N]obody who agrees with them can possibly be a dramatist..." (Epistle Dedicatory to *Man and Superman*). One need not be scornful of Shaw's wish to "convert the nation." During the first half of the twentieth century the English nation was converted to many socialistic ideas, and Shaw could take some credit for this. But another conception of drama is implicit in this description of the several points of view that all embody part of the truth. Also there is hyperbole as well as humor in the idea that the whole nation was Shaw's audience. In fact, his plays were addressed to the educated bourgeoisie of all nations and were about that class, whether his characters wore tailcoat or toga, pinstripe trousers or doublet and hose. Shaw came to manhood in the century of the second great wave of philosophes, and, with the others, he helped the educated middle class to criticize itself. Ibsen had touched their guilt feelings; Shaw touched their funny bone. This is to say that Ibsen showed their complicity in crime, whereas Shaw showed incongruities, inconsistencies, and absurdities, both in the crimes and in the complicity. What comedy may lack in depth, it can make up in scope. The subject matter of Ibsen's tragic plays is forever the same. In his comedies, on the other hand, Shaw would "cover the field": war and peace, the capitalist system, education, biology, religion, metaphysics, penal law, the Irish Question, the family, the various professions (medical, martial, clerical) . . . anything and everything.

It is in the prefaces and attendant pamphlets, articles, and treatises that the field was covered in extenso. The plays did what plays do: they brought certain crucial conflicts into sharp focus. Indeed one might well say that it was in the prefaces and the like that Shaw did his best to convert a nation, whereas in the plays he provided comic relief. But it was comic relief of a highly ironical kind, because in it the subjects of the prefaces are seen, not in a simpler form, but in a form that is even more complex, being more human and concrete. The difference between preface and play has sometimes been viewed as one between the propagandist and the artist, the latter being considered "universally human." Shaw's critics are free to choose their terms, and even to invoke shibboleths. To me, however, it seems mistaken to think of the plays as any less social in their commentary than the prefaces. Surely comedy was always the principal vehicle of sociological thought until academic men had the unhappy idea that the comic sense was not necessary in this field and founded the science of sociology. In any event, Shaw's comedies bring social principles to the final test, asking what they mean in the lives of human beings. Some critics will perhaps see a claim to the "universally human"—a claim to be asocial, parasocial, metasocial—in Shaw's own statement that his plays present a conflict of free vitality with various abstract principles and impersonal institutions. Yet just as the principles and institutions are specific ones, and Shaw's satirical thrusts are directed at them, so the free vitality is seldom merely the Life Force in the abstract but is to be found in the actual life generated in a character by Shaw the comic artist.

A recurring type in Shaw's comedies is what, with apologies to Nietzsche, we may call the superman: a human who is not divided against himself but is all of a piece and lives directly and happily from the primal vital spring. Caesar, Undershaft, and Joan are examples. There are no such people in the comedies of Aristophanes or Plautus, Machiavelli or Jonson, Shakespeare or Molière. Superior people stem from the epic and tragic tradition: and so, if Ibsen can be said to have given tragedy a comic twist, Shaw can be said to have given comedy a tragic one. Yet even tragic heroes are traditionally supposed to have a flaw, whereas the Shavian superman is flawless, an Achilles invulnerable even in the heel. Perhaps only one great tragic writer regularly risked such protagonists: Corneille. And the result is that his tragedies verge upon comic effects, including some that were not intended.

Invulnerable in himself, as a dramatic creation the Shavian superman has not proved invulnerable to dramatic criticism. There are obvious dangers to the comic art in the presence, at its center, of a man who (like Undershaft) knows all the answers, especially because it is not just verbal answers that he knows but practical ones. For drama is *praxis*. The plot of *Saint Joan* is not helped by the fact that the heroine could do no wrong if she tried. That she pleads guilty at one point in the trial is only a momentary hesitation that makes her final position the more heroic. Similarly the Shavian Caesar's vanity is only the charming humanizing foible of a great man, not a flaw undermining his greatness.

But has criticism been as ready to see why Shaw created this sort of hero as it has to note the reasons why he should not have done so? Such a "why" might not be especially significant if it were explored in biographical, psychological terms, citing factors in Shaw's life that impelled him to seek flawless heroes, but it surely has much interest in relation to modern social drama. It relates to what Ernst Bloch has called *das Prinzip Hoffnung*—the principle of hope as the very foundation of the modern radical outlook, as it was of the religions and mythologies in the eras of their full vitality. And, just as the religions and mythologies had a golden age in the past that one could hope for the return of, or a heaven in the sky that was eternally there, so modern radical philosophy has a future in which this earth is a home for men.

When society is fate, a historical fate, the dialectic of drama will be found in an interplay between epochs. One sees this first, as Ibsen did, as an interplay between past and present: the theater exhibits a present into which the past ("ghosts") erupts. But, as Ibsen also knew, this is a simplification. There is a third factor: the future. And if art has a normative function—"it is always a writer's duty to make the world better" (Samuel Johnson)—the future is suffused by a definite sentiment, namely, hope. Indeed, one must perhaps say that, in the modern situation, if art is to have something positive about it, the most likely locus of the positive will be the future, for golden ages in the past have become as inconceivable as heavens in the skies. The past, far from being golden, hangs like lead around the necks of modern characters. The past is the dead weight of failure pressing upon the present and tending to kill the future. Such is the modern view of the past, personal and neurotic, social and historical. Thus, unless the modern artist is to acquiesce in a blank future, a future murdered by the past, he has to postulate and imagine a positive future: he has to work directly with his hopes; he has to build directly with such actual and vital hope as he can find within himself.

Ibsen the thinker certainly believed this. Ibsen the artist felt on firmer ground with the past and present, hence the fact that most of his plays provide a far more desolate image of life than his proclaimed philosophy. Shaw and Brecht, although they lived in a time of yet greater public catastrophes, by that very token felt themselves close to whatever positive solutions were to be found. They clearly resolved, at whatever cost to their art as art, to inject a far larger positive element into their work than Ibsen had usually done. For them, even more than for him, art was not for its own sake, but for the sake of the future. Like Ibsen's, their art would help to exorcise the ghost of the past—"let the dead bury their dead"—and help to terminate the life-in-death of the present. Less ambiguously than Ibsen's, their art would help "us dead" to "awaken."

In itself this would have been sufficient reason for them to discontinue Ibsen's investigations of neurotic weakness. If they can be meaningfully referred back to him at all, it would be to his one or two attempts at a simply positive hero, notably Dr. Stockmann in *An Enemy of the People* (1882). Such a superman was to find a place in both Shavian and Brechtian drama, though in different guises, corresponding to different nationalities and generations. Shaw's most characteristic and impressive superman is Undershaft, a radical critic of normal bourgeois procedures and shibboleths, yet himself a hero of bourgeois civilization—and a scintillating bourgeois intellectual too. If we look in the plays of Brecht for characters who are solid and all of a piece, who are always right and always do what is right, we shall find them only in the guise of the rebel as revolutionary: examples are Pavel in *The Mother* (1932) and several of the Communards in *Days of the Commune* (1949).

There are not many such supermen in Brecht or even in Shaw. Both playwrights remained Ibsenites to the extent that they dealt primarily with divided characters, if not with neurotic weakness. Pavel is a revolutionary from the outset, but the protagonist is his mother, who is not a revolutionary until near the end: meanwhile the play has shown her inner divisions. Particularly the Brecht characters who have universally been found most human and interesting—Mother Courage, Galileo, Azdak—are divided people, brave and cowardly, passive and active, good and bad. Even in Shaw, the superman did not always have to be protagonist. He could fill a character role such as that of General Burgoyne in *The Devil's Disciple* (1897) or Sergeant Meek in *Too True to Be Good* (1931).

Shaw generally placed his supermen over against men who were all too human—the typical products of a given epoch and class. In these encounters he was able to give the age-old contrast of ironist and impostor a thoroughly actual and relevant treatment. And his own divided nature preserved him from supermanic dramaturgy on the scale of Corneille: the ironist did not defeat the impostor too easily. Some plays, such as *Heartbreak House* (1919), are principally about impostors and contain no outright supermen. In some, such as *John Bull's Other Island* (1904), the emphasis is strongly on a single impostor (Broadbent). Again, a favorite Shavian device and achievement is the ironist-superman who ironically turns out not to be a superman after all, but only too human. Such are Bluntschli (*Arms and the Man*, 1894) and Tanner (*Man and Superman*, 1903). Nor is it true that a Shavian character who embodies free vitality must have superman capabilities. He may be an impotent priest such as Father Keegan (*John Bull's Other Island*), or a senile crackpot such as Captain Shotover (*Heartbreak House*).

He may be a she. Shaw was a feminist, not only after the more political and abstract fashion, but in his human and artistic instincts. He tended to identify both himself and free vitality with the External Feminine and to identify the enemy with the society-ridden male. Hence, if we are looking for the positive element, for bridges to the future, for foundations of a socialist humanism, his women are just as important as his supermen. And this can be true in the least political of his comedies. *Pygmalion* (1913), for instance, is the tale of the incubation and liberation of a woman. With Tanner and the rest, Henry Higgins is a superman *manqué*, a clever ironist who proves to be an impostor, a Pygmalion who is only a Frankenstein.

A woman is the key to a Shaw play that has been widely misunderstood. *The Doctor's Dilemma* (1906), a play that will also permit us to illustrate another fact about Shaw the social dramatist: namely, that he delights to drive his critique beyond its ostensible main point to another point that is its dialectical opposite. Sometimes the very topic is not the ostensible one but another and contrary one. So with the "dilemma" represented by the choice between saving the life of an immoral genius or that of a moral mediocrity. This dilemma itself is thoroughly immoral. Only God can rightly assume such powers of life and death. A mere man can only plunge into folly or worse. The mere man in Shaw's play chooses to believe that his hand is pushed toward sacrificing the immoral genius by a solicitude for the latter's wife, who can thus be kept ignorant of her genius's immorality and so preserve her romantic image of him. However, we the audience know that it is not solicitude but desire that is forcing the man's hand: he wants to marry the widow. The "dilemma" is a false one, and its falsity is brought home to him in dramatic action. When he meets the now-widowed lady, he finds that she has already remarried. He is amazed, because it has never occurred to him that she might have found him resistible. "Other people" are a somewhat unreal category to him, pieces on a chessboard. His error over the widow springs from the same complex as his error in setting up a false dilemma.

Would it be fair to conclude that the social drama of the medical profession became a "universally human," or at least wholly psychological, drama? No. In drama, every subject must be humanized, must be steeped, as it were, in the essence of humanity; but surely *social* and *human* are not opposites? The topic here is private enterprise in medicine. The author's view is that medicine should be socialized. He is discreet enough not to state this view in the play. His play will show—in the flesh, as it were—private medicine as it exists. At one pole there are the more obvious impostors, the outright fools, who are lined up at the outset. The doctor-dramatist James Bridie complained that they are *too* foolish (in *Shaw at 90*, edited by S. Winsten [London, 1946]), but then Shaw exhibits the less foolish kind of impostor in the protagonist, the man of the dilemma, Sir Colenso Ridgeon, a superman who, like Tanner and Higgins, is not a superman at all.

Sir Colenso is less of a superman than he supposes, but Jennifer Dubedat (the widow) is more fully human than she has seemed. She does not really need an inspiring, mendacious image to live by, after all; nor can she consent to be a marionette on Ridgeon's string. In counting on his idea of the inevitable female reaction, Ridgeon leaves out of account the woman, the human being. And so the parable remains political. Medicine should be socialized to free us from the caprices and fantasies of the Ridgeons, and all the more so if they can disguise their self-centered wishful thinking as objectivity and generosity. Second proposition: there exists a counterforce to Ridgeonism, namely, free vitality, that is sometimes (and not at all accidentally) embodied in women. Paradox: precisely where Ridgeon looked for compliance as the feminine contribution, he met with resistance and indeed with his comeuppance.

The social drama, as practiced by nongeniuses such as Brieux, ran into fatal clichés. That Shaw just did not notice the limitations of Brieux is an index of his missionary zeal and of the strength of his commitment to a social criterion in drama. "Incomparably the greatest writer France has produced since Molière" (as Shaw calls him in the Preface to *Three Plays by Brieux,* 1909), Brieux was the kind of playwright that the propagandist-in-a-hurry in Shaw could not help envying, yet some deep intuition as to where his own calling lay prevented the envy from growing into emulation. Let those who once considered that Brieux rather than Shaw really came to grips with social problems take note that today Brieux cannot be seen as coming to grips with anything, whereas the playful Shaw must be seen to have tackled, in play as well as preface, the main problems of the era.

"We are coming fast," Shaw wrote in one of his 1896 theater reviews, "to a melodramatic formula in which the villain shall be a bad employer and the hero a Socialist." In his first and third plays, completed in the early 1890s, he had provided a socialist critique of capitalism without recourse to this formula. In the first, *Widowers'*

Houses, it was as if he set out to make the bad employer his hero and the rebel against capitalism his villain. Yet that, though it "sounds like Shaw," is not exactly it, either. The capitalist Sartorius is a scoundrel who knows he is a scoundrel, whereas his adversary Trench is an exploiter who thinks he is outside the whole process of exploitation. Comedy has always been less inclined to scowl at iniquity than to laugh at a lack of self-knowledge, and so it is in this comedy of nineteenth-century capitalism, as in all the rest of its author's work.

Shaw's third play, *Mrs. Warren's Profession* (1894), is founded on an innocent girl's discovery that her mother is a procuress and ex-whore. This would make mother a villainess and daughter a hero-ine if melodrama were true to life, but actually—and comedy has as its yardstick the actuality of society, of life as people live it—in-nocence is not of itself heroic, nor is membership in an antisocial profession (and for Shaw all professions are conspiracies against the public) an act of personal iniquity. If Mrs. Warren has a sin, it consists only in a belief she shares with most of mankind, namely, that you can't buck the system: if you can't lick 'em, you join 'em, and she has joined 'em. In the end, her daughter, for her part, re-ally *is* a heroine, to the extent that she is trying to buck the system: she has taken that first step, which nowadays would be called "dropping out." But she has also ceased to regard her mother as a villainess or herself as more wronged than others who are living on tainted money. For what money is *not* tainted? Under capital-ism, you can either (as worker) have your earnings stolen or (as capitalist) do the stealing and live on the proceeds.

These two early plays are socialist not only in implying that so-cialism would be the remedy but also in their rendering of the *comédie humaine* generally. Just as the ultimate source of trouble in *Ghosts* and *Hedda Gabler* is both social and unnecessary, so the ultimate source of trouble in *Widowers' Houses* and *Mrs. Warren's Profession* is social and unnecessary. When the Mrs. Alvings are truly liberated, when the Heddas don't give a damn about scandal, life will be different. When there are no landlords to exploit slum-dwellers, when there are no white-slavers to buy and sell sex, life can be better. Meanwhile it is ridiculous to condemn the individual landlord, pimp, or whore: ridiculous, deserving of ridicule, a proper object of laughter, a proper subject for comedy. What is needed, then, for the comic play on these themes is the plausible capitalist, the worshipper of the god of Things As They Are, and, opposing him, the idealistic rebel against capitalism who does not even know that the stocks and shares he lives off are investments in the same shabby business as the landlord he denounces. Or a procuress and ex-whore who is a very honest, agreeable, intelligent woman utterly devoted to a daughter who, well brought up as she is, will undergo a trauma when she finds out what money she has been well brought up on...

The two plays present capitalism in miniature, and in this they could be regarded as models for Brecht's *Threepenny Opera* (1928) and *The Rise and Fall of the City of Mahagonny* (1930). The perspective of all four comedies is suggested in some lines of Simon O. Lesser:

> The attitude of most comedies is that of an urbane and tolerant friend, amused rather than censorious about that blonde he saw us out with the night before... Other comedies are caustic and the reverse of indulgent, but they suggest a scale of values against which the shortcomings and misdeeds of the characters seem trivial... [G]ranted that the little people [this kind of comedy] set before us are far from admirable, they, and by inference we ourselves, are no worse than anyone else.[7]

Shaw called the two types here adumbrated *Plays: Pleasant and Unpleasant,* a phrase that he used as the title for all his early plays (1892 to 1898). The "unpleasant" play—exemplified by *Widowers' Houses* and *Mrs. Warren's Profession*—was certainly a precision tool in social criticism, a dialectical tool for which their author has scarcely yet received due credit. You can smile all evening at the amusing crimes of Sartorius and Mrs. Warren; but if, on your way home, you realize that the whole social order is run in this way, you smile on the other side of your face.

Shaw, for his part, seems to have found the "unpleasant" mode constricting. Like Swift, he "served human liberty," and the schematic early plays afforded his enterprise far too little elbow room. They had, for example, no room for his supermen and, although they had room for rebellious women such as Blanche Sartorius and Vivie Warren, they kept the rebellion within too narrow bounds. Even the impostors were miniatures compared with those to follow. Shaw once spoke of the need a dramatist has to let his characters rip. That is what he was not able to do in the earliest plays; the mold in which the plays were cast seemed to forbid it. There is far more freedom later, in two respects: first, there is the growing freedom of the playwright as he learns his craft and gives his genius its head; second, characters are placed in situations in which *they* have freedom in its ultimate form—real freedom of choice on crucial issues. Both kinds of freedom had been lacking in *Widowers' Houses*. Not only had the journeyman playwright acquired no kind of ease or daring in handling the structure, but inside the box of his plot, and in the box (with one side missing) of the Victorian stage-scene, he presented a version of humanity hemmed in by the capitalist system. It was cutting, even devastating, writing, but no wind of freedom blew from that stage to that audience. One thing needed was that characters should not just be worked upon by circumstances, but should themselves work on the circumstances. History, by all means, can determine their mode of existence; but they in turn must work upon history.

Saint Joan (1923) could not have been written by the Shaw of the early 1890s. He would not have known how to let Joan rip. In this play we breathe the air of human freedom, and again this is both an artistic, technical matter and a matter of the outlook defined by the art and the technique. The closed, boxlike form of the nineteenth-century well-made play was progressively abandoned by Shaw. As a chronicle, *Saint Joan* is rather compact, but that it *is* a chronicle at all means open windows, fresh air, amplitude.

Half a dozen years after the première of *Saint Joan,* Bertolt Brecht wrote *Happy End,*[8] which a couple of years later had grown into *Saint Joan of the Stockyards.* It can serve here as a cue for continued analysis of *Saint Joan* itself and for an exploration of the difference between Shaw and Brecht. The relation between the two drama-tists was never closer than here, because *Saint Joan of the Stockyards* owes much, not only to *Saint Joan,* but also to *Major Barbara.*

As usual with Brecht, one can begin with surprise at how much he saw fit to borrow. "A Salvation Army officer forsaken by God" could be considered the central image of *Major Barbara,* and Brecht appropriated it. That the officer is a girl, with all that femininity connotes of delicacy in feeling and ardor in aspiration, is not lost on Brecht, either. And the general reason for the loss of God is the same in both authors: the dependence of the otherworldly institu-tion upon a capitalistic world. However, although both authors rely upon a materialist analysis of the Salvation Army, they approach the subject from opposite ends. Shaw shows that the teetotalism of the Army, being promoted by brewers' money, is compromised at the start: the "idealism" of an Army officer has to be either ignorant or corrupt. Realizing this, Major Barbara feels drained, devastated, abandoned by her God. She will remain in this state of mind and heart until a niche is found for her within the existing social order. The finding of such a niche is the psychospiritual solution to what Shaw has ironically portrayed as a psychospiritual problem. Brecht, on the other hand, is little concerned with the usefulness of capital-ism to the Salvation Army. He is concerned with the usefulness of the Salvation Army to capitalism. If his Joan, too, suffers a psycho-spiritual crisis (and she does, though the phrase itself begins to let us down in a Brechtian context) it is from the sensation, not of being deserted, but of being cheated. God has not gone: he was never there. Joan discovers not a void of unbelief, but an active atheism that offers an alternative to deity in the idea of Man On His Own—man's fate is man himself. It is at this point that one can imagine the playwright Brecht asking whether, if one Shaw play wouldn't do his job for him, another might serve the purpose. Although *Saint Joan of the Stockyards* is mostly a *Major Barbara,* ultimately it is indeed a *Saint Joan:* for Barbara turns into Joan when Brecht's protagonist moves from false to true consciousness and from passivity disguised as action to action that is positive and revolutionary.

Brecht probably noted what most of Shaw's critics have missed: that Shaw himself goes part of the way toward making Joan a revolutionary leader whose final support comes from the people. She is his only nonbourgeois superman (even his Caesar is bourgeois in spirit, as is his super-king Magnus), and this fact yields much more broadly conceived political drama than Shaw was wont to attempt. In the great scene that is the turning point of the story, Joan stands forth as the patron saint of all future National Liberation Fronts:

> Common folks understand . . . they follow me half naked
> into the moat and up the ladder and over the wall . . . You
> locked the gates to keep me in; and it was the townsfolk
> and the common people that followed me, and forced the
> gate . . . I will go out now to the common people, and let
> the love in their eyes comfort me for the hate in yours. You
> will all be glad to see me burnt; but if I go through the
> fire, I shall go through it to their hearts for ever and ever.

Unlike Shaw's Major Barbara, Brecht's Joan Dark has, in the Communist Party, an alternative to both the Salvation Army and big business. However, she is not permitted a true martyrdom, like Shaw's Joan, but only a fake one: her death is a "setup," and so she remains in death what she has been in life: a victim. The politics of *Saint Joan* and *Saint Joan of the Stockyards* are thus revealed, in their respective endings, to be diametrically opposite.

Shaw calls for a democracy of supermen that shall be worthy of his democratic superwoman. Brecht appeals for solidarity among those people (the working class, the victims) by whom the myths of sainthood will be shattered along with the social order that the myths serve to flatter and conceal.

In nothing is the difference between Shaw and Brecht more marked than in their presentation of the capitalist villain. Both authors are at the top of their form: Undershaft is one of Shaw's most telling stage creations, and Pierpont Mauler is one of Brecht's. Underlying both creations is the Marxist principle that the individual capitalist is not to be equated with the system. To Shaw, this means that whereas the system may be rationally flimsy and morally outrageous, the individual capitalist may be rational, plausible, intelligent, and charming. To Brecht, it means that, although the system may be omnipotent and devoid of conscience, the individual capitalist may well have a sense of guilt but that, sensing also his own powerlessness, he will hold on to his position, anyway, seeing no alternative:

> Just think, if I—who have much against [the system], and
> sleep badly—were to desert it, I would be like a fly ceas-
> ing to hold back a landslide.

Thus Mauler in *Saint Joan of the Stockyards* (scene 8). Therefore, although he does not feel sorry for mankind, because "mankind is evil," he is distinctly sorry for himself as the presumably nonevil exception. He pities himself as he pities slaughtered cattle: both are true victims. The alleged victims—members of the working class—are just those who, being bad, meet with a bad fate.

One could elaborate indefinitely the different schemata behind Undershaft and Mauler respectively. The artistic result is two characters who stand at opposite poles of comedy. Undershaft is a maker of comedy—of amusing speeches and of dramas that will have a chilling comedic effect to begin with and a happy ending later. He is an entertainer, entertaining his workers in a model factory, entertaining Shaw's spectators whenever he comes onstage. Even in his family's home, he is the Father As Entertainer. If Undershaft represents comedy as the highest possible degree of *charm,* Mauler's effect is so close to the opposite pole of *nausea* that some will want to deny him the epithet "comic" altogether. What also may strike some people as uncomic is that he is so emotional; whereas Undershaft is cool, keeping his head in every crisis, Mauler loses his head throughout, suffering vociferously—the aggrieved victim of a social system in crisis. And what a system! Brecht reported that when he first studied capitalist economics, his reaction was not, "How unjust!" but, "It will never work!" To the extent that it did work, it kept its helpers and servers at fever pitch watching the fluctuations of the market. Thus the Pierpont Maulers experience the extreme tensions of the roulette player.

If we think such painful tensions out of place in comedy, we are forgetting the sufferings of, say, Jonson's Morose or Molière's Harpagon. But comedy, to use Brecht's word, *alienates* the emotions so that we feel no sympathy. And alienating the emotions so that we feel no sympathy, comedy is the exactly correct vehicle of this author's intention and philosophy. We are to recoil from Mauler and his colleagues in horror and disgust, and we do so because they are made ridiculous, that is, because they are seen through the eyes of comedy. Thus, to those who would assume that comedy might somehow make such figures pleasant and therefore acceptable, there would be several answers. One is: no, this is "unpleasant" comedy. A second is: no, the danger would lie in the more direct portrayal of gangsters as villains, whereby their villainy, conveying emotional intensity, gains a fascination by no means reduced in being called *evil* fascination. One could see a Hollywood movie of that era, such as *Scarface,* and draw the conclusion: "Scarface's life was good while it lasted. And how can one be upset by a premature death in a society that offers such empty living? Better to live dangerously. Gangsterism has glamour." Conclusions of this sort can be blocked by such "alienation" of the action as we see in Brecht's gangster play *The Resistible Rise of Arturo Ui* (1941) or in *Saint Joan of the Stockyards.*

In Andrew Undershaft and Pierpont Mauler we find our socialist playwrights equally determined to remove a mote from the public's eye—but not the same mote. For Shaw, the target is the audience who will exonerate the system by characterizing the businessman as bad. For Brecht, the target is the audience who will exonerate the system by characterizing the businessman as *human.* Shaw is portraying a businessman who is not merely human but *super*human. Brecht is portraying one whom the folklore of capitalism will see as a superman (man of distinction, VIP, member of the power elite) but who is actually subhuman, a worm. The difference, here, between Shaw and Brecht reflects the passage of time between the writing of *Major Barbara* and the writing of *Saint Joan of the Stockyards,* yet not so much the steady ticking of the clock as the gigantic happening of World War I, a dual happening that consisted of the destruction of one world and the boldest attempt since the French Revolution to bring a new world into existence. Although he is an orphan and a rebel, Undershaft still very much belongs to the Victorian salons he despises. There still *exists* a world of salons in which his brilliant repartee is not really unwelcome. Mauler, on the other hand, is truly homeless, has nowhere nice to go, is trapped between the stock exchange and the stockyards. Whatever Undershaft's objections to the upper-class London of his wife and son, he actually enhances its claims on our respect by adding to the formal elegance of its furniture, dress, and accent his own elegance of word and thought. He is its crowning adornment; so that, from the vantage point of the 1970s, although we may cry, "Obsolete!" we cannot restrain a sigh of longing for the snows of yesteryear. But Mauler's world has no more aesthetic appeal than the slums where his class-enemies live. Like the slums, it is ugly, nasty, stifling, and macabre—a kind of Inferno.

Saint Joan of the Stockyards is not just a play that happens to be different in kind from *Major Barbara* because time has passed, nor even because in that time a war and a revolution occurred. It also reflects deliberate conclusions on the subject of social theater that Brecht reached during the 1920s. That was the decade in which he put together his theory of an Epic Theater—*epic* in the sense of *narrative*, as opposed to lyric or dramatic. Richard Wagner had perfected a *lyric* theater, and in this had been echoed even by poets who did not need music, from Yeats to Maeterlinck. Ibsen had perfected the modern "dramatic" theater: *dramatic* in the classic, Sophoclean-Racinian tradition, with its unity of time, place, and action; *modern* in its psychological, indeed psychoanalytical, emphasis. Brecht's scheme of things began with the rejection of Wagnerism and Ibsenism. As for Shavianism, he would not so much reject it as develop it—to an extent that would have made it unrecognizable to Shaw.

The essence of Shavianism in dramaturgy was the assumption that the modern world could best be placed onstage in the form of serious parody—a double form of parody, as it turned out, because Shaw consistently parodied both the behavior of men and the patterns of dramatic art. In his mind, the two were so closely related as to be at essential points identical:

> The truth is that dramatic invention is the first effort of man to become intellectually conscious. No frontier can be marked between drama and history or religion, or between acting and conduct.[9]

Just as Marx proposed to stand Hegel on his feet, so Shaw proposed to stand all the nineteenth century's idealisms on their feet. Hence, notably, his subjection of melodrama, in theater or in life, to the test of reality. For such purposes, already in the 1890s, he was demanding a nonillusionistic stage:

> For him [William Archer] there is illusion in the theatre: for me there is none ... To me the play is only the means, the end being the expression of feeling by the arts of the

actor, the poet, the musician. Anything that makes this expression more vivid, whether it be versification, or an orchestra, or a deliberately artificial delivery of the lines, is so much to the good for me, even though it may destroy all the verisimilitude of the scene.[10]

Now what has just been called the essence of Shavianism was never challenged by Brecht. On the contrary, his plays, like Shaw's, are to a very large extent parodies both of conventional plays and of conventional behavior. In the passage just quoted, Brecht would no doubt have been dissatisfied with the phrase "expression of feeling," but at the same time he would have enthusiastically accepted Shaw's invitation to a nonillusionistic theater in which "versification, or an orchestra, or a deliberately artificial delivery" would not be out of place.

Perhaps the most damaging thing ever said about Shavian theater was Egon Friedell's remark to the effect that Shaw's message was like a pill that he had covered with the sugar of entertainment, and the nice thing was that you could suck off the sugar and put the pill back on the plate. Seeing how much truth there was to this, Brecht resolved to write "Shavian" comedies that could not be disposed of in this way. Such are the theory and practice known as Epic Theater. Brecht once said his efforts could all be summed up as an attempt to restate in theatrical terms the famous thesis of Marx: "The philosophers have only *interpreted* the world in various ways: the point, however, is to *change* it." Shaw had of course wanted exactly the same thing but (as the young Brecht would see it) had been too nice to his audience, who took from his plays merely what they wished to take. The early theoretical work of Brecht is taken up with a condemnation of "culinary" theater—theater in which you just enjoy eating, as in a restaurant. It seemed to him almost as if the guests in the modern theater-restaurant swallowed all their food without chewing it. Perhaps the answer was to serve them crunchy solids instead of smooth fluids? Certainly one must not, as Wagner had done, melt down the whole meal into a single smooth liquid, but, rather, break it up into dishes of various and contrasting kinds.

Brecht was aware of a cultural situation that was being discussed in his time and has been discussed since, particularly by writers of German background, from Herbert Marcuse to Hannah Arendt. Modern bourgeois civilization—to use the food metaphor in another way—*devours* everything, good or bad. It not only pours forth musical rubbish in the elevator or supermarket in the form of Muzak: it is equally capable of serving up the "Ode to Joy" from Beethoven's Ninth Symphony in a radio or television commercial and at the same time claiming to be spreading "culture" around. Against this kind of exploitation the music of Beethoven is as helpless as the young Mrs. Warren before the white-slaver or a coolie before a colonialist. Being dead, Beethoven can do little about it; but what of the living artist?

Brecht's answer was that he can make his art less fluid and saccharine by means of crunchy and pungent ingredients known as alienation devices. The German for alien is *fremd*. Marx had seen the worker under capitalism as *entfremdet* (alienated). Brecht proposed actually to make alien (*verfremden*) the familiar elements of the theater experience. A paradox, yes, because alienation is the problem and the antagonist, and communism will mark the end of alienation. But communism is a good way off, even in socialist countries. Meanwhile the artist can resist being consumed, can help to prevent the whole inherited culture from being trapped between the Leviathan's jaws and gobbled up. Brecht's theater is an attempt at a different kind of communication. The result would inevitably be that some would not receive any message at all; but those who did receive one would know that they had. It would not be lost in the fine print. It would stand out. It would command attention, and perhaps even incite to action.

It was with such ends in view that Brecht discarded so many of the treasured devices of traditional theater. The lighting was to be plain white and diffused over the whole stage. In this way the cult of *Stimmung* (mood) would be countered. To the same end, illusionistic scenery must go, for the paradox of scenery that "looked like the real thing" was that it induced dream states in the audience. What was needed, instead of a hypnotic trance, was alertness. Actors would have to change their ways. Instead of attempting a hallucination of unrealities suddenly present ("I am Dracula"), they must exhibit realities that can be recognized as such and have thus belonged to our past ("This was a man"). Instead of the Stanislavsky actor who spoke in the first person and the present tense and absorbed all stage directions into a living illusion of the actual thing, Brecht proposed an Epic actor who seemed to be using the third person and the past tense; as for the stage directions, they could be read aloud, at least as an exercise.

This is not the place to itemize every feature of Brechtian theater, either in its early (Epic) phase or in the final phase, when Brecht was beginning to substitute the term Dialectical Theater. Too much theory would be misleading, at least if accompanied by too few looks at the practice. One must take care, as was suggested above, not to assume that Brecht's theories correspond exactly and in all ways to his practices. Even if they did, practice is no more deducible from theory than the beauty of a landscape is deducible from a map. Just as the Ibsenite drama could never be deduced from existing notions of social theater, and Shavian comedy could never be deduced from free-floating notions such as discussion plays and propaganda, nor yet from Shaw's own prefaces, so Brecht's achievement as a playwright, even as a social playwright, could not be deduced from theoretical writings, even his own. On the contrary, it is possible to make bad mistakes about the plays by assuming that they conform exactly to what the theories prescribe.

Whenever active artistry is at work, many concrete elements come into play that escape the net of general ideas. You may read in Ibsen's workbooks that "marriage for external reasons ... brings a nemesis upon the offspring," and this idea is obviously in *Ghosts:*

yet it neither makes *Ghosts* a good play nor gives it its particular tone, style, and character, its mode of being. This latter stems (if the source can be isolated in a single phrase) from Ibsen's *ironical use* of the idea and of all his other materials. So, too, with Shaw: many of the ideas of, say, *The Intelligent Woman's Guide to Socialism* (1928) are also found in the plays, sometimes in similar phrasing, but they neither constitute the merit of the plays nor give them their life as theater, as art. *A dramatic context ironizes:* and to say "dramatic irony" is often a little like saying "dramatic drama." A Shavian dramatic context sometimes ironizes to the point of conflict with the presumably intended idea. Thus it is not clear whether Shaw solved all his problems in the final act of *Major Barbara.* One may feel that Undershaft is so strong a character that an intended balance is upset and a desired synthesis is missed.

One would like to turn the attention of critics exercised by Shaw's opinions to something far more pervasive in his work than any particular opinion, and far more likely to endear him to some, while deterring others: namely, his habit of teasing. His opinions come from here, there, and everywhere, but his teasing tone is, somehow, his very self: it is present throughout his plays and his other writings. Shall we ask what his various avowals signify and not ask what this central fact about him signifies? That would be like being seduced and not asking who seduced us.

Teasing is a complex phenomenon, but it is easy to see at least two ingredients as it applies to Shaw: humorous acceptance of failure to persuade, and a degree of aggression toward the unpersuaded. On the few occasions when Shaw did not tease, he expressed complete exasperation. Teasing may be regarded as indicating either a disguised acceptance of defeat or a good-natured refusal to accept it, and it is not surprising that some have seen Shaw's humor as just another weapon of an optimistic fighter, while others have found in it a tacit admission of both defeat and defeatism. But these are not the only possible explanations. It is also possible for a man to be thinking "*Even if* we fail, *even if* we are mistaken..."

When Tolstoy expressed disapproval of Shaw's humorous approach to religion, Shaw replied: "Suppose the world were only one of God's jokes, would you work any the less to make it a good joke instead of a bad one?" That a man allows for failure does not mean that he thinks it is inevitable; and both Shaw's teasing and his humor in general serve to communicate neither optimism nor pessimism, but rather to *ironize* whatever topic *arises,* and so serve to make the thought dialectical and the form dramatic. The pessimist can surely find in much of the teasing an admission of difficulty—of possible impossibility. The optimist can congratulate the teaser on his admirable poise, the confident way in which he gets on top of his subject, but the shrewd psychologist will want to stress that, by teasing, Shaw ensures that he is always in an active relation to his audience: whenever he is not pushing, he is pulling. To be sure, what those who reject Shavian theater reject it for is commonly what those who relish it relish it for. Here is an author who "never lets you alone." You are either stimulated and delighted or provoked and disconcerted.

Such is the concrete Shaw, as opposed to the ideological Shaw. Of Brecht, it has been said that, although his views were Communist, his concrete existence contradicted those views. Even if this formulation is correct, it need not be taken to be as damaging (either to Brecht or to communism) as has been assumed. Some tension between existence and idea is surely inevitable. No Christian is merely an embodiment of Christianity. If such a person existed, he would not, in any case, turn out to be a Christian *artist.* Always more concrete than theory, art must give a different account of the world, unless by sheer lack of merit (as with Brieux) it fails to be art. To the political artist, art presents a particular opportunity, which is not—as is commonly thought—simply to restate his political views and thus to extend the political battle to another front, but, instead, *to test abstract principles in concrete situations,* to show what politics means in the lives of people. Contradictions enter the picture automatically: because the concretely human is the writer's special field, when he brings it into play, it brings with it the con-tradictoriness of people. Bertolt Brecht was a contradictory man, so is the present writer, and so are you, dear reader. Why not, also, Brecht's Galileo?

> ...ich bin kein ausgeklügelt Buch,
> Ich bin ein Mensch mit seinem Widerspruch.[11]

> ...I am no wiredrawn book,
> I am a human being with his contradiction.

It should, therefore, come as no surprise that the socialist hu-manism of Brecht is more adequately rendered in a many-sided and problematic work such as *The Caucasian Chalk Circle* (1945) than in the more explicit presentations, closer to Marx and Lenin, such as *The Mother* or *Days of the Commune*. Again the author's sense of humor—and specifically his ironizing of everything—is our best clue. When, as in the two plays just mentioned, Brecht writes of class-comrades, he abandons this irony—understandably, to be sure, as it was likely to turn against them. Yet it was evidently hard to find anything to take its place: a friendly attitude, however commendable morally and politically, has no particular aesthetic merit, no energy as art. Another author might perhaps have found another solution. Brecht the artist, like Shaw the artist, cannot be severed from his sense of humor. By his lyric gift, eked out by Hanns Eisler's musical genius, Brecht was able to raise both *The Mother* and *Days of the Commune* well above the common level of political theater, but to see what he can really do—even when he is writing about socialism itself—one must turn to works that have been steeped in his irony.

Ernst Bloch[12] has written that, in the work of all the great poets and philosophers, there is a window that opens upon Utopia. One might add that sometimes (as in Shaw's *Back to Methuselah*, 1921) it is open too wide. What is engaging about *The Caucasian Chalk*

Circle is the irony in the Utopianism, particularly in the wake of a prologue that presents the Soviet Union as much closer to Utopia than it actually was. In this play, Brecht used the idea of the Lord of Misrule, who for a brief interregnum turns the existing society and its values upside down. If the existing society is an antihuman one, this would mean substituting a genuine humanism. To be human for a day: that is the formula. There is a catch in it. What we are likely to get is a flat, unbelievable virtuousness. Brecht does not give us this, arguing that if the whole society was monstrous, then even the misrule would be grotesque: in its origin a fluke, it is by nature a freak. The fact that by definition it will have no future affects its character: it is only a truancy, not a liberation. All of this would have remained so much theorizing, except that Brecht was able to write the poetry and the comedy, the narrative and the character, by which the word became flesh—by which the Lord of Misrule became *ein Mensch mit seinem Widerspruch* (a human being with his contradiction): Azdak, the disenchanted philosopher as quasi-revolutionary activist.

Does the irony undercut the author's activism? As with Shaw, there will be those who think that it does, with the justification that, as they read or see the play, they find themselves responding more fully to the despair than to the hope; and it is always likely, a priori, that despair will outweigh hope in a work of art, because despair is an established fact that tends to pervade the past and the present, whereas hope tends to be just a project, located as it is, in that frail, as yet merely imagined, spot, the future. But it seems to me that Brecht has linked despair and hope in lively dialectical interplay; and that although there are many moments when despair predominates, hope remains at the end: which is all that hope need do. It need not bring in the kingdom. It need only survive. The question is whether the good society is felt, nostalgically, to be in the past (that is, to be over), or whether it is felt, hopefully, to be in the future (that is, in the making), felt to be a possibility and "up to us," something we can work on, a matter of praxis. The old notion of the golden age has little meaning in *The Caucasian Chalk Circle* until it is inverted. We, the audience, return to the golden age when we see Azdak inverting our rules and laws. In thought, Azdak returns to a golden age when he nostalgically recalls the popular revolt of a former generation. On the other hand, the age of Azdak is no golden age, but an age of war and oppression in which, by a fluke, a little justice may be done. That, for Azdak himself, revolutions are identified with the past, is what is wrong with him. The era of Azdak itself has the transitory character of the Saturnalia, in which, after the brief interregnum, a Mock King goes back into anonymity, but the important prologue suggests a *regnum* that is not *inter*. The ultimate ironic inversion (among many in the play) is that a golden age should be envisaged not in Arcadia but in the state of Georgia. In this way, what is planted in the minds of at least a sympathetic audience is not a memory, a fantasy, or a dream, but a possibility. That this should be open to doubt, and that certain audiences can respond differently, is a tribute to the dialectical complexity of the piece, the subtlety of Brecht's method.

"What is a modern problem play but a clinical lecture on society?" Bernard Shaw asked in 1901.[13] If the works of Ibsen, Shaw, and Brecht may fairly be described as modern problem plays, then our answer must be that they are much else besides clinical lectures on society. They are tragedies, or comedies, or tragicomedies of so special a kind that only close analysis can reveal their peculiarity, let alone their merit. They are dramatic art, and they are dramatic art in motion: we see the "problem play" developing from one Ibsen play to another, from one Shaw play to another, from one Brecht play to another. There is also development from one *author* to another. And because people are individuals and unique, geniuses (if an Irishism may be permitted) are even more individual and unique. The problem play, ultimately, was what Ibsen or Shaw or Brecht made of it; yet there is reason to say that it remained the problem play. Although it has been my aim in this essay to suggest that far more art and artifice went into this form of play than has sometimes been assumed, it has equally been my aim to demonstrate that the social drama was indeed social, from *Ghosts* and *Hedda Gabler* to *Widowers' Houses* and *Mrs. Warren's Profession,* and from *Major Barbara* and *Saint Joan* to *Saint Joan of the Stockyards* and *The Caucasian Chalk Circle.*

References

1. Sebastian Mercier, *Du théâtre* (1773), as cited in Romain Rolland, *The People's Theater,* trans. Barrett H. Clark.

2. Alexis de Tocqueville, *Democracy in America,* Part II (1840).

3. Georg Lukács, *The Sociology of Modern Drama* (Budapest, 1909).

4. Inaugural Lecture, Copenhagen (1871).

5. Bertolt Brecht, *On Experimental Theater* (Stockholm, 1939).

6. Bertolt Brecht, *Notes to "The Mother"* (1933), trans. Lee Baxandall (New York, 1965).

7. *Fiction and the Unconscious* (1960).

8. Actually, he disowned the play. The title page carries the name Dorothy Lane. Some have said it was written by Elisabeth Hauptmann. Yet the present author's attribution seems also very plausible.

9. Bernard Shaw, Preface to the Pleasant Plays, in *Plays: Pleasant and Unpleasant* (1898).

10. Bernard Shaw, in *The Saturday Review* (April 13, 1895).

11. C. F. Meyer, *Huttens letzte Tage* (1871).

12. In the following three paragraphs, I am drawing on the article "The Caucasian Chalk Circle (II)" beginning on page 195.

13. Bernard Shaw, "Who I Am and What I Think," *The Candid Friend* (London, May 1901).

Brecht, Bertolt (1898-1956)
1969

*During the sixties, I wrote the Brecht entry in several encyclopedias,
notably,* The American People's Encyclopedia *(Grolier, 1964),* Col-
lier's Encyclopedia *(Crowell-Collier, 1968), and* The Encyclopedia
Americana *(1966, 1969). All the material is subsumed in the much
longer entry I wrote for my old friend John Gassner, who prepared most
of* Reader's Encyclopedia of World Drama *(Crowell, 1969) before his
untimely death; the book was completed after that by Edward Quinn.
IF ANYONE IS READING THIS BOOK AS AN INTRODUCTION TO
BRECHT, IT WOULD BE WELL FOR HIM OR HER TO BEGIN WITH
THIS ITEM. The same goes for browsers in bookstores and libraries.*

GERMAN POET, THEORIST, STAGE director, playwright, Bertolt
Brecht was born on February 10, 1898, the son of a Protestant
father (Berthold Brecht) and a Catholic mother (née Sophie Brez-
ing) at Auf dem Rain 7, Augsburg, Bavaria. He was christened
Eugen Berthold Friedrich. Berthold Sr. worked at the Heindel
paper factory in Augsburg and was eventually to be its managing
director. Both parents hailed from Achern in the Black Forest.
1904 to 1908: Volksschule. 1908 to 1917: Realgymnasium. The author's own account appears in a letter to the critic Herbert Ihering:

Elementary school bored me for four years. During nine
years of being lulled to sleep at the Augsburg Realgymnasium I didn't manage to be very much help to my teachers.

But by 1913 he was a published writer of remarkable accomplishment, as both prose and verse printed in the school paper *Die Ernte*
(*The Harvest*) attest. His first play, *The Bible*, appeared there in January 1914. In this year, Brecht came before a general public, starting to publish in the *Augsburger Neueste Nachrichten*. Some of the
Brecht items in this paper are nationalistic. The young poet steps
forth as the patriot of Kaiser Wilhelm's war. Yet at least one commentator has questioned the sincerity of the nationalism, in view
of poems stating other attitudes and in view of the greater sophis-
tication of the standpoint in items written earlier. By 1916, certainly,
the profile of the Brecht the world knows is clearly seen in such a
poem as "The Song of the Fort Donald Railroad Gang," as remarkable a work as any eighteen-year-old, except Rimbaud, has ever
been known to write.

Graduating from high school in 1917, Brecht continued to live
at home (Bleichstrasse 2, Augsburg) while beginning to study medicine in nearby Munich. He was even able to stay in Augsburg when
inducted into the army in 1918, his service being limited to the duties of a medical orderly in the local barracks. (The story that he
acted as a surgeon and actually amputated limbs is a legend created
by Brecht himself). His famous poem "Legend of the Dead Soldier" dates from this period: it was to be the only work of his cited
by the Nazis as their reason for depriving him of German citizenship in 1935. 1918 was also the year he wrote his first mature play,
Baal. It was too indecent to find any immediate producer. Brecht's
father offered to pay for it to be printed but only on a condition his
son did not accept: that the family name not appear in the volume.

Though peace had come to the world, 1919 was a year of the
greatest storm and stress for Germany and for Bertolt Brecht. It

was in this year that he had his first taste of politics, and his only direct contact with revolution, the unsuccessful revolution that his native Bavaria underwent. He belonged for a time to the Augsburg Soldiers' Soviet and to the Independent Social Democratic Party. That bitter disenchantment followed is indicated in the play that grew out of this chapter in his life, *Drums in the Night*, as also in the poem "Ballad of the Red Army Soldier" (the "Red Army" of this work being almost certainly the Bavarian, not the Russian one). This was also the time of a love affair with a girl called Bie Banholzer, who bore him a son. (He was named Frank, after Wedekind, but was later consigned to an orphanage and was finally killed on the Russian front in World War II.) 1919 was an *annus mirabilis* for Bertolt Brecht the poet. Though not all the products of his pen from this time have survived, many of the poems published later in *Manual of Piety* were written then.

In 1920 Brecht's mother died. His poem on the event expresses heartbreak in a remarkably direct way. It was at this point that he moved from Augsburg to Munich (Akademiestrasse 15). The Munich years were marked by a close friendship with the playwright Arnolt Bronnen (later a Nazi, later still a Communist sympathizer); by marriage to Marianne Zoff, daughter of a Munich theater man; and by the birth of Brecht's first legitimate child, Hanne (today the actress Hanne Hiob, an occasional guest artist with the Berlin Ensemble). In these years, too, Brecht not only wrote plays but had them produced. Here the principal event was the production of *Drums in the Night* at the Munich Kammerspiele in 1922, which led to Brecht's being awarded a national prize (the Kleist Prize) through the influence of the critic Herbert Ihering. The first productions of *Jungle of Cities* (also called *In the Swamp*) in 1923, and of *Edward II* in 1924, were less successful with the public and the critics but equally important for the young playwright.

In 1924 Brecht settled in Berlin (Spichernstrasse 19). His first marriage fell apart, and in 1926 Brecht had a son (Stefan) by the actress Helene Weigel, whom he married two years later and stayed married to for the rest of his life. It was in this period that Brecht found his way to the kind of drama he intended to create, the play *A Man's a Man* making the decisive breakthrough from his early manner (lyric, balladesque, expressionistic) to what he was to call Epic Theater (narrative, objective, political, didactic). And this achievement was by no means a purely aesthetic matter. In October 1926, he wrote to a friend: "I am eight feet deep in *Das Kapital.*" It was also his habit to seek out personal mentors, and two such were important at this stage: the left-wing, but not strictly Marxian sociologist Fritz Sternberg and the Marxian, but anti–Communist Party, Karl Korsch.

The early plays and the publication in 1927 of his book of poems *Manual of Piety* gave Brecht a solid reputation in literary circles. His work reached a wider public for the first time with the Berlin production of *The Threepenny Opera* at the Schiffbauerdamm Theater (première August 28, 1928). The now world-famous "musical" not only stayed in the repertoire of that theater until the advent of Hitler (when all such works were banned), but was played all over Germany and Central Europe generally. Two successful films were made from it on the same set, one French, one German. But success stopped at the water's edge. *The Threepenny Opera* was not to be done in London until after World War II. In 1933 it ran briefly (twelve performances) at the Empire Theater in New York and was not even a succès d'estime.

The money Brecht made from *The Threepenny Opera* bought him the time to write less successful works. *Happy End* (1929) was a flop, but it was also the starting point of a major Brecht play that the author worked on intermittently for the next three years: *Saint Joan of the Stockyards.* Meanwhile there were three more important premières: *The Rise and Fall of the City of Mahagonny* (Leipzig, March 9, 1930), *The Measures Taken* (Berlin, December 10, 1930), and *The Mother* (Berlin, January 15, 1932).

It was especially the two last-named works that stamped Brecht as a Communist, for in them he very forthrightly identified himself, not only with Marxist philosophy in general, but with the Communist Party in particular. It did not, of course, follow that the Party accepted the attentions of its enthusiastic wooer. This was, moreover, the era of Stalin's ascendancy in world communism: there was no friendliness in the movement toward any form of modernism in art. And style was not the only stumbling block. Party critics of *The Measures Taken* had grave reservations about its content. For, like other young converts, Brecht had a tendency to be "more royalist than the king."

How the tension between Brecht and the Party critics would have worked out will never be known. Hitler's rise to power (1932 to 1933) ended such luxuries. On January 28, 1933, a performance of *The Measures Taken* in Erfurt was broken up by the police, and proceedings for high treason were instituted. The burning of the Reichstag on February 27 precipitated a period of terror. Brecht had seen it coming, and he slipped across the frontier, with Helene Weigel, on the following day. Their two children, Stefan and Barbara, were smuggled out later. After a few months in Switzerland, Brecht was enabled, by the well-to-do writer Karin Michaelis, to make his home in Denmark for the next six years. Black years for Europe, they were highly creative ones for Brecht. Compulsory withdrawal from politics left him all the more free to write. He completed a big play he had begun in Berlin, *Roundheads and Peakheads;* wrote *The Private Life of the Master Race, Mother Courage and Her Children, The Trial of Lucullus,* and *The Life of Galileo;* and began *The Good Woman of Setzuan.*

Hitler invaded Poland on September 1, 1939. Already in the summer of that year Brecht had considered Denmark too hot to hold him. The Nazi Embassy had long been harassing him there, and a Nazi invasion of Denmark was already talked of. He moved his family and collaborators to Stockholm, where the sculptress Nina Santesson made them welcome in her home on Lidingö Island. When Sweden too feared a Nazi invasion, the Brecht "ensemble" moved on to Finland and the estate of another wealthy woman, Hella Wuolijoki. The play *Mister Puntila and His Man Matti* was originally written in collaboration with Miss Wuolijoki, who, indeed, continued to regard herself as its coauthor to the end—possibly with justification. *The Resistible Rise of Arturo Ui* was written on Miss Wuolijoki's estate in March 1941.

Marxist refugees from Hitler had gone off in various directions: some to fight in the Spanish War, some to live in the "Socialist Fatherland," a compact and rather important group to settle in Mexico City. It would not seem that Brecht seriously considered the first two possibilities—either one might easily have meant death—but he would probably have found his way to Mexico had not one member of his entourage, Margarete Steffin, been refused entry. In May 1941, the whole group obtained visas to enter the United States and proceeded to cross the Soviet Union, but Miss Steffin never made it beyond Moscow, where she died of tuberculosis. On July 21 the group—Brecht, his wife, the two children, and Ruth Berlau, who was both his mistress and an invaluable collaborator—landed in San Pedro, California. With a little money from the actor Fritz Kortner and the composer Kurt Weill, the family settled down in a small frame house in Santa Monica.

Brecht was in America over six years, and seemed fully prepared to stay longer, yet he sank no real roots in American life. For one thing, America did not welcome his works. (As for the talents of Helene Weigel, a great actress, she was "used" in exactly one American film, for the space of about ten seconds, in a nonspeaking role.) But again, exclusion from social activities left Brecht free to write, and to the American years belong *The Visions of Simone Machard, Schweyk in World War II,* and, above all, *The Caucasian Chalk Circle.* He made strenuous efforts to get this last produced on Broadway, but there were to be no Broadway productions of Brecht plays till the sixties (and then only unsuccessful ones). The only productions Brecht had anything to do with while he was in America were a small off-Broadway production of *The Private Life of the Master Race* (1945) and a limited run of *Galileo,* first in

Hollywood, then at the Maxine Elliott Theater, New York (1947).
But meanwhile his works had begun to appear in print in America. The books led to college productions of the plays. And, after
he had returned to Europe, an American audience for Brecht, located mostly in the universities, did grow up.

When *Galileo* opened at the Maxine Elliott on December 7,
Brecht was already in Europe. There had taken place on October
30 a grotesque little tragicomedy, not on the stage of any theater,
but on the floor of the Caucus Room of the Old House Office
Building in Washington, D.C. Here Bertolt Brecht was cross-
questioned by the House Committee on Un-American Activities.
It was a case, as one wit put it, of the biologist being studied by the
apes. Brecht found himself in this position, less because he was a
"Hollywood writer" at a time when Hollywood was being combed
for "conspirators" than because he was a friend of the Eisler brothers, one of whom (Gerhart) was an agent of the German and/or
Russian Communist Party. And someone in American "security"
suspected a connection between the Eislers and the J. Robert Oppenheimer case. (Since the Committee broadcast the hearings on
the radio, the "Brecht program" could easily be recorded by any listener who possessed the right sound equipment; today it can be
heard on a Folkways recording.)

Bertolt Brecht's next resting place was the upper floor of the
pleasant, chaletlike Swiss house overlooking the lake of Zurich.
From this spot (Feldmeilen) he tried to orient himself in a Europe
that offered him various opportunities. One possibility was to buy
a house in Salzburg and write for a much refurbished Salzburg
Festival. With this in mind, he acquired Austrian citizenship—
never relinquished. He was also in touch with Benno Frank, cultural officer of the U.S. Army in Germany, and it seems Frank
would have placed Brecht back in his native Bavaria had the State
Department not suddenly issued a warning against "promoting"
Communists. Frank then commended Brecht to the attention of
the Russian cultural officer, Colonel Dymshitz. Dymshitz ar-

ranged for Brecht to be made welcome in East Berlin, which is where he then spent his last half dozen years.

With historic and by now well-known results. On January 11, 1949, *Mother Courage* had opened at the Deutsches Theater in East Berlin with Helene Weigel in the title role. Brecht and Erich Engel directed it with a "scratch" company of actors. At this point the Berlin Ensemble was just a group within the larger organization of the Deutsches Theater. Not till 1954 were they to have their own building, the Theater am Schiffbauerdamm (today the full title would be Das Berliner Ensemble am Bertolt Brecht Platz). But during the first years of the fifties, Brecht and Helene Weigel converted their group into the most impressive theatrical ensemble in the Western world. Possibly Brecht's writing suffered; but possibly, too, it was worth it. In any case he still did some writing: poems, theoretical prose, adaptations, and one full-length play, barely finished at his death, *Turandot*.

If people had raised political questions about Bertolt Brecht in 1932 and in 1947, they were obviously going to raise them during the fifties. His conduct on June 17, 1953, became a storm center of controversy, and has remained so. (Günter Grass came out with a play on the subject in 1965.) On that day, the workers of East Berlin rose in revolt against their government. Brecht wrote the Party chief, Walter Ulbricht, an expression of his loyalty. According to one account, his letter to Ulbricht also contained much criticism of the regime, but Ulbricht struck it out when giving the letter to the press. This account is denied by Käthe Rülicke, who was acting as Brecht's secretary at the time. Another witness states that Brecht did propose to include such criticism in the letter, but that Miss Rülicke herself persuaded him not to. Certainly he did not declare his solidarity with the rebels.

1956 was another year of decision. The leader of the intracommunist revolt against Ulbricht, Wolfgang Harich, named Brecht as someone who was sympathetically close to his group. That was in October. But Brecht had died in August and could not testify. His widow has stuck by Ulbricht through thick and thin, and apparently would not wish anyone to think her husband ever did otherwise. Brecht kept a journal in which, it is said, he wrote down various unpublishable criticisms of Ulbricht and others. In the widow's view they remain unpublishable to this day, though, it is also said, she has taken the precaution of stowing a copy or two in the vaults of banks in the West.

Again, the main fact is that Brecht did *not* take a public stand against the East Berlin regime. On the contrary. He chose, finally, if for a mixture of reasons, to live in the East, and to give the regime some very solid support. His attacks, quite naturally, were on Western misdeeds. In January 1953, for example, he sent off telegrams to Albert Einstein, Ernest Hemingway, and Arthur Miller asking them to do something about Ethel and Julius Rosenberg. He was concerned with the threat to world peace presented, in his view, by the United States, and he was happy to receive (1954–55) the Lenin Peace Prize (then still called the Stalin Peace Prize). Ironically, his acceptance speech, delivered in Moscow, was translated into Russian, at Brecht's request, by Boris Pasternak.

Brecht's life ended with some theatrical triumphs. In July 1954, the Berlin Ensemble played *Mother Courage* at the Théâtre des Nations in Paris, and in June 1955, it played *The Caucasian Chalk Circle* under the same auspices. These prize-winning events laid the foundation of that international success that Brecht's work was to meet with all over Europe in the late fifties and throughout the sixties.

The Bertolt Brecht described by friends who saw him in his last year—the film director Erwin Leiser, the playwright Max Frisch—was a sick man. Knowing the trouble was with his heart, he said to Leiser: "At least one knows that death will be easy. One tap on the window and ..." The tap came a little before midnight on August 14. One of the doctors who signed the autopsy was Müllereisert, a boyhood friend whose name is familiar to readers of *Manual of Piety*. Brecht lies buried today beneath the windows of his last home (Chausseestrasse 125) in the same cemetery as the remains of his second favorite philosopher, Hegel.

Bertolt Brecht was nothing if not the creator of a new theater. New in all departments. Lighting, for instance. One of the first things the stranger notices in the Brecht theater in East Berlin is that the lighting is different. There are no gelatins on the lamps. All the light is "white." So a Brecht play has a different look even before we see *what* is on the stage. Costume, for instance. No one had ever seen a costume play that looked like *Mother Courage* or *Galileo.* Nor was the difference the accidental one of a guest designer or a special brainstorm. A view is taken of costumes that extends from one play to another. For one thing, they are not seen as costumes at all, but as clothes, which have been worn before. Or stage design. "This is neither naturalism nor any of the departures from naturalism that we know about," students say who have examined the stage created by Brecht's designers (chiefly, Caspar Neher and Teo Otto). These designers usually started from a bare stage and placed on it whatever objects the action of the play required. Art? The art is in (a) the design of each object, and (b) the placing of the objects. Spectators were often surprised how drastic the logic was. For example: if the action, though set in a room, makes no use of walls, you present a room without walls. Not naturalism; but Brecht called it realism.

Sometimes the setting, instead of creating the mood (which in Brecht it never is supposed to do), is in direct contrast with the mood. Not a new idea in itself, but not an exhausted one either, and most people felt they *had* seen something new when they witnessed the interaction between setting and actor in the Pope scene of *Galileo.* Here there was the added piquancy that the setting is actually the costume. More precisely: what had been "setting"— the Pope's robe on a dummy—becomes costume as it is transferred to the Pope's body; and when he is fully dressed, it becomes "setting" again, because he is submerged under it.

Music, too, is used as comment, and therefore often in direct contrast to the moment and the word. In his book *Composing for the Films,* Hanns Eisler suggests that this should be a principle of movie music, replacing the present assumption, which is that music is mood music and always either reinforces or embellishes. Eisler composed his best music for Brecht, and his idea is an application of Brecht's most famous idea, *alienation* (*Verfremdung*).

Fremd is German for "alien." Hegel and Marx had made a very important principle out of *Entfremdung,* the normal German word for alienation or estrangement. *Verfremdung* is Brecht's word for the process of *making* alien or strange. Now since it is well known that alienation, especially in the writings of Karl Marx, is an appalling phenomenon—the estrangement of the worker from the ownership and meaning of what he works at—it will be asked: how can the Marxist Bertolt Brecht actually *call for* alienation?

But already in Hegel alienation is a positive as well as a negative thing. More important, perhaps: it is necessary. As Herbert Marcuse likes to put it, Hegel proved the power of negative thinking, proved, indeed, that thinking *is* negative by virtue of being analytic—it takes apart. Conversely, "positive thinking" blurs distinctions, dissolves meaning in a perhaps inspiring fog. In which fog we live our lives. To use a metaphor that brings us back to Brecht, we need to step *away* from a picture to come *closer* to seeing it.

In what Brecht called the bourgeois theater, an author's aim is to make the audience think: "This man is brilliant: he sees such things as I never saw." It was Brecht's ambition to make his audience say: "What this man shows me is no creation of his brilliance, it is the real world, which I realize I was out of touch with till he reminded me." This kind of "reminder," in Brecht's view, is not—is no longer—effected by naturalism. It requires the *alienation effect*. (Here the word *effect* [German *Effekt*] also gives trouble. The right sense is suggested by our use of the plural, *effects*.) In order that the buzz and blur of the circumambient world should become defined sound and image, the world itself has to be pushed away a little, even pushed to one side a little, and looked at askew—as Hogarth and Daumier knew. In this way, the world is "made alien" in order that it may be "made known." The logic is paradoxical, but what is involved is not a trickiness in reasoning, but complexity in the experience of discovery and realization. Colloquially, we say "I suddenly realized," but the suddenness comes at the end of a process, and the process does not resemble driving straight ahead on a highway. Rather, after a sharp turn left, immediately followed by a sharp turn right, one "suddenly realizes," *with a jolt,* that one is still moving ahead in the original direction. The jolt has defined the direction one is moving in for one's emotional system. It is an alienation effect.

Brecht often addressed himself to the topic of the *A Effect* (in German *V-Effekt*) in acting, and it may well be that the most radical changes he demanded in the theater, other than in the writing, were in the acting. "Three devices," he wrote, "can contribute to the alienation of the words and actions of the person presenting them: 1. the adoption of the third person, 2. the adoption of the past tense, and 3. the speaking of stage directions and comments." This meant that, in early rehearsals or classroom exercises, the dialogue of a scene should be translated from the first to the third person and from the present to the past tense and that an actor should read all stage directions aloud as they occur. A Brechtian playwright will sometimes even write scenes in the third person and the past tense, in which case no such translation is called for. A celebrated example is to be found in Brecht's own play *The Caucasian Chalk Circle,* and it will be noticed that the narration also includes what would normally be considered "stage directions and comments":

> . . . And she rose, and bent down, and sighing,
> took the child
> And carried it off.
> As if it was stolen goods she picked it up.
> As if she was a thief she sneaked away.

It is Brecht's thesis that, if an actress will practice enacting such an incident, while another performer reads the lines, she will eventually find she has acquired another way of acting, another *style,* the style of the new theater.

How does this differ from the style of the old theater? Precisely by alienating the narrative—and with it the character the actor is presenting. The difference has sometimes been understood thus: "In the pre-Brechtian theater, and notably in the Stanislavsky theater, the actor is completely identified with the character; he *is* the character, and *we* can completely identify ourselves with *him, we* are the character. In the Brechtian theater, on the other hand, the actor openly disowns the character, shows both himself *and* the character. By not identifying himself with the character, he prevents *us* from making the identification. Instead of losing ourselves in the character, we look at it from the outside." This is correct but exaggerated. In no theater could there be *complete* identifications, or spectators would be rushing onstage to save the Desdemonas from the Othellos. In no theater could there be complete detachment, or the spectator would simply be excluded—and would detach himself from the whole occasion by going to sleep or walking out. A degree of identification is contained in the very idea of enactment. It is a question of what degree. And the whole difference of opinion on the matter represents a concern with *degree.* Brecht experimented to the end of finding out what *degree* of identification is needed and for what. If the aim is pathos, then you must make the identifications as nearly complete as theater art will permit, and this has been done in all the pathetic domestic dramas, from Victorian melodrama to radio soap opera, of the past hundred years. Conversely, if the aim were comedy, there would be nothing new (in that sense, nothing Brechtian) about resisting identifications. A traditional way of resisting identifications is for a comedian to break out of any role he may be playing and talk to the audience. If Brecht was an innovator in this area it was because he introduced this principle into dramaturgy itself: his characters often "break out" of a scene and address the audience. Generally, the songs, too, represent such a breakout, in contrast to the songs of the American "musical," which are made continuous with the dialogue.

Lighting, costume, stage design, music, acting, and, last but not least, playwriting itself: Brecht wanted to "make it new" in all these departments and took steps to do so both as writer and as stage director. One could even add directing to the list of departments, except that what it primarily means is the coordination of all the others. "Audience" is not, in this sense, a department, either. You wouldn't expect a section on "the people who eat" in a cookbook, and audience is not a category parallel to the theater arts themselves. On the other hand, just as cooking exists for eaters and no one else, so theater exists for spectators and no one else, and if a theater theoretician does not speak of them at *one* time it is because he has them in mind (in the back of his mind, perhaps) *all* the time. Every kind of theater represents a particular kind of operation performed upon the audience, and Brecht's originality consisted in his determination to perform a different operation on them.

What operation? In Brecht's pronouncements of the late twenties and early thirties, there is heavy emphasis on the didactic: the theater is to instruct. In his "Short Organum" (1948) the emphasis is shifted to pleasure: the theater must please. Brecht's shift in emphasis has sometimes been taken as a mellowing or even as simply a retreat to a more traditional position, as if his earlier preoccupation with teaching was later regarded as a waste of time. But this is to ignore much of what Brecht said in the later theoretical writings, as well as his later practice as a playwright. And the change of theory reflects a development in the practice. It is the development from plays of the period 1928 to 1934, which he himself labeled didactic (*Lehrstücke*), such as *The Exception and the Rule,* to plays of the period 1938 to 1944, such as *Galileo, Mother Courage,* and *The Caucasian Chalk Circle.* And of these latter, it could be said that, while they are less didactic in form, they are more instructive in effect. Brecht's development was from a rather puritanic and perhaps even undialectical didacticism to a much fuller presentation of the dialectics of living. Correspondingly, he became dissatisfied with the name he gave his kind of work in the late twenties—Epic Theater—and at the end of his life was toying with the term Dialectical Theater.

There comes a point at which the distinction between pleasing and instructing does not help us anymore, for what Brecht wishes to do is not flatly either to please people or to instruct them. It is something closer to waking them up. In the eighteenth century already, Schiller had complained that in the theater the Muse "takes to her broad bosom the dull-witted teacher and the tired businessman and lulls the spirit into a magnetic sleep by warming up the numbed senses and giving the imagination a gentle rocking." This describes just what the German theater was still doing in Brecht's youth, and while the older playwrights continued to purvey sleeping pills, the young Brecht manufactured an alarm clock.

The bedroom he planned to place it in was not that of the businessman. The positive emotional content of the new theater has to do with productivity and corresponds to the joy of planners and builders. Indeed, in a society where the planning and building is rational, the worker on these tasks will find them reflected—jubilantly taken up in symbolic form—in the drama. The new theater will also have a negative emotional content. It will show impatience with whatever impedes the planning and building, anger at whatever opposes or wrecks it. These two bodies of emotional content will produce their own characteristic rhythm in the theater, will outcrop in plays that have a characteristic movement. First, there is the rhythm of joy, the movement toward fruition and achievement, best exemplified in Brecht's own work by *The Caucasian Chalk Circle*. Second, there is the rhythm of rage, the movement toward defiance and resistance, best exemplified by *Mother Courage*.

Anger and defiance were, of course, commonplaces of the social drama even before Brecht. But they seldom worked: that is to say, they only touched the surface. Millionaires could be roused to cry:

Strike! from their seats in the orchestra, but their zeal had subsided before they reentered their waiting limousines. What Brecht, on the other hand, says about anger in the scene devoted to the subject (*Mother Courage,* scene 4) reveals what he has in mind for the theater. Getting worked up for an hour or two has no value. We need to generate enough anger to last a lifetime. Or rather, since we probably have that much already, we need to tap it, to make it available. This, as psychoanalysts know, can only be done by indirection. The indirections of Brechtian theater—its devices and "effects"—are ways of doing it. There could therefore be no greater error than to imagine that the purpose of Brecht was to exclude emotion. He sweeps aside facile tears because his concern is with deep passion, and he shares with religious thinkers the assumption that deep passion is seldom neutral but tends to be tied to convictions, to belong, as it were, either to God or the Devil. The Brechtian drama taps those deeper springs of feeling which, like the sentiment of faith as described by Saint Paul (an allusion found in *Mother Courage,* scene 4), can move mountains.

None of the innovations listed above (or any others that could be added) was to Brecht in the first instance an aesthetic matter. In that respect, he was not an "avant-garde" writer at all: none of his idiosyncrasies claim any interest in themselves. And even his later homage to pleasure brought with it no innovations that had the purveying of pleasure as their specific purpose. So what *is* he doing with his audience? It would be a fair summary of what has been reported here to state: he is helping the audience to *see* certain things and to *feel* certain things. But to this must now be added that the help is not extended because the "certain things" are interesting in themselves, let alone just because they are "there." It is extended because, in Dr. Samuel Johnson's words: "It is always the writer's duty to make the world better."

When, little more than a year before his death, Brecht was asked: "Can the world of today be represented on a stage?" he replied in the affirmative—"but only if it [the world] is regarded as transformable." For him, the stage is concerned with what men do to men and nothing else. And, unlike Jesus Christ, he believed that they do know what they do. They have chosen to do what they have done, and could choose otherwise. A description of their activities "makes no sense"—would have no point—if this were not true. Therefore even the most descriptive-seeming episode in a play must really be, not descriptive at all, but normative. It implies either praise or blame. It moves history along, if only by a minute, invisible step, toward a different future. It is likely that, to Brecht, the most important statement in all history was this:

> The philosophers have only interpreted the world in various ways; the point, however, is to change it.

It is the eleventh thesis on Feuerbach of his favorite philosopher, Karl Marx.

Days of the Commune
1971

The BBC (London) produced a radio presentation of Days of the
Commune *in 1971. What follows was written as both a radio talk on
that occasion and an article in the BBC's weekly journal,* The Listener
(December 9, 1971).

WINSTON CHURCHILL ONCE SAID he learned his history of England from Shakespeare's chronicle plays. It is a vulnerable remark,
since any historian, even a very amateur one, can have a field day destroying Shakespeare the historian, beginning with the fact that the
real Richard III was quite a nice chap. I say: "beginning with the
fact." It is always by citing facts that one sets straight any piece of historical interpretation. The trouble with this is that there is no piece
of historical interpretation that cannot be brought into question by
reference to facts that don't fit in with it, or don't seem to fit in with
it. A question suggests itself. Is to interpret history inevitably to fal-
sify it? And, if so, is there a factual test by which this can be proved?

The question had best be elaborated thus: are there people who
judge history entirely by facts? There are certainly people who
would have us believe they do. I am thinking at the moment of
people who tell us the Marxist interpretation of the Paris Commune is discredited. In their sense, it was never credited. It is

precisely an interpretation, which is to say that it has assumptions behind it as well as conclusions up front. And people who tell us they reject the conclusions are only bringing up facts and forgetting to tell us they never accepted the assumptions. All of which helps us answer our question. It is not really by factual tests that interpretations are rejected. Only an omniscient god could reason from sheer knowledge of the truth. Mere human beings reason, at best, upon a mixed basis of facts and assumptions. Assumptions both about facts and about nonfacts. One should therefore be a little suspicious of what is offered as a purely factual refutation of historical interpretation. One should ask the interpreter: don't you have any *ideas*? And, if you do, can I not proceed to question them on what purports to be a factual basis? Nietzsche said there are no facts, there are only interpretations.

These remarks were suggested by my reading of *The Fall of Paris* by Alistair Horne. "Out of the fabric of the Commune, Karl Marx was to weave social and revolutionary myths," Horne writes. Well, perhaps. But out of his own study of the Commune, Horne develops a myth of another kidney. His book is a cautionary fable, in effect advising young people today not to throw their weight into revolutionary movements because in the short run they will fail like the Commune; and if in the long run they succeed, it will be a horrible type of success like that of Stalin.

I wouldn't criticize Horne for thus exploiting history to point to a moral that obviously means a good deal to him. I would criticize him for seeming unaware that he does this, and hence for presuming to criticize others for doing it. Long ago it was said: history is philosophy teaching by examples. In the nineteenth century the ambition of historians went beyond that, and some historians thought they could show exactly what happened, resting content with a modest omniscience. They were wrong. History remains philosophy teaching by examples. As decisive in any modern as in any older history book are the assumptions the historian makes in advance of any of the facts he presents.

Now if this is true of historians, it is even truer of historical playwrights. The authors of even the greatest history plays—perhaps above all these authors—have had only a very specialized and narrow interest in history. History has only attracted their attention where they thought it would help them make a favorite point, a point they had already made in their nonhistorical works. *Saint Joan* is the principal modern history play. It is also the quintessence of Shavianism. It enables the author to make again points he had made in *Major Barbara* and other nonhistorical plays. It is extremely vulnerable to historical criticism. One can show, for example, that it is unlikely that Bishop Cauchon was anything like that. At the same time, Shaw's critics inevitably resort to presuppositions of their own, which also have their vulnerabilities.

Playwrights, however, often don't mind being told that they got their history wrong. They are likely to retort that their real interest, anyway, was in the present: something in the past had caught their attention because it seemed to belong not in the past at all, but in the present. Also, this something seemed not to be merely fact but what Alistair Horne quite rightly calls myth. It is only when history can also be seen as myth that it's of any use to the playwright. Sometimes the figure he picks is already what we call a legend and has already collected around himself much that can hardly be considered fact. Jesus. Napoleon. Even Galileo is a mythic figure in this sense, it being by no means certain that he either dropped things from the leaning tower of Pisa or said: "Eppur si muove."*

Bertolt Brecht wrote three other history plays besides *Galileo: The Mother, Mother Courage,* and *Days of the Commune. The Mother* and *Days of the Commune* belong together in a series of *historical* events that Marxism has, to be sure, made *mythic,* a series that begins with Robespierre and ends with Stalin. *The Mother* is by far the

---

* This ground is gone over more thoroughly in the article "*Galileo* (I)" above. I return to the territory in my preface to *The Recantation of Galileo Galilei* in the volume *Rallying Cries* (1977).

simpler of the two, being, in essence, on that classic theme of radical theater: conversion from defeatism to militancy. *The Mother* is also far less "historical"—a piece of domestic fiction, rather, against a historical backdrop. There is domestic fiction in *Commune* too, but history is no backdrop. The family story is placed in the political storm center. It has been said that in *Mother Courage* Brecht presents a worm's-eye view of history. A plebeian view, anyway. The blacksmith's shop seen by the anvil rather than the hammer. For Mother Courage is at heart thoroughly passive. She has capitulated and she accepts, and she isn't going to change her mind like Vlassova in *The Mother.* Such has been the life of the people through the ages.

In 1848 the Communist Manifesto announced another type of plebs: the common man as insurrectionary. Unhappily, the 1848 revolutions hardly showed him as such. Marx had to wait till 1870 to 1871. That was precisely the importance of the Paris Commune for him and that part of the world that would follow him. For if we take "myth" to be that which men make out of fact to inspire themselves with—a possibly nonfactual past out of which they propose to make the fact of a different kind of future—then myth is all the more important, and it is all the more important that, out of the facts, men make *this* kind of myth, rather than *that.* At the very least, it is important *what* myth they do make: what myth of the American Revolution, the French Revolution, the Russian Revolution, the Chinese Revolution—what myth of the 1871 Paris Commune. After all, many of those who speak most contemptuously of mythmaking when it is a matter of the Paris Commune are suddenly very acquiescent when it is a matter of a claimant to the Messiahship of some two thousand years ago.

"Workingmen's Paris," Karl Marx predicted, "with its Commune will be forever celebrated as the glorious harbinger of a new society. Its martyrs are enshrined in the great heart of the working class." Or again: "Paris, working, thinking, struggling, bleeding, almost forgetting the cannibals at its gates in preparing for a new society, radiant in its historic enthusiasm." This second quotation from Marx was reprinted during the 1960s in the Berlin Ensemble program of *Days of the Commune*. Beside it was placed this quotation from Bertolt Brecht: "The great public thought-processes and discoveries directly answer urgent needs, the brain of the population works in broad daylight." Had anything like this actually happened in Paris 1871? Here is a standard, non-Marxist account, from the *Columbia Encyclopedia:*

> At the end of the Franco-Prussian War in 1871, the Parisians opposed the national government headed by Adolphe Thiers and the National Assembly at Versailles. Thiers, after failing to disarm the Parisian National Guard, fled in March to Versailles, and the Parisians set up a communal government, while the victorious Prussians affected neutrality. The Versaillais began a siege. The Communards, whose aim included economic reforms, represented many shades of political opinion. As the long siege drew to an end, however, they fell under the sway of extremists, who shot hostages, including the Archbishop of Paris, and burned the Tuileries palace, the City Hall and the Palace of Justice. On May 28 the Versailles forces entered the city. Severe reprisals followed with more than 17,000 people executed, including women and children.

I call this account "standard," meaning that I assume its authors would consider it dispassionate and objective. That is, of course, the question. Just being critical of both sides is not necessarily to have a godlike completeness of vision, and one of the main categories used begs one of the main questions at issue. This is the word *extremists*. The nice people with suitably different shades of opinion fell under the sway of another sort for whom, however, the scholarly contributor can find no word outside the vocabulary of the *New York Daily News: extremists*. The word removes them from consideration. A moment's thought tells us that that is the raison d'être of such words: to remove from consideration. Also interesting in the rhetoric of our encyclopedia entry is that, while the killing of one man and the burning of several buildings are attributed to "extremists," the killing of seventeen thousand human beings by the other side is mildly termed "a reprisal."

All of which I bring up to gain a proper hearing for Bertolt Brecht. If he is not more dispassionate and objective than these other writers, he is not less so.

The writing of *Days of the Commune* was suggested to Brecht by his reading of a play by Nordahl Grieg, *The Defeat.* Following history, both Grieg and Brecht show that the Commune: 1. practiced humane restraint, 2. was consequently vulnerable, and 3. ended in defeat. For Grieg the conclusion was, "How noble this defeat was, caused as it was by taking a humane position." For Brecht, the conclusion was, "If taking a humane position entails a victory for inhumanity, we had better 1. deplore it, and 2. be ready to do different next time." I have stated the difference between Grieg and Brecht so as to make Brecht sound the more sensible. He has a strong point, and it should be allowed to come out at once. He is making a critique of that liberal idealism that would romanticize defeat and hence reconcile us in advance to being defeated in future. Any army officer knows better, knowing that he wouldn't fight at all except for the one purpose: to win.

What did the Communards see as their purpose?

> The right to live, yes. But how did we propose to put it through? Freedom, yes. The freedom to do business, to live off the people, to plot against the people to serve the enemies of the people! Is freedom to *lie* also guaranteed? We permit the election of cheats. By a people bewildered by school, church, press, and politicians! And where is our right to occupy the Bank of France which holds the wealth *we* have accumulated with our bare hands? With that money we could have bribed all the generals and

> politicians, our own and Bismarck! We should have con-
> centrated on one point: *our own* right to live.

This is Langevin, Brecht's realist, talking on May 22, 1871, when it is too late. Geneviève, whom he is talking to, says, "Why didn't we do it?" and he answers, "Because of freedom, which people understand nothing of. Unlike any regiment fighting for its life, we were not prepared to renounce personal freedom until the freedom of all was won." Geneviève says: "But didn't we just want to avoid staining our hands with blood?" And the answer comes: "Yes. But in this struggle there are only blood-stained hands and severed hands."

The military comparison in this passage is a point well taken. Of course, the soldier in battle forgoes his freedom till the battle is over. His uniform and gun show that he has already agreed to stain his hands with blood in order not to have his hands cut off. If we grant the premise here, we have to grant the conclusion. The premise is that the reasoning by which non-Marxists justify war and wartime Machiavellianism between nations also justifies war and wartime Machiavellianism between classes.

It is Brecht's way to slip such conclusions up on us. You cannot reject him unless you rejected him far back in the argument—where the presuppositions lie. It is perhaps curious that a playwright who liked to claim that he appealed to reason and encouraged discussion liked also to push his stories to the point where discussion is impossible and where reason is suspended in the horror of it all. After all, if you wanted to discuss, mildly, whether perhaps there weren't pros as well as cons to anti-Semitism, you would hardly lead off with a brief film of the gas ovens in action. But that is the kind of thing Brecht does in his plays. And the Hanns Eisler music makes its contribution: far from encouraging skepticism, it refuses to take no for an answer. Its very charm lies in a certain cockiness: "I'm right, and you're wrong, so there!"

If Bernard Shaw's comedies retained something of the quality of parliamentary debate, being the product of the classic era of parliamentary debating, Brecht's plays show the Parliament a Cromwellian contempt or, if you prefer, assume that it is too late for debating, that the age of debate is bankrupt and finished, and that the practice of debate, at this point, would be the merest hypocrisy. The Communards are defeated because they engage in debate. That way valuable time is lost: it is too late. Even more, it is too soon. The battle is still raging. Again, the military metaphor applies, and again, it is something more to Brecht than a metaphor. The battle is lost because our side has taken time off for parliamentary debate. This is an indication that it does not regard the enemy as truly a military enemy: one who will kill you if you don't get to him first.

> The proletariat stopped halfway. Instead of proceeding with the expropriation of the expropriators it was carried away by dreams of supreme justice. Institutions such as the Bank were not seized. The second error was the unnecessary magnanimity of the proletariat: instead of annihilating its enemies it tried to exercise moral influence on them. It hesitated and gave time to the Versailles Government to collect its forces.

This is Lenin speaking, Lenin who was taken to his tomb shrouded in a Communard flag, and *Days of the Commune* is the purest Leninism, the purest tribute to Lenin's interpretation of Marxism. It will be persuasive to you exactly in proportion as you are receptive to Leninism in general.

We are all receptive to the idea that it's better if our side wins, but the application of this idea to the Commune entails difficulties. What appealed to Marx in the Commune was not exactly its capacity for winning, as if it were some new kind of shock troop or an ultimate weapon. It was that the common people took over. Themselves. Not leaders whom they appointed, let alone leaders who appointed themselves. Common folk ran the city of Paris for a matter of weeks. Why not forever? Lenin accounts for the failure in part as a matter of mere bad judgment as to exactly what should be done on a given day. But surely his main criticism is of the very character of the Parisians: they were too good. You've got to be bad to win, as Machiavelli had said long before, and as Brecht said in a number of his plays, most famously perhaps in *The Good Woman of Setzuan*. Since the proletariat would never spontaneously be bad enough, Lenin devised the Communist Party to provide the ruthless leadership and make the ruthless decisions. His party won. But at the end of this road stood Stalin, a man who lost all contact with the common people and all belief in the people's initiative.

Days of the Commune is a very dated play in 1971 because it does not acknowledge the dangers inherent in the severity it advocates. However, if the Leninism of the play has, in my view, dated, the Marxism has not. When Brecht accepted the Stalin Peace Prize in Moscow in May 1955, he told his hosts the most important teaching of socialism was that a future for mankind could be seen only from underneath, from the standpoint of the oppressed and exploited. Surely Brecht was right, even if he couldn't see that this was a criticism of them and theirs. If one looked for any analogy to the Commune in the past two decades, it would be precisely to Prague 1968, Budapest 1956, and, in a degree, Berlin 1953 that one would turn, granted that the analogy is not exact, and was complicated by the plans of the United States to cooperate with socialist uprisings for antisocialist purposes. In any event, there is still vitality in the idea of popular insurrection and popular government, and this vitality is present in Brecht's play, not merely by way of verbal formulations but even more in depiction of character and mores and action. Lyrically, too: two of the songs have been sung to Eisler's music in these English words of mine by present-day American radicals. Especially the second one seems to dramatize the Black Panthers.

RESOLUTION

In view of our great weakness you established
Laws that kept us long in slavery
But let all these laws henceforth be disregarded
In view of the fact that we wish to be free:
In view of the fact that then you threatened
Us with cannon and with bayonet
We henceforth resolve to fear a wretched
Way of living more than death.

In view of this sad fact: that we have no coal
And who has no coal has frozen feet
We have all decided just to go and fetch it
For that is the only way to get some heat:
In view of the fact that then you threatened
Us with cannon and with bayonet
We henceforth resolve to fear a wretched
Way of living more than death.

ALL OR NOTHING

Who, O slave, is going to free you?
Those who stand in darkness near you
From the lowest depths shall hear you
In the darkness they shall see you
Other slaves are going to free you
For it's all or nothing, none or everyone!
By yourself you lose all battles
Grab a gun or keep the shackles
For it's all or nothing, none or everyone!

Who'll avenge your scars and bruises?
You on whom the blows descended

Are by all the weak befriended
We'll decide who wins or loses
We'll avenge your scars and bruises
For it's all or nothing, none or everyone!
By yourself you lose all battles
Grab a gun or keep the shackles
For it's all or nothing, none or everyone!

Who will dare? You ask in sorrow
He whose misery's past bearing
Finding finally the daring
Joins with those who are declaring:
We won't wait until tomorrow!
Now it's all or nothing, none or everyone!
By yourself you lose all battles
Grab a gun or keep the shackles
Now it's all or nothing, none or everyone!

The Threepenny Opera
1976

The only Berlin Ensemble production that ever bored me was The
Threepenny Opera. *There were reasons, chief of which was the after-
the-fact Marxism of the staging: the directing was more Marxist than
the play, and Macheath became all bad. At the time of the Lincoln Center production of* Threepenny *this totally negative view of Macheath
was reflected in the press and other public discussion. I wrote the following piece for* The Village Voice *as an objection to this trend.*

LILLIAN HELLMAN HAS SAID THAT the great plays of our time are
Threepenny Opera and *Mother Courage.* I would add that a song
named "The Solomon Song" is at the heart of both, and that they
are really the same play.

"Vanity of vanity, saith the Preacher [that is, Solomon], all is
vanity," says the Bible, and its commentators explain that the reit-
erated word means emptiness, nullity: our life begins and ends in
nothingness—a leitmotiv of literature, especially modern literature, especially Brecht and Beckett. "There is indeed no more to
add: the world is poor and men are bad." There Mr. Peachum rests
his case, and many have assumed that Brecht rested his there too.

Those who assume otherwise point to his Marxism, which in
turn points to a world that is rich, where men are good, and, to be

sure, Marxism is either explicit or implicit or both in much of Brecht's later work. It is explicit in his *Notes to Threepenny Opera,* written later, as also in the new ending that was found for the *Threepenny Film* in 1930. *Threepenny Opera* itself, though written only two years earlier, is another matter. Its politics do indeed seem to be summed up in the chorale at the end, as Marxist critics have not been slow to state:

> Combat injustice, but in moderation:
> Such things will freeze to death if left alone.
> Remember: this whole vale of tribulation
> Is black as pitch and cold as any stone.

Or, as Beckett would say: nothing to be done. It is true that the social relationships in the play depict the capitalist system, seen in a Marxist way, in miniature, but without the Marxist solution, without a rebellious and liberating proletariat. It is a kind of semi-Marxism that only reinforces the sense of defeat inherent in the social order that Marxism seeks to replace.

One reason I call *Mother Courage* the same play as *Threepenny* is that it is imbued with the same sense of defeat. "The Solomon Song," sung in both plays, externally speaking comes as a digression in both plays, but is no digression thematically speaking:

> King Solomon was very wise
> So what's his history?
> He came to view this world with scorn
> And curse the hour he was born
> Declaring all is vanity.
> King Solomon was very wise
> But long before the day was out
> The consequence was clear, alas,
> And wisdom 'twas that brought him to this pass:
> A man is better off without.

In *Mother Courage,* the subject of the song is given as "the useless-ness of the virtues." In *Threepenny,* there is a song called "The Fu-tility of All Human Endeavor." In neither play is Marxist optimism invoked. I was present at a meeting of the Communist Youth (East Berlin, 1949) when the radical teenagers complained bitterly to Brecht himself of the pacifistic pessimism in *Mother Courage.* "An insult to our heroes fighting in wars of liberation all over the world," one boy said. Both *Mother Courage* and *Threepenny* dramatize class struggle, but in neither case is any development forward to a new synthesis, a higher stage of civilization, in any way affirmed.

But another kind of optimism is to be found in both plays—an optimism not grand and world-historical but apolitical, personal, temperamental, irrational, if you will, and yet not devoid of much clever, cynical rationality.

The premises of the Brechtian pessimism are a universe without God and a world without ethics. All heroic and saintly quests have become vain: the Holy Grail is not there, and our Don Quixotes are all Sancho Panzas. What room is there in this scheme of things for *any* positive element? Those who look in *Threepenny Opera* (and other early works of Brecht) for idealism will look in vain. The positive element is not idealistic but erotic and, as such, amoral. It would seem that even in the bleak climate of Brecht's early plays man cannot be discouraged from pleasure seeking—the pursuit of an orgasm to put it physiologically, the pursuit of hap-piness to put it philosophically. The only god that is known to have won Brecht's allegiance is a Chinese god of happiness that he en-countered in the form of a statuette of a little fat man. And, as against Stalin, he was the god that didn't fail.

Clearly, the possibilities for happiness, even for pleasure, in that climate, are very circumscribed. "The wickedness of the world," says Peachum, "is so great you have to run your legs off to avoid having them stolen out from under you." Yet good times can be had if you are prepared to meet two conditions. The first is simply to recognize the narrow limits within which you must work: don't attempt to be more than a small-time hedonist—no paradises, no heavens, no Utopias, no Free Worlds. The second condition is willingness—also on a small scale—to be a crook, lie a little, steal a little, and keep your mouth shut at certain times . . . I am outlining the philosophy of the woman Brecht called Courage. The play *Mother Courage* "explains" that, ultimately, this philosophy doesn't work. Nonultimately, however, it did; and it was really a nonultimate notion anyway.

It has often been remarked that, while *Mother Courage* is a very sad tale indeed, for about two-thirds of the evening Brecht's audience is chuckling. There is a conclusion to draw here other than that Brecht was witty. It is that his character Mother Courage was having a good time, was as near to happy as mere human beings get: she had a lot of fun, she gave and took much good humor and warmth. Even in his somberest book of poems, *Manual of Piety,* Brecht could report:

> Almost all men give thanks for their birth
> Before they receive their handful of earth.

Still, philosophically, the emphasis, in *Mother Courage,* is on the negative, and Courage's willingness to accept small mercies and commit small offenses is not recommended by the author. In this, the later play parts company with *Threepenny Opera,* for, as I see the earlier work, its final word, if it has one, is that in a big, bad world the best thing is to be a small, bad man. A good time is to be had, not, it is true, by all, but by those who meet the two conditions.

I know Mr. Peachum doesn't agree with me. At the end of *Threepenny Opera,* a reprieve comes by mounted messenger for the small, bad man—Mr. Macheath—who had been headed for the gallows, and Mr. Peachum says: "In reality [the] end is bad. Mounted messengers from the Queen come far too seldom, and if you kick a man he kicks you back again." It is a joke that goes all the way back to Brecht's source, *The Beggar's Opera,* by John Gay (1728), where Macheath is reprieved because it is an opera and frivolous.

If there is a problem for critics in *Threepenny Opera*, it's in deciding what to take literally and what ironically. There is also such a thing in comedy as a double twist whereby irony is not accepted as such. Brecht duplicates Gay's ironical ending, but the irony is that he has removed the irony, and the point, in *Threepenny Opera*, is that a mounted messenger *has* come from the Queen, and it isn't the first time. Macheath—people like Macheath—bear a charmed life, are reprieved, and, having escaped from jail, if they are reimprisoned, escape again. And again. And again. If *Mother Courage* audiences chuckle, *Threepenny* audiences roar with laughter: quite provably, this is one of the great entertainments of the twentieth century, the show above all shows in which the repulsive debacle of modern history becomes delightful masquerade.

The dolce vita of Fellini's film was not *really* dolce. At the center of those good times was misery. Macheath, on the other hand, by a little crookedness, earns himself a very good time indeed. If *Threepenny* is about capitalism, its conclusion is that, bad as the system is, and totally without historic prospects, you can have a good time in the holes and corners of it, the nooks and the crannies. No irony: this good time is good.

And here is the deeper reason why *Threepenny Opera* cannot express socialist optimism: it is too optimistic about capitalism. If in *The Good Woman of Setzuan* Brecht shows you can't be good under capitalism, in *Threepenny* he shows you can be happy under capitalism—if you're prepared to be bad. Granted, of course, that everything is relative, especially happiness, and you may not be very happy or happy for long.

It isn't just Mr. Peachum who disagrees with me. Mr. Brecht himself had quite different things to say in his Notes. But then he was inclined to change the meanings of his works after the fact. It was after the fact that he added lyrics to *Threepenny* in which the audience is warned against going after little crooks like Macheath while leaving at large crooks like the top Nazis. Brecht seems to have hoped that such inserts would successfully moralize this otherwise amoral work. Too late. Tagging on a few moralistic lines cannot change the temper and tone of a three-hour masterpiece. Besides, my point about Macheath is only reinforced by the later additions. Thus: until we have brought to heel the giant adventurers of big business and imperialism, there is no reason not to tolerate the dwarf adventurers of small business and "highway robbery." Mother Courage says: "We're prisoners. But so are lice in fur." Macheath is a prisoner of a certain economic system. That's the fur; he is definitely a louse.

"The Solomon Song," vehicle of the ostensible pessimism of *Threepenny Opera*, has this to say:

> And here you see our friend Macheath:
> His life is now at stake.
> So long as he was rational
> And took whate'er there was to take
> His fame was international.
> But then he got emotional
> And though the day is not yet out
> The consequence is clear, alas!
> Emotion 'twas that brought him to this pass:
> A man is better off without.

"This pass" is mortal danger. Macheath is about to be placed in the death cell. He will be saved from death only by an intervention that, Peachum says, wouldn't happen in real life. But Peachum is not Brecht. And later Brecht is not the Brecht who wrote *Threepenny Opera*. And early Brecht believed life could be good while it lasted. "Emotion" (Eros) was not fatal to Macheath, or not immediately so, and nothing in any case lasts forever.

If Macheath does not embody saintliness or heroism or any idea of virtue, he does embody Eros, the Life Force. In other respects the most negative of "heroes," he is in this respect decisively positive. Brecht's Notes say no: they have it that it is not passion that drives Macheath to the whorehouse each Thursday, and thus enables the Peachums to plan his capture on a Thursday; it is the bourgeois sense of order, dictating that what is done on many Thursdays must be done on all. This is a joke *made only in the Notes.* In the original story, Macheath is obviously driven by lust like Brecht's other early "heroes," especially Baal, whose reincarnation Macheath is. One of the lyrics speaks of his "sexual submissiveness," but that *is* simple irony—the singer is Mrs. Peachum—and Macheath "submits" to sex, just as Baal does, with delicious, self-indulging passivity. The Chinese god of pleasure, Baal, and Macheath are all one.

In a late work of Brecht's, next to a picture of the Chinese god, these words are printed: "happiness, that is, communism." *Threepenny Opera* dates back to a time when Brecht had not yet really "found" the positive part of communism, and so happiness was officially nowhere. Unofficially, I have suggested, it subsisted in nooks and crannies. A Marxist might put it that this happiness was to be found specifically in the petty bourgeoisie and *Lumpenproletariat,* themselves nooks and crannies between bourgeoisie and proletariat. He might add that, later, Macheath would have to choose between being forced down into the proletariat or taking a job as a guard in a concentration camp.

Behind the whole story lies one of the supreme comic masters of all time, Jonathan Swift, for it was he who gave Gay the idea for *The Beggar's Opera.* The image Swift created was that of a "Newgate pastoral." Pastoral literature portrayed a golden age of love and perpetual youth: conflict and death were simply wished away. Swift saw comic, satiric possibilities in equating this unreal other world with the ultrareal world of jailbirds and whores. An exquisite irony! And again we find Bertolt Brecht doing some further ironizing on his own. More important, we again find him taking away much of the preexistent irony, for the point he would above all make is that, in the interstices, the cracks, of our prosaic, life-hating society, a certain degree of "pastoral poetry" (death-defying erotic fun) remains "quite a thought," even a real possibility. *Threepenny* is even more of a Newgate pastoral than *The Beggar's Opera*.

The Measures Taken
1977

It is utter folly to be wise all by yourself.

—La Rochefoucauld

My work on the translation of The Measures Taken *was spread over a longish period because, in the sixties, Jerome Robbins planned to stage the work and wanted to see several different drafts of my translation, reflecting different approaches to the language. The Robbins production never happened. And the following Note was not written till 1977 when Saul Elkin staged* The Measures Taken *for the State University of New York at Buffalo. I was in no way trying to cover the ground but rather to pinpoint a single issue: to isolate what seemed likely to embarrass our Buffalo audiences and forestall that embarrassment with a little candor.*

1977. THE GOVERNMENT OF THE United States would like the government of the U.S.S.R. to respect "human rights."

Sarcastic commentators have not been slow to point out that the rights implied—notably, habeas corpus—are not held by the citizenry of most countries in the world—are not held, even, by most of the countries designated "friendly" to the United States. One of the "friendliest," Iran, is indeed one of the most unfriendly to those rights and to all individual freedoms.

That, we say, is politics, and we think perhaps of Brendan Behan's remark: "I'll never make a politican, I've only got one face."

If we are cynics, we leave the matter there: "rights" are something that belong to ideology and propaganda; in practice they can be, and are, discounted. We all preach rights; we just don't practice what we preach.

One thing wrong with cynicism in this case is that it overlooks the fact that many honorable and intelligent persons have not preached—have not believed in—such rights. One of these persons is the father of Western philosophy, Plato, who, in *The Laws* 942AB, wrote:

> The principal thing is that none, man or woman, should ever be without an officer set over him, and that none should get the mental habit of taking any step, whether in earnest or in jest, on his individual responsibility: in peace as in war he must live always with his eye on his superior officer, following his lead and guided by him in his smallest actions... in a word, we must train the mind not even to consider acting as an individual or know how to do it.

This is Plato in what is sometimes called his Spartan vein, and there is a clue in the word *Spartan,* in that what distinguished Sparta was the subordination of all other elements in its culture to the military factors.

There can be little doubt that the chief model of social order throughout Western history has been the military model, and of this proposition the converse is that whenever a regime has made order its highest priority it has by that token proclaimed the military state. Prussia is a famous example, and in the Articles of War of the Prussian Army in the time of the author of *The Prince of Homburg* and *The Marquise of O.* we read that a Prussian officer must obey his superior "even against his own honor." And if this strikes you as a peculiarly Prussian extremism, remind yourself that the founder of the Society of Jesus had laid it down that, faced with a conflict between individual conscience and obedience to the Order, the Jesuit must commit himself to obedience. Ignatius Loyola had transferred the military discipline of his soldiering youth to a religious Order—an idea of genius, perhaps, but hardly an idea of liberty.

It is, of course, only in countries where the citizens have won those individual rights that there is any broad contrast between military and civilian law. In such countries, civilians may well be shocked by Bertolt Brecht's *Measures Taken* because of its clear-cut defense of the right of the group to liquidate the individual in the group interest. Even they, however, would probably not be shocked if the story were placed in a wartime setting. Noncivilians could hardly be shocked (unless they are also stupid) since no general could run a battle except on the assumptions about solidarity and obedience that are made by Brecht in his play. Ethics aside, the practicalities of strategy and tactics require that when a decision is taken by the High Command it be carried out by the soldiery.

But our Western audiences have three more reasons for being shocked at *The Measures Taken:* 1. that, as they see it, the situation depicted is not a wartime situation; 2. that the disciplinarians are Communists, who we have been brought up to believe are our mortal foes; and 3. that the individual sacrificed is not a traitor, malingerer, or fool but the "good guy" of the outfit, apparently getting his for his very goodness.

The first two of these three reasons are at bottom the same, for Karl Marx proposed to regard the struggle between the peoples and world capitalism as a war, a universal civil war—the class war. The only ethics, therefore, would be, in a clear sense, military ethics. "We derive our morality," Lenin put it, "from the interests of the proletarian class war."

And the third reason for being shocked at *The Measures Taken* is particularly poignant since, for the Western spectator, that good guy, punished for his very goodness, is himself. For obviously every spectator who is not a Communist and therefore does not identify himself with the Party when he sees this play, identifies himself with the Young Comrade—except, no doubt, when the latter identifies *himself* with the Party and agrees to his own execution.

Now it is a well-known part of the Brechtian theory that we must not identify ourselves with the protagonist, at any rate not to the extent we have expected to. In the light of this principle it was quite cunning of Brecht to permit us an identification with the Young Comrade then, suddenly, to shock us out of that identification. At this point, indeed, we withdraw angrily from our entanglement in history with the word *No!* on our lips.

Well, such is dialectical drama. Brecht suggests, in a note, that if you wish to learn something more after playing the part of the Young Comrade, you should play one of the Agitators; after which you should try singing in the Control Chorus; switching roles in a political psychodrama in order to get the feel of the other standpoint.

And dialectics works both ways. An actor who had sung in the Chorus or played an Agitator would have it borne quite strongly in on him, when he then played the Young Comrade, to what extent Brecht wrote sympathy into that role, gave it a certain dignity, brought it to the verge (though not over the verge) of pathos.

> And we looked and in the twilight saw
> His naked face, human, open, guileless...

In the New Testament, there is a story of a zealous young man who thought he could win the Authorities over to his view of things. He was wrong. They put him to death. Yet "all that sat in the Council, looking steadfastly upon him, saw his face, as it had been the face of an angel." The New Testament tells the story from the young man's viewpoint: he is Stephen, the first Christian martyr. And it is interesting that Communist Party critics, back in 1930, wished Brecht had taken Stephen's—the Young Comrade's—side, just as his "bourgeois" readers and spectators still do.

A nondialectical drama, one concludes, would have suited everybody, while very likely boring everybody too. *The Measures Taken*, as we have it, suits nobody. But it also bores nobody and, I venture to think, has something in it for everybody.

The Rise and Fall of the City of Mahagonny
1979

In the forties (as far as the United States is concerned) Brecht was a blank; in the fifties, a smudge;* it was in the sixties and seventies that his name became a banner headline, which was a very mixed blessing. For example, it got Mahagonny *produced at the Metropolitan Opera House, and—despite a John Dexter production with many strong points—the bigness somehow made him small, the glare of light had the effect of darkness. But in the following Notes, written for the program at the Met, I sought to help make the occasion a grand one.*

WHAT HAS BEEN, SO FAR, THE GREATEST *moment in twentieth-century theater?* The drum scene in *Mother Courage* as suggested earlier? Another keen suggestion would be: the end of the first act of *Mahagonny*—number II in the libretto—that whole sequence, or perhaps the exact moment when Jimmy Mahoney says, "Du darfst es" (Yes, you may).

---

* "[I]t is difficult to escape the feeling that Brecht speaks only to Bentley, and that Bentley speaks only to God." (Walter Kerr, *Herald Tribune Book Review*, April 5, 1953.)

You may what? Anything. You may think the unthinkable. You may *do* the unthinkable. In fact, until this conclusion was reached, something seemed lacking—even in the paradise of booze and sex that was Mahagonny. Paradise was—isn't it always?—boring. Peace is illusory. Real in Nature are the hurricane and the typhoon. Real in *human* nature, in human society, are hurricanes and typhoons of a different, even superior, order: World War I, the crash of 1929 . . . Nature has nothing to teach humankind:

> Wir brauchen keinen Hurrikan
> Wir brauchen keinen Taifun
> Denn was er an Schrecken tun kann
> Das können wir selber tun.

> We do not need your hurricane
> We do not need your typhoon
> Because anything typhoons can do in the way of
> horrors
> We can do on our own.

"Mahagonny" and T. S. Eliot's "Waste Land." To continue our playful quiz: Was the publication of *The Waste Land* in 1922 the greatest moment in twentieth-century poetry? It certainly ended nineteenth-century poetry, and proclaimed the end of nineteenth-century civilization, doing with words what World War I had done with tanks and shells. By that token, it looks back—how desolately!—to the age when the poet invited you to "grow old along with me, the best is yet to be." *Mahagonny* is more modern. It looks forward. This is no cause for rejoicing: the worst was yet to be. Hitler and the Holocaust—typhoon of typhoons—were yet to be; for Jimmy Mahoney they were already in the cards. The barbaric thirties and forties are inherent in this masterpiece of the twenties. (*Mahagonny* was completed in 1929.)

One of Brecht's friends has said that Brecht invented the word *Mahagonny* (not even in German identical with the word for mahogany) after seeing Nazi storm troopers in the streets and thinking they looked like wooden soldiers. Significant is that most intellectuals of those days dismissed Hitlerism as merely silly, while Brecht recognized its tremendous negative dynamics, recognized a destructive force that, like modern weaponry itself, could overwhelm the planet we live on.

"Mahagonny" and the Holy Bible. That Brecht once described the Bible as his favorite book has widely been received as a mere joke, and indeed he did not spend many of his adult hours poring over the holy book. Even so, from his early upbringing, he had a mind full of biblical imagery, and the phrases of Luther's translation sprang incessantly to his lips. Nor is this just a matter of wording and form. A modern "point," for Brecht, will most often be a Christian "point" stood on its head. Mack the Knife will be captured on a Thursday so that the day of his (presumed) execution and "passion" will be a Good Friday. In *Mahagonny,* the Hebrew conception of "Babylon" is never far away, nor is the Hebrew prophet's prevision of an end to all things. Christian images hover that are postbiblical.

In *Major Barbara,* a play that deeply influenced Brecht, Bernard Shaw told us that Hell was nowadays located in the slums of the big city: poverty was the modern Damnation. Add to this suggestion the very different idea, also proposed by Shaw, that Hell is a perpetual vacation, and you have the two main premises of the Brecht-Weill work. The combination of Brecht's words with Weill's music communicates the intuition and experience of such Hells much more vividly, more disturbingly, than Shaw's comedies. Brecht and Weill re-create an Inferno that Dante would have recognized as his own.

"Mahagonny" and "Wozzeck." Alban Berg's *Wozzeck* is another amazing product of the 1920s: a great drama of a century earlier became this century's greatest opera. In maintaining that the great opera *Mahagonny* is, in the last analysis, a great *play,* I intend no deroga-

tion of Kurt Weill. Nor would I revive the Wagnerian notion of Music Drama. In my view, all good opera is music drama in Wagner's sense—that is to say, the music itself is dramatic. All Mozart's operas are music dramas: the music makes what one might almost call Shakespearean plays out of brilliantly serviceable but brittle and in themselves not very dramatic libretti. Mozart always gets the better of Da Ponte, and Berg gets the better of Büchner, even though the latter was a great playwright. *Wozzeck* is not the same sort of work as Büchner's *Woyzeck,* on which it is based. For one thing, Berg enlarges many of the emotions so much that a difference of degree becomes a difference of kind. Büchner's characters are changed. A non-Büchnerian world is created. In *Mahagonny,* on the other hand, a non-Brechtian world is *not* created, nor are non-Brechtian characters. A single vision, a single mind controls all, and it is not that of Kurt Weill.

I can be wrong about this, and I know Brecht himself inclined sometimes to another view. A composer was to him a sibling rival, and by the time he heard the full score of *Mahagonny,* he began to wonder who was winning. Around this time Brecht began to prefer to work with Hanns Eisler, who seemed more easily kept within bounds. Later, Eisler started to prepare music for *The Good Woman of Setzuan,* but Brecht stopped him in his tracks because he was "using too many instruments." "This is not going to be an opera," said Brecht, handing Eisler's job over to another and yet more submissive composer, Paul Dessau.

Brecht's notes to *Mahagonny* indicate that at the time he was willing to accept opera if its definition could be changed. Later on he generally avoided opera altogether. Are Dessau's two Brecht operas (*Lucullus* and *Puntila*) exceptions? Yes and no. They are indeed *called* operas. But in the more effective of the two, *The Trial of Lucullus,* the one on which Brecht collaborated with him, the music is pretty much reduced to percussive accompaniment of the text. Sublime sound effects, like his contribution to Brecht's *Coriolanus.*

Is the City of Mahagonny all bad? The Mahagonny Brecht originally imagined was a place that appealed to him—a place where people had fun. The philosophy that Brecht worked out before he espoused Marxism in the late twenties was not *totally* negative. True, one could not reach happiness by being good. And if one was bad beyond a certain point, one was so conspicuous, one was likely to be brought down in some big crisis or other. The answer, as I argue in my piece on *Threepenny* elsewhere, was to be bad but in a small way, like Mack the Knife: such a man would at least have fun till his luck ran out. The Mahagonny Brecht invented in the midtwenties, or earlier, was populated by Macheaths, and it was clear the inventor was happy to be in their company. The Brecht-Weill Mahagonny is something else. Something opposite. The previously innocent hedonism is now guilt-laden, nasty, noxious, perverse. "Fun" is now as sinful in this Brechtian, materialistic work as in the worldview of Christian puritanism. Yes: the City of Mahagonny is all bad.

Is the opera "Mahagonny" really an opera? Any conceivable audience is going to have fun with the (sinful) fun of the work: what can you do with "Oh, moon of Alabama" except love it? But loving it, you are wallowing in its wickedness and munching what Brecht thought of as its culinary deliciousness.

Brecht once said he would be remembered only by a single line in *The Threepenny Opera* (the opera that is *definitely* not an opera). That line runs: "Erst kommt das Fressen, dann kommt die Moral"—"Till we've had dinner, morality can wait." Audiences relish the spunky cynicism that is in *The Threepenny Opera* and reject or ignore whatever else is in that immense work. Will the audience of the Metropolitan Opera House be so cavalier with *Mahagonny*? No one can stop them, if they insist. Fun is there to be shared, as food to be eaten, and Brecht himself was later to reaffirm the ancient and Aristotelian view that the purpose of theater is precisely to give pleasure. *Mahagonny* gave pleasure willy-nilly before Brecht arrived at that conclusion, and Kurt Weill's score is *pure* fun. At any rate it is much closer to being pure fun than Brecht's libretto is, and some fun-lovers will therefore wish this opera were being performed in a language they did not understand. But is it an opera? Is Brecht's text a libretto? Is it not, as I have been saying, a play?

For that matter, is it really a play? In the program at the Met, my piece ended with the previous paragraph. In the same program, I found that Andrew Porter, a music critic I respect and regularly read, said just the opposite: *Mahagonny* is an opera because Kurt Weill wrote a score for opera singers, and actors cannot sing it. Q.E.D. The key word in my question—an opera? a play?—would seem to be the word *really.* What is really so, what is real, what is reality? Let metaphysicians tackle that one, but let me add something modestly pragmatic to Mr. Porter's proposition. Actors can, too, sing *Mahagonny,* and have—ever since 1930—not, to be sure, in the very first production (Leipzig) but certainly in the very second one (Berlin). Mr. Porter will counter that the music had to be adapted to the actors, and adaptation meant simplification and reduction. He will therefore reiterate: so the actors did not sing that score after all, and for the reason I gave in the first place, that they could not. I stick to my pragmatism. I have heard Weill's score sung as written, and not only at the Met but in productions that musicians thought more highly of, and I have to make that most pragmatic of all comments: it did not work. Obviously I have no way of proving this, but at least I can explain what I mean: at those performances one had a strong sense that something was being muffled—some *other* sound was being muffled, not the musical one—and one realized, upon reflection, that the Muffled Man was Bertolt Brecht, lying bound and gagged, on the ground, his *words* not coming through. So much in *Mahagonny* does not come to us in music alone—too much, if I may let my own presuppositions show, for an opera. And suddenly in a good performance by actors, with only moderate hurt to the score, it all does come through: an abundance of meaning, with all manner of fun and feeling attached, is released. On balance then *Mahagonny*-given-as-a-play is a bigger work, more moving, more satisfying, more amusing, than *Mahagonny*-given-as-an-opera. My conclusion is confirmed by arithmetic, if not by philosophy: more is more.

Brecht–Bentley Correspondence
1980

Our opponents are the opponents of mankind. They are not "right from their point of view": the wrong consists of their point of view. They may have to be as they are, but they do not have to be . . . They are not men, they are leprosy, and they must be burned out like leprosy.

—Bertolt Brecht

Nothing will repay a man for becoming inhuman. The aim of life is some way of living, as flexible and gentle as human nature; so that ambition may stoop to kindness, and philosophy to candor and humor. Neither prosperity nor empire nor heaven can be worth winning at the price of a virulent temper, bloody hands, an anguished spirit, and a vain hatred of the rest of the world.

—George Santayana

Kurt [Weill] had to get away from Brecht: he never could be a communist.

—Lotte Lenya, *PLAYBILL,* March 1980

I WAS IN TOUCH WITH BERTOLT BRECHT from 1942 to 1956, and it would not surprise me if letters, now forgotten, turned up from any of those fourteen years. I did not keep copies of most of my letters to him, but I have recently been supplied by the Brecht Archive with Xerox copies of a number of these: I gather that the Archive has others in its possession. Not all of Brecht's letters to me have survived as far as I know, but I have about twenty originals. I also have letters from secretaries and colleagues of his, which, I was told, were authorized by him.

Hearing about some of the above facts in the late seventies, an American scholar asked if he could bring out all Brecht's surviving letters to me in a Festschrift. I informed him that, for this, permission from the Brecht estate or its representatives would be required. I did not particularly wish to go through the grueling process of suing for approval from these people, letter by letter, but if he, the prospective editor, could get blanket approval, sight unseen, I would release copies of the letters. Such permission was requested and refused.

Wishing to include the complete text of three Brecht letters in the present volume, I this time sent Xeroxes of the letters to the Suhrkamp Verlag in Frankfurt, the firm that controls Brecht publication rights. An argument ensued that dragged on through most of 1980. The upshot is that the full text is not given here but, instead, excerpts and a paraphrase of what is not excerpted. Parts of other letters also appear here.

During 1945 and 1946, a negotiation was in progress for the publishing firm of Reynal and Hitchcock to bring out a multivolume edition of Brecht's plays under my editorship. They were in process of publishing my first book on drama, *The Playwright as Thinker*, through which their editors had gained some sense of Brecht's stature. The suggestion that they take him on in a big way as a Reynal and Hitchcock author came, of course, from me, and in a letter dated February 27, 1946, Brecht set forth his own editorial ideas for the project. One of them was that I should accept his friend Elisabeth Hauptmann as an associate. I had already jibbed at that, having had experience of this particular collaboration already: Frau Hauptmann had helped with my translation of *Master Race* in 1943 and 1944. But Brecht insisted, and I complied.

All of which is relevant here only as explaining why Brecht took an interest in the appearance of *The Playwright as Thinker* that spring. I was encouraged to think that he and I might put together a publishable correspondence, starting out with a response by Brecht to what I had said about him in the book. In the second letter I wanted to print here in full, he led off with:

> Your suggestion that I should take your book as starting point is legitimate. I am reading it with real enjoyment and slowly. Your first thesis—that throughout the *whole* modern epoch the issue is Naturalism—is a real clarification of things, and I think I see why you did not use the word Realism—it is still too much of a shock for many.* And it's true that modern theater begins to provide the natural history of human society; the poetic and artistic elements are in no contradiction with this. So let me have a little time for my reading; such things should not get disposed of in a hurry. (Incidentally your wife should definitely translate the book into German. It won't be hard to find a publisher, once the printing presses have started up again over there ...)

I don't remember if I answered this. No such answer has turned up as yet in my files. But Brecht clearly did continue with his reading and did pick up my suggestion that we should enter into a discussion in depth on the Brechtian theater. "Our treatment could follow the schema enclosed," he wrote in the third letter I had hoped to print in full, enclosing a page of "possible points."

One thing in what I had published about Brecht (as reprinted above, on page 31) had irked him; it was the notion that, if he was

---

* In all editions of *The Playwright as Thinker,* except the first, I did use the word *Realism.* But BB read the first edition.

not one of the supreme figures like Shakespeare, this was because ours was not a time of greatness and fulfillment:

> What I like about your method [Brecht wrote in this same third letter, dated just August 1946] is always the *tabula rasa* it provides. Important is only that we stand up for our own time, and regard its transitional character as possible greatness. No longing glances in the direction of times of fulfillment—those deceiving images of the good old days that we carry in our heads.

He then tackled *The Playwright as Thinker* head-on:

> It seems to be absolutely correct to look on bourgeois Naturalism, with its social reformism, as the beginning of the new theater, but to get to a great age of theater, one must reach much further back than Ibsen, namely, back to the revolutionary time of the bourgeoisie. Poetics aside, the mirror Ibsen holds to nature is very much clouded over. Compare Shakespeare! And what monotony and rigidity of form! And if reality is exhibited in order that it might be influenced, it is also true that, in Ibsen, reality is reproduced as a total illusion, nothing missing but the fourth wall.

Brecht next came to the crucial question of exactly what he was claiming for his theater:

> ...I am not claiming the epithet Great for a particular dramaturgy, I'm only guarding against the usual neutralizing talk, which even you do not always come out against sharply enough—all those pacifying hints that we are dealing only with the ephemeral, provisional, nonbinding, that it's a matter of mere experiments, whereas actually it is a matter of an attempt to establish the experimental as

a defining function of theater. (Bacon's experiments* are not themselves what count. What counts is the definitive introduction of experiment into the sciences.) The very diverse theatrical forms are by no means attempts to arrive at a final form: only the diversity itself should be final. Nor is the introduction of the experimental into dramaturgy just a matter of forms. Actually, the spectators should be transformed into social experimenters, once the critique of reflected reality has been opened up as a man's source of artistic enjoyment.

My reply to this has survived, as I had now decided to make carbon copies of letters: it seemed they might be destined for publication. This is the full text:

Dear Brecht:

I gather from your letter that you do not today think of Epic Theater as the one and only theater of the future. In your Notes to *The Threepenny Opera*, however, you wrote: "Today...only the Epic form can enable the dramatist to find a comprehensive image of the world." Have you changed your mind? This question is not malicious; nor am I merely curious to learn the history of your mind. I am a little puzzled by your reasoning. Have you really explained the difference between Ibsen and Shakespeare, for instance? Is it really true that the poet of *Peer Gynt, Ghosts,* and *When We Dead Awaken* is monotonous? Is it true that his forms are rigid? And even if it were so, would a comparison with the Elizabethan Age explain it? After all, many of the Elizabethans wrote very woodenly. Or am I missing your point?

---

* What experiments? He caught cold and died after "experimenting" on a chicken. Were there any other experiments? He had no laboratory. Was he not a theorist rather than an experimenter?

I think I understand you and agree with you when you write: "The very diverse theatrical forms are by no means attempts to arrive at a final form: only the diversity itself should be final." But what are you saying about Bacon? Could you elaborate your distinction between Experimentalism as something provisional and Experimentalism as something much more important and lasting? You are right in thinking that it is too easy for people, especially for historians and critics like myself, to assume that our own age is purely an Age of Transition while certain other times were ages of fulfillment. The present is of course pure transition from past to future, and the present age *must* always seem purely transitional; fulfillment on the other hand is something that can be recognized only after the event. All this is true. Nevertheless not all ages are equally great, and one is bound to have some opinion of the greatness or un-greatness of one's own period. My own impression is that the generation 1880–1920 was a much more fruitful one than that of 1920–1945.

To you as a creative artist this may not be important. You will do your work and let others decide how good it is at their pleasure. You are indifferent to my historical and critical judgments for yet another reason: you are not only an artist but a teacher, a fighter, a "propagandist." You have a conception of art which few understand. I think I am probably not one of the few. You will have to explain yourself. The explanation you gave in "Writing the Truth: Five Difficulties" was not enough. I felt that you brushed aside all modern art except your own kind. You brushed it aside; you did not really cope with it. I would welcome two things: a brief account of your philosophy of art and—but this can wait a little—an account of Epic Theater that deals with some of the difficulties raised by Edmund

Fuller some years ago and, more recently, by myself (*The Playwright as Thinker*, pp. 259–61).

These are troublesome demands. But I think you will do yourself a service if you can help American readers and playgoers to see the difference between "Brechtism" and the impossible vulgarities of "proletarian literature" of which the most impossible is Socialist Realism. Like Shaw you are more eager to explain your politics and your morality than your art. This is your privilege. But I warn you that you will never make any further advance in America unless you can dispel the illusions and doubts that at present surround your kind of enterprise. They will not listen to your message until they are "sold" on your art.

Yours ever

Eric Bentley

I got no answering letter. The answer, it seems, was his now famous essay "A Short Organum for the Theatre." Although this was not ready until a couple of years later, a first draft is reported to have been written in summer 1946. "The discovery," writes James K. Lyon in his *Bertolt Brecht in America*, "that a sympathetic collaborator and promoter of his works like Bentley did not understand his theories well enough . . . seems to have been the catalyst in Brecht's writing this early version of the 'Short Organum.' The reference, in his letter, to Francis Bacon, the title of whose famous work Brecht consciously imitated in the title of his own treatise, connects that work with this discussion Bentley triggered. If . . . Brecht did write a first draft of the 'Short Organum' that summer, it arose . . . in response to . . . the reading of Bentley's book *The Playwright as Thinker* and the wish to have his theories explained satisfactorily [by Bentley] to American readers in a forthcoming edition of his own plays."

Considering the problems with which Brecht was confronted in 1946, 1947, and 1948, it is hardly surprising, in any case, that he did not continue the correspondence with his young editor. What he obviously decided to do was encourage me to become more familiar with his work in the hope that I would more and more share his point of view. And so it was that I was his houseguest in the summer of 1947; a visitor to his home in Zurich in 1948; and one of his assistants in Munich in 1950.

But in Munich something happened that proved a kind of turning point. Evidently Brecht decided to handle an important matter through an ambassador, for his friend Ruth Berlau took me out to dinner only, when we got to dessert, to reveal as much. "Brecht wants me to sound you out." "Something he couldn't tell me himself?" "He didn't want to overwhelm you. He knows you and I gossip together and even know how to cuss each other out!" (This was not Ruth's vocabulary. She spoke to me in German—with her Danish accent. I answered in the same tongue—with my Anglo-Saxon twang.)

"Why aren't you one of us?" "Us?" "Oh, you know what I mean. I'm not afraid of the word! Communism! Or just antifascism if you want to call it that! Why aren't you?" "Well, I *am*...sort of... partly...All my best friends..." "Pah, we've read your book! And don't you have a new piece saying Brecht would be a better writer if he gave up Marxism?" "Not exactly, what I said was..." "We know what you said. We are asking if you are ever going to change!" "Change?" "Yes, change. Brecht says, if all these rumors are true, and the Russians are about to take over West Germany, it'll be very good for Bentley, because they'll carry him off to Moscow and reeducate him. He'll learn a lot!" "You're joking." "Oh, no, I have a very important message for you." (She took a deep breath and leaned across the table.) "Brecht is tremendously impressed with you. Thankful too. He knows what you have done for him in America. So much. It's wonderful. You *represent* him there. But that's the question. Do you? Can you? On the aesthetic plane, yes, but don't you know what Brecht's aesthetic is? You do. But you 'disagree' with it. That's what's wrong. Doubly wrong since Brecht is, well, *anti*-aesthetic! Content before form, you understand? If you're antifascist, progressive...why aren't you consistent...why don't you follow through?" "Well, Ruth, where to begin? One of my closest friends, Arnold Kettle, before I even met Brecht, was a Communist. Arnold and I argued all the time . . ." "About what? What couldn't he satisfy you on?" "Oh, the usual stuff—the Moscow Trials . . ."

At the mention of the trials, Ruth blew up. Literally *stood* up in the restaurant and shouted: "Du bist so dumm"—"you are so dumb! Ignorant too! What do *you* know about the Moscow Trials?" "Well, I did look into them. And I didn't think they were on the level!" "That's it, then. I have to tell you this: you can *never* represent Brecht in America while you represent reactionary views, while you are . . . on the other side in the fight!"

Neighboring guests in the restaurant had turned to look at the shouting Dane, but the latter sat down quietly, paid the bill, and became entirely polite again. I thought maybe the incident hadn't happened. We were both a little drunk after all. Or that it wasn't serious.

Ruth never referred back to this conversation, nor did Brecht ever mention it. But, alas, it had happened, and it was serious, and, except for the swearing, Ruth meant every word of it, and did speak for her master, whether or not he had told her to handle it just as she did.

Such was my experience of the Cold War. Not being on the Communist side of it, I was placed, by them, on the anti-Communist side. And, in the fifties, in the midst of those giant antagonisms, I even came at times to believe this was true. I look back at some of my writing of that period and note now (though I had clean forgotten in the intervening decades) that I had allowed myself to be assigned a role in the Cold War, had foolishly allowed myself to assume that if one was not a Communist, one was an "anti-Communist."

As for Brecht, he would sometimes seem to forget—or choose to ignore—that he and I were supposed to be on different sides of the barricades. Not long after Shaw died in 1950, I was with Brecht in East Berlin and he asked me, quite as if I had been a fellow Stalinist, was it true that Shaw had appreciated the greatness of Stalin?

(I was naturally very surprised to learn later that Brecht himself had privately denied the greatness of Stalin. It was in private that he had talked the other way to me: no one within earshot.)

Brecht died in 1956, but the Berlau edict of 1950 survived him. I was not to be the carrier of the flame. I was not to be trusted. Or as Helene Weigel, his widow, put it in so many words to the Brecht scholar John Fuegi: "Bentley is our enemy."* And enemies fight. There was a war of the translations and productions, with East Berlin, as usual, asking everyone which side they were on. The stage designer Teo Otto wrote me:

> Because I did not join the campaign against you as trans-
> lator and antipode of Steff [Stefan Brecht] I have lost
> contact with Helli [Helene Weigel]. It was demanded of
> me that I declare myself against you but, as I say, I refused.

Well, especially for us dialectical thinkers, there's another side to everything. In a letter dated November 12, 1949, which discusses the holes I had picked in (a) his "Short Organum for the Theatre," and (b) his play *Days of the Commune*, Brecht wrote:

> For the rest you are pretty much the only person with
> whom I discuss such things and to whom I write about
> them—if also too little. After all that you have done for
> me, there can be no estrangement from my side because of
> sharp criticism of this or that play from your side: you are
> fully entitled to this.

He went on:

> And please don't let yourself get bitter about my hesitation
> in having you direct plays in the commercial theater. This

---

* "Er ist ein ausgesprochener Feind von uns"—a definite enemy of ours.

has nothing to do with whether I regard you as a "Westerner." (What a term!) Following your defense of my theory—actually the only one there is [*die wirklich einzig dastehend ist*]—a directing job by you would be taken as representative and exemplary. But since theory and practice are separate, and I have not yet seen anything directed by you, and since further my own efforts are still only in a beginning stage, I would prefer that you should practice first in our theater. If you see any chance of this, I would do much to help. Meanwhile, please, no bitterness! For the rest, I prefer the university productions to the commercial ones.

Cordially your old Brecht

To which he added a footnote as follows:

We are now trying to bring out several of your works in the *Neue Rundschau* or in *Sinn und Form:* they are first-classic.

Yes, he wrote "classic," not "class"; he always enjoyed such play on words.

In a letter to me of the year 1954, Brecht said:

About your critical abilities, everyone agrees, except perhaps for a few blockheads; even if a few non-blockheads deplore your appalling lack of political education ... Let me make a suggestion. I have put together a collective [*Arbeitsgemeinschaft*] for dramaturgy. The participants—a period of one to two years is envisaged—draw an income from the Academy, namely 1200 marks a month, and have access to the Berlin Ensemble and the universities. We've already got a notable young Dutch poet and an interesting young playwright from Munich. I'd like to give you an official invitation ... The proposal should at least show you the value I set on your collaboration ...

Did he value this collaboration even while I remained so appallingly lacking in political education? Or did he hope to educate me? Was I being invited to East Berlin, at the height of the Cold War, as friend and ally? Or as heathen to be converted—"enemy" to be brainwashed? I decided to let a little time go by before deciding. But history had no time. Two years later Bertolt Brecht was struck down. The Berlin Ensemble would not again express interest in my "collaboration" until 1980 when a request came from their dramaturg for permission to perform my play *Are You Now or Have You Ever Been.* He ventured to wonder if I would make any trouble about this.

To letter three, as mentioned above, Brecht appended the following possible points for discussion:

> That the plays were written in an age of revolutions and world wars. In phases when social orders dissolve, literature does not simply dissolve with them: a part of it belongs to the dissolving factors.
>
> 1. Continuing the tradition: significant theme, rich narrative, great roles.
>
>   Examination of the themes. Lethal character of the bourgeois ethos in bourgeois relationships: *The Good Woman of Setzuan.* Productivity as the basis of the new morality in *The Caucasian Chalk Circle.* Truth as a commodity in *Galileo.* Ignorant goodness in *Saint Joan of the Stockyards.* Et cetera.
>
>   Examination of the narratives.
>
>   Examination of the roles: Baal, Galy Gay, Callas, Joan Dark, Mauler, Galileo, Courage, Simone, Schweyk, Grusha, Azdak, Shen Te, Peachum, Polly. Et cetera.
>
>   (Compare the efforts to come to grips with classic forms in Picasso and Stravinsky.)

2. The NEW. Dialectical realism.

　a) Realistic attitude to the theme.
　b) Realistic attitude to the audience.

The legend that the doctrinaire dominates the element of entertainment should be combated. It is an impression that comes from class division in the audience—classes whose interests are being attacked seldom feel they are being entertained! But in the bourgeois classics and in the works of antiquity, one had both: the instructive and the entertaining and no contradiction is imputed.

Question: Will you be translating the Notes to *The Threepenny Opera*?

Incidentally: It may interest you that the reviews I received from Vienna where *The Good Woman of Setzuan* was produced during the summer are on quite an idiotic level, since the poor fellows take it all to be symbolic. They interpret the conflict between Shen Te and Shui Ta as eternal, universally human, et cetera. One should really explain sometime the difference between symbol and parable [*Gleichnis*]. A parable is a simple, realistic reflection of a historical situation, a situation that is ephemeral or rather that should be made ephemeral.

The tearing apart of Shen Te is a frightful act of bourgeois society.

The Influence of Brecht
1986

The following piece was originally a talk given at the conference "Brecht Thirty Years After," at the University of Toronto, Canada, October 1986. About a hundred people from East Berlin were on hand, and I expected, mistakenly as it turned out, that some of them would be present at my talk. Hence the "we here today" of page 362 below.

I SHALL NAME THREE FALLACIES.

Begin at the beginning. A new star is found in the heavens. Stars, in astrology, have influence. New star, new influence. A recent instance is Samuel Beckett. A whole battery of astrologers have established that he has a prominent place in the heavens. They deduce from that that he has influence. They are correct. They even prove they are correct. I read an essay just the other day making it quite clear that the plays of younger dramatists are the quintessence of Beckettism. What I'll call the First Fallacy is the assumption—the taking it for granted—that this is a good thing. The plays that are full of Beckettry are not equally full of talent. So what is the question before us? It is whether these plays would have been worse or better without Beckett's influence. Unanswerable. How could one ever find out? Luckily, all I need for my argument here is the fact that the influence of Beckett is not, in any of the evidence, *shown* to be a good thing. It is possible that some of the Beckett epigones would do better left to their own devices. Or influenced by someone else. To go further than this, one would have to look in detail at particular examples and their whole context. The next conclusion to reach is that the reason for celebrating Beckett's alleged influence has, in the last analysis, little to do with celebrating the authors influenced. The aim is to celebrate Beckett. Beckett has influence because he is big. And he is big not least because he has influence. So what is wrong? Primarily, I suppose that, when we thought we were talking about literature as such, we find we were talking only about public relations. We were talking only of the way in which the astrologers call further attention to their star. No doubt they have every right to do this. But, contrariwise, we have every right to object to the confusion of one subject with another.

The second fallacy of influence lies in the fact that the word is not clear, and that it is not clear because it is a blanket term, and the blanket covers far too large a bed. What *is* influence? When Jesus appeared in the sky and said, "Why persecutest thou me?" Saul of Tarsus, a Christian-baiter, became the Christian saint Paul. That's influence: impact unmistakable and total, Saul taken over by Jesus. If only literary influence were as clear and simple! Some scholars have thought it *was* as clear and simple. If Poet *A* says the sky is blue, and Poet *B*, later, says the sky is blue, these scholars see what happened as the influence of *A* on *B*. The second fallacy of influence is the assumption that *post hoc* must be *propter hoc*, which is still a fallacy when the examples given are complex. Those who do not allow for the possibility of this kind of error are allowing neither for accidental coincidence nor for natural affinity and confluence. Did Charles Darwin influence Alfred Russel Wallace or vice versa? The two men put forward the same theory of evolution at the same time. Science was converging on the same conclusion from two sides. Does this never happen in the arts? Something very like it is happening all the time in the arts. Here it is not usually a convergence on an idea. It is more often that the influences of *A, B, C,* and *D* become so mixed that it is unreasonable to cite any one as *the* influence.

What about cases when *post hoc is propter hoc,* cases when, for one reason or another, we know that words were transferred from an earlier text to a later? If such transfer be automatically called influence, we have a third fallacy, the fallacy involved in assuming that if Writer *A* draws on Writer *B, B* is necessarily influencing *A.* Writers you quote do not necessarily influence you: they are "necessarily" being made use of, being exploited, by you. In such cases influence is only a possibility. Did the quotations in T. S. Eliot's *Waste Land* influence Eliot in the writing of his poem? It is possible that in some degree they did. What degree, though? One cannot take the measure of it. One certainly has no sense of other minds bearing down on Eliot and changing his course. One definitely has a sense of *his* changing *their* course: the quotations *are* influenced by their context in Eliot's poem.

It is appropriate to introduce Bertolt Brecht's name at this point. In the songs to *The Threepenny Opera* was he influenced by François Villon? The songs are, to a considerable extent, based on Villon ballades. Insofar as the spirit of those ballades is carried over into German by Karl Klammer, the translator, and Brecht, the adapter, Klammer and Brecht are surely being influenced by Villon. All translators and adapters are obviously influenced by their source. Yet there is a fallacy—Fallacy Three—here if we assume that the word *influence* covers the case even approximately. One can argue that the young Brecht, and not only in *The Threepenny Opera,* was influenced by Villon, but one can argue, at least as persuasively, that he was not so influenced, but that he merely made use of Villon when it was convenient and amusing to do so. What people take to be the spirit of Villon in such work could in fact be simply the spirit of Brecht. which had much in common with that of Villon. In this case Villon came in handy but was probably not necessary to the formation of Brecht's spirit and style. Finally, as far as Fallacy Three is concerned, when what we have is a source on which a writer is drawing, it is *gratuitous* to speak of influence; the word *source* does cover the case. So I shall not speak of the influence of John Gay on the *The Threepenny Opera,* much less that of Nordahl Grieg on *Tage der Commune*—"much less" because, if Grieg's play were an influence and not just a source, it would be a negative influence, it would have influenced Brecht, not to say what Grieg said, but to say the opposite. In a crass, literal sense, provocation *is* a form of influence. You are powerfully affected by what powerfully provokes you. And words are free—you can use them as you choose. But negative influence is sufficiently different from the positive kind as almost to require a separate word. For the prime function of influence is positive. It is to inspire.

Every inspired writer is inspired, in part, by other writers. This is probably as it should be. It is certainly as it is. And the same thing is true in the other arts. Beethoven liked to have the scores of Handel and Mozart to hand. He was influenced by them. It is therefore legitimate to ask of any artist: who influenced him? The answer should have, at the least, biographical and historical interest, even if it does not reveal any secrets of the art that results. It can be amazing how unerringly an artist finds the predecessors who can and will influence him. They will not always be the greatest. What the artist looks for is not merit on any terms but assimilable merit, congenial, relevant merit: merit that happens to meet his need of the moment.

Sometimes a major talent is influenced by a minor one. It can be asked: how could influence like that be called inspiration? Let's take a problematic case: the influence of Eugène Scribe, and Scribean drama generally, on Henrik Ibsen. It could be argued that Scribe did not inspire Ibsen but merely provided him with a formula. But this is unfair to Scribe who came to Ibsen, so to speak, possessed of much more than a mechanism. If the cleverness of an Agatha Christie or an Alfred Hitchcock were just a mechanical formula, then anyone who learns a little of that, shall we say, arithmetic? could write a Christie novel or direct a Hitchcock film. Scribe had talent of their sort. It has its own *je ne sais quoi.* To take over something of its real quality, and not just the externals of a method, one has to be inspired by it. (If *inspiration* is too romantic a term for your taste, call it an infection that one has to catch.)

Brecht and influence. First, the influences *on* Brecht. I do not propose to enumerate them. The ground has been gone over many times, perhaps too many times. What of the ground that has not been gone over quite so often? Writers acquire their status by having the influences on them noted and approved. It places them in a Tradition. You or I after all can pay someone to prove that you or I are descended from William the Conqueror. A writer can find scholars to prove his descent from Homer or the *Urvater* of his choice. Such games become boring only when scholars continue them after they have ceased to be needed. Ceased to be needed by their author, that is. They may still be needed for the scholars' academic advancement. But the boredom inflicted on the reader will now rub off on the author. He is now that most passé of all creatures, a leader of a former avant-garde, hero of yesterday's tomorrow.

Sidestepping, then, the main body of information about literary influences on Brecht, let me make one or two possibly marginal comments. First, influence of the great. Brecht was little influenced by the greatest names in German-language drama: Lessing, Goethe and Schiller, Hebbel and Grillparzer, even Kleist. Ibsen had no positive influence on him, nor did Chekhov or Pirandello. But Bernard Shaw's influence is marked on *Saint Joan of the Stockyards.* It is not limited to use of source material. And it is in part negative: Brecht is reacting against Shaw.

About Brecht, Shaw, and Shakespeare. In his youth, Shaw had had to deplore the influence of Shakespeare on the English stage. He embarked upon an anti-Shakespearean campaign in order to free that stage for modern drama. People laughed, but the laugh was on them: GBS knew what he was about. The dramatist Brecht emerged in a different place and at a different date. It was his privilege, as it was not Shaw's, to let Shakespeare *inspire* him. A professional enthusiasm for Elizabethan theater in general probably had more to do with Brecht's so-called epic forms of the twenties than anything further afield, such as Chinese or Japanese theater, of which, even later, he knew much less than the thousands of Western students who today can see Peking Opera and Kabuki and Noh.

The final result of all the polemics and all the scholarship about influences on Brecht is that these influences have come to be overstressed. I have already suggested how that could come to be. First, there was a needed polemic to legitimize Brecht, to establish his place in a dynasty. Second, there was the need of scholars to publish articles and their way of elaborating points and repeating facts ad nauseam before a halt is called. It is an irony that discourse that begins as an effort to raise Brecht's status ends by lowering that status. For to overestimate a writer's dependency on other writers is to underestimate his *in*dependence, his individual strength, his originality. I am reminded of discussions of Brecht's plagiarisms and near-plagiarisms. Critics who take pleasure in pointing these out are so carried away that they fail to note how Brecht made his borrowings his own. In *The Threepenny Opera* he might use whole lines of Klammer, but the song as a whole could only have come from one hand, his own. I am also reminded of discussions of Brecht's politics. Both critics who want to show him very much the Marxist, and those who want to show the reverse, direct our attention to what Brecht had in common with others, Communists or non-Communists, and not on the individuality of his thinking and his writing, his own persona as a poet.

What of the influence of Brecht's collaborators on Brecht? No one was more inclined than he was, in conversation at least, to credit this collaborator or that. Yet in the text that results from collaboration what one hears is one voice, recognizable only from the other works of the one poet, Bertolt Brecht. And these other works had other collaborators.

It is known that the play *Happy End,* except for the songs, was written by Elisabeth Hauptmann. I see no problem therein. She wrote in the Brecht manner, and not surprisingly came up with second-string Brecht. Some of my colleagues believe that she wrote most of *The Measures Taken.* I have no special competence to judge the facts, but any one of us has the right to say that, if she did so, all that is thereby proved is that she could write better Brechtian prose than that in *Happy End.* And we have some questions waiting for any scholar who might prove that X number of lines in *The Measures Taken* did in fact come first from the typewriter of Elisabeth Hauptmann. For instance, before she went to that typewriter, what discussions had she had with Brecht? Given his capacity to be Svengali to any Trilby, couldn't he have told her what to write, perhaps even verbatim?

Note what has happened to my argument now. Asking what influence Frau Hauptmann might have had on Brecht, I find myself declaring that *he* had an influence on *her.* Someone may retort that, being his *Freundin,* she must surely have had an influence on him. But this is not literary influence. I see no evidence that the literary persona of Elisabeth Hauptmann had any influence at all upon Brecht's own writing, whereas it is obvious that *Happy End,* if not written by Brecht, was written by a Brecht epigone.

Those, if any still live, who believe in the possibility of collective authorship can find little comfort in the works of Brecht. *Mitarbeiter* are acknowledged, if in small type and on a separate page, but nowhere is the presence of a second personality felt in the finished work. If the claim that Frau Hauptmann wrote Brecht has a future, it can only be accompanied by the theory that she learned to write like him. He was a dybbuk, if you will, and spoke from inside her.

I come finally to the influence of Brecht on posterity. This is to speak again of public relations. At an early stage of a great writer's career, his Public Relations Director may well decide to establish that he is not as iconoclastic as he seems. He is in a great tradition. He is great among great predecessors. Thus, the music of Schoenberg is shown, not to be arbitrarily new, but to spring from Wagner and Brahms and other worthies. But, later, Schoenberg's Public Relations Director must do an about-face. The greatness of the same music must now be established by the fact that it is welcome to the bright spirits of the younger generation. An appeal to the Fathers gives place to an appeal to the Sons. It is understandable, then, that people who wish to pay tribute to Brecht should cite his influence. Their tribute seems to increase Brecht's importance. But they have fallen into the trap of my First Fallacy, and have forgotten that the influence of a good author can be bad. The influence of Shakespeare was bad at the time when Shaw declared it so: his case for liberating the London stage from Shakespeare was a sound one and, incidentally, did not invalidate his case for a Shakespeare differently seen, as by W. Poel's Elizabethan Stage Society.

The influence of Shakespeare. The word *influence* is vague in itself and is made vaguer by its object: influence of what part of Shakespeare, what feature of Shakespeare, what connection of Shakespeare's? When we try to answer this question, another question opens up. Is it Shakespeare himself who is having the influence, or things that have grown up around him, for instance, the Victorian style of producing him? Even if we decide it is the latter, we still have to ask if Shaw, attacking the production style, by necessity of polemic rather than logic, didn't have to tackle Shakespeare too? GBS used the famous phrase "Better than Shakespeare" about himself, though with a question mark that people then omitted. Even the omission belongs to the polemic. The thrust of the whole transaction was that Shaw really *was* better—for the London stage at the time—than Shakespeare.

Back to Brecht. Influence of Brecht is influence of *what*, exactly, in the Brecht oeuvre? The influence of his dramatic theories on theatrical producers? The influence of the Berlin Ensemble? The influence of Marxism as championed by Brecht? These questions, so different from each other, get mixed up—utterly confused—in our discussions of them.

At least one of the questions brings an abrupt change of subject. I have been treating the subject of influence as that of the influence of one writer upon another, the inspiring of one author by another. This is a matter of writer psychology. Energies of one writer pass over into another. But when we talk of influence on audience, that is something rather different. An audience as such will not be inspired to artistic creation. When we say it is influenced, we mean that something from the work of art will stay with it, will not be water off a duck's back. There is an impact that, on the one hand, and, most obviously, is emotional and, on the other, and more mysteriously, is spiritual and intellectual.

How *much* influence can any art have on its audience? The only limit, emotionally, is the limit of each recipient's own emotions. A big work will touch his heart as deeply as his heart can be touched. Spiritually and intellectually, he can feel stimulated, challenged, enlightened. It is even conceivable that his opinions can be changed, which would be influence indeed. In the theater, this seldom happens. In any art, it seldom happens and is seldom the aim. If minds are changed by anything but circumstances, they are changed by the principal idea carriers: philosophers, theologians, even politicians. Dante, one can confidently assume, has not changed as many minds as Aquinas: if it is possible for anyone to convert you to Catholicism, a priest or a philosopher is more likely to do it than a poet. If you *think* a poet has done it, you may well be deceiving yourself: the poet probably came along after the real persuading, if any was needed, had been done. Thus, if someone is going to become a convinced Marxist, he is likely to be convinced by Marx himself, and not to the same extent by Marxist poets. If you ask me if Brecht had an influence on the *world*, politically, I would answer: very little, and not always influence of the kind he sought. The influence of words, after all, is often, in all contexts, quite different from what is intended.

Brecht's influence on theater? Certainly very marked, not only in Germany, but in France and England. But is this a good thing? Who can say? Besides, what is good? I'm sure we here today are not agreed on that. In politics, we are not. Are we agreed in other areas? Yes, we probably could agree that British Shakespeare production changed sharply after the visit to London of the Berlin Ensemble in 1956. Most of us think it changed for the better. It adjusted itself anyway to *us,* the audience of the later twentieth century, especially in becoming earthier, gutsier, what Brecht called more realistic.

In England he influenced playwrights, too. Was *this* good? Probably Edward Bond would tell us it was good for him; but for my part, I don't know if it was. These things are hard to gauge. Who knows what Edward Bond would have been without Brecht? Maybe less dryly didactic and better. But I don't know that. A writer, when influenced at all, is often influenced in several ways at the same time. Brecht may have made Bond better in one way, worse in another. Since one doesn't have an uninfluenced Edward Bond to compare with our Edward Bond, we come here to historical *ifs,* ever a frustrating and futile category.

What I was asked to write about was Brecht's influence in America. The main reason I didn't want to should by now be evident. And I had other reasons. One is that much that is called Brechtian in the United States, well . . . Brecht can't be blamed for it, or can be blamed only for writing his theoretical essays. Students—teachers even more—love it when an artist has a theory. It keeps them busy, possibly earns the teachers money and promotion and confirms in them a belief that the arts are there to illustrate theories of the arts. A play is there to be a tragedy, or to be naturalistic, or to be epic theater.

It is widely assumed that Aristotle announced the three unities, and that Sophocles then sat down to write *Oedipus Rex.* Brecht must have thought of Epic Theater in about 1916 and then written *Baal* to exemplify it. Within their chosen field—vocabulary (terminology, nomenclature)—what academics most enjoy is words to conjure with. Epic Theater: two words to conjure with. *Gestus* and *Verfremdung:* two more—and even better because they have no

English equivalents. Thoughts that are really deep can only be expressed in German. Hegel established that long ago, and Brecht's theoretical essays provide further evidence. This way American scholars are kept busy writing whole paragraphs—pages—chapters—on what any single German word means. The same words provide translators with food for feuds. So, alas, Brecht's theoretical writings have had an influence in America: a bad influence.

What about his poems and plays? Poetry works on people so quietly and internally, one can hardly speak of its influence till it is fruitfully seen, if it ever is, in later poetry. American poetry has not become Brechtian. Nor has American drama, though I am far from insisting that it should have. When Brecht's influence *is* seen, if it is not the influence of his essays, probably misunderstood, it is the influence of the externals of his theatrical technique. For it is easy enough to ban colored light, to expose the lighting equipment, and so on. One even hears actresses hopefully mimicking the mannerisms of Lotte Lenya or coming on real butch, arms akimbo, legs spread as Mother Courage, hoping that this is "Brechtian." (I have seen the style of a cabaret singer ruined by the effort to be "Brechtian.")

Nor is it just the essays that are misunderstood. Everything is misunderstood. When *The Threepenny Opera* opened in New York in 1954, I asked why the actors kept bumping into each other. Inevitably I was told: "That's Brechtian; deliberate roughness of texture, closeness to real life, the result of *das plumpe Denken*." I am not exaggerating: I am describing, without distortion, what influence ends up as, namely, the influence of what had not been said in the first place. No fallacy here, just error. But important because it is something that has happened before and can happen again.

What remedy is there, short of putting an end to all human stupidity? One thing that would help is to reduce human belief in influence, specifically the influence of the great. Greatness does not impart greatness. It creates epigones: many little fish swimming around the one big fish. Epigones hope for reflected glory. But glory reflects rather dimly and becomes much less glorious. It is legitimate for the small to try to grow, but, in many situations, their purpose will be less well served by following on than by breaking away. Disciples have to find the energy to become rebels—or, better, voyagers.

Richard Wagner had many epigones, and a break with Wagnerism then became appropriate. Henrik Ibsen had many epigones, and a break with Ibsenism became appropriate. And now, because Brecht has had all the adulation, all the cult following, that any writer could ever aspire to, a break with him, and what he stood for, has become appropriate. This is by no means to say the adulation was undeserved. Today Wagner and Ibsen have no epigones. Wagner and Ibsen are the gainers. The greatness is all theirs. Our view of the big fish is no longer obscured by shoals of little fish. So it can be tomorrow with Brecht if those who are now dependent on him can change course and emulate his independence.

Dramatic Poetry Was Reborn in Germany
1989

Nineteen eighty-nine was the year in which the Berlin Wall came down as the Soviet Union began to collapse. Brecht had been dead, of course, for thirty-three years, but it was hard for some people to believe that, after the shocks of 1989, even his soul went marching on. For me, it did. Nineteen eighty-nine could even be seen as its liberation. I felt all the freer to speak of his work in nonpolitical, artistic terms.

The following pages are taken from a lecture at the first Yeats International Theatre Festival in Sligo, Ireland, 1989. My announced topic was "the poet in the modern theater," and I was permitted to range beyond the confines of Yeats's plays to poetic drama generally. Of course, Brecht had to be mentioned and "placed" in this context—not, happily, in the context of Marxist thought or Soviet practice.

UNTIL THE EIGHTEENTH CENTURY, dramatic poets were people who supplied a demand, the demand of the acting profession and the institution of theater as a whole. It is in the eighteenth century that we find the poets finding the theater and all its works beneath them, and Byron, early in the nineteenth century, is a spokesman for the whole elite when, in several of the prefaces to his plays, he indicates in no uncertain terms that he does not wish his work distorted and degraded by theater people: he is publishing his plays that they may be read, and read in seclusion.

Now actually Byron was familiar with theater and had been performed there. At least one of his plays would have quite a stage history after his death. Even so, he did usher in the era of the closet drama, and few closet dramas invited performance. Not that the literary drama, in this sense, was new. Milton's *Samson Agonistes*, surely, is a literary drama. It has been performed, and people have enjoyed its performance, though I would say they enjoyed it, not as theater, but as a poetry reading, and poetry readings are to theater as oratorio is to opera: the readers of the one and the singers of the other are rooted to the spot, do not interact, do not make eye contact with each other, do not—in short—act. (There are of course no costumes, no stage sets, and so on, but these elements are only ancillary, not essential, to the drama.)

In the twentieth century, many of the poets wished to return to the theater but few of them knew how. Many assumed all they had to do was have their closet dramas recited onstage. This only resulted in poetry readings—onstage and in costume. We must assume that such poets did not recognize the organic connections between dramatic poetry and the institution of theater and preeminently the actors. They offered poetry in the theater but not poetry, in Jean Cocteau's famous phrasing, of the theater. How do these differ? Cocteau suggested that, in a way, theater of the theater is cruder: you cannot make your stage set with silken threads, invisible from a distance, you must use thick and thus visible ropes. This "thickness" is not necessarily vulgarity, though dramatic poetry is certainly inclined to be less dainty than nondramatic. (Jacques Barzun says Brecht wrote poetry with barbed wire.)

How does Shakespearean drama differ from Milton's *Samson Agonistes*? As far as language is concerned, the difference is not least that Shakespeare is more worldly in the sense that his characters are of the world, not necessarily being what we call earthy, for many are far from it, but in belonging to the street or, if off the street, to worldly institutions: the court, the law court, the church. We hear the language of politicians, lawyers, soldiers, churchmen. Shakespeare is much closer to spoken English than is Milton, and I doubt if even the most stylish or stylized form of drama—say the *Oresteia* or the *Phèdre* of Racine—can take us as far from the language people speak as the lyric poet. William Wordsworth was a celebrated champion of simple and "real" language, but he didn't use it in his greatest poem, *The Prelude,* whose blank verse is on this account much closer to Milton than to Shakespeare.

When one says *language,* one thinks first of vocabulary, but what makes Shakespearean verse more dramatic than that of Milton or Wordsworth is as much a matter of meter and rhythm. His rhythms are much more irregular because he retains so much of the jaggedness of actual talking. Except in his earliest works, he does not always even fill up the blank verse line. This is not monologue but dialogue, and people interrupt each other. Their doing so is part of the ongoing agon of dramatic action: a to-and-fro, a battledore and shuttlecock. Monologues themselves can be dramatized by being demonologued: they are, if they are dramatic, dialogues in disguise. The disguise may be crass, as in Cocteau's famous monologue in which the speaker holds a telephone throughout and we live with an active sense of someone at the other end. But even Hamlet's monologues are not monologues: they are dialogues with himself—could even be seen as dialogues with the audience—an implied nod, and "don't you think so?" after every assertion.

Dramatic poetry is based on actual speech and, more important, dramatic poetry is going to be actually spoken. Taken from speakers of the language in the first place, it is going to be returned to the speakers of the language—onstage. And here the meaning of the word *speaker* broadens out, for, in the encounters of human beings with each other, speech, prescribed by words, is acted out not only by the vocal cords but by other parts of the body as well, and not only by the hands and arms, which make the more deliberate gestures, but by an ensemble of all the body's parts. My subject here is body language, which is the actor's language, whatever the priority we may give his talking words. Even a film actor when only his head is seen in a given sequence is using manifold body language, as we note in his management of eyebrow and eyelash, the eye itself, and also the less subtly expressive parts of the face, the wrinkled brow, the jutting chin.

Writers of closet dramas had bodies and no doubt knew it but were not interested in the actor's body. Even when they returned to the theater, they did not expect to return to that, and their failure is part of a larger failure, the failure to realize that while literature in general presents characters, dramatic literature in particular presents characters (and only those) who are also roles. A role is a character-to-be-acted. Thus the playwright has not only to conceive of a character, he has to provide the actor with the means to act it, provide him with the opportunity to, as it were, draw the outline of the character and also bring it into high relief. Many of the would-be poetic playwrights, closet playwrights, simply did not have this ability. Some, maybe, had it but neglected to train and develop it; others saw this element as playacting in the pejorative sense, something vulgar.

My mind jumps here to Henry James, who tried in vain to become a great playwright. One conclusion James reached was that to make drama you had to throw much cargo overboard to save the ship. He saw the exigencies of theater as negative: his characters would be diminished by being dramatized. Now I am not saying that the characters of James's novels lend themselves to dramatization, but I am saying that if they were dramatized something would have to be, not subtracted, but added *that they might become roles.* Let the mind jump to Charles Dickens for an illustration of an obverse phenomenon. Dickens at his worst can certainly be called stagey because he always made sure, even in novels, that his characters were roles as well, which is why his people can walk right out onstage speaking his lines in any dramatization that is made from them. James's characters might, indeed, become vulgarized by any attempt to make them into stage roles. The life that James gave them derived not from dialogue, but from a subtle, discursive prose not made for speaking and projecting aloud. And Dickens is considered vulgar by guardians of literary refinement.

Is a thick rope necessarily more vulgar than a fine thread? What James may have had more reason to fear than vulgarity was the role-playing in itself. But an actor's job is role-playing: therefore the playwright who provides the play the actor enacts must be sympathetic to role-playing, and to that vision of life as role-playing that is invoked more than once by Shakespeare and was both a philosophy and an obsession to Pirandello. *Totus mundus facit histrionem*—all the world plays the actor. A playwright may tell you he disagrees with this idea, but if he then writes a play, is he not paying tribute to it? I am proposing no answer to this question except that, as far as drama is concerned, the idea of role is not minor or marginal but major and central. And it has many aspects. For instance, why is *Hamlet* the most effective of Shakespeare's tragedies? Not for any reason that you will find in scholarly accounts of the play, which, when not preoccupied with details, are concerned with the complexities of character or the nature of tragedy. *Hamlet* holds the stage beyond any other tragedy because of the opportunities it affords the actor. I am not speaking of the play's popularity merely. *Hamlet* is not necessarily the play with most *in* it, but for most people it is the play you will get most *out of* should you see it tonight: in the hands of anyone but a bad actor, it is the play in which, in the four hours it takes up, a human destiny is most completely acted out. Prospero is just as interesting a person, but Prospero is not as good a part, as actors who rashly undertake it learn at their cost. But if much remains controversial about *Hamlet,* and will be discussed forever and ad nauseam, one feature, not often remarked, should be clear and unequivocal: the Prince of Denmark is the ultimate *role.*

When the nineteenth century built an Ivory Tower for the poet, and told him "as for living, your servants can do that for you," they were placing him at the farthest remove from Shakespeare's Globe Theatre or any other theater that has a lively audience and playwrights working for it. And it was asking too much to think that poets born and bred in the Ivory Tower could, by merely walking over to some Globe Theatre, become playwrights. What they would do was lecture the Globe Theatre folks on the merits of the Ivory Tower. Thus the Symbolist poets of the 1890s and the German Expressionists of the early twentieth century had much in common with them. Dramatic poetry was reborn in Germany, not with the expressionist outbursts of 1910, but with Bertolt Brecht's reaction against them in his first mature play of 1918 to 1920, *Baal*. If the expressionists had gazed at the stars above, Brecht brought his audience down to the mud below. An unseemly exercise, which unfortunately led, in turn, to an unfortunate cult of mud later (not just a nostalgia of mud but an obsession with it). Still, this rebirth from below had been necessary, and Brecht was not the only one to act accordingly. What was first noticed about Samuel Beckett's plays in the fifties was their muddiness, so to speak, their locus in lowlife and degradation. What took time to notice was that Beckett was a poet of the theater. The garbage cans were stuffed with poetry.

Now preoccupation with the lower, rather than the higher, life of mankind is no virtue—it is a limitation—but one of its positive meanings in the context I have defined is that it lends itself to role-playing. Indeed, in such notably "bourgeois" authors as Brecht and Beckett, it was itself role-playing. Both of them were clowning, pretending to be Karl Vallentin or Charlie Chaplin or Buster Keaton. Again, while the higher man in drama (see Corneille passim) has no body (except for fighting and dying purposes), the lower man, in theater as perhaps elsewhere, is all body, is that which eats, drinks, excretes, copulates, sweats, loses its balance. With his repertoire of high purposes, Corneille could write the drama of an imagined high order of being. With their lowlife repertoire, Brecht and Beckett could write the drama of the common man stripped of those illusions that the uncommon man has hidden him behind.

A role is a character made projectile by the admixture of certain exaggerations. ("Art is exaggeration," Gide said.) Thus a character might be Brecht, a Self-Portrait, and the role would become Baal or Macheath. The character, in such cases, remains in shadow, in the background. The role comes forward into the light, strutting, swaggering: *that is Mack the Knife.* It is interesting to read the life of Beckett and find that the characters behind the roles of Didi and Gogo were Beckett and his wife wandering around occupied France during World War II. How terribly prosaic that wandering must have been! It becomes dramatic poetry when Mr. and Mrs. Beckett are transfigured, not upwards into Cornelian heroes, but downwards into bums, into clowns. (That Mrs. Beckett has turned into a man will surely not offend feminists: this is no male master.)

I would not argue that dramatic poetry in the twentieth century is condemned to dwell forever in Brecht's whorehouses or Beckett's garbage cans, though it is certainly interesting that even T. S. Eliot, who turned in desperation to the drawing-room play, had been at his best, dramatically, in the little unfinished Sweeney Agonistes play. He had also been slumming in the London music halls—in search of authentic theater, finding, in that line, Marie Lloyd, a great comedienne of English lowlife.

Brecht and Beckett diverged from closet drama not just in turning to lowlife for subject matter but, even more signally, in coming to terms with the acting profession as it existed in their time. Original writers have a perennial quarrel with that profession because it is always stuck in some earlier mode that preceded the writers' originality. Thus Bernard Shaw had to discredit the ladylike (and gentlemanlike) acting of 1890 in order to stage plays like *Mrs. Warren's Profession.* In their turn, Brecht and Beckett encountered actors unable to assimilate their work, let alone to take hold of it and project it. But, like Shaw, they also encountered new talent—or, alternately, old talent that happened to be ahead of its time—and, before they died, they had found people who could give body to their dreams, three-dimensional stage life to their poetry. The other side of this notable, if small, social phenomenon was that, in a society where only a few groups of people would take readily to their work and champion it, one of those groups, both for Brecht and for Beckett, was the acting profession. Even today, in the 1990s, it is the actors who give both Brecht and Beckett the strongest support. And while neither playwright may be said to be welcome on Broadway, or other such places, both have been integrated into the institution of theater, on the initiative of the actors and their colleagues, the directors. Lord Byron, and other closet dramatists, may be looking down from Parnassus with a certain envy.

THE BRECHT MEMOIR

1   *817 Tweny-fifth Street, Santa Monica, California; June 9, 1942.* My first meeting with Bertolt Brecht. Him, forty-three. Me, twenty-five. I was teaching freshman English at UCLA and in my spare time turning my Ph.D. thesis into a book about hero worship in German and English literature. I had just discovered a German poet, Stefan George, who fleetingly became something of a hero to me: his was at the time the only photograph adorning my apartment walls in Westwood Village. My Stefan George studies led me to the home of a member of Brecht's circle of friends, the philosopher Theodor Wiesengrund Adorno, who gave me a batch of his manuscripts and sang me songs of his own, twelve-tone composition. (The most hideous shrieks I've ever heard outside of horror movies: had he discovered a thirteenth tone?) I think I saw him only once again. That time he explained to me that *The Caucasian Chalk Circle* was not really Marxist (many people in those days explained that something or other was not really Marxist), it was, "what do the Americans call it? Technocratic."

One contact with new German music led to another: the Brecht composer Hanns Eisler turned up one evening in the home of a UCLA musicologist. Before he arrived, my host warned me that Eisler was the famous (or was it notorious?) composer of the red anthem "Comintern" and other such scandalous items. When later we asked Hanns about these, he professed to have forgotten them. "Oh, I dashed off a number of little songs, marches and the like— that was in the fight against Hitler, before '33—all forgotten now!" And when Stalin dissolved the Comintern in 1943, Hanns bounded to the piano and "dissolved" his Comintern anthem in a succession of harmonies that made the original tune quite disappear.

To talk as he did, I would later learn, was a policy decision: to have a present and future in the United States, Eisler had decided to lose his past. He even seemed to believe his own fictions. I have heard him denounce the whole Brecht and Eisler oeuvre as mere ephemera: "the great modern democratic poet is not Brecht, it is García Lorca!" But this declaration was made "under the influence" (*in vino non veritas*), and the inebriation itself had its reasons: by then (1947) Eisler was under tremendous strain as a target of the Un-American Activities Committee and its big brazen brother the FBI. Back in 1942, he was cheerful enough and gave full play to his natural ebulliency. I recall attending a concert with him in Royce Hall, UCLA. In the intermission he spotted his old teacher, Arnold Schoenberg, standing in the lobby. Today, more than forty years later, I can still see those two small men with the huge eyes, Schoenberg tight—in lips and body—motionless, unsmiling, almost unspeaking—Hanns flitting about him with rapid gestures and broad smiles and a flood of flattering words.

I also retain a distinct image of Hanns at the Hollywood Hotel working at a small upright piano on a Brecht cantata. On that occasion he listened to the tale of my troubles with UCLA: I made my older colleagues jealous because I was such an eager beaver. So I was being dropped from the faculty, the reason given being that I was a scandalous character and talked about sex too much in class, too much, that was, for the taste of my Mormon and Christian Science students. Eisler proposed that I say I was suspected of communism, and *that* was why they were laying me off. It's possible he believed this was true even though I kept telling him I wasn't even a Marxist. In Brecht circles there had to be an explanation for any problem on political lines. Hanns provided it in the present case and offered to help organize the mass movement that would "spontaneously" rise up in my defense and result in my being rehired . . . This idle chatter was broken up by the entry into the hotel room of another person of considerable importance in American history—and in the life of Hanns Eisler—the playwright Clifford Odets. In 1942 the relationship between those two was unshadowed. Later Odets would make "full disclosure" of his Communist past (such as it was: it was meager) to the Un-American Activities Committee, and Eisler would in effect declare him a nonperson.

But it wasn't Adorno or Eisler who opened the Twenty-fifth Street door to me, it was the movie director Herbert Kline (*Forgotten Village*), and I had come to *his* door because his wife, Rosa, was taking my freshman English class. I'd given her a C-minus for a paper, telling her it wasn't a critical essay as assigned, it was a *New Masses* editorial. Both the Klines then let me know that left-wing editorials met with their enthusiastic approval, and in their home I met a goodly section of Hollywood's left-wing crowd, though the man who stands out in my memory was not of the Left at all. This is Max Ophuls, later the director of *La Ronde,* who talked to us one night after dinner of G. W. Pabst's (alleged) contributions to a Nazi film about the fall of France. Triumphant violence and slaughter on-screen with lovely harp music on the soundtrack— I'm remembering what Ophuls said, I've no idea if it's an accurate description of the film.

It was when I was telling Herb Kline about a student of mine who had a hand printing press and wanted to print some poems on it that the name of Brecht came up. For the first time in my life, I think. (The Brecht editor John Willett says I listened to records of *Threepenny Opera* in a college room in Oxford during the 1930s. This may well be, but I doubt that the name of its "librettist" had made an impression.) Back in Los Angeles, Stefan George was ousted. For one thing the student-printer preferred living poets to dead ones, new poems to old. I also discovered one could not be devoted to both Stefan George and Bertolt Brecht; and my hero worship was about to be transferred from the one to the other. The photo of George would come down off my wall, and I would soon be having my own photo taken with Bertolt Brecht—by his girlfriend, Ruth Berlau.

Both George and Brecht wrote about Hindenburg. I showed Brecht my translation of George's poem "The War." He laughed out loud when he came to these lines about Hindenburg: "supported on his stick, there then descended from the colorless suburban house of the dullest of our cities a forgotten, unadorned old man: he answered the hour's need and rescued what, after all, the screamers and gesticulators had brought to the edge of the abyss: the Reich." "Das ist natürlich ganz albern," said Brecht, "that, naturally, is quite fatuous." (*Albern* and *läppisch* were favorite words of his: they both meant fatuous, silly.) It was not long since he had depicted another moment in Hindenburg's life, not 1914, but 1933, the moment when Hindenburg appointed Hitler chancellor. This was in the play *Arturo Ui.* (Another moment in Hitler's life was when, in 1944, a bomb went off that was intended to kill him. It had been placed under the table by Claus von Stauffenberg, a disciple of Stefan George.)

The house on Twenty-fifth Street was small, and I was shown into Brecht's bedroom, which was also his study. He had few or no books, but there was a typewriter, and copies of *Freies Deutschland*—which I later found to be a Communist magazine published in Mexico City—were strewn about. In the typewriter was the very thin paper, folded double, which I later knew to be characteristic of the man. It was on this paper—the cheap tissue used for carbon copies when you have no onion skin—that I first saw any of the work of Brecht. He handed me a couple of sheets while he looked over the samples of my own work I had brought along.

My first impression of the man himself is hard to recapture at this distance in time. I believe I took Brecht for a truly proletarian writer on the score of his current lack of cash and his style of living and dress. This was naïve of me—the man was bottomlessly bourgeois—yet the charm and power of the encounter had their source in just this naïveté and especially in the fact that I had no sense of being in the company of a famous man. Quite a contrast to those meetings with Brecht that young people were to have in the 1950s, when the cropped head and the tieless shirt were well known in advance from a score of photographs and a hundred anecdotes! For all I knew, Brecht might have had a trunkful of ties under the bed, and it could have been by chance that he was tie-less at the time...or, as I say, it could have been because he was a proletarian writer.

Most famous writers would have made sure that before I left, after our first interview, I did have a sense of their fame. Remarkable about Brecht was that he didn't bother about this. Here we see the human value of what I came later to recognize as a certain deliberate depersonalization of things that Brecht brought about. He did not try to find much out about me. He did not invite me to find out much about him. As in his plays, two people would encounter each other for the sake of what they have to do together. I was a student of German and of poetry. He was a German and had written some poems. So? I would translate *him*.

On the spot. And with him as collaborator. He already knew enough English to have a pretty shrewd idea if a given expression corresponded to the German. "Wirklich, ich lebe in finisteren Zeiten!" That was the first line on one of the bits of tissue paper he had handed me. What did it mean? "Really, I do live in dark times"? *Finstere Zeiten* means "dark ages." Was the reference to *the* Dark Ages? (I had no idea of any context.) "Nein, nein," said the quiet staccato voice. Then, after a puff at the cigar (not yet "the famous cigar"), "Nein, ich meine *diese* Zeiten, Herr Bentley, *unsere*— auch in Los Angeles kann es finister sein, nicht wahr?" "No, I mean *these* times, Mr. Bentley, *ours*—even in Los Angeles, it can be dark, can't it?" He was teasing me. That too I would later regard as characteristic. (At least once he would refer to me as Baby-Face Bentley.) At the time it was simply new...Well, what about *wirklich*? What did one say for that in English? "Actually," "of course," "oh, yes," "it's true"? To each of these suggestions of mine, the quiet, sharp voice said, "Nein! Nein!" And Brecht shook his head decisively. We were discovering together that, in our effort to translate his poetry, we could not get past the very first word.

Maybe I didn't yet know enough German? I was still taking courses in that language (at UCLA). When Brecht first heard me speak his native language, he smiled. I blushed: "Do I sound that bad?" "On the contrary," said he, "you sound that beautiful! You speak the language of Goethe and Heine, only slightly corrupted by Stefan George, and of course even *his* language is 'beautiful' too!" All my German at that time came out of books—good books, luckily. "We don't speak beautiful German anymore," says Brecht, "we all sound like the Führer!"

At subsequent sessions, he read his poems back at me. He may have read slowly because he doubted my ability to follow if he read fast, but in any event what I remember is the loving care that his quiet, thin voice lavished upon each word. Compared with George, the poetry, too, seemed quiet and thin. Incidentally, I was taken aback at the word for housepainter in this poetry—as a standard way of referring to Hitler. Was this just *Daily Worker* cartoons in verse? Was it poetry destined to live and quietly die in the *New Masses*?

> Der Anstreicher spricht von kommenden grossen
>   Zeiten
> Die Wälder wachsen noch
> Die Äcker tragen noch
> Die Städte stehen noch
> Die Menschen atmen noch.
>
> The housepainter speaks of the great times to come
> The forests are still growing
> The fields are still bearing fruit
> The cities are still standing
> The people are still breathing.

Brecht made a long pause at the end of every line, letting the images hang in the air. What he wanted me to realize, he said, before I started translating, was that this writing was *ungeheuer delikat*. "Frightfully delicate": the phrase surprised me at the time for the left-wing talk I had heard was all for blunt forthrightness, even when it was not positively hostile to beauty and refinement.

Poetry, says Robert Frost, is what does not come through in translation. This truth was empirically established by Brecht and myself, but luckily it is a truth that all are agreed in advance to defy, and a half-truth at that. A lot of poetry just as problematical as Brecht's has come down to us in more languages than one—with whatever changes along the way . . . Although something must have happened to my student's hand press, for I never saw anything in print from it, I had begun the "impossible" task: translating poetry, translating Bertolt Brecht.

For a while nothing was said about publication, but then Brecht wanted his poem "To the German Soldiers in the East" to be printed. With him it was always a matter of the place and the time to publish something, considered not personally or "literarily," but politically. People in America should now read what he had to say about the German soldiers in World War II (which, perhaps consciously, was the opposite of what George had said of the German soldiers in World War I). So I translated that poem and sent it to *Partisan Review*. The choice was politically inept since the *PR* people were violently anti-Communist, but then, being anti-Communist (that is, formerly Communist), they knew about Brecht. In fact they had run a "big" article about him by Clement Greenberg (not yet a famous art critic) in 1941. So I was upset when Dwight MacDonald (not yet a famous movie critic), rejecting the poem for the magazine, told me how outrageous he considered its sentiments to be. (The Germans were barbarians at the gates of a supercivilized Russia . . . In 1965, an editor of *Partisan* was to ask me please not to fight the Cold War when criticizing the Brecht theater in East Berlin. Maybe it's good that times change?) "To the German Soldiers in the East" appeared in the *Rocky Mountain Review*, late 1943.

For me T. W. Adorno had been the link between Stefan George and Bertolt Brecht. He was also a link between Arnold Schoenberg and Bertolt Brecht. From 1942, I taught at the much discussed progressive school, Black Mountain College in North Carolina. At that school, my guide, philosopher, and friend was a Schoenberg protégé, Heinrich Jalowetz.[1] It was Jalowetz who gave me an introduction to the Viennese poet and stage director Berthold Viertel—the "Bergmann" of Christopher Isherwood's novel *Prater Violet*. In June 1942 Viertel directed scenes from Brecht's *Private Life of the Master Race* in German at the Barbizon Plaza Hotel in New York: Herbert Berghof was in it. Later that year Viertel gave me a copy of the German script they had used and told me Brecht wanted me to translate it. It was my second real commission. The first was to translate *Tales from the Vienna Woods* by Odön von Horváth for a refugee producer, or would-be producer, named Leo Mittler. Nothing came of this, and my translation is lost. I got no money either from Mittler or Brecht but I was thrilled by both commissions and had soon finished work on *Master Race*. A staged reading was presented at the college on February 26, 1944. Fritz Cohen, formerly of the Ballet Jooss, later of Juilliard, was at the Hammond organ with a splendidly distorted harmonization of the Horst Wessel lied. That April, Radio Station WWNC in Asheville broadcast our performance, and around this time Jay Laughlin of New Directions accepted the play for book publication.

On December 22, 1943, the tenth anniversary of the Reichstag Fire trial was commemorated in Carnegie Hall. The whole political spectrum from the fascist Batista to the Communist Browder was represented. Brecht read a statement in my translation. Later I wondered about a comment on this text to the effect that it was in excellent English. BB's advice to me had been: "Don't make the English too good. It should have a German accent, *nicht wahr? Ich bin kein 100% Amerikaner, wie?*"—"I'm not a 100 percent American, understand?"

The statement was one of two pieces Brecht had me translate around that time in defense of the current Communist line on Germany. (The German people were anti-Nazi. Army divisions much needed on the Russian front had to be left at home to keep

the people in line . . .) Brecht said that with the help of the novelist Lion Feuchtwanger, his friend and collaborator, I could get the
second and longer piece published in the *Saturday Evening Post*.
Actually, I could get no magazine to publish it at the time. A little
later the Party changed its mind about the German people—they
weren't undiscourageable democrats, their minds had been poisoned by fascism—and the piece ceased to be what was called in
Brecht circles *aktuell*—topical. Indeed, Brecht lost the original
German manuscript, and the item survived only in my English
translation. That the Communist Party could go so fast from one
view of German character to its opposite has been taken as mere
opportunism. But a radical uncertainty existed all along, and
would continue to exist in the future. I noticed it in Brecht. On the
one hand, he would preach, "Trust the people," and prate confidently of the *Weisheit des Volkes*. On the other hand, on the least
provocation, he would angrily give up the German people as hopeless, "and I know my Germans," and so on.

There was an "on the other hand" also to his anti-Americanism.
If the Americans, too, were hopeless, they were also not so hopeless and were to be distinguished from their more completely
hopeless Ruling Class. They were human, and he liked some of
their habits so much he affected them: not shaking hands upon
being introduced, for example, or saying "So what?" an expression
that did not exist in German until Brecht first said, "So was?"

2 *Lexington Avenue and Twenty-third Street, New York;
June 12, 1945, the world première of Brecht's Master Race in
an auditorium belonging to City College.* The words *New
York* bring up other topics and particularly Brecht's old friend (that
is, former girlfriend) Elisabeth Hauptmann, who was living at 243
Riverside Drive. "She can't say 'it's raining' without looking over

her shoulder to see if J. Edgar Hoover is eavesdropping." This is what I was told of Frau Hauptmann by another German woman, Therese Pol, daughter of the composer Paul Dessau, a report that is not really to Frau Hauptmann's discredit since, in the light of the Freedom of Information Act, we know now that J. Edgar Hoover generally *was* eavesdropping. But paranoia is still paranoia even when provoked.

At the time I used to visit her regularly on Riverside Drive, Frau Hauptmann was masterminding a magazine pleasantly entitled *The Protestant.* She told me how glad she would be to arrange for me to write for it: it was the most progressive magazine in America. Looking through a few back issues, I noticed that it was not the most Protestant magazine in America.

Frau Hauptmann was also masterminding Dorothy Thompson, then possibly the most influential columnist in the country. The needed intermediary between these two powerful females was a male Communist named Hermann Budzislavsky—later a VIP in East Germany—who had contrived to become Ms. Thompson's "private secretary." When I turned up at the Hauptmann apartment for a Brecht session, Frau Hauptmann would be on the phone telling *lieber Budzi* what should be in the next Thompson column, and a few days later I would see that it *was* said in that column.

If Dorothy Thompson's politics were "corrected" by Frau Hauptmann, Ms. Thompson didn't know it and was furious when, later, she found out. But Bertolt Brecht's lines were sometimes corrected by Frau Hauptmann, and it was fine with him. "Yes, yes," he would tell me, "let that stand." In my opinion, she ruined one scene in *The Private Life of the Master Race* and her handiwork still stands in the editions, German and English. It was a scene presenting the terrible fact that the Communists fought with the Social Democrats even in the Nazi camps. The original scene presented simply the horror and irony. Frau Hauptmann didn't buy that. With her, policy and ideology came before facts and loyalty to them. We were having a United Front at the time—well, weren't we? Of course. "We" Communists were working with "us" Social Democrats. Of course we were. Therefore what must happen is that the quarrelers become friends when threatened by the Nazis. Friends and heroes to boot, since they were to refuse, on pain of torture, to give each other away. Only a few lines needed to be added to the scene, so it was a heroism achieved with a minimum of labor. Brecht brought the lines in the following day, and I translated them:

> (*SS Guard appears.*)
> GUARD: You people have learned nothing. Who was it shouted "You betrayed the people"?
> (*No one speaks.*)
> GUARD: We'll shove you in the bunker till you pass out. I'll give you five seconds to speak up. Then the bunker!
> (*Five seconds of silence.*)

It had been the Communists who said, "You betrayed the people." A Social Democrat declined to turn him in.

Frau Hauptmann also took it as her function to adapt the play to local conditions and assumptions. A Brechtian hero faces death and leaves a message for the son who will survive him: "Be true to your class." But in 1944 people like *lieber Budzi* were taking over Vice President Henry Wallace, who had announced that ours will prove to be the century, not of the proletariat, but of the common man. So I was instructed by Frau Hauptmann that my American text would read: "Be true to the common people." And the line remains to haunt me because some years later when I went down to the East Village to see a performance of the play, a shrill voice in the theater lobby reached my ears: "Bentley obviously doesn't know German, he has translated the word that means 'class' as 'common people'!" It was a German-speaking person denouncing me to the management. (He may also have been an FBI man. Walter Winchell had announced on the radio that Bertolt Brecht would be present and make a speech that night. The FBI sent someone to check it out. He reported that the speaker was not Brecht but Professor Eric Bentley of Columbia University. There were only about a dozen people in the house.)

Frau Hauptmann also made a suggestion that throws a certain light upon Brechtian theater as a whole. The scenes of life in Germany under the Nazis were all written, but she proposed that I go to the Forty-second Street Library and find documents on which they might *seem* to have been based. Had I done so, the play would have become 100 percent authentic, historical, truly a Living Newspaper. Each scene was to be headed by a relevant eyewitness account or legal document, but, whether from laziness or disinclination, I never got around to what would have been quite a problematic piece of research; and the scenes have yet to receive such "authentication."

Early in 1945, when I was teaching in Minneapolis and Brecht was living in California, we received an offer from an off-Broadway production outfit entitled The Theatre of All Nations. Brecht was later to comment, with reason, that this number of nations was too many for the purpose, but *The Private Life of the Master Race* was produced, and the prospects originally seemed good. Erwin Piscator, the eminent German director whose name people associated with Brecht's, though actually he had never directed any of Brecht's plays, was to direct, and the great Albert Bassermann would appear in the cast. However, by the time I got in from Minnesota, Piscator had quarrelled with Brecht and had been replaced by Berthold Viertel. When I entered the Brecht-Berlau apartment, 124 East Fifty-seventh Street, Brecht was on the phone, yelling about one of his favorite subjects: *Verbrecher*—crooks. Evidently the voice at the other end had spoken of the producers as Big Crooks because Brecht was yelling: "No, no, no, *little* crooks—we can't even sue them to any good effect!"

Brecht would always shout and scream when things went wrong in the theater. His paranoia was as outrageous as that of anyone I've ever met, with the single exception, perhaps, of the critic F. R. Leavis. Brecht found hostility and sabotage everywhere, and, though often he didn't know who the "enemies" were, he wouldn't hesitate to define them as Nazis. Sometimes he would claim that the rows he made were part of a deliberate plan to improve standards. This claim only made his wild accusations the more unconscionable, yet there was something suspicious in the speed with which the screaming maniac could become a good imitation of a wimp. ("Thou whose exterior semblance doth belie/Thy soul's immensity!") That is how he looked, at least to the casual observer, in the Lexington Avenue bus after rehearsal in the gray workshirt worn, student fashion, outside the pants and the peaked cap that was supposed to make him look like a Worker but actually made him look a shade mousy, not to mention the three-days' growth of hair often on his chin. Probably the younger generation in the 1980s finds this last feature rather dashing, but in the 1940s the unshaven look was not chic.

Remarkable how Brecht could blend with the world of lower-class Manhattan—the subways, the buses—and yet be at heart so thoroughly alien from it. I retain an image of him sitting silently in a half-empty IRT subway train, rather late at night, idly scanning the headline of a paper being read by someone opposite. Referring to the Polish "government in exile" in London, it ran: POLES REJECT RED BORDER. Brecht nodded, a tired smile on his lips, and said in his very distinct English with its Germanic guttural Rs, "Rrred borrrder rrreject Poles!"

The Private Life of the Master Race was so bad that Brecht wanted to prevent it from opening. As the author, and this no doubt was very European of him, he expected to be the autocrat of the breakfast table. Contracts could be torn up, he assumed, at will. New York had news for him: once he had signed a contract he had ceded many of his powers. This powerlessness, the feeling of it, greatly exacerbated his natural paranoia. "If I can't stop the show, I'll exclude all critics! Viertel, arrange with Bentley to keep all critics out!" His idea was now that if his producer would not act on his behalf, those closer to him would. But we couldn't. And then that sabotage that Brecht was so willing to accuse others of was practiced by the Meister himself. The actress playing his Jewish Wife couldn't be replaced? Then he'd fix *her*. "Give Viertel these revisions!" The "revisions" were simply cuts. Any parts of the dialogue he thought were handled badly he cut right out: they amounted to at least half the scene. Dramaturgy was no longer a consideration. The scene was now such that the audience wouldn't be able to follow it. Important was only to destroy the actress and defy the producer.

The opening night was a fiasco. Brechtian devices such as would be declared brilliant a few years later all over Western Europe came off awkward and sophomoric: for example, an SS Man played by a black actor in white face.

An ill-prepared orchestra in the pit stumbled through Eisler's parodies of Nazi band music: it sounded as if they were trying to play the real thing but failing. Elisabeth Bergner sat in the wings and wept. Viertel and myself, in the back row with many empty rows in front of us, applauded at every opportunity with simulated enthusiasm.

Jay Laughlin took some of us out for a beer afterwards and announced that all the copies of the book of the play that he had sent for sale in the lobby had been stolen—by the producer? Next morning, except for the mild Lewis Nichols in the *New York Times*, the reviewers chirped and chortled at that which always brings sunshine into their bleak souls: the failure of something "highbrow." Brecht asked Ruth Berlau to have all the reviews cut out for publication in his collected works later.

Like all theater people, Brecht could assume for the moment that nothing in the whole world mattered except what was happening on a stage in his own show, yet he differed from most playwrights in not assuming that the failure of a production was the failure of a play. Also, his political activities, while they paused, did not totally stop because there was a show on. One day, when I

turned up at 124 East Fifty-seventh Street, a compact, rather otherworldly gentleman was just leaving. "That was Dr. Paul Tillich,"
Brecht said. I asked what *he*—a Protestant theologian—could be
doing here. Brecht sternly gave me to understand that he and
Tillich were busy building a New Germany. Yes, Tillich was a social democrat but "I," said Brecht, "always tried to be the link between communism and social democracy." (Actually, he tried never
to say anything bad about communism or anything good about social democracy: that was how United Fronts, in those days, got to
be United.) Years later Mrs. Tillich was to tell me Brecht had
worked hard on converting Paul *from* social democracy *to* communism. (There are churchmen in East Germany today who support
the Communist regime. What a coup for Brecht if he could have
won a "star" like Tillich to support the CP cause!)

German Communists in New York did not always support the
cause of Bertolt Brecht. I had got to know Franz Weiskopf—a
Czech national who wrote in German and attended meetings of
what I took to be German CP functionaries—at a time when he
wanted me to translate him—a project that didn't work out since
for some reason I was not acceptable to his publishers, Alfred A.
Knopf, Inc. But I used to get invited to his apartment where I drank
in the atmosphere. It was there that I learned, though I hardly knew
it at the time, the true relation between orthodox Communist writers and Brecht. The fact was that *some* of Brecht's work was considered very fine. "But a lot of it," Weiskopf said quite flatly, "is
shit." He went on to assure me, since I was Brecht's translator, that,
in the interests of solidarity, he would never reveal this publicly.

On the contrary, he gave a party for Brecht, I remember, a nice,
down-at-heel party, in his nice, down-at-heel Greenwich Village
apartment, with the one picture on the wall, a cartoon by Arthur
Szyk of Hitler getting his comeuppance, stuck into the plaster with
thumbtacks. (Another Szyk cartoon inspired a large part of Brecht's
Schweyk.) An inner circle of young left-wingers knew who and what
Brecht was and sat at his feet. He took such things in stride, and

mildly told us that Schoenberg had made a contribution to music in his day but that, of course, Eisler had now gone far beyond him. Considering that most of us hadn't heard of Eisler that was quite a testimonial. I never knew, and still don't, whether Brecht believed what he was saying. I soon learned, however, that in his swaggering vein he was given to pronouncements of this sort.

He would swagger more freely in Ruth's apartment than away from home, and he would swagger more freely with an audience of one—such as myself, with Ruth bobbing in and out—than in company. By "swagger" I mean pace to-and-fro waving that cigar and getting himself excited. Under such circumstances the topic would turn to himself—where else? If I had ventured on the word *creative,* he would toss off: "Anyone can be creative, it's rewriting other people that's a challenge." (At a later time, he came up with a corollary. Because the lyrics to *Galileo* had first been written in English, he had the job of translating them into German—to fit music composed to fit the English. He was sweating as he listened to the music and toyed with the syllables and accents. Translator now, not creator, he turned to me and said: "I now know your job is harder than mine.") He would complain that Thomas Mann had (allegedly; I never heard it confirmed from any other source) described him as "der leider sehr begabte Brecht," "the unfortunately very gifted Brecht." "And their rules and criteria," he was addressing himself now to teachers and critics, knowing that I myself was both, "they can all be ignored, defied, and should be. Climax two-thirds of the way through? Unity of action? Who says so? *They* say so. I say: Why?" On the other side, when he heard someone had said his *Galileo didn't* have unity of action, was amorphous and "episodic," he was eager to exclaim: "Just the contrary! They think I just meander along, stick things in at random. Actually, I work from a chart posted on the wall. I connect everything with everything else. D'you see the connection between the first scene and the last? In both, Galileo is *imbibing,* milk, in the beginning, a goose at the end. Because he is the same man: greedy . . . Of course you only appreciate this the *second* time you see the first scene. The second time is the first time you really 'see' a play! So don't ask what I think of your critics who never see a play more than once! Today's critics! Today's society! Only when there's a socialist world will there be a world for *my* work!"

It was sometime in 1945 that my first book on the drama was accepted for publication by a newish firm in New York, Reynal and Hitchcock Inc. I suggested that they publish the collected works of Brecht, and they picked up the suggestion. I was to be general editor, though, on the insistence of Brecht, I had to accept the collaboration of the formidable Frau Hauptmann.

My book *The Playwright as Thinker* infuriated Erwin Piscator who wrote me, in a letter dated May 27, 1946:

> ...[T]he one-sidedness of your description [of me] may be very dangerous for me at the present time. If you were older, riper, and more realistic I could perhaps ask you, "How much money did you receive for sending out such a 'steckbrief' for a refugee or such a political defamation?"

But Brecht was interested enough to accept my proposal that we embark upon a publishable correspondence about theater with my book as point of departure. I wished to challenge the excessive claims for the theory of Epic Theater that Brecht had made earlier in his career; and eventually he did claim less and did present a far less heretical view of dramatic art. However, he was not ready to do this in 1946, and the correspondence broke off. The answer came two years later in the form of a long essay entitled a "Short Organum," which I forthwith arranged to have translated by one of my graduate students and brought out in *Accent* magazine.

It was in the mid-1940s that Brecht gained some slight acquaintance with Broadway. On the whole, he was not amused. Even by *The Glass Menagerie*, one of the best American plays of that time.

Or by what may have been *the* best: *The Iceman Cometh.* "If you open a play with the image of a roomful of sleeping men," said BB, "the audience will take the hint." He *was* amused by Orson Welles in the Cole Porter musical *Around the World,* but, failing to discern any color scheme in the costumes and sets, declared Americans color-blind. Ingrid Bergman? Even those who did not applaud her acting in *Joan of Lorraine* praised her beauty. Brecht found her "ugly as night." He enjoyed rejecting Nordic models and gloried in what was blatantly non-Aryan. Parallel to the racial bias was the social. Aristocracies are bad; peasantries are good, if poor enough. Therefore the former are ugly, the latter, beautiful. In clothing as well as in face. In Brecht plays, the good guys wear the browns and grays of the peasantry; the bad guys, the bright and brilliant colors of the aristocracy. If you took up such themes with Brecht in conversation, as many of us did, he would point out that we have let Italian Renaissance painters dictate our criteria of feminine beauty. He commended to us—the women of Africa.

Brecht regarded The Federal Theatre (1936 to 1939) as the best news there had ever been about theater in America. "In America," he said, "things are better when they're worse. What the American theater needs today [1947] is another Depression. When Americans are prosperous, theater is something they can't afford." He would sometimes claim that he liked American musical comedy. He had seen very little of it. And what he conceived it to be like one can deduce from the fact that he regarded his own *Caucasian Chalk Circle* as a contribution to the American musical stage.

3   *Meanwhile back in Berlin.* Behind him in Germany, Brecht, in 1933, had left his elder son, his elder daughter, his father, his brother, various ex-girlfriends, and some of his closest friends and co-workers, such as the stage designer Caspar Neher and the stage director Erich Engel. So he was hardly in a position to argue, as many refugees did, that people had either to leave Germany or resign themselves to being regarded as Nazis. Some of his closest associates, notably the playwright Arnolt Bronnen and the actor Heinrich George, did support the Nazis. I never heard him speak of them, though I know he denounced George in a poem—one of those exercises in grandiose self-righteousness that Communist culture delights in. Supporters of Stalin have still not been treated that roughly. Also, Brecht didn't treat all Nazi supporters alike. The critic Herbert Ihering was excused, yet he had praised the regime in fulsome terms in a book he wrote on the actor Emil Jannings (and, for all I know, elsewhere). What excused him was that he had been such a good friend to Brecht, being the first critic to recognize his genius. I mention this less to fault Brecht than to show that, in a pinch, his criteria were not political. The *terms* in which I heard him excuse Ihering were as follows: "Well, *wissen Sie*, Ihering was never a Marxist. He wasn't Jewish. He was a *Berliner*. A fixture in Berlin—like a lamp-bracket on a Berlin apartment wall." I asked BB if he had Ihering's book on Jannings— I had managed to root out a copy in a bookshop, though someone solicitous for Ihering had torn out the title page where his name must have appeared. "No: but I'm sure that what he said in favor of the Nazis was absolute minimum. Just enough to preserve his... place on the wall."

4 *The Coronet Theatre, Los Angeles, California; July 31, 1947.* Let me drop some names: I was seated beside Peter Lorre, behind Ingrid Bergman, and in front of Charlie Chaplin. Lorre alone would have been enough: he is probably the most intelligent actor I have ever met, even making allowances for the fact that, in front of the young Professor Bentley, he too much enjoyed showing off his erudition. ("Was sagt Heidegger dazu?"—"What does Heidegger say to that?") It is the first night of *Galileo*, and Lorre is telling me how *he* would do the play, how he would do other Brecht plays, and, yes, he would do *all* of them, he has known since the 1920s that BB is *the* dramatist, *the* poet, of our day... Brecht is nervous just before curtain time. He runs out of the theater to the nearest drugstore, exclaiming: "Ich muss ein Seven Up haben"—"I must have a Seven Up."

I had been staying at Jay Laughlin's ski lodge in Utah and drove down to Los Angeles with Maja, my wife and collaborator. The Brechts put us up in their garden house. I recall that the walls of the bathroom had been papered by Brecht's wife Helene Weigel with Chinese newspapers. She was an excellent cook and a hospitable hostess: bourgeois regularity? No. Brecht led a double life that made him hard to keep tabs on. He might be at his family place for supper, but he had installed Ruth Berlau in a house a mile or two off, and he would characteristically repair to her place during the evening, very likely returning "home" in the morning to work in his study. Maja and I would be driven between one house and the other at need, occasionally taking in a call at the Peter Lorre residence, which was on a grand scale. Horses! For Lorre, to be a star was to have one's own stable. He also had his own Frau Hauptmann on the premises. No, not as mistress, but as counselor and friend: she called the position "private secretary." (What is a public secretary?)

Slightly unnerving, chez Brecht, the comings and goings. Only Helene Weigel seemed to have settled in, to really reside there. How she managed to cook for people who showed up at different and unpredictable times one never knew. The son and daughter—Stefan and Barbara—were already showing the symptoms of whatever that malady should be called from which the children of the conspicuous so often suffer. Signs of strain, of wear and tear, and, yes, of rebelliousness...

It seemed hard for Brecht to sit through a meal with family and guests. He would flee to his room before dessert. One would discover at some point that he had run to his couch and a detective novel. (He read them in English, his command of the language being much greater than people thought who heard him speak it.)

The rebelliousness of the Brecht children has its importance for the student of Brecht: the children were the only channel through which rebellion could come to Brecht and stay. He would meet with someone like Ruth Fischer, née Eisler, rebel against Stalinism, call her a swine and prescribe that she be shot. One of his son's friends was a son of Viertel named Hans who reports that Brecht would shout that *he* should be shot, repeating the key word several times: shot, shot, shot! Hans adds, however, that this was only when carried away and that Brecht didn't really mean it: he was very friendly to Hans later. That is the point. He would let the children rebel. He would say he wouldn't, but still he did. About such as Fischer, there can be little doubt that, if empowered, he *would* have condemned her to death. Treason to the Soviet Union was treason *tout court;* only slowly, and at that incompletely, did BB come to see Stalin himself as traitor, "honored murderer of the people." Stefan Brecht and Hans Viertel were "Trotskyites" (perhaps the quotes are uncalled for) who had to be tolerated even in a home where tolerance was not preached. They helped to prevent Bertolt Brecht's mind from becoming entirely closed.

Strange how little has been said by memoirists and biographers about Brecht as a father.[2] Even I, who was not in the Brecht home often, have some vivid memories. *Item:* his daughter Barbara (this was in Zurich, and she was a young woman now) slamming the door of her room on both parents as she shrieked: "You can take your social significance and shove it!" *Item:* BB asking me to send money (this in Munich later still) to his son Stefan and adding rather savagely: "Why do I send it? He'll probably spend it on whores."

A "bad father," then, like many another writer? Yet a "correct," bourgeois father in the end, for, in his will, he did not order his estate on the *Chalk Circle* principle of "to those who can best use it," but left everything to his widow, the other women in his life (past and present), and the three surviving children. (The full story of the will—or rather, wills—is too long to tell here, and even now, in 1988, not all the facts are known.)

Helene Weigel held open house every Sunday evening. They were very nice occasions socially, unpretentious, warm, with beer and an item or two of Weigel's cooking. Hostess was a very good role for this actress, even if Host was not something her husband could bring himself to be. He would deposit himself in a corner where people had to come and seek him out, whereas she would flit about and make sure that any who felt unwelcome changed their minds. The guests were mainly German, and most of the conversation was in that language, but two types of people were present and no more: those for whom communism was the answer to everything, and unpolitical people from theater and film, like Charles Laughton. Peter Lorre was a necessary guest as being maybe the only one who comfortably straddled the two worlds, as well as being fluent both in German and English. In memory stays a moment when the words *Der Kommunismus* rang out loud and clear and was followed by a knock on the door. Conversation stopped. Had the FBI heard the word and sprung into action? In strides a round little man with a broad ironic smile and very keen eyes. "Der Kommunismus?" he asks loudly, "der Kommunismus?" It is Peter Lorre.

Brecht left America the year before Henry Wallace ran for president but the Wallace movement was under way and Brecht saw the imminent campaign as the Final Conflict. "It's Wallace or World War III!" he would exclaim and look you challengingly in the eye. The apocalyptic character of the man's vision relieved him of all liberal illusions about the Nazis: he was convinced from the outset that they would draw the line nowhere. In some of his moods he would describe all friends of capitalism as Nazis. When I told him I was flying to Europe by Youth Argosy, an outfit that arranged cheap chartered flights for students and was having difficulty getting recognition in the airports, Brecht was immediately certain that the major airlines would arrange for a Youth Argosy plane to sink in mid-Atlantic. He gravely advised that I make other arrangements.

And my own relation to this milieu? In Brecht's eyes at the time, I *had* to be seen as belonging, like his friend Laughton, to the unpolitical men, the uninstructed, the naïve. There was no alternative except to be "one of us." Because I saw no purpose in a pretense of argument (real argument being excluded, certainly), I allowed myself to be placed in this category, as far as BB himself was concerned. But I tried to get a point through to him that I thought might be of importance: my sense was that, if his allegiance to the Soviet Union was strong, his allegiance to his own literary career and destiny was even stronger. Though I knew I would not persuade him to admit as much, I felt that I might get through to him if I said: "Whatever the validity of Marxism or Stalinism, if we wish to make a future for your work in America, it must be through your cogency as an artist, not your rightness as a philosopher." I was able to tell Brecht that most of the ideas in his "Short Organum" were not dependent on Marxism, let alone Stalinism, for their validation.

Not that, even in those early years, I ever fully saw myself as a champion of the "Organum" or of any of Brecht's theoretical writings. Even he never realized this but thanked me as late as 1949 for being, apparently, not only *a* champion but *the* champion of his "theory." His antipathy for individualism was such, I suppose, that he could not conceive that anyone might wish to champion, not a theory, or its philosophical background, but a practice, a person practicing. Am I saying that I was impressed not by Marx and Stalin but by Brecht? Not that, either. Marxism was important to me. I was and am deeply influenced by it. But I have never been a Marxist. On Stalin, like some others, I had no consistent position, but this was a period when Winston Churchill himself could speak quite loudly of "Stalin the Great" and, at a time when I abandoned pacifism for support of the Allied cause in World War II, I too did some blathering of this sort. The curious can find a little such blather in my first book, which came out in 1944, and which caused me to be labeled a Stalinist by Philip Rahv, Sidney Hook, and many others. I mention this here, however, only in order to make, yes, "full disclosure," and not because my short-lived approval of Stalin had much bearing on my continuing relation with Brecht. He never noticed my limited and ephemeral support for Russia. What he noticed was that I was never a Marxist; what he thought he noticed was that I championed his ideas about theater; and what he perhaps failed to notice was that I was championing his work, his genius, and therefore himself. The Communists in New York, like Weiskopf, were telling me: "Brecht is good insofar he is Communist," but what I was privately concluding was that Brecht was good insofar as he was Brecht. (And he was not Brecht completely. Sometimes he was just Marxism or some other *ism*. And then, according to me, he was less good.)

Though young and in many ways diffident, I even tried to influence Brecht. I hoped to broaden his mind, though I knew he held what the rest of us regard as breadth of mind in contempt. "Broadminded people," he said once, "see three points for and three points against every proposition. The two sides cancel out. Three minus three is zero..." What I had read of the left-wing controversy over Realism rather bored me, and I realize now it should have bored me—or bothered me—utterly. Each of those wretched writers sought to take Realism and ram it down your throat. And while the "discussion" was null and void intellectually, it was dynamite politically: say the wrong thing and you went (if you lived in Russia anyway) straight to the Gulag or to the next world... Of course I did not know the political dimensions of the situation in the early 1940s, but, recognizing intellectual emptiness when I saw it, I (1) resolved to omit the word *Realism* entirely from my book-length account of modern drama (*The Playwright as Thinker*),[3] and (2) sent Brecht a copy of *Mimesis* by Erich Auerbach, a book which makes a supremely rational use of the word *Realism*. I'd be

surprised to hear that he ever read one word of it. The critical
works at hand, when I visited Brecht later, were by his old adversary, and longtime slave of Stalin, Georg Lukács, who probably did
more than any other critic to empty the word *Realism* of meaning.

5.   *Charles Laughton.* He, of course, was the star of *Galileo*
and the latest man of power who was supposed to give BB
the status he felt he was entitled to. A very strong mutual
admiration society was created. No praise for Mr. Laughton could
be too high in the opinion of Mr. Brecht. No praise for Mr. Brecht
could be too high in the opinion of Mr. Laughton. "I believe him
to be the most important living dramatist," Laughton wrote me,
adding in a postscript: "This is pretty strong and you could never
print this but I believe there is Shakespeare and then Brecht."

That was in 1948. As yet Laughton could not believe Brecht and
Eisler were really identified with the Communist movement.
When FBI men haunted the Maxine Elliot Theatre in 1947, he
couldn't "for the life of him" tell why. "Eisler, a Communist? Nonsense: his music is just like Mozart!" But the times they were
a-changin', and even such as Charles Laughton saw, if not the light,
then the darkness. He *had* associated with Communists, but please
teacher, he didn't mean to! What could he do to atone? Repent?
What was Galileo's word: recant? He would do it. He would es-
pouse the New Conservatism. He would direct a play with a different message indeed from what those rebels preached: *The Caine
Mutiny Court Martial.* Even when the captain is a dangerous nut,
a crew has no right to rebel because it's more important that authority should be respected than that justice should be done. Questioned about this by the press, Laughton simply declared, "Them's
my sentiments." So when *Time* magazine ran a cover story on
Laughton (March 31, 1952), and portraits were included of all the

great men he had portrayed, there was an omission: Galileo Galilei. And if Laughton repudiated Brecht, Brecht repudiated Laughton in an epigram: "Speak now of the weather and bury that man for me deep in the earth who, before he'd spoken, took it back."

Actually, Laughton took nothing back: he hadn't been on the point of speaking. This friendship was all public relations, though not without its humanity. Laughton could get so tired of luxury that he'd forsake his gourmet cook and run over to the Brechts' where "Helli" would fix him a chop. But he was never accepted, chez Brecht, as what he was: a man trying to be honestly homosexual. (Honestly? Well, as much as was possible in those days without risking instant ruin. On a movie set, in front of the crew and a large crowd of extras, a director had shouted, "Charles, Charles, *must* you come on as a flaming queen?" and Charles had answered by extending his middle finger and shouting back, "Sometimes, my dear man, even in Hollywood, the truth will out!")

Charles had got his boyfriend cast as Andrea—the second-best part in *Galileo*. The boyfriend didn't deserve the part, as I pointed out to Ruth Berlau. She agreed. She told me everyone agreed, including the nominal director, Joseph Losey. "Then why isn't he replaced?" "Because," Ruth told me, "Brecht doesn't want to hear about such things." "But you—you could talk to him!" "No, no!" "Surely he wants the best actor for the" "No. This is a subject that cannot be brought up in Brecht's presence." Curious: because, otherwise, Brecht was a single-minded champion of his own interests. (Soviet communism is homophobic, and even T. W. Adorno said "Totalitarianism and homosexuality belong together.")

The full text of Charles Laughton's letter quoted above reads as follows:

> My dear Bentley:
>
> I owe you many apologies for not replying to your appeals about Brecht before.
>
> I believe him to be the most important living drama-

tist. At the same time, I have never been able to understand either yours or anybody else's translations of his plays. As far as I have got is to be able to dimly see the great architecture. I also understand that you didn't like my translation of *Galileo,* so the situation between us is not an easy one. If I allow you to say, "I believe Berthold Brecht to be the most important living dramatist," and if the general public is anything like myself, they will see my name stuck on something they cannot understand, which is somewhat of a black eye for me. At the same time I feel all kinds of a heel that I am not doing everything I possibly can for this great writer. I would certainly like to be a help, and not a hindrance.

Suggestions, please, and very warmest personal regards.

Sincerely yours,

Charles Laughton

P.S. I also feel that the actors as a whole failed this great man miserably in our production of *Galileo.* The demands he makes on actors are much the same as the demands that Shakespeare made on the actors in the Elizabethan days. This is pretty strong and you could never print this, but I believe there is Shakespeare, and then Brecht. To this end I have started a Shakespearean group, training a bunch of American actors and actresses in the business of verse speaking and prose speaking. We have been working together some 8 or 9 months, three evenings a week for three hours, and I believe that in another year (it will take no more, but will also take no less) we shall be the best team of speakers in the English language. I am doing this solely with the aim of getting a company together that can play Brecht's plays. I want to see *Galileo really* performed, and *Circle of Chalk* and *Mother Courage,* and the rest of them. I am devoting all my spare energies to that end.

6 *The Thornton Wilder connection: 1946 to 1948.* Wilder had spent time in Germany before 1933 and, according to Ruth Berlau, the ostensibly original production scheme of his play *Our Town* (1938)—actors breaking out of the story to talk to the audience, a stage only partially transformed into the illusion of a fictive place—was a "steal" from Brecht. This is, of course, a gratuitous assumption since (a) the scheme could have been stolen from others, such as the Russians, and (b) it may not have been stolen at all. But the allegation is noteworthy as connected with the obsession that everyone in Brecht circles had with the Eminent, the Successful, in a word, the Powerful. (Noteworthy also as reflecting Brecht's own paranoid suspicions. John Willett reports that as late as 1956 Brecht was accusing Wilder of "pinching idea of [BB's only partially written novel about Julius Caesar], then writing offensive letter." No such letter seems to have survived.)

Brecht would send Paul Dessau running to beg Stravinsky to make an opera from a Brecht libretto—and Dessau was a "Brecht composer" who wished to do the job himself. Brecht tried hard to get a Big Name, preferably Archibald MacLeish, to accompany him to his confrontation with the Un-American Committee in 1947. And then there was Thornton Wilder. Brecht had been tipped off (by whom?) that Wilder was *the* big name who might be able to put over the BB plays in the United States. (Kurt Weill could help, W. H. Auden might be able to help, but Wilder could more than help, he could . . . he could . . . !) So in the winter of 1945 to 1946, a meeting was arranged with the distinguished author of the possibly plagiarized *Our Town*. Since nothing came of it, Brecht had me run after Wilder and tell him to translate *The Good Woman of Setzuan*. This is the answer Wilder sent me in a letter dated July 3, 1946:

> When I met Mr. Brecht last winter I told him of my admiration for *Der gute Mensch* and my hope of being able to translate it. I could not promise, though. I was just out

of the Army and could not foresee what projects of my own might take shape. After the shilly-shallying moods of re-adjustment I began to catch on to a subject and I returned the text with regret to Dr. [Paul] Czinner and wrote a note to Mr Brecht saying that I could not undertake the work after all. There's one translation I've committed myself to, though, that'll interest you. I'd rather you didn't tell Mr. Brecht, though, for it would appear to have been a choice made in values rather than one reflecting personal relations . . .

Wilder is referring to a Sartre play, and I think he did prefer Jean-Paul Sartre to Brecht, too, as did my friend the Nietzsche scholar Walter Kaufmann. Nor was Sartre the only one thus preferred. I received a postcard from Thornton Wilder in (?) 1948 that contained the following *NB:* "Lorca may not be as influential as Brecht but he's better any day." (Which, as I reported above, was what Eisler also had said. Was it a thought that haunted a whole generation?)

7 *W. H. Auden: 1947 to 1948, 1953 to 1954, 1959 to 1960, 1964 to 1965.* Auden has been quoted as saying that Brecht is a person one could easily imagine facing a death sentence and that he himself would enjoy being the executioner. Ruth Berlau, on the other hand, reporting Brecht's view of Auden, is obviously aware only of very high esteem. What actually went on?

Auden often got the rough end of Brecht's stick, and after his death received an even rougher end from the Heirs when they commissioned a *Mahagonny* translation from him without mentioning that they had Marc Blitzstein making another translation at the same time.

My own firsthand reporting, here, amounts only to a marginal note. The first bad treatment Auden received at Brecht's hands might have seemed my doing. Auden, with his friend Jimmy Stern, had translated *The Caucasian Chalk Circle.* As often, Brecht expressed dissatisfaction with the result. Why didn't I try a version? "Not unless Auden and Stern withdraw of their own free will," was my reply. "Ask them to: they will," said Brecht; so I wrote Stern. In a letter dated December 9, 1947, Stern replied: "I did not know that I had 'got across with Brecht.' I'm sorry he didn't like my translation of the *Kreidekreis.* I'm sure he'll like yours better. I never could understand why you didn't do it in the first place. Betrayed? Good Lord, no. Not even surprised..."

Not even surprised, Stern had BB's number, and in a letter to me dated (?) January 5, 1948, Auden added: "I have no contract with Brecht that would get in your way, and of course I have no objection to any negotiations you may make. Good luck with them. *You'll need it.*" The italics are mine, but the innuendo is all Auden's.

My next contact with him came in 1953, when Brecht said he would endorse my version of *Mother Courage* but that I should have Auden collaborate with me on the lyrics. No full-scale collaboration took place, largely because Auden was fairly happy with *my* lyrics, but he *did* send me the following advice from his lair on Ischia in a letter dated October 31 (?1953):

> The first thing to decide is whether we should try to make the translations fit the Dessau music or ignore the latter entirely. Personally, seeing that they are chants, not operatic song, i.e. the music is subordinate to the words, I am strongly in favour of the latter course, since it makes it infinitely easier to make a translation that is readable. However, you are the translator and must decide. If you want to keep the original music, there are one or two spots where your words don't fit, e.g. "Lucky all mortals

who have none" has the first accent in the wrong place.
Let me know what you think.

Six years passed. In July 1959, I find myself writing Auden in his
Tyrolean retreat of that time:

> You will recall that in 1953 you helped me with the lyrics
> from the play [*Mother Courage*] and expressed the thought
> that you might help me more later if necessary. Well, you
> seem to be the only person who would be accepted by both
> myself and the Brecht family as to what is a good script! . . .
> They would like to hear what you think of my script . . .

This elicited a cable from Kirchstetten, Austria, reading:
"Translation seems perfectly OK to me writing, Auden."

I don't think Auden did "write" anything further at that point,
but a little later on I find him offering assistance in court if I
should have further difficulties with the Brecht estate:

> The documents seem clear enough and, needless to say,
> Jimmy Stern or I would confirm our share of the proceed-
> ings in court, if your lawyers advise an action.

In 1964, the *Mother Courage* negotiation was resumed. The National Theatre (London) would do the play in my translation, but
with "lyrics by W. H. Auden." The joke this time is that he had a
secret collaborator—myself. For it happened that we were both
artists-in-residence in Berlin for the winter of 1964 to 1965, and so
I was able to drive over and work with him anytime he wanted . . .

This is all trivia. Less trivial is the contradiction existing between Brecht's desire to have Auden's name on the plays and the
lack of real sympathy either for Auden's work or persona. This I
might have inferred quite early on from a brief exchange between
Brecht and myself in Santa Monica that went something like this:

EB: Auden was brought up an Anglican.

BB: "Church of England"?

EB: *High* Church—the closest to the church of Rome.

BB: Ah, yes! Isherwood says, "Now there's nothing left but the height."

EB: That was some years ago. He's reconverted now.

BB: Seriously? Oh, well, I could handle that. Do something for me. Bring Auden over some time. I can deprive him of those illusions in short order.

EB: In one meeting?

BB: In about twenty minutes, yes.

But if Brecht misunderstood Auden, Auden, I felt, returned the compliment, which feeling came through to me most strongly on an occasion when I asked Auden who would be the right American composer to provide the music for a Brecht play and Auden suggested Samuel Barber. Since I know Auden fully appreciated the quality of Barber's style, I can only conclude that he was not really in touch with Brecht's. In this sense I can agree with the Russian dissident Joseph Brodsky, who thinks Auden should have had nothing to do with Brecht. (Brodsky's reasons are political, mine are aesthetic.)

Talking with Auden, I came to find his whole relation to *Deutschtum* profoundly ambiguous. His prejudice—pose, if you will—was anti-Gallic. Already before Hitler, it was Germany he went to, not France or Italy. But his Teutonicism was only skin-deep. I heard him—this must have been in 1964 or 1965—lecture in German. He was fluent, even fast-speaking. But the grammar was all wrong. German is all a matter of word-endings, and Auden didn't care how any of their words ended: he knew the stems and talked on and on without a word of English, even invoking flourishes of colloquialism...

8 *Zurich, 1948.* In the 1940s Brecht had two hairbreadth escapes. The first was in Moscow in 1941. Had he stayed a week longer, it seems likely that he would have disappeared into the Gulag, as his one-time girlfriend Carola Neher—the Polly of the *Threepenny Opera* film—had already done. (Tretyakov, his Russian champion and translator, was simply shot.) The second was in New York in 1947. Just before he left for Europe, the FBI decided to detain him in America for questioning. But instead of using the phone or Western Union, they sent the instructions from Washington to New York by mail. These arrived too late, and the bird had flown.

Financed by the Guggenheim Foundation, I followed in 1948. Let me try to recapture several images.

One: Brecht in his new, temporary home near Zurich; his confrontation with the Un-American Activities Committee in Washington five thousand miles away. He has a small phonograph and is playing a disk recording of that confrontation for Dessau and me. When we've heard it out, he provides several extra details: that one of his lawyers had advised him to say he had been a card-carrying Party member, since otherwise the Committee would fault him by forging such a card; secondly, that he would have pleaded the First or Fifth Amendment but had been advised that, as a foreigner, he was not entitled to, so instead he declared that, no, no, no, he had never been a Communist; and thirdly, that the Americans weren't as bad as Nazis because they let a man smoke even during a grilling, and that this enabled him to pause and think out his answers between inhalations.

Two: Same location, one day later. Enter Dessau with music manuscript on which he has written the music for the "Song of the Water Seller" in *The Good Woman of Setzuan*. When Dessau sings and plays for us at the upright piano, and I praise the music, Brecht says: "It's good but it's not right, it's opera, it's concert music, it's not a work song." His words bring him to his feet; he starts to indicate (not fully embody) the role of Wang, makes us imagine a pole across his shoulder, and begins to speak-sing. He does not sing Dessau's tune, or any tune, but croaks out a rhythmic pattern—if there's a tune it is one the composer won't remember. He'll remember the rhythmic pattern, which will bring to his composer's mind the appropriate melody. I know this because another image I retain is that of Dessau coming in next day with a big smile on his face. "Is this it?" He plays and sings. It is Brecht's performance *plus a tune.* Brecht, acknowledging a bull's-eye, laughs with pleasure. I think to myself: "Then maybe he did write the tune of 'Mack the Knife' as I've heard him hint that he did!" Dessau has made himself into Brecht, I also think, as I observe that he's copied BB's Roman hair-do and his clothes (gray work-shirt and so on).

Three: Brecht in the small picturesque commuter train between his pretty suburb of Feldmeilen and downtown Zurich. He doesn't approve of Switzerland, so Ruth has told me, because the Swiss workers are happy—when would they ever rebel? And he dislikes the picturesque in general, which in itself is to dislike Switzerland. Eisler even told me Brecht hated Beethoven because of the hieratic stance, the sacred holier-than-God sound. *Violins in themselves bothered him:* my theory on this was that he could never get out of his head the story of Lenin listening to Beethoven's *Appassionata* Sonata and declaring music *too* beautiful because it tempts you into stroking your brother's head and forgetting that he'll bite your hand off. And so it is that Brecht detaches himself from Switzerland even more decisively than he had from America when he lived there. Yes, on the Swiss train he is even more absent than on the IRT. And where does the fantasy of the great realist wander off to? Where but Mother Russia, though the script in his hands, and from which he reads to me on the train (less noisy than the IRT), is ostensibly Greek: his *Antigone.* What he's reading is the narrative of an invader's disastrous bloody defeat. At the end, he looks up from the page to say with flashing eyes, "Stalingrad!"

A fourth image: Brecht at the movies in Zurich. Ruth has arranged for the three of us to see a film we are all familiar with: *The Gold Rush.* Brecht was big on happiness, friendly to hedonism, especially in his youth, but—by that token, maybe—was far from the happiest of men. He was not neurotically unable to relish the elementary pleasures—eating, drinking, sex—but the World (as seen very politically) was too much with him and made him, in his own words, lose his enthusiasm for lovemaking, while even eating seemed something squeezed in between battles. Sometimes, surely, he must have made love *with* enthusiasm? I have certainly—in Zurich and elsewhere—seen him eat and drink at leisure and with ample enjoyment. Never did I witness him having a better time than at *The Gold Rush* in Zurich. He was murmuring and gurgling with relish even when not laughing out loud. An especially memorable moment came when Chaplin disposed of the villain in the film by having an avalanche descend on him: in a trice he has fallen into an abyss. Brecht laughed, poked me in the ribs, and whispered: "Our playwrights would have taken twenty minutes to get rid of the man!" I rather think there is more theater wisdom in this off-the-cuff comment than in any hundred pages of his abstract theorizing and programizing.

There was another good Brechtian moment—*Image Five*—that afternoon at the movies. There were newsreels in those days, followed by some cute little feature story or turn. Today the feature was a performer who could balance a pile of cups on his head. And even a few on his chin! Brecht loved all that with the love of a six-year-old child, and, when the over-serious Professor Bentley hinted that, still, this was trivial and useless stuff for us realists and reformers, Brecht was quite firm in his defense of art for art's sake. "You see," he explained afterwards with smiles and much animation, "more is more. If you can add something to life, *anything,* that's good! Who cares if it's just a *small* addition! That man added!" (Hanns Eisler used to say that the *Gebrauchskunst*—functional art—of radio commercials in America made him long for a country dedicated to art for art's sake.)

9 *Brecht the bad correspondent.* In his lifetime, Brecht was the man who never answered letters. We know now that he answered all the letters he wanted to answer. I for one should have realized this at the outset and let him ignore letters he wished to ignore. Instead I made myself a nuisance by pestering him with demands for replies. Thus it is that the first sentence of his first letter to me (1945) reads: "Sie haben ja ein abhscheuliches Temperament"—"You certainly have a frightful temperament." Later he had kinder if not truer things to say of me. And he told this anecdote:

> One day a man came into a cigar store and said to the owner, "Give me a cigar." The owner was speechless but laughed and handed over the cigar. Next day the man came again and again said: "Give me a cigar." This time the owner hesitated but then handed over the cigar. But when the man came yet again on the third day and asked for a cigar, the owner was ready for him and stood firm. "Please!" said the man. "But can you give me a reason why I should give you a cigar?" asked the owner. "Certainly," said the man, "I'm the man you give a cigar to every day."

10 *Austrian intermezzo, 1949 to 1950.* The residency that BB took up—now a world-historical fact—was Berlin but the citizenship he acquired—not without some brouhaha in the world press—was Austrian. He proposed to play a role in the Salzburg Festivals and was in and out of Salzburg in years when I happened to be in and out of Salzburg in a different connection indeed, a connection with the Salzburg Seminar, which had recently been set up by some Harvard students at Schloss Leopoldskron. Were the two of us a living example of détente? The seminars were certainly part of the apparatus of the new American imperialism—a liberal part, by all means—and we only narrowly and accidentally missed getting BB to the Schloss as a distinguished speaker. Brecht in this period was effectively entering the service of the new Russian imperialism—"socialism" imposed on non-Russian territory by the Red Army—but there was no wall as yet in Berlin, and Brecht was continually issuing invitations to such as myself to be his guests in the East. I was present at the moment at some social gathering in Salzburg when he conceived—improvised in conversation—his preferred Austrian play, a *Salzburg Dance of Death*, never to be completed, in some words such as these:

> Rich people cannot understand why they die; it seems so unfair. So they go to Death and say: "Couldn't something be worked out? Surely there are enough poor people to keep you busy?" Death says all right, so long as they make it clear to him, when he approaches on professional business, which *are* the rich ones. A sign is agreed on, and for a while the new system works well. The poor die and the rich bid fair to be immortal. But the latter have overlooked one small point: Death has a bad memory. How should he not have? There are so many poor people who have to die. And now, watching out for a sign given by the rich takes up time and attention. Death does not manage to maintain the efficiency of the early days of his compact. One day he lets a rich man die. Receiving the indignant protests of the still-living rich, he makes a slight effort. It is no good. He is on the downward path, and soon is as indiscriminate as in the past. You can't make deals with Death.

Since the critic Kenneth Tynan later became Brecht's chief champion in London, it is pertinent to mention that he and I worked together in Salzburg in June 1950. I directed E. E. Cummings's *Him;* Ken played the title role. What principally came of the collaboration was not a good production. I didn't believe in the play strongly enough to do it justice, and Ken at the time was busy reaching the conclusion that he was not an actor. What came of the collaboration was conversation. "Who *is* this Bertolt Brecht?" was the question on Ken's mind, and I dealt with it—at least to the point of arousing enough curiosity to lead to further developments.

The next contact between us was when he arranged for the National Theatre to stage my version of *Mother Courage* in 1965.

11   *Berlin, 1949 to 1950.* It was not just in Salzburg, but also in Berlin that Brecht was cast in the role of Mr. East, and I in that of Mr. West. In 1949, the Soviet Union tried to isolate Berlin by blockade, but the United States defeated this intention by flying supplies in from Frankfurt. I was one of the supplies. I got to Berlin by special permit on a U.S. Army plane, and my mission for "the West" was to give some talks in the western sectors of Berlin and to meet with the cultural officers in the U.S. military government. An incidental observation I made was that the same U.S. Army that on principle excluded homosexuals had actually let quite a few in and was now hunting them up so they could be "Cultural Officers" and run the culture of occupied Germany. Everyone knows that to-be-gay-is-to-be-sissy-is-to-be-cultured, and perhaps this is where Gay Liberation really started. One of these officers told me that when he'd been asked: "Are you bi-zonal?" he'd replied: "No, just bisexual," and his superior officers thought it a wonderful joke...

Despite the blockade, things could be more relaxed in those days than they became later: there was, for instance, no difficulty in phoning the East from the West in Berlin. Nor did the American authorities seem to hold it against me when the first thing I did in West Berlin was ask the way to East Berlin.

Brecht and Weigel both seemed welcome to the higher-ups in the U.S. military government. "Budd Schulberg's brother is going to show us Hitler's film about the 1944 officers' plot," Ruth Berlau announced. That was at the HQ of military government in Dahlem, and I recall that Weigel was delighted to receive food-stuffs from the PX provided by Schulberg and his friends. (Monster ingratitude! A little later on, Brecht and Dessau would write a song representing those who had received food packages from America as traitors.)

January 11, 1949: a landmark in theater history—Mother Courage *opens in East Berlin.* The special permit had not arrived in time for me to attend, but I made it to a performance soon thereafter, and it was a landmark in my life. Many details are clear in memory after thirty-five years, including surrounding circumstances. The Berlin subway was totally unlit at the time of the blockade, both the trains and the stations, and one could only find out where one was by asking some passenger who was familiar with the territory. The city had not yet been rebuilt after the bombings, so one went to see *Mother Courage* in terrain reminiscent of the Thirty Years' War, all ruin and rubble. Walking from the Friedrichstrasse station to the theater, one shuddered a little passing the windowless building the Russians were using as a prison. Brecht hadn't been sure I'd make it to the theater that night, and indeed it was curtain time when I arrived and every seat in the house was occupied. However, he had gone to the trouble of waiting for me in the lobby. Muttering "Pünktlich, pünktlich!"—"Punctual, punctual!"—he grabbed a chair and pushed both me and it into a side box just above the stage...

When the curtain came down on this wondrous piece of modern theater, Brecht had left, so I went to Weigel's dressing room and later walked her home, "home" at the time being the Hotel Adlon. Another Brechtian situation! The Adlon had been the Waldorf Astoria of Berlin. Now most of it was rubble, but a surviving section housed the Brechts, and housed them in the Brechtian lifestyle: a big room for Weigel and Brecht here, and just down the hall, Ruth Berlau's smaller room.

I already knew most of the Ruth Berlau story as it has since been publicly told in James Lyon's *Brecht in America* and elsewhere—the baby boy she'd had by Brecht, his death, her committal to Bellevue by Brecht—but Ruth didn't know I knew, and in the American years did not confide in me. However, on this visit to Berlin, I learned from Ruth of Weigel's jealousy. Brecht would go on the assumption that, since Marxists despise jealousy, they are not jealous. Ruth knew better. She knew Brecht himself was the most jealous of men. For that matter *she* was jealous of Weigel; but she held her own. "Why, Weigel doesn't even know his favorite brand of cigars!" she protested, while admitting that this ignorance provided the opportunity for her knowledge, for her kind of caring. "I like your ring, Ruth," I said one day on this trip. "It's from Brecht," she said. "Is it silver?" I asked. "Oh yes," she explained, "you know: gold for marriage, silver for love."

En route for the Adlon, I reported to Weigel that everyone, including myself, had been in tears during her final scene. "Is this all right in a play by Bertolt Brecht?" "Maybe," she said with a satisfied smile that actually read, "Certainly, and I love it." On the other hand, she was pleased to be able to give a "Brechtian" account of the means by which a supreme emotional effect had been achieved. In the same final sequence in which Courage goes out alone into what seems an endless night, her cheeks were hollow, as if she'd lost ten pounds since the scene before. "How do you do that?" "Shall I tell you my secret?" "Definitely!" "I remove my dentures. And there's nowhere onstage to put them, so I hold them in my hand till just before the curtain call."

The "silent scream" Weigel emitted after she had pretended not to recognize the corpse of her son had not been "discovered" yet when I saw the play. It *was* a discovery, not something thought out. "One night," I heard her tell later, "no sound came out, it was as simple as that. After the show I got compliments on this 'idea.' I kept it in, so now it *is* an 'idea.'"

I don't know if Brecht wanted the public to know Weigel took her dentures out, but he did want them to know how such things as silent screams come about. He told this story about Peter Lorre in *A Man's a Man,* 1931. Lorre was told to turn pale onstage. When he asked how an actor could possibly do such a thing on command, Brecht said: "Have some white paint ready in a bowl upstage, then turn away from the audience and smear your face with the paint. When you turn around, they'll see you've also turned pale."

Again, I don't know if BB wanted either the public or the critics to take up just those matters but he did want the critics to describe more, and judge less. "What they say about my plays doesn't matter, my plays will survive the critics, but what they say about my productions matters very much because what they write is all that posterity will know of the subject."

It was during this Berlin visit that Ruth took me to a meeting of the Communist Youth, euphemistically called the Freie Deutsche Jugend, where Brecht was going to talk and be talked to. Many of the kids seemed willing to let Brecht explain things to them—his play or the world—but breathing hotly down his neck were the zealots. The play was just antiwar, pacifistic, wasn't it? Well, Brecht said, picking his words carefully, it presented *a* war, and that war was a wholly bad one with people on both sides the losers. But what then does your play do, the zealots countered, for our heroes, fighting for socialism in wars of national liberation? The voices asking the questions are excited, but the playwright resorts to his own alienation effect, cooling what might have been a shouting match into a scene from his treatise-in-dialogue-form *Messingkauf:* "There was, of course, no socialism in the seventeenth century."

The zealots no doubt were all set to ask why he had to write about the seventeenth century when Brecht cleverly interrupted to ask if anything in the form of his play had caught their attention.

Oh yes, the form was quite strange and in places perverse. How can you stop the story to have Eilif sing and perform a sword dance? Brecht took the kind of pause he had made famous before the Un-American Committee in Washington: giving himself time to think while taking a long slow puff at his cigar. "Two answers to your question. First, there are places and times where and when people do such a song and dance. Second," and this with a slight smile, "*warum nicht?*"—"why not?"

The "free" German youth of 1949 had spent their infancy under Hitler and were now spending their adolescence under Stalin and Ulbricht. Ruth took me to a session Brecht had one day with professional acting students. He had a question for them. Why this profession and not another? What made them want to be—of all things—actors? Many of the answers came close to a statement James Dean made a few years later to the effect that acting, for him, had to do with being neurotic: not that it necessarily proved to be a cure, a therapy, rather it was the way one's neurosis expressed itself, worked itself out. "You're all Americans!" Brecht said with a laugh. "This is exactly what I used to hear at the Actors' Lab in Hollywood!" "Well, Herr Brecht," said one bold soul, "what would you have liked us to say?" "There are more good answers than one," Brecht replied, "but there *was* one I heard not long ago that I especially liked. Its Charles Laughton's answer: 'I like to imitate great men.'"

Another question: "I'm asking you to play a Berlin policeman. How will you go about it?" Here a boy who had some Stanislavsky-type training in Weimar made a speech about telling himself he *is* a policeman until he *becomes* one by (though this was not his language) sheer intensity of identification. There followed some discussion of the psychology of acting, the conclusion another calculated interruption by Brecht: "No one has suggested going out on the street and watching policemen. Listening to them. What about *observation* as an actor's first task? No introspection; one's insides are invisible except by X-ray. Observation of *others.*" "But Herr Brecht," says a timid voice, "just imitating, copying, isn't that going to be too flat, literal, naturalistic?" Brecht's voice gets much louder. "*Nein!* No! Who has acted policemen best?" (Silence.) "Oh come on, *you* know! Even if he *was* banned under Hitler, banned for *playing* Hitler—Yes, exactly, Charlie Chaplin. Or what about the Keystone Kops?"

Of course, these students had already done some homework on Brecht and had questions for *him.* "We've read about Epic Theater, the Alienation Effect, well, the new kind of acting you ask for, has it ever happened, did anyone ever get it right, have any of your plays ever been acted in that completely new way?" "Well, I've seen The Thing Happen at moments and, wait a minute, there was one whole performance that had It. When we were rehearsing my *Round Heads and Pointed Heads* in Copenhagen, the Nazi Embassy put pressure on the Danes and the play was banned. However, we learned we could legally present a rehearsal—just not a finished performance. How could we make a legally clear distinction between a rehearsal and a performance? 'Hm,' said one actor, 'in a performance you don't have a script in your hand: if you have a script in your hand, that makes it a rehearsal.' Actually, the actors had memorized their lines, but I sent them onstage that night with scripts in their hands. These scripts got in the way of the action—constructively! Broke up the smooth lines. Came between the lover and the shoulders he needed two hands to embrace. In other words brought about the Alienation Effect, provided a more complex contour for the composition, added style." "And on subsequent evenings, Herr Brecht?" "Unfortunately, the actors learned to take the scripts in stride. Smoothed everything out. Returned to the performance they had been giving before the ban ... Such was my one evening of Epic Theater!"

Mother Courage established the Berlin Ensemble as the great theater company of our time, and early in 1950 *The Private Tutor* proved that the art of Brecht, Weigel, Busch, Neher, and the others could be handed on to the younger generation. It was a production without the oldsters, without "stars"; but *all* the young people in it seemed to be stars. That was the achievement, and in retrospect it seems amazing that the Ensemble reached its peak so quickly. I would see the company again in 1956, 1960, 1964 to 1965, and 1967. It was always good, and probably the best in the world, but 1950 remains the annus mirabilis. Even the sardonic Brecht was euphoric that year. Delighted with my delight over *The Private Tutor*, he bubbled over: "Write me a telegram in English to send to Hambleton!" (This was the American producer of his *Galileo*.) "Saying what?" "*Private Tutor* something you must produce in America. Come at once!"

It must have been about that time, too, that Brecht told me he had at last and definitely inherited the crown. When I asked what crown that was, he explained that the German theater always had a king. In his youth, it was Gerhart Hauptmann: in his early maturity it was Georg Kaiser; now it was himself.

Hambleton did not come, at once or otherwise, nor would anyone else from the professional American theater. As late as 1954 I offered *Mother Courage* to Lawrence Langner of the Theatre Guild, suggesting that he might try it out modestly at his summer theater in Westport, Connecticut. He replied:

> Dear Eric,
>   OLD [*sic!*] MOTHER COURAGE is a wonderful play but too misery for the good old summertime as well as the good old winter time, so am returning same . . .

At that, he must be given higher marks than my own New York agent whose only comment, on reading the same masterpiece, was "is this supposed to be a play?"

My relationship with Brecht also reached a peak in 1950; and then it fell. The pains of the later process were no less because the problems were professional and political rather than personal. A main cause of trouble was an article I had brought out in *Theatre*

Arts magazine, late in 1949, about the first half of the twentieth century in theater. For while I attributed to Brecht an importance ("the most original dramatist now writing") the world had not yet conceded him, I also stated that his mind was in bondage to Soviet communism. The way Ruth Berlau was to put it was: "You said Brecht would be a better writer if he were not a Communist: you're crazy!" But this is to anticipate.

12 *The Kammerspiele, October 8, 1950:* **Mother Courage opens in Munich.** In Italy during the summer I'd heard that Brecht would go to Munich in the fall to direct *Mother Courage* at the Kammerspiele. Unable to reach him beforehand, I drove north, turned up early at the first rehearsal, and sat in one of the directorial chairs onstage. When Brecht arrived he took in the situation at a glance and grinned: "Der Bentley natürlich, pünktlich wie immer!"—"It's Bentley of course, punctual as ever!" After rehearsal he asked the Kammerspiele people to hire me as an assistant. They declined, but I took the position anyway, without salary—alongside the two paid assistants, Ruth Berlau and Egon Monk, the latter a young director from the Berlin Ensemble (later director of very fine TV presentations, shown on public TV in America, such as *One Day* and *The Oppermanns*). This meant that I not only attended all rehearsals but that I met with Brecht and the two other assistants most evenings in his hotel room. For two or three hours we would discuss the day's rehearsal—its pluses, its minuses, the conclusions we should draw, the action we would plan for the day following. I came to regard such meetings as central to the production process, and wished later I could have persuaded American colleagues to hold them.

There were fringe benefits also to my presence in the hotel room. I would be present when journalists interviewed Brecht, and he would always say, as I offered to leave, "No, no, stay, we may need your collaboration." A literary moment comes to mind. A journalist was telling Brecht that Marcel Proust was the great French novelist of the century. As imperturbably as he had announced the superiority of Eisler to Schoenberg, Brecht admonished his interviewer: "Well, no; for us, Anatole France is more important."

On the whole, the Munich production of *Courage* could be deemed as dazzling, as moving, as much fun as the Berlin production. Built like a washerwoman, and seeming to belong utterly to the workaday and desperate world of Mother Courage, Therese Giehse in the title role might be considered less Brechtian than Weigel in that she did not comment from outside but got thoroughly inside the role, Stanislavsky-fashion. But I thought she was ideal.

I was now anxious not only to translate but direct the Brecht plays. To be sitting in Brecht's rehearsals and evening staff meetings during those autumnal weeks would be my chance to see exactly how he did things. He was the quietest director I've ever seen at work. Some people said he was *too* quiet and didn't intervene enough; but this was an illusion. He felt that a flow, a continuum, was needed to get the actors' creative juices working. Energy had to be generated or "nothing would happen," and it is the aim of directing to cause "things" to "happen." Quietness can help and is not just an abstention. The actors (I am close to quoting Brecht's own words here, also Ruth Berlau's when she was quoting him) must sense that the silent director is on the edge of his seat paying attention: they must feel watched, listened to, appreciated. In the comic passages, Brecht's silence would be punctuated by very quick and spontaneous laughter. This might tell an actor that a passage he had supposed humdrum was in fact hilarious. Or it might express appreciation of his talent. Either way, it was economical and unobtrusive directing.

"You must know," Brecht would tell us would-be directors, "how to go with the flow when you interrupt; never interrupt when it would stop the flow. Save comment for later." In other words, he realized, as much as Stanislavsky, that it's the actor who creates the living performance. Much as Brecht admired Meyerhold, he would never have said, as Meyerhold is supposed to have said to an actor, "You roll up into a ball: I'll throw you."

Naturalism was a bad word in Brecht's vocabulary, yet I think it must be applied to his voice work with actors. Many of the German actors made all plays sound grandly declamatory, like Schiller. Brecht wanted, on the contrary, to sound down-to-earth like Büchner. So when they made his lines sound like Schiller, he would send them out with Egon Monk and me for coaching in the desired kind of speech. We had to completely change their speech melody. If an actor had a long speech, we would break it down into short units that could be treated as quick remarks in a present-day conversation. "How would you say that, talking with me now, or to your wife at breakfast?" With some difficulty, the actor would find what ought to have been the easier—the more natural—way of phrasing and intonation. This was Brecht's answer to *Wallenstein*.

If Brecht fired actors, it would usually be because they were too noble. In Zurich, the unfavorite actor of both Brecht and Weigel had been Will Quadflieg, a "noble" Hamlet, Brecht's ideal casting for Hamlet being Peter Lorre: "Shakespeare himself says Hamlet was fat." Two actors were fired during the *Courage* rehearsals in Munich. One was a girl with a beautiful soprano voice. "*Too* beautiful," said Brecht. "The stage becomes a concert platform when she sings. Also, she's only giving us notes, bypassing the words, which don't express beauty but complacency to an almost insolent degree. We need an actress who can play the complacency, the insolence." We got one. Her soprano was not super-fine, but this pleased Brecht. "Not a singer performing in a hall; a girl singing in a kitchen." The other actor to be fired was a young man who played the angry soldier in scene 4 (the capitulation scene). He wanted the scene to generate anger as it went along, but what

Brecht had written was someone already in a towering rage when the scene begins. This gives the actor a harder assignment and probably seemed to him the wrong way to write a scene: he expected to be given the opportunity to work up anger. That is what Brecht called "the old theater." The "new theater," like Chaplin, prefers to plunge in medias res. Then again, our young man simulated strong emotion by merely increasing the decibels. "You shout so loud I can't hear you," said Brecht. Effects that the "old theater" got with shouts, Brecht got by mutterings and whispers.

If the vocal work could be called naturalistic, the "blocking" could be called stylized, almost mannered, definitely pictorial and formal. Brecht would go through a scene like a movie director, noting every "frame" in a sequence. Every "frame" had to please him as a piece of visual art, and, once the show was running through without a break, he had Ruth make still photographs every few seconds. (The click of her camera had driven Charles Laughton to threaten to kill her with his bare hands if she didn't stop.)

When I say "almost mannered," I have in mind groupings and movements of Brecht's that he seemed to introduce as often as possible in all his plays. His pet hate was actors in a straight line or symmetrically disposed across the stage. His preference was, for example, a solitary figure in one corner, and a clump of figures at a distance (a clump, not a row). As to movement, he had been struck, when young, by the way Frank Wedekind (after whom Brecht named his elder son) would walk straight across the stage close to the footlights. To the end Brecht would have two things to say about actors' "walks": First, don't walk a pace or two; make it a walk clear across the stage. Second, don't walk while talking, or even while someone else is talking; walk in silence, make a dramatic pause out of your walk, let the only sound be the sound of your feet. Here Brecht the director was carrying out the plans of Brecht the dramatist: these "walks" are not mere movements, are in no way decorative, but are action, and action powered by some high dynamic such as aggression or anger.

He would not always claim to know in advance what move was best—or whether movement was needed. Even though he'd written the script, he was not one of those directors who work out all the movement in their heads beforehand. At the end of the capitulation scene, Mother Courage, he said, might walk off, or she might just stand there. There were these alternatives, and indeed several others, and he put Frau Giehse through her paces trying out half a dozen ways of ending the little scene. A whole morning was spent on this: getting her up, sitting her down, changing the cues on which she does this or that. An American director would undoubtedly have consulted *her* along the way. Brecht was the European dictator-director in that he didn't consult actors. Frau Giehse was, of course, free to tell him anything that was on her mind at lunch afterwards, but he did not allow discussion during rehearsal. (It was at lunch that I asked Frau Giehse if she always allowed her director to push her around as Brecht had done in preparing the end of the capitulation scene. "Only if he's a genius," she replied.) If an actor wanted to try out an idea, he could say so before the rehearsal started, and Brecht would say: "Don't explain, don't justify, but by all means show me. Show me right now." And he was often happy to accept an idea that was entirely the actor's own. The actor playing the Dutch Cook in Munich thought the man would be more interesting if he didn't just have a Dutch accent but gave the impression of thinking in Dutch and only translating into German. He took lessons in Dutch so he could find the Dutch words for the German speeches in Brecht's script. *Something was added to* the role, and Brecht was delighted.

What that actor did enriched the comic texture of *Mother Courage,* the significant premise being that the highly uncomical tale does have a comic texture. In conversation Brecht took no umbrage at my notion that his Epic Theater, untraditional as it might claim to be in relation to tragedy, was in the tradition of comic theater. Brecht was not only witty in himself but was never happier than when teaching young actors to be witty. To an actor who kept laughing, presumably hoping to get the audience to laugh with him: "The more laughter onstage, the less out front." To an actress who got the giggles while rehearsing: "A—, if it's really that funny, you should pay the price of admission." An American visitor, hoping to be associated with a Broadway production of *Mother Courage* asked Brecht if he had advice for the American actors. Answer: "Tell them to play the comedy—the tragic elements, the ideas, all that will take care of itself."

The American visitor was Edward F. Kook, president of the lighting company that supplied all the Broadway theaters with their lighting equipment. Before going to Germany, he had read me to the effect that Brecht used white light only. "It can't be true," Kook said, "you just don't know lighting. I'm going to Germany to see what they actually do." He went, and I received an airmail postcard from him that read: "You are 99 percent right." Back in America, he told me the 1 percent was steel blue, which of course is as near to white as you can get without being white ...

Brecht's banishment of colored light from the theater certainly required explanation and of course received it from the Meister himself in his theoretical essays: the theater should reveal, not conceal; illuminate, not leave in obscurity; demonstrate openly, not beat about the bush; and so on and so on. His old friend Caspar Neher had another explanation. After World War I, in the inflation period, power shortages were rife, and radically affected the theater. Should they shut down? Revert to candles, gas, or arc lamps? Well, the more affluent theater people had cars, and the big sporty cars of the era had external headlights, rather easily detached. Neher invented "Brecht lighting" by detaching headlights and using them as stage floodlights. This lighting was (a) white, and (b) very intense: *a* plus *b* equals BB lighting.

13 *Teo Otto in Munich—and after.* "Die Wahrheit ist konkret," it was Brecht's pleasure to declare: "Truth is concrete." Certainly his own abstract ideas were mostly attempts to universalize the practice of certain individuals: the acting of Frank Wedekind, Albert Steinrück, Karl Vallentin, Helene Weigel, and Peter Lorre; the stage—and costume—designs of Caspar Neher and . . . Teo Otto.

Brecht was the first to concede that it was Otto who found the way to stage *Mother Courage* and especially how to present the wagon, namely, on a turntable revolving in the opposite direction—opposite, that is, to the wagon's wheels. A notion simple to the point of naïveté in terms of mechanics, yet in terms of effect in a theater, sensational! Teo Otto designed the Munich production; and I enjoyed bettering a friendly acquaintance made in Zurich in 1949. He, Ruth, Dessau, and the Viertels were the only ones in "the gang" with whom I ever got on first name (*Du*) terms.

Let me mention two of the many things I learned from Teo Otto. *First:* have the scenery ready at a much earlier point in rehearsals than is the custom in London and New York—the costumes even earlier, so that the actors can rehearse in them for weeks. *Second:* don't design the costumes on reading the script; wait till you see the actors. Design your costumes for those particular bodies, those specific personalities. Draw the actors before making any other sketches. Then draw clothes on the actors you have drawn. This way the clothes will *be* clothes, and not traditional "theater costumes"—such is Brechtian Realism. For BB and his collaborators abolished the costume play in the very act of recreating the history play. Backstage a whole technique was worked out for making the scenery look old and the clothes look worn, a technique that had begun, perhaps, in 1928 with the ironing of grease into the pants for the *Threepenny Opera* . . .

Of Brecht's own clothes, my colleague John Fuegi likes to say: "He would spare no expense to look poor," and the principle applies to the Brecht-Otto stage. No painted canvas, no three-ply wood or the like. For their *Mother Courage*, the Bavarians went out and chopped down forests, then "spoiled" this superb new wood with a blowtorch to make it look old and worn. Ruined postwar Munich could afford what Broadway never in this world could have even considered.

In awestruck tones, since she was a good bourgeoise herself, Ruth confided to me: "Teo is a *real* proletarian!" (The rest of us were fake proletarians.) Luckily, Otto didn't play the role assigned: real proletarians love bourgeois comfort and bourgeois culture when they can get them, and Otto could get them, *had* got them. Outside of his superb talent, his main quality was gentleness. Second only to Ruth he was the warmest person in that entourage, and second to none he was the gentlest. So I had to feel guilty later when I found out that he had got on Helene Weigel's enemies' list as a result of his loyalty to the friendship formed with me in Zurich and Munich in 1949 and 1950. This is what he wrote me several years after Brecht's death:

Lieber Eric Bentley
  ...habe auch wenig Freunde in Ost und West—das macht nichts...da ich die Kampagne gegen Dich als Übersetzer und Antipoden von Steff nicht mitmachte, habe ich den Kontakt mit Helli verloren. Man verlangte, ich sollte mich gegen Dich erklären aber wie gesagt ich habe das abgelehnt. Hab eine schöne Zeit. Wir hören von einander.
  Dein, Teo Otto

Dear Eric Bentley
  ...also I have very few friends either East or West—it makes no difference...Because I did not join the campaign against you as translator and as antipode of Steff [Stefan Brecht] I have lost contact with Helli [Helene Weigel]. It was demanded of me that I declare myself

against you but, as I say, I refused. Have a lovely time. Let's hear from each other.

Yours, Teo Otto

Teo was a man of the Old (pre-1933) Left. Tired and disappointed now, his position, finally, was not too far from that of Caspar Neher, who, sharing none of Brecht's political enthusiasms, had, during the Third Reich, simply kept as low a profile as possible. "Die Politik ist eine Hure," he informed me: "Politics is a whore."

14 *Again, Munich, autumn 1950: a restaurant (name forgotten).* I've said Brecht was a quiet director. He was so confidently so that he allowed visitors in at any and all rehearsals, which is in strong contrast to most American directors, who either think rehearsals are a great big secret and / or are afraid that they'll be caught out throwing a tantrum. I've also said that Brecht himself was given to the occasional tantrum: at which time he would give what I used to call his Hitler imitation—screeching till his voice broke! And it is in the logic of history that he would find more "Nazis" in Munich than he had in New York.

But he "found" them too easily. He sat there "finding" them with two scientific instruments: the light meter and the stopwatch. The light meter was in his hands so he could check that "they" gave him enough light on the stage. He would run up on the stage, light meter in hand, to demonstrate that "they" had not given him the intensity of white light that he had demanded. "But that's all we have, that's the maximum!" "Then increase the maximum! Go out and buy more powerful bulbs!"

The stopwatch was supposed to solve one of the main technical problems of *Mother Courage:* long pauses between the scenes. Each scene change had to take place in that number of seconds that BB would allow. When his stopwatch told him "they" were taking more seconds than that, he would have a fit. He would demand that the stage manager be brought out onstage, and then he would bawl him out in language both harsh and raunchy. Having some acquaintance with American workers, I was surprised that a stage manager would take it—with fifty to a hundred invited guests in the orchestra! This stage manager not only did so but accepted an order from Brecht that in America would simply have been disobeyed. Brecht told him to do the whole scene change again. This entailed taking off stage everything his men had just put on, putting back what was on before that, and then restoring what was on in the first place. All this was done and, I assume, in something like the time the stopwatch dictated, for Brecht grunted and let the performance continue...

During the lunch break, he would take a twenty-minute nap in a little room in the theater set aside for the purpose. One day, however, he came galloping down the stairs, roaring that they had locked him out, they, of course, being the Munich *Scheisskerle* (shitheads), the NAZIS! Ruth whispered in my ear that she was going to run upstairs and check this out. In a minute, she returned and whispered something in Brecht's ear. For a split second he was in shock. Then he slunk back upstairs. What she had told him was that he'd made a mistake and tried the wrong door.

Still Munich is (not just was) the home of Nazism, and we encountered the real thing during an otherwise delightful Oktoberfest—an annual event in the city with much bock beer and wurst and, even in 1950, the kind of side show that had aroused BB's interest in "another kind of acting" some thirty years earlier. Brecht and Ruth and I were in a tent having a couple of those beers when students at a nearby table started singing traditional German "student tunes." I say "tunes" because I wasn't catching any of the words till I saw the face of Brecht turn purple. And then I thought Ruth and I were going to have a case of apoplexy on our hands. Suddenly, though, he got up. Ruth and I rose with him. Brecht kicked over the bench we'd all three been sitting on and stalked out. We followed. "Genug! Das ist genug!"—"Enough! That's enough!" The song he'd walked out on had been about the *Saujud,* Jewish swine;[4] and indeed it proved that we had been hearing several anti-Semitic compositions, one after the other. When we had put some distance between us and the Aryan swine, and were again seated, Brecht's voice carried an incredible intensity of feeling. No "alienation" now. He looked me in the eye and said savagely: "And they say these people have changed! Good liberals now, are they? I know this sort! They will never change! And in the East, they know this. Over there these hoodlums would be behind barbed wire! And never, never would they be let out."

The thought that the Nazis were in our midst, and that we were in the midst of Nazis, remained with us throughout our stay in Munich, and at a late rehearsal Ruth asked that Frau Giehse, as Courage, jump, as it were, out of her role and "point her finger at the Nazis in the audience." This was to be when she sang:

> War's just a business proposition
> But not with cheese, with steel instead!

Only when I remarked that this would damage his play, since antiwar propaganda was not in the character of Mother Courage, and it is important for the scene that the actress show Courage's belief in the war, did Brecht turn Ruth's suggestion down.

When people asked me if Brecht was 100 percent Communist, I used to answer, no, only 99, but the women in his life: 101 percent. It was Stalinist communism I was talking about. The actors who opened in the Berlin *Mother Courage* as the Cook and the Chaplain left not long thereafter for the West. Helene Weigel asked why. "Well," explained one of them, "it isn't very pleasant to be noticing how, in the East, people—your colleagues sometimes—disappear one day and are not seen again." Weigel replied, "Wo gehobelt wird, da fallen Späne."—"When you plane the wood, the shavings fall." "It's just," one of the actors rejoined, "you fear that your turn will come to be a shaving."

When, in that autumn of 1950, Helene Weigel passed through Munich and joined Brecht, Ruth Berlau, and myself, I had to feel that the Communists were in our midst, and I was in the midst of Communists. Whether or not those three conferred about Eric Bentley, I did receive an invitation from Ruth that turned out not to have been entirely her own idea. To dinner in the restaurant of her choice, and she chose a good one. After dessert she got right to the point: "Brecht wants me to sound you out." "Something he couldn't tell me himself?" "He didn't want to overwhelm you. He knows you and I gossip together and even know how to cuss each other out!" (This was not Ruth's vocabulary. She spoke to me in German—with her Danish accent. I answered in the same tongue—with my Anglo-Saxon twang.)

"Why aren't you one of us?" "Us?" "Oh, you know what I mean. I'm not afraid of the word! Communism! Or just antifascism if you want to call it that! Why aren't you?" "Well, I am . . . sort of . . . partly . . . All my best friends . . ." "Pah, we've read your book! And don't you have a new piece saying Brecht would be a better writer if he gave up Marxism?" "Not exactly, what I said was . . ." "We know what you said. We are asking if you are ever going to change!" "Change?" "Yes, change. Brecht says, if all these rumors are true, and the Russians are about to take over West Germany, it'll be very good for Bentley, because they'll carry him off to Moscow and reeducate him. He'll learn a lot!" "You're joking." (I half-realized how black the humor was. In Russia I would all too soon have gone the way of Tretyakov and Carola Neher.) "Oh, no, I have a very important message for you."(She took a deep breath and leaned across the table.) "Brecht is tremendously impressed with you. Thankful, too. He knows what you have done for him in America. So much. It's wonderful. You *represent* him there. But that's the question. Do you? Can you? On the aesthetic plane, yes, but don't you know what Brecht's aesthetic is? You do. But you 'disagree' with it. That's what's wrong. Doubly wrong since Brecht is, well, anti-aesthetic! Content before form, you understand? If you're antifascist, progressive...why aren't you consistent...why don't you follow through?" "Well, Ruth, where to begin? One of my close friends, Arnold Kettle, before I even met Brecht, was a Communist. Arnold and I argued all the time..." "About what? What couldn't he satisfy you on?" "Oh, the usual stuff—the Moscow Trials..."

I did not know at the time that Brecht was supposed to have said of those who were condemned in the Moscow Trials of the late 1930s: "The more innocent they are, the more they deserved to die."[5] But I did learn then and there that I had cited a crucial, perhaps *the* crucial, issue, for Ruth at once blew up. Literally *stood* up in the restaurant and shouted: "Du bist so dumm"—"you are so dumb! Ignorant too! What do *you* know about the Moscow Trials?" "Well, I did look into them. And I didn't think they were on the level!" "That's it, then. I have to tell you this: you can *never* represent Brecht in America while you represent reactionary views, while you are...on the other side in the fight!"

Neighboring guests in the restaurant had turned to look at the shouting Dane, but the latter sat down quietly, paid the bill, and became entirely polite again. I thought maybe the incident hadn't happened. We were both a little drunk after all. Or that it wasn't serious.

Ruth never referred back to this conversation, nor did Brecht ever mention it. But, alas, it had happened, and it was serious, and, except for the swearing, Ruth meant every word of it, and did speak for her master, whether or not he had told her to handle it just as she did.

"And don't you have a new piece saying Brecht would be a better writer if he gave up Marxism?" So they knew about the *Theatre Arts* piece, and Brecht must have thereupon decided that my "unpolitical" position wasn't as harmless or as unpolitical as he'd supposed. Perhaps I would come into the Communist movement just

in order to be Brechtian Number One in America? An offer had
been made to me. Was it an offer I could not refuse?

Hardly. For though, at this distance in time, I cannot measure
the magnitude of my desire to be important in Brecht circles, to be
his exclusive or near-exclusive translator, editor, and so on, I did
know Brecht had misjudged the political difference between us. I
don't mean I was at the opposite end of the political spectrum.
That he could have handled. When not too busy explaining that
they were really Nazis, he had a soft spot for reactionaries, businessmen, men of power, enemies you had to respect. He preferred
dealing with them rather than with liberals and non-Stalinist radicals—with a very few exceptions in this last category, such as Karl
Korsch. Just as a fanatic Protestant hates a Catholic more than a
Buddhist or a Hindu, so Communists of the Stalin era loathed the
Social Democrat more than the reactionary. Now my own politics
had been wobbly. I had wobbled all the way over from absolute
pacifism to an excessive enthusiasm for the Allied war effort,
headed as it was by Marshal Stalin. But the only party I'd ever been
in was the Independent Labour Party. That was in my Oxford days
of the 1930s. It represented the kind of socialist I was and have
been ever since: Social Democratic, not Communist.

Though I did not enjoy being named, later, as an Enemy by Helene Weigel, I would at any time have heartily accepted the word
opponent. Not of course in every respect. I can direct *A Man's a
Man* and feel complete sympathy with what I conceive it to be saying. And so it is with many of BB's works. But on socialism there
was always the deep disagreement. Perhaps I had been too quiet
about this in the beginning from fear that Brecht would never let
me get to know him if he realized how much of his thinking I rejected. Later on, he would find out; did find out; and declared the
disagreement unacceptable. I must either agree to agree or ... ?

During Brecht's lifetime, I was not actually thrown into outer
darkness, though I often felt I might be. I had to assume that Ruth
reported our fateful conversation to her master but he never fol-

lowed through by telling me I could not represent him in America or that he considered me reactionary and "on the other side in the fight." He had let me manage many of his American affairs before 1950, and he continued to do so afterwards. When an American, in this period, wrote him about rights to a play, he referred him to me, saying I knew more about his affairs in America than he did himself. He continued to assign me various production and publication rights until his death, and a letter to me of 1954 shows that Brecht continued to regard me as politically salvageable (that is, convertible to communism):

> About your critical abilities, everyone agrees, except perhaps for a few blockheads; even if a few non-blockheads deplore your appalling lack of political education...Let me make a suggestion. I have put together a collective for dramaturgy. The participants—a period of one to two years is envisaged—draw an income from the Academy... and have access to the Berlin Ensemble...

Which was exactly continuous with what he had written me shortly before our Munich crisis:

> Don't let yourself get bitter about my hesitation in having you direct plays in the commercial theater...I would prefer that you should practice first in our theater...If you see any chance of this, I would do much to help.

It was not until his heirs took over that I was definitely placed on the enemies list. Clifford Odets and Charles Laughton were, of course, already on it. And it was not long before the three of us were joined by the very person originally chosen to denounce me: Ruth Berlau. Though dead, she's still being denounced in the 1980s by the Winifred Wagner of East Berlin's Bayreuth, Barbara Brecht.

15 *Chausseestrasse 125, East Berlin; June 1956.* At an Ibsen celebration in Oslo, the Norwegian capital, I got to know the chief drama critic of East Germany, Fritz Erpenbeck, who, from his days of exile in Moscow earlier, had defined a position on Brecht that at first blush looks much like my own: Brecht is a great writer, but one need not embrace his theory of an Epic Theater. In Oslo, I have defended Ibsen the individualist against Brecht the collectivist. I am not aware that Brecht has been becoming more critical of Stalin in his last years or that he has been in close touch with the young Wolfgang Harich, leader of the dissidents among Berlin Communists. Actually, I have heard Brecht speak of Stalin's "greatness" even after our fracas of 1950. I am not sure that I want to go to East Berlin to see him.

But of course I go. (Is that the meaning, perhaps, of the whole story I'm trying to tell?) I go: "pünktlich wie immer." Stalinism was indeed deeply troubling. (To Brecht also, but I didn't know that yet.) But fundamentally I was never an *ism* person, and though Bertolt Brecht professed to be an *ism* person, one might say *the* ism person, what I had felt was that really he wasn't. Or that he wasn't in relation to me.

I got a shock. Brecht presented himself as soon as he knew I was there. A physically shrunken Brecht. A Brecht who had lost his looks. (In his own way, severe, gaunt, a little haughty, Sphinx-like, he had been good-looking.) Shrunken in the body, swollen somewhat in the face, flaccid. And without that familiar and so distinctive voice. What voice he still had kept sinking to a hoarse whisper. Gallantly—and he did have his own gallantry, had no self-pity that I could ever descry—he bade me welcome back to Berlin. I hope I didn't show signs of shock; but he assumed I *would* show such signs and said his health had not been "too good"; he was "etwas reduziert," "in reduced circumstances." I told him the commonplace thing: that I was very, very glad to see him again. And he saw the reality behind the commonplace.

Being a dramatist ("the most original dramatist now writing") he could read a subtext anytime. Seeing my eyes, he also felt my vibrations. He knew all.

BB arranged for me to see three new or newish productions: *Trumpets and Drums, Playboy of the Western World,* and *The Caucasian Chalk Circle.* As usual at the Ensemble, I was much impressed every time. Each time it was theater with a dimension more than theater, even good theater, as I had known it in other countries, and as I had just been "covering" it for several years as dramatic critic of the *New Republic* in America. What was that extra dimension? Communism?—tell it to the *Daily Worker*! Walter Kerr, then with the *Herald Tribune,* had written in 1953 that Brecht speaks only to Bentley, and Bentley speaks only to God. Myself, I didn't feel that close to Godhead, certainly I had my less supernatural readers, albeit not as many as Walter Kerr, and I tried, with whatever unsuccess, to convey to them the impression that, initially Brecht on the printed page, later Brecht on the stage of the Berlin Ensemble, made on me. If I failed, it was my failure, not his.

After the three evenings in his theater, a talk with Brecht in his apartment at 125 Chausseestrasse. (The "arrangement" was now that Weigel and Brecht lived in the same house but on different floors, each with a bell at street level. Ruth Berlau had her own place within walking distance. She could pride herself it favored Brecht's special preferences—not just his cigars but the kind of chair he liked, and so on—but actually she had lost him in his last years, not to Weigel, but to the younger generation, girls such as Wolfgang Harich's wife, Isot Kilian. Ruth was drinking herself to death.) Brecht wanted to know my impressions of the three shows I'd seen. Were standards being kept up? Was anything wrong? Or lacking? Well, I said, *The Playboy of the Western World* was *all* wrong, beginning with the East Berlin interpretation of the word *Western* as meaning non-Communist (what American politicians call the Free World). That was laughable. And from it came a ridiculous interpretation of the playboy himself as a would-be Hitler. J. M. Synge had never thought of anything like that, so why should they, pirating his work, as I gathered they had? (It was still protected by copyright.) Oddly enough, in the twilight of his days, it was Brecht who was the easygoing worldling and I who was the zealot. "Oh, well," he shrugged, "what else could we make of the play in this benighted land? We couldn't possibly reproduce the Irishness and the wonderful humor." "Then why do it at all?" I asked harshly.

The subject had to change. I had loved *Trumpets and Drums,* and thought that any historical-geographical errors in it were irrelevant. I held no brief for Farquhar's *Recruiting Officer,* on which it was based, and saw no reason why it should not be fooled around with when the fooling was in such excellent taste and in so effectively light a vein. You can't be pretentious if you are pretending to nothing! The show had high style. Another rediscovery of art for art's sake? Good in any terms, the production seemed to me especially salutary in the East, where the critical emphasis had been all too heavily on content as against form, message as against manner. On this BB could emphatically agree with grins and many nods of the head. Ever since the 1930s, he reminded me, he had tried to make the pundits of the East see that, while he agreed with them on message and content, *this was no reason to neglect form.* What's wrong with form? He knew he didn't have to explain this to me! Was I not his formalist friend? (He could disown me when I went too far. Very well. This too was a living arrangement.)

By this time, Brecht was longing to talk about his own masterpiece, which I had translated, *The Caucasian Chalk Circle.* Had the production let me down in any way? Or? No, no, I answered, I had had the time of my life. It was the greatest modern theater in my life since *Mother Courage* in 1949. I had basked in its glory. Pick holes here and there? Perhaps. The Dessau music was so hard on the singers, one couldn't always make out the words, and wouldn't one maybe have welcomed music more conventionally tuneful? "You sound like *our critics* now," says Brecht, referring to the disapproval of all musical modernism in East Berlin. I reminded him of my "sympathy" with Erpenbeck, despite the abyss between us. "Extremes meet, huh?" says he, mischievously.

"Now let me ask *you* something," say I. "Was Ernst Busch as Azdak exactly what you had in mind?" "He's a great actor. He's my actor too," says Brecht, "but no. There was a dimension missing this time." "Ah?" "Yes, he missed the whole tragic side of the role." I was so fascinated by this comment, I had no comeback. Bertolt Brecht favoring tragedy? Finding in this comic, realistic role a "whole tragic side"? A tragic side is not what East Berlin wished to hear about when words like *renegade* and *traitor* came so much cheaper! In Brecht's mind, when he wrote the role of Azdak, must have been Ignazio Silone and Arthur Koestler and their disenchantment with Communist revolutionism. *And is not that the kind of thing Azdak is all about?* I had noticed a book open and face downwards on Brecht's desk; it was Koestler's account of his Communist phase and what followed . . .

During all this I was alone with BB except that Frau Hauptmann kept coming in and going out for no apparent reason. Was she keeping an eye on us? Taking note when she heard things that shouldn't have been said by either of us? I thought of the culminating scene in Brecht's *Galileo* where the scientist's former student visits the great man for the last time. Galileo's daughter is now his jailer, and views the visitor with suspicion. Frau Hauptmann seemed worried that Brecht might hand me something he shouldn't by way of a remark or a joke. She would correct him now and then. For instance, he had a lot of fun with a Louis Armstrong record that someone had sent him, on which Satchmo sang "Mack the Knife." The lyrics were thrown to the winds, and Louis Armstrong was singing the familiar tune to any syllables that fit, such as "Lou-is Armstrong, Lot-te Len-ya . . ." Frau Hauptmann didn't want me going to America to announce that this was acceptable to

East Berlin! "Decadent!" said she, "American colonialism!" "*Aber doch,*" said BB, "still and all, *das ist ein Neger,* that is a Black."

Since I arrived in Berlin—city of rumors—I had caught the rumor that Brecht had been writing subversive stuff, even on Topic *A:* Joseph Stalin. Five years earlier there had been a large portrait of J. S. on Helene Weigel's wall. It was gone now. (Destroyed, I wondered, or relegated to the cellar against the day when J. S. might be rehabilitated?) If only I were the former student in *Galileo,* and he that great man, he would now pass to me a copy of his anti-Stalinist writings, and I would smuggle them out of East Berlin under the very nose of the watchful Frau Hauptmann.

Mere fantasy: Brecht's little "Stalin (that is, anti-Stalin) poems"[6] were to be totally secret for years to come, and indeed were semi-secret till they were officially published in 1982. If Brecht had daring thoughts, he didn't usually dare to make them known. Osip Mandelstam wrote a Stalin epigram, read it to friends, was exposed, and didn't live very long after that. Mandelstam's epigram called Stalin's mustache "huge laughing cockroaches." They were still huge laughing cockroaches when Brecht made an imitation of them, sporting it on his own upper lip, and was photographed as Stalin. The difference is that the photograph, taken in the 1940s, was not shown till 1978.

Brecht must have known that what I wanted to talk about was that Twentieth Communist Party Congress in Moscow at which Khrushchev had recently "told all" about Stalin, but I did not force the issue, and he seemed to be steering me away from such matters of state. He wanted to talk theater. "So this is what I get for being the aesthete and formalist of the family," I was thinking. Brecht was saying: "Helli thinks Ethel Merman would be the best American Mother Courage. Could we get her?" "Alan Schneider has written us saying he wants to direct the play but with Helen Hayes in the part. Could she hack it?" "They tell me it would be easier to arrange an American visit for the Ensemble if Walter Kerr came over and reviewed our shows. Can we get him to come?" "Tell me about *My Fair Lady*. Is it something we could put on with our Regine Lutz as Eliza?"

As for my own plans in New York, what had happened to the Leo Kerz production of *A Man's a Man*? He (Brecht) had wanted the play put on during the Korean War: it would have had a lesson in it for America. And Howard Da Silva's interest in *Chalk Circle*? Had that too come to nothing? I laid my current project before BB: I wanted the rights to *The Good Woman of Setzuan* for Uta Hagen, Herbert Berghof, and myself. With these in hand, we would offer the play to his old and trusted producer, Hambleton. Frau Hauptmann was listening hard. Brecht nodded and said, "*Gut, die Hauptmann* will put it in writing."

On my mind throughout was that I was looking my last on Bertolt Brecht. As for him, he was well aware of his condition, but there was nothing to do with the scene except underplay it. Büchner, not Schiller. "Thank you so much for coming. Write me from New York." "Definitely. I trust you'll be fully recovered very soon."

16 *Truro, Massachusetts; August 16, 1956.* Would Hambleton take the play? And us three with it? With his partner Norris Houghton, he came to my summer place on Cape Cod to tell me yes. I was already writing the English lyrics at a small reed organ I'd purchased for the purpose in the Wellfleet antiques shop: I still have it. The day was August 16. On that same day—melodrama à la Chaplin but flatly true—I received a cable from Johannes R. Becher, minister of culture in the German Democratic Republic, inviting me to a memorial meeting in East Berlin. Bertolt Brecht had died of heart failure.

I didn't go to Germany: told myself I couldn't afford it. I think now I just didn't want to face "those people"; anyhow, contented myself with a return cable expressing sympathy.

Charles Laughton had also received "the cable." It fluttered his Hollywood dovecot. He called his lawyer: what should he do? The lawyer called the FBI and reported CABLE RECEIVED FROM RED COUNTRY. The FBI expressed its satisfaction at being informed and consulted, and gave a green light for Charles, also, to send a cable expressing sympathy.

I wrote the obituary that appeared in the *New Republic* issue of August 27. Writing today (1985) I might use different language here and there: I do not sympathize with today's anti-Communists, nor accept the worldview now called anticommunism, but I am still anti-Communist in the simple sense of being against what passes for communism in Russia.

BERTOLT BRECHT (1898–1956)

If at this moment I could write impersonally of Brecht I would say, "We have just lost our leading dramatist," but this is a man who has played a large, perhaps inordinate, part in my own life, and I am oppressed with the dull pain and inarticulateness that follows the death of a friend. And since the pain is mine, not his, anything I do manage to say is likely to sound outrageously egocentric. But it is this or nothing.

We were not intimate in the sense that we ever spent even months constantly in each other's company, and it is likely that he did not feel as intimate with me as I did with him. However, after the long periods of not meeting, I always felt welcomed back as a member of the family. The last of these reunions took place just two months ago. Brecht had had a heart attack in the spring, and was in Berlin just for a doctor's appointment. He kindly snatched an hour out of the trip for a talk with me. I can see him now rising from his chair, despite his weakness, and with all the correct, very German and bourgeois graciousness that was essentially his to shake me by the hand. We talked of this and that—of Louis Armstrong singing the Moritat, of *My Fair Lady* as a possibility for his Ensemble—and I can never forget that when I told him how Shaw's plays were being edited and cut now that he was dead Brecht said: "One must never die." His voice was gone as a result of the illness, but the old, Confucian smile still played around the set, thin lips.

He was a Communist, and I am anti-Communist, but I do not think people on my side have understood him very well. In theory he often showed disrespect for individuals and individualists, yet I had the experience of being his political enemy and his personal friend, and I must record that the friendship was given precedence over the enmity. At the throne of grace, like many others of us he will have to plead Inconsistency.

At a banquet in Oslo last May I found myself seated next to some of the leading critics and academics of East Germany, and they had no trouble at all in explaining What is Wrong With Brecht from "the Marxist viewpoint." "For one thing," said one of them, a rival Communist playwright,[7] "he thinks no one but him understands Marx..."

He liked individuals, and was himself highly individualistic. His depreciators have to explain what it was in him that could take hold of you even though you didn't agree with him and he supposedly valued agreement above all else. He was, in the strict sense, the most fascinating man I have ever met. There were times when I hated him, but there were no times when I did not love him.

ERIC BENTLEY

17   *Lotte Lenya and the aftermath.* The relationship of Brecht with Weill lies outside the scope of this eyewitness account of the former, since I never saw the two men together. I witnessed only the aftermath through an acquaintance with Lotte Lenya, but of course I recall things Brecht would say about Weill. He was catty on that subject, not only hinting that he himself composed the best tunes, but indicating that Weill had gone wrong where BB had gone right in the handling of American exile. "Pity Weill was born somewhere else," he would say with a wicked grin. "If the Americans didn't have a law against foreign-born presidents, he'd have made it."

What I am calling the aftermath consisted of my becoming an Enemy of the Brecht heirs, and a great deal of time was consumed in epistolary dispute and litigation. We never got before a judge or a jury, though at one point I submitted a motion for Summary Judgment to Judge Frederick van Pelt Bryan, who said no, and at another point we would have gone before a judge the following day at 9 A.M. had not an out-of-court settlement been reached on the phone at 9 P.M. Both sides spent quite a lot of money on lawyers, and sometimes the results were ironic, as when I for the first time in Brecht-Bentley relations received a check in four figures (from the Lincoln Center production of *Chalk Circle*) and my lawyer asked as his fee exactly the amount I had earned...

Rather than rehash all this shabby detail, which might well bore me as much as my readers, let me tell a story that suggests the coin had a reverse side to it.

When my relations with the Brecht coterie were good, my relations with Kurt Weill's entourage had been bad, a fact that reflects the tension that had existed between Brecht and Weill since 1930. I am shocked today to pick up correspondence from the 1950s that bears witness to hostility between me and Lotte Lenya. It was partly my fault. As critic for the *New Republic,* I had been excessively snotty about the 1954 opening of *Threepenny Opera:* there was sibling rivalry between me and the adapter, Marc Blitzstein.

Not surprisingly Lotte Lenya wrote East Berlin of her preference of Blitzstein to Bentley, and so on and so forth.

Luckily she and I were both people who did not know how to bear a lasting grudge and a business correspondence we began to have in 1961 burgeoned into cordiality by 1964. After that (I find I have some seventeen letters from Lenya in my files) my admiration for Lenya's work proved to be not altogether one-sided, and when I sent her my Hanns Eisler record album (*Songs of Hanns Eisler*, Folkways, 1964) she wrote me a bubbly letter that I would blush to quote in full, though I cannot resist citing the crowning compliment: "It's quite wonderful to hear all those songs, and you do them so well that I am afraid you might become a close competition to me."[8]

Bentley–Brecht Correspondence

There are eleven letters here, eight of them to Brecht. Three dots indicate omissions. Only letters three and ten are reprinted from a carbon copy retained by me. I did not usually make any carbon or other copies; indeed some of these communications are just hurriedly scribbled (or "scribble"-typed) postcards. The letter (two) to Jay Laughlin came back to me, in Xerox reproduction, through the kindness of James Lyon. Letter four is taken from the *New York Times*. Letters five through eleven (except for ten) are all taken from indistinct photocopies supplied by the Brecht Archive in East Berlin: where these are illegible, it is so noted in the texts below. Eccentricities and inconsistencies of abbreviation, capitalization, and so on, have been retained: these were highly informal communications, never intended (except for three and four) for publication.

1. To Berthold Viertel, an undated letter obviously written in March or April of 1945. It reflects the disillusionment that had followed the enthusiasm of 1942 to 1943. Even at that, it makes the same distinction between Brecht the Man (often outrageous) and Brecht the Artist (always gifted) that W. H. Auden used to make. The Schnitzler mentioned here is Heinrich, Arthur's son, who at the time was directing Master Race *in California. The Roberts is one Ernest Roberts, producer of the* Master Race *in New York.*

Dear Mr Viertel:

I'm sorry my resentment against Brecht seemed to get transferred to you...

I am not angry with you; but with Brecht I am, so much so that I regret having translated his play at all; it was a service he does nothing to deserve. For a couple of years I have been Brecht's only staunch supporter in the American liberal and literary press. I have spent much of my time and not a little small cash in trying to get his play produced. The result is that I now receive a wire from one person telling me that another person says that Brecht is consulting his lawyers about my actions. Meanwhile Brecht declines to reply to all my communications. He has been told about the Roberts affair and about everything else that concerns his play. But he has neither good manners nor elementary decency. He lives out his own theory that it is impossible to behave well in this society.

But for Schnitzler and Roberts I would wash my hands of the whole thing at once. However, these two men are working on the play, and I shall not tell them to desist unless Brecht himself writes to me and gives a full explanation of his conduct. It is his fault that both Schnitzler and Roberts are already involved; he knew about both projects from the start; and he did not write to me to stop them. Schnitzler's production is already in rehearsal. Roberts has been kept hanging around for weeks. Personally I do not see that S's production can be cancelled at all; and Roberts can only be repudiated if Brecht wants to act very unscrupulously—as a man like him, I suppose, does.

I believe I have stage rights, and not merely book rights, to the play, but of course I shall not use these rights. Brecht can consult his lawyers; I shall not consult mine (I don't have any). No. I shall do what Brecht wants, if he will only tell me *what he* wants, and tell me himself. When this is over, I wash my hands of Brecht. I shall apologize to Roberts if his production is cancelled, pleading that Brecht is an irresponsible and dishonest man. I shall not be interested in my rights to the play; in fact I think I shall sell them; I would like *not* to be connected with people of this sort.

Now let me apologize to you again for implicating you in the affair. I will be happy to help you with your article [on BB] if you will yourself negotiate directly with the KR [*Kenyon Review*] first. Nothing is altered between *us*. Nor does my opinion of Brecht's art change. He is like Dubedat in *The Doctor's Dilemma*—a scoundrel but an artist.

All the best,
Eric Bentley

2. *To James Laughlin, publisher of New Directions, February 28, 1946. My correspondence with Laughlin had begun, I believe, with a letter of August 17, 1943, beginning: "As perhaps you know I am interested in Bert Brecht…" It goes on, "Mr Brecht…is very unbusinesslike, so I venture to write to you on my own responsibility. One of the mss. [sent me by Brecht] is quite definitely among the best work [sic] of recent times… This is* FURCHT UND ELEND*…" Later items in the correspondence with Laughlin find me furious with Brecht, as in the foregoing letter to Viertel.*

…Brecht has now signed a contract with R & H [Reynal and Hitchcock]. He suggests me as his general editor but upon impossible terms. I'm to do all the dirty work and Brecht is to boss everything. Unless he withdraws his demand to supervise the whole show I must be counted out. I've had enough of Brecht and his female followers. He even asks that my introduction contain no criticism of his work!…

3. *Internal evidence indicates that this undated letter was written in August 1946.*

Dear Brecht:

I gather from your letter [dated just August 1946 and quoted in "Brecht–Bentley Correspondence" above; see page 343] that you do not today think of Epic Theater as the one and only theater of the future. In your Notes to the *Threepenny Opera*, however, you wrote: "Today . . . only the Epic form can enable the dramatist to find a comprehensive image of the world." Have you changed your mind?

This question is not malicious; nor am I merely curious to learn the history of your mind. I am a little puzzled by your reasoning. Have you really explained the difference between Ibsen and Shakespeare for instance? Is it really true that the poet of *Peer Gynt, Ghosts,* and *When We Dead Awaken* is monotonous? Is it true that his forms are rigid? And even if it were so, would a comparison with the Elizabethan Age explain it? After all many of the Elizabethans wrote very woodenly. Or am I missing your point?

I think I understand you and agree with you when you write: "The very diverse theatrical forms are by no means attempts to arrive at a final form: only the diversity itself should be final." But what are you saying about Bacon? Could you elaborate your distinction between Experimentalism as something provisional and Experimentalism as something much more important and lasting? You are right in thinking that it is too easy for people, especially for historians and critics like myself, to assume that our own age is purely an Age of Transition while certain other times were ages of fulfillment. The present is of course pure transition from past to future, and the present age *must* always seem purely transitional; fulfillment on the other hand is something that can be recognized only after the event. All this is true. Nevertheless not all ages are equally great, and one is bound to have some opinion of the greatness or un-greatness of one's own period. My own impression is that the generation 1880–1920 was a much more fruitful one than that of 1920–1945.

To you as a creative artist this may not be important. You will do your work and let others decide how good it is at their pleasure. You are indifferent to my historical and critical judgments for yet another reason: you are not only an artist but a teacher, a fighter, a "propagandist." You have a conception of art which few understand. I think I am probably not one of the few. You will have to explain yourself. The explanation you gave in "Writing the Truth: Five Difficulties" was not enough. I felt that you brushed aside all modern art except your own kind. You brushed it aside; you did not really cope with it. I would welcome two things: a brief account of your philosophy of art and—but this can wait a little—an account of Epic Theater that deals with some of the difficulties raised by Edmund Fuller some years ago and, more recently, by myself (*The Playwright as Thinker*, pp. 259–61).[1]

These are troublesome demands. But I think you will do yourself a service if you can help American readers and playgoers to see the difference between "Brechtism" and the impossible vulgarities of "proletarian literature" of which the most impossible is Socialist Realism. Like Shaw you are more eager to explain your politics and your morality than your art. This is your privilege. But I warn you that you will never make any further advance in America unless you can dispel the illusions and doubts that at present surround your kind of enterprise. They will not listen to your message until they are "sold" on your art.

Yours ever
Eric Bentley

4. *To the* New York Times, *November 10, 1947. The part of the letter they did not print—they themselves used asterisks to indicate an omission—is lost. Reference is to the Hollywood production of* Galileo, *evidently compared by a* New York Times *correspondent to Barrie Stavis's* Lamp at Midnight.

ADVOCATES BRECHT PLAY

To the Drama Editor:

I do not know the play which your correspondent prefers to Brecht's. But I have just seen Brecht's play on the stage, which your correspondent apparently has not. I shall not compare it with Shakespeare or call in the aid of Miss [Margaret] Webster, but I shall say this: that it is unwise to condemn Brecht's play before you have seen it performed, and that in my opinion Charles Laughton's production of it constitutes the big theatrical event of this decade. Mr. Laughton did not choose the play merely as a vehicle for his talents—though that would be a good enough reason if one considers what Mr Laughton's talents really are. He chose it out of admiration for the play as a play and as an important statement about science and social ethics. I saw his performance in Los Angeles three times. It is an astonishingly beautiful and instructive thing, and something different in kind from even the best thing one sees on Broadway.

Eric Bentley
Minneapolis, Minn.[2]

5. An undated postcard apparently sent from Salzburg to East Berlin in late 1949.

Dear Brecht:

I want you to read Erich Auerbach's *Mimesis,* published by Francke in Zurich. It is the best history of the idea of Realism that I know, much profounder than [Georg] Lukács.

In the background of the idea Verfremdung would you say the work of [Theodor] Lipps or [Wilhelm] Worringer was important? They elaborated the conception of *Einfuehlung,* which is, in a way, your starting point. I am interested in finding the broader setting of your dramaturgy.

By the way, one of the parts of the ORGANON I like best is the part on [illegible word or words] the Gestus. This is at the same time original and classical. You started out as an anti-Aristotelian critic. But the ORGANON champions 2 great Aristotelian notions: first, that pleasure is the end of art as of life and, second, that the heart of drama is plot.

People say: "But after all Stanislavsky cannot be held responsible for all the excesses of his followers. And he didn't have a System: he had an Approach useful in all styles." Question: what in Stanislavsky's books is useful for Narrative Realism (my name for Epic Theatre)?

yrs E.B.

6. *A postcard to Brecht's secretary, Ilse Kasprowiak, with address American Express, Paris, dated October 18—the year has to be 1949. The present book being no place for business correspondence, the businessy part of the message is omitted.*

…Eine Frage für Brecht. In dem Teil des ORGANONS wo er Hamlet resümiert, sagt er, dass Hamlet umkehrt, als er Fortinbras sieht und beneidet. Das ist nicht wahr. Er kehrt viel später um und aus anderen Gründen. Auch schlachtet er nicht seine Mutter usw. WAS MEINT DER BRECHT? Ich frage, der englischen Uebersetzung wegen. Es wird schwierig sein, diese Resümierungen von Shakespeare in Shakespeares England zu drucken. Oder habe ich nicht recht verstanden? Ihr Bentley

…A question for Brecht. In that part of the ORGANUM where he provides a resumé of Hamlet he says Hamlet turns around when he sees and envies Fortinbras. This is not true. He returns later and for other reasons. Nor does he slaughter his mother etc. WHAT DOES BRECHT MEAN? I ask because of the English translation [of the ORGANUM]. It will be difficult to print these summaries of Shakespeare in Shakespeare's England. Or have I got it wrong? Your Bentley.

7. *A letter from EB in Salzburg to BB in Berlin, prefaced by a message to BB's secretary: "I must write in English because I have to explain some complicated matters. You'll see that Brecht reads this?" Again 1949; the date is given as November 12–15.*

Liebes Fraülein: Ich muss auf Englisch schreiben, weil ich schwierige Sachen zu erklären habe. Sie werden sehen, dass der Brecht dies liest? . . . viele Grüsse, EB

Dear Brecht: I'll see that your revision [of the *Hamlet* passage in his *Organum*] and your footnote are used in the English version.[3] Not that I am quite happy about the footnote—but it's your affair. I'm not happy about it because it introduces a principle not explained in the text: the idea that you can *change* the play and make it definitely different from Shakespeare's. Carry out this idea, and you'll have a *Hamlet* as different from Shakespeare as the *Dreigroschenoper* is from *Beggar's Opera*. I have no objection to such re-creations—provided that the result is NOT called an interpretation of Shakespeare. Interpretation and adaptation are in principle different things. You seem to me to blur over this distinction.

Your ironic remark about the golden West is doubtless justified as far as the West is concerned, but are you never ironical about the East? The fate of men like [Theodor] Plivier and Lukács is of interest, surely.

I bring this up because I have read your play *Tage der Commune*. [Kurt] Hirschfeld [Dramaturg at the Schauspielhaus, Zurich] says it's meant to refer to Berlin under the blockade, the Soviet blockade. And yet your play shows a city attacked only by capitalism. Is the analogy very exact? If Western troops are in Berlin and are engaged in a struggle, the struggle is with Russia and not with Germany. I see no equivalent to this in your 1871 situation. Or rather: to accept your version of the story one has to accept the Marxist interpretation of 1871 in its entirety, and one has also to accept the Russian interpretation of 1949, i.e., one has to think that the Communists in the East zone stand for rule of the Germans by the Germans in the fullest and sincerest way. Can you *really* believe this? [A couple of paragraphs that follow are very indistinct but the following statements can be made out:]

I don't know whether this letter will estrange you. Since you don't write anyway, the estrangement could not perhaps, for practical purposes, be more complete than it already is. But I want you clearly to understand that I write as a proven admirer of your work, as one who has been called in the *New York Times* a "Brecht Disciple." I do not think *Tage der Commune* is a good play. Considered stylistically it is made up of imitations of your own earlier work. It seems to be lacking in all freshness and spontaneity. A big disappointment. [The prospect of E. B.'s directing *Setzuan* at the Oxford Playhouse is then mentioned.] Of course I could choose a play by someone more friendly to a Westerner like myself, but I still have an admiration for your best work, an admiration that will survive our disputes or even our friendship. [The signature is just "Yrs E. B." after the news is given that twelve university productions of BB have been arranged by EB in America.]

8. *This letter is dated November 18, and the year must again be 1949. It is almost complete. Above a Salzburg address is written: "I hope you now have my article MODERN GERMAN STAGE-CRAFT? I wish you'd send any criticisms. It's in the KENYON REVIEW which I mailed to you. Something for Neue Rundschau?"*

Dear Brecht: It was a great pleasure to have your letter [dated November 12, 1949, quoted above in "Brecht–Bentley Correspondence," page 349] and to learn that no damage was done. I would indeed like to work with you in the theatre before proceeding to direct your plays myself. The difficulty is a practical one: I would have to know exactly *when* and *where*. As things are, I could scarcely accept employment at the Deutsches Theater even if you wanted to offer it to me. But when is your next production? It is possible that I could arrange to be present at most of the rehearsals. However, I need to know very soon.

My present plans are to be in Italy during December, and in January [1950] to produce *Setzuan* at the Oxford Playhouse, England. I take it I have your permission to undertake such a production as this...

I am directing a month of theatre for advanced theatre students in June 1950 at this Schloss [Leopoldskron]. Could you come? For a week? Or a couple of days? We would give you an official invitation which might facilitate your entry into Austria... A visit from you would be very important to me. I have been able to do much more for you here than at Minnesota, because the students here come from many different countries and take home what I say to various communities. A French translation of *Puntila* has already come about in this way. An Italian version of *Galileo* will be made. My production in England will be another pioneer job.

I doubt if you are right in suspecting that my gifts lie more in the theoretical than the practical direction—it is simply that you *know* more of my theoretical work. My temperament seems to me to lead more to directing than to writing. I would gladly be a director who also writes (not a writer who also directs). But I can't say that America seems to offer me the chance I need.

However, you must have realized that I am too little in sympathy with the present-day Communist parties, as led by Russia, to go over into the other camp just because they are more interested in theatre. I agree with very many of your criticisms of the West, but I think that the East is even worse. In West Germany it is true that ex-Nazis are getting encouragement, but what about the Deutsches Theater? This morning I bought a book by [Herbert] Ihering[4] published a few years ago. In it I find a clear and unambiguous endorsement of Hitler and even a picture of [Emil] Jannings "in the liberated city of Danzig, October 1939."

I think it quite possible that the Communists will throw you overboard one day, as they are rumoured to have thrown over Lukács in the past months and so many others in the past years. From their point of view you are indeed a "formalist" etc etc: even [Erwin] Piscator, whom I talked to in New York [summer 1949], levels this charge at you. But perhaps I am irritating you now?

As to your Hamlet question, what you say in your letter seems more moderate, and I think it is acceptable. I'll think about it again. [A half legible signature follows an illegible message and greeting.]

9. This must be 1950. The letter is dated simply July 1, and again is going from Salzburg to East Berlin.

Dear Brecht: The well-known Italian manager and director Luchino Visconti wants to know if I could direct PUNTILA for him in Italy and in Italian during the coming season. It would be a full-scale production with the best actors. His season of theatre will probably be the outstanding event of the next two years as far as Italian drama is concerned. Naturally I am very eager to do this job, and since I saw *Puntila* in Zurich and Munich, and also discussed it with you in Berlin, I feel I could do you justice. At present my intention is to return to America in September but if you will approve Visconti's proposal I shall try to arrange to come and study with you during September and October... Since the planning of my future depends on decisive action now I hope you will help me.

... Very sincerely, *Eric Bentley*

10. In Italy in 1950 and 1951, I experienced a small triumph and a less small setback. The triumph was my production of The Exception and the Rule *with the Teatro Universitario di Padova, headed by Gianfranco De Bosio, a production that ended up gloriously at the National Festival in Bologna. The setback was the collapse of the Visconti plan for me to do a first-class production of* Puntila *in Rome, with Paolo Stoppa as Puntila. I sued Stoppa for nonpayment of what he owed, and won; but this was Italy, and my lawyer took all the winnings: all! Letter Ten belongs to 1951 and is dated January 27. It went from Padua to East Berlin.*

Lieber Brecht:

Hier sind die zwei wichtigsten Artikeln über meine Brecht-Aufführung in Padua. Sehr intelligent sind sie nicht, günstig sind sie schon ... Auch die Fehler dieser Artikeln sind symptomatisch ... Zum Beispiel, der eine Kritiker schreibt, dass Altruismus der Beweggrund des Kulis war.

Die Première war ein grosser Abend. Ausverkauft—1200 Zuschauer. Ein freches Publikum und zum Teil ein unwissendes. Die Musik von Dessau war "fischiata" (?deutsch: verpfiffen). Auch die pantomimischen Teile, die ich zusammen mit einem französischen "Expert" [Jacques Lecoq] gemacht hatte. Aber jemehr der eine Teil des Publikums sich ärgerte, desto mehr wurde der andere begeistert. Am Ende: Beifall, Beifall, Beifall, Die Musik, muss ich sagen, ist sehr schön, und wir haben fast die ganze Partitur gespielt. (In der Pariser Aufführung, wurden nur zwei Stücke davon gespielt.) ... Auf der Bühne, benützte ich das Rundhorizont der COURAGE. Es war wunderbar für die ganze Reise des Kaufmanns—mit—der Dessauer Musik and den Pantomimen des Lecoq ...

Die Aufführung ist bei weitem meine grösste praktische Errungenschaft im Theater. Es ist das erste Mal, dass ich (ungefähr) zufrieden mit meiner Arbeit bin. (Da ist auch viel, was ich gerne ändern möchte—aber das sind Sachen, für die man Geld braucht:

ohne Geld kann man einen grossen Realismus nicht schaffen!) Eine Brechtsche Aufführung. In München lernte ich sehr viel.

Die ganze Stadt Padua redet davon... Zaiotti, der Chef des Festivals von Venedig, war hier. Die Vorstellung hat ihm gefallen... Wann kann ich eine englisch-sprachige Aufführung [von *Ausnahme*] leiten? Fahre jetzt nach Rom. *Puntila* soll in März stattfinden... Viele Grüsse

[*EB*]

Dear Brecht,

Here are the two most important articles about my Brecht production in Padua. They're not very intelligent but anyway they are favorable... Even the errors in these articles are symptomatic... For example, one critic writes that the Coolie's motive was altruism.

The première was a great evening. Sold out—1200 spectators. The audience aggressive and in part ignorant. Dessau's music was *fischiata* (whistled at). So were the pantomimic parts which I created in collaboration with a French expert [Jacques Lecoq]. But the more one part of the audience got mad, the more the others waxed enthusiastic. At the end: applause, applause, applause. The music, I must say, is very fine, and we played almost all of the score. (In the Paris production, only two bits of it were played.)... On the stage, I used the cyclorama of MOTHER COURAGE. It worked wonderfully for the Merchants whole journey along with the Dessau music and Lecoq's pantomimes...

The production is by far my greatest practical achievement in the theater. It is the first time that I've been (more or less) satisfied with my work. (There's also a lot I'd like to change, but these are things one needs money for: without money one cannot create a grand realism!) A Brechtian production. In Munich I learnt a great deal.

All Padua is talking about it... Zaiotti, head of the Venice Festival, was here. He liked the production... When can I direct an English-language production [of *The Exception*]? Now on to Rome. *Puntila* should be on by March... Best wishes, [EB]

11. This letter went from Rome to East Berlin, February 21, 1951.

Lieber Brecht: eine Katastrophe ist geschehen. Das Theater hat entschieden, PUNTILA in dieser Spielzeit nicht zu machen. Und das Angebot, das Stück auf Oktober zu verschieben, hat wahrscheinlich nur den Zweck, mich jetzt nicht bezahlen zu müssen.

Eine Schweinerei. Aber Sie wissen wie das Theater ist? Das Theater in Italian ist alles von kleinen Gangsters organisiert. Die wussten, dass ich den Winter in Europa passiert habe, um diese Regie zu machen. Und ich glaube, sie wussten schon in Dezember, es wäre unmöglich PUNTILA zu machen, haben aber nichts gesagt. Es war sehr "convenient" mich da zu haben, falls sie keinen Erfolg mit *Death of a Salesman* haben würden. Aber sie haben Erfolg gehabt. Leider. Jetzt sagen sie, sie haben die Schauspieler für PUNTILA nicht... aber Sie können sich vorstellen, was für Diskussionen wir gehabt haben—Sie kennen ja den Broadway, also es ist dasselbe—Schwindel, Heuchelei, man wird Verrückt, weil niemand sagt, was er meint, alle sagen andere Dinge, und aus Diskussion wird "shadow boxing."

... Arbeitslos bin ich also. Mein Versuch ein Regisseur zu werden klappt nicht... Andererseits, mit dem was ich gemacht habe, war ich verhältnismässig zufrieden. Mir und dem Publikum habe ich gezeigt, dass ich wirklich ein Regisseur bin. Ich bekam soeben die Presse von Genova—über AUSNAHME UND REGEL. Ein grosser Erfolg. Die grösste Zeitung sagte sehr schöne Dinge von Ihnen und fand die Regie "stupenda"... Alles gute, Ihr alter E. B.

Dear Brecht:

A catastrophe has happened. The theater has decided not to do PUNTILA this season. And the proposal to postpone it till October probably has the sole aim of not having to pay me.

A bad business. But you know how it is in theater? In Italy, the theater is run by small-time gangsters. They knew I spent the winter in Europe in order to direct this show. And I think they knew as early as December that it wouldn't be possible to do PUNTILA. But they said nothing. It was very convenient to have me on hand, in case they had no success with *Death of a Salesman*. But it's a success, alas. Now they say they don't have the actors for PUNTILA... but you can imagine what our discussions have been like—you know Broadway, and this is the same—swindling, hypocrisy. You go crazy because no one says what he means. They all say something quite different, and discussion becomes shadow boxing.

...So I'm unemployed. My attempt to make it as a stage director has not clicked...On the other hand, I was relatively happy with what I did. I showed myself and the public that I really am a director. I just got the reviews from Genoa—EXCEPTION AND RULE [which was on tour]. A big success. The largest newspaper said very fine things about you and found the direction *stupenda*. All the best, Your old E. B.

Notes

1. I performed the speaker's part in Schoenberg's setting of Byron's *Ode to Napoleon,* and we sent a disk recording made with very primitive equipment to Schoenberg. The latter wrote Jalowetz in somewhat imperfect English (letter dated September 8, 1943):

   > As soon as I had opened the package I played the records. Let me tell you at first that what you have achieved in training Mr. Bentley and in accompanying this difficult piece is so excellent that it gives me again an opportunity of beeing [*sic*] proud about my pupils. It is really a pleasure to see how superior all of them are to everything which figures as masters in our present time. I have no idea what Mr. Bentley's voice is like. From the records no such sonority emerges which shows whether this voice has the compass (as to pitch) and the number of shades essential to express one hundred and seventy kinds of sarcasm, hatred, ridicule, derision, contempt, condemnation, etc, which I tried to portray in my music. It is also not to see whether the voice possesses the dynamic scale necessary to all that. But especially it is impossible to find out whether the voice has the "euphony" without which success of the recitator with the snobbish New York audience would be impossible. On the other hand I was astonished how well everything was done as regards rhythm and declamation. I consider this as very excellent and if, in New York, they find a good answer to the problems before-mentioned, I would say that Mr. Bentley would be qualified for this performance...

2. But in some cases this is explicable. My friend James K. Lyon was allowed to see certain material *on condition that* he say little or nothing about Brecht's offspring. When he asked me if I thought he was wrong to accept such a condition, I answered, no, not if he told his readers about it. However (in *Bertolt Brecht in America*), he did not tell his readers about it.

3. This fact is borne out by the edition in print in America in 1988. The word *Realism* crept back in—carefully defined, I trust—in some earlier editions.

4. Hardly a common expression in English, it is all too common in German, and its use in the third act of Berg's *Lulu* was the reason why Arnold Schoenberg refused to help finish the orchestration of that opera.

5. The report that Brecht said this in 1935 was not made till 1960. In the *New Leader*, December 30, 1968, I gave reasons for not taking such a report too seriously. The reporter, Sidney Hook, angrily exclaimed that I was impugning his veracity. I had only meant to suggest that memory—certainly after twenty-five years—plays strange tricks. But Henry M. Pachter wrote to the magazine to aver that, in thus daring to differ with Mr. Hook, I was insolent (*New Leader*, April 28, 1969).

6. The most outspoken of them runs as follows:

> the czar spoke to them
> with gun and whip
> on Bloody Sunday. then
> there spoke to them with gun and whip
> every day of the week, every work day
> the honoured murderer of the people.
> the sun of the peoples burned its worshippers.
> the most learned man in the world
> forgot the communist manifesto.
> the most gifted student of Lenin
> punched him in the puss.
> when young he was conscientious
> when old he was cruel
> young
> he was not god
> who becomes god
> becomes dumb.

7. Hedda Zinner, not so incidentally the wife of Erpenbeck.

8. I did ask permission to print two of her letters in full but Lenya's executors refused. It seemed they didn't wish the public to find out what she thought of Stefan Brecht.

Notes to Correspondence

1. Edmund Fuller criticized Brecht in *One Act Play Magazine*, April 1938.

2. In lieu of the lost passage, let me supply this excerpt from a letter to my editor, Harry Ford, dated August 12, 1947: "We drove down to Los Angeles to see

the Brecht *Galileo* which was really magnificent. I still don't think the play great, but the ensemble of play and production is very fine. Laughton's performance is very brilliant and also—which is more remarkable—very solid. The production is the first satisfactory Brecht yet seen in America... The whole affair was very encouraging and fascinating..."

3. The revision and footnote were provided in a letter from BB to EB dated October 31, 1949. They were incorporated in the English version included in Toby Cole's *Playwrights on Playwriting,* but, as far as I know, nowhere else.

4. Ihering, the first important critic to recognize BB's gifts in the early 1920s was in the late 1940s working at the Deutsches Theater.

Postscript

I still think I was right to keep myself in the background upon first publishing this collection. After all, it was to be a memoir of Brecht, not an autobiography. At the same time I was uneasy when friendly readers found my Brecht memoir mysterious and when less friendly readers found it evasive or disingenuous. Reading the memoir now, I see that my determination to be self-effacing left holes in my narrative and perhaps prevented the reader from learning what I was up to.

What I feel might be misleading, when I read the memoir now, is the detached tone. Brecht is onstage playing to the hilt the roles I assign him, striding, gesticulating, at times even screaming. I am the quiet spectator or reporter. Not that I (often) wasn't. Not that he didn't scream. I was the interviewer; he, the interviewed. He expected it to be that way and was used to getting it that way. He was creating his own image in the minds of his admirer, and why not? Who was I to feel insulted at receiving no comparable attentions in return? But when I hear people remark that he concealed so much from me, I can only retort that this "so much" was as nothing beside what I hid from him. Even in the memoir above, I admit withholding differences of opinion, lest they break up the relationship we did have. But the real withholding was that of my soul—spirit, if you prefer—both when we first met and later when he assumed he knew me pretty well.

Most readers of the memoir probably already had some idea who Brecht was and knew by what strange turns of fate this deeply German writer had come to be living in the neighborhood of Forest Lawn and Aimée Semple MacPherson's Temple when World War II was at its height. What they could not be asked to guess were the equally strange turns that brought me there. Brecht's starting point was Augsburg, Bavaria. Mine was Bolton, Lancashire. I come of what a snobbish brother of mine called sturdy yeoman stock. My paternal grandfather put us on the path Up-From-Wage-Slavery. From being a simple mover of furniture, he acquired a horse and van and created Joseph Bentley, Bolton, Limited, Removal Contractors. Inheriting this business with his brother, my uncle Frank, my father acquired first, a second horse, then a steam van, and later the motor vans that were to be seen in that part of Lancashire for some decades. In short, my family was enacting the same drama as millions of other families of the Western World in this era: the drama of upward mobility from the depths of poverty to the dizzy heights of the lower middle class. After I had left for America, my father would be mayor of the town.

My mother was equally interested in the journey to gentility but what she gave me in earliest childhood was far more intense than social ambition. It was faith: religious faith, implicit, unquestioned, ardent, total. We were Baptists and devout churchgoers, Sunday School–goers, too. My mother's idea of a normal Sunday was church in the morning, Sunday School in the afternoon, and church again in the evening.

I say my mother *gave* me faith. I should say rather that she strove mightily to give me faith and that at first she was successful. Only this would explain the fact that the fullest experience of happiness I've had in my more than seventy years was the moment each night when Mother would come to my bedside to hear me say my prayers. What is bliss? Negatively defined, it is absence of qualm or anxiety. Positively, it is a delight in blending, merging with Mother, with Nature, with God.

She was fully successful at first and intermittently successful for some years thereafter. After that, bliss became a will-o'-the-wisp, not always recognized as such. What had intervened? Non-faith. Doubt. Unbelief. Where does *that* come from? I have no memory of it but Mother told me later that when she first told me, in outline, the life story of Jesus, I said, "Is that true, or is it a legend?" Her reaction, she said, was amazement that I knew the word *legend*. Even if I was only four, I had already had at least one experience that created radical doubt. At three, two lumps, like two small eggs, swelled up on my neck. A doctor, I was told, would come and remove them. I was in my baby chair (operations were performed at home in those days) when this man approached me, razor in hand. Doubtless, it was a scalpel, but what I was familiar with was my father's open-blade razor. He had a large black mustache with wax tips, like Kaiser Billy. I had a clear image of what was happening: a Giant was coming to cut me up. I screamed. My mother was present, after all, and standing just behind the Giant: her job was to save me. I can see her clasped hands now, and the anxiety in her face, but she made no move. The world belonged to the Giant, and the Giant, advancing, said to the now terror-struck me: "Be a man."

I realize that persons who ask (among other malign questions), what causes homosexuality? and who, in any case, love to attribute any uncongenial human traits to traumas of infancy, will now pounce. Be it so. The gestalt of this little scene was burned into my consciousness and my unconsciousness: one's self as infant in the baby chair, the all-powerful male Giant-with-the-knife poised for the fatal blow, and, in the background, the mourning mother, either helpless or will-less, but doing nothing, accepting impotence as her role.

A small child who fastens on a grown-up word like *legend* will be congratulated on his brilliance, but what he has actually done is intuit that one day he may sorely need the word, and more than half a century later I would have to write a play called *From the Memoirs of Pontius Pilate* in which I separated the legendary Jesus from the historical. As for belief and unbelief, the second had been added to the first but had not replaced it. I oscillated painfully between the two forever after. Later, I found the phenomenon encapsulated in a single sentence of Montaigne's: "We are double in ourselves, so that what we believe we disbelieve and cannot rid ourselves of that which we condemn." It is a principle that articulates itself in a myriad ways, as I realized when a friend told this story about me. He had ridden the subways of Berlin with me after the city was divided in two in 1949. He said that, when the train was in the Western stations, I made heads turn around by aggressively worded anti-Western remarks, but that, as the train made its way to the first East Berlin station, my position changed so blatantly to an anti-Communist one that, really, I should take care or I might be arrested. My first reaction when I heard this story was to feel flattered: it sounded like the story of an effectively Socratic gadfly. But when I let my mind dwell on it, I could only remember the torment that had always attended my feeling for the truth of *A* when I was openly espousing the truth of *B*, its opposite.

At puberty, the young Baptist is asked if, unlike those Christians who are baptized without their permission in infancy, he is going to be baptized into the faith. For my part, I loved my mother, and I loved Jesus (or what I took for him), and I said yes. I was baptized by total immersion in what resembled a small swimming pool just below the pulpit of Claremont Baptist Church on Saint George's Road. I had high expectations of the big moment. (Also low expectations, disbelieving what I believed.) I liked the minister, was even prepared to have a bit of a crush on him. But when he held me in his arms, and lowered my head into the water, I came up chilly and dripping and learning that wet clothes cancel out romance, even romance with God. It was not long before I told the minister I had difficulty believing. In reply he sent me a religious greeting card with this sentence from John's gospel: "Whosoever willeth to do His will shall know of the teaching, whether it be of God." I read it many times and decided I understood it but had not found it to be true. I had after all willed to do His will when I expressed the wish to be baptized. But I did not know whether the teaching was "of God."

Nor was I ever to find out. Worse: the terms of the question were beginning to disintegrate when, in pursuit of education and gentility, I won a scholarship to Bolton School where the official religion, affirmed by hymns and prayers every morning, was not confirmed by the teachers who made the strongest impression, nor by the books they gave me to read. What does the word *God* mean? What would it mean to know the "will" of a God? But of course the spirit of contradiction works both ways, and even while the ideas of the Free Thinkers were seducing my adolescent spirit, the will to believe asserted itself, too; as vigorously as its opposite. If philosophy represents a pure will to know, while religion reflects the will to believe, then my nature was ever religious rather than philosophical. And when, later, I came to devote myself to the arts, the art that held a unique fascination for me was the art that since Greek days has itself been fascinated by beliefs: the art of the drama. I would learn that other kinds of drama have also been proposed, particularly in our day, with its drama of the bedroom and the front porch. When I was a professional dramatic critic, it was a foregone conclusion that my reviews of such plays would be negative.

In my undergraduate years—at Oxford where another scholarship in the same cause brought me—I was still not prepared to break with organized Christianity, but I sought out its least organized, least theological institution: the Society of Friends. That was my negative reason for joining it. There was a positive reason: its pacifism. I was not yet of university age when Oxford students voted that they would never fight for King and Country, but I was caught up in that surge of antiwar sentiment while still at Bolton School. One of my teachers knew Robert Graves, and I read

Graves's *Goodbye to All That* along with other already famous products of World War I like *Death of a Hero, Memoirs of a Fox Hunting Man,* and the poems of Wilfred Owen. It wasn't clear to me (still isn't) that the New Testament preached pacifism, but it had a pacifist element, and guided by Tolstoy one could isolate and endorse this element. I was prepared, at the time, to be politically as simplistic as Tolstoy. The world seemed headed for a war that would destroy civilization, but this could be prevented if enough people would refuse to take part. My will to believe, more and more detached from any theology, could lead me to believe in this.

Communism was the sophisticated thing, in the mid-1930s, for student rebels to believe in, but I was not sophisticated. I wasn't upper class enough for Oxford proletarianism. I felt that immediately on hearing Philip Toynbee make Communist speeches at the Oxford Union. How, without the right accent and self-assurance, would one ever get into a club like that? Literary communism appealed to me but only in a literary way. The plays of Auden and Isherwood were in the Communist orbit and opened up for me a vision of a lively new kind of theater, especially if they had music by Benjamin Britten. But the odor that came off all these men was unmistakably Public School. Marxism was something (I thought) that they must have picked up on their expensive vacations on the Continent.

I don't know why I didn't feel the same way about Aldous Huxley, whose *What Are You Going to Do About It?* I championed against C. Day Lewis, a future poet laureate, who at that time wrote a Communist riposte to Huxley under the title "We Aren't Going to Do Nothing." Huxley, too, belonged to the English upper class's argument with itself, but what he had to say about war reached many of the rest of us, even the most class conscious and suspicious. What he was writing in that period met my needs, and since the will to believe carries with it a will to act on one's beliefs, commit oneself to them, I, who had broken with churches, joined two pacifist organizations, The Peace Pledge Union and the

Oxford University Pacifist Association. I was the first chairman of the latter, and in this period, for the only time in my life, I joined a political party, the Independent Labour Party.

What would happen if war broke out and neither civilization nor myself disappeared from the scene? It was a question I had to answer in 1939. But how could I? Initially I was able to float along on assumptions made earlier. As a pacifist, I would declare myself a conscientious objector and enter a camp for such. Indeed I was in a camp near Birmingham when news came that I had won the scholarship to Yale, which I had applied for the previous winter. Would the British government give me an exit permit? It did. After the blackout I'd left behind me in Birmingham, the neon lights around New York Harbor announcing WRIGLEY'S SPEARMINT were an astonishment. I had left the continent where everything had ended and come to one where nothing had begun.

But for me there began a new double life. Outwardly, it was business as usual, which for me meant continuing my studies, distinguishing myself. My life as a scholarship boy was a continuous success story from my entrance into Bolton School at eleven, to my entrance into University College, Oxford, at eighteen, to my promotion to Senior Scholar at New College, Oxford, in 1938 and now to my two-year term as Commonwealth Fellow in the United States. I had the choice between Harvard and Yale and chose Yale because they would let me get the doctorate in less time. I now placed myself in competition with the intellectual athletes in America as I had already done in England. My friend Richard Ellmann, the famous biographer-to-be, won the Porter Prize for the best doctoral thesis of general human interest in 1942; I had won it the year before.

"Keeping up appearances" is usually spoken of slightingly, as if one's duty were to keep up no appearance and run naked, but looking back I'd say that a degree of professional proficiency and success was what preserved my sanity and kept me, most of the time, from thoughts of suicide.

This year 1939 was not the first in which my life had been in danger of total collapse. But the last time this had happened—when I was eleven—the crisis was overt: what doctors then diagnosed as "nervous breakdown" was accompanied by high temperatures, fevers and chills, nightmares and hallucinations. The crisis of 1939 was both better and worse, better in that there were no visible or measurable symptoms, but worse in that their very absence left me facing, in full consciousness and good health, the fact that my world had blown away: I was no one and inhabited nowhere.

I don't know if anyone who did not live through the 1930s can imagine the state of mind of those who did. In addressing my own sons, I must say: *Since you will have illusions of your own, try to bear with us in ours.* Until September 1939, I thought any general war must destroy civilization (as today we presume that World War III would do). But when World War II came and life for many of us continued, I discovered I had never really believed war would come at all. I had been naïve enough to assume that the nations just would not do it. And one consequence of my naïveté was that I had in no way prepared my psyche for war, for any role in war, least of all the role of a war resister, which, for one of my class, can be a harder role than that of a soldier: in uniform I'd probably have been assigned to noncombat duties, out of uniform it was jail or picking up broken bodies on the battlefield in an ambulance unit.

If my body escaped to America, my soul did not. *Coelum non animam mutant qui trans mare currunt.* If only I'd been running away from war to a country really at peace, life would have been simple and understandable. But I knew from the first that peace, for America, was precarious and could end any time. And what disturbed my spirit was not my unpreparedness for soldiering but unpreparedness for conscientious objection in wartime. Pacifism had not been more to me, I was learning, than making sure war did not come. And my religious training had taught me not to cast oneself for a heroic role without the specific strengths it would require. A nonsaint should not play at saintliness, nor nonheroes at heroism.

Well, the American fellowship would be a reprieve, not a solution or a refuge. It would buy me time to find out where I stood. Perhaps I could coast a while longer on the formulas I had been living by in England? In New Haven, Connecticut, I looked up a Friends' Meeting House and attended a couple of Sunday services. They were not helpful. I learned that some Quakers were moving away from pacifism. And everyone present was American and still remote from war itself.

Had I miscalculated in coming to America? I could have stayed among the pacifists in England until it became intolerable, if it did, and then I could have joined the army with millions of others at that time. I really didn't know why I hadn't stayed home. With hindsight I suspect that the part of me that impelled me towards flight was not political. The "home" I was fleeing was not the British Empire, it was 152 Markland Hill Lane in Bolton, Lancashire. It was a flight above all from my mother, which will come as no great surprise to the few among my readers who knew her. She was a powerful Victorian matriarch. As a child I had worshipped her. As an early teenager, I had an intense crush on her. If I rebelled in my late teens, I was still in awe of her and fearful of incurring her displeasure. I knew she laid claim to infallibility in theology, so it was not easy to drop the Baptist faith when it meant dropping her. And at least as troubling as religion was sex.

My mother, a Yorkshire woman born in 1883, celebrated no wedding anniversaries because her eldest was born less than nine months after marriage. She had known nothing of sex then, and didn't learn much more later. As a young man I learned that she never knew how to exercise birth control. Babies just came. There were none after me. Just before I was born, my father had an accident and was in Manchester Royal Infirmary for many months. No sex with his wife afterwards, I imagine. She had never liked it anyway, she gave me to understand. It was brutal, dirty, and you couldn't imagine Jesus doing it.

I don't know if she knew about homosexuals, but when I was fifteen or so I had a big crush on a boy in my class at Bolton School, and Mother went to consult the only woman teacher there. She was worried about us keeping company too much. We were not having sex. I had already played with other boys' genitals now and then, but I didn't connect those small events with the adoration I now felt for Derek. I would go to his home and instead of playing games or talking we would just lie together on the couch, touching but not carnally. I've seldom had more blissful hours than those, and they enable me to understand the "Oriental" respect for absolute stillness and Walt Whitman's affirmation of sheer loitering.

The teacher told Mother that such things were common in boys' schools but that the boys got over it later, and I suppose that, since I got over Derek, or he me, Mother imagined the "problem" had evaporated. The dualism characteristic of my life in general made my sexual experience and inexperience also ambiguous and contradictory. Although the flavor of the feeling for my own sex seemed to me as innocent and delicious as that of strawberries, I knew the horror in which it was held by persons of my mother's background, and I developed a terror at the possibility of being found out—a continuation of the fear, verging on panic, of having my masturbations found out. I gather that the liberated generations of today are no happier than we were, but surely they must be miserable for other reasons. For us the stigma of being found out would have been unbearable. But the strain of hiding was so great I had to run away, from Bolton, from Britain, whenever an opportunity offered, as in 1939 it did.

When I read the lives of upper-class homosexuals like Christopher Isherwood, I envy them. They had to pay attention to the taboos—Isherwood left the sex out of his early book accounts of his life, and Auden addressed love poems to lovers whose sex was unspecified—but they could arrange to live in "gay circles" and have an abundant love life. Myself, even after I'd run away from home and moved in the privileged circumstances of an Ivy League campus, I was too shy to hunt out the like-minded. After two years of Yale, I was still a virgin as far as women were concerned, and I had made a carnal connection with exactly one fellow student who, like myself, pretended to be straight. You may ask how, in that case, anything ever happened? Through fantasy. Scott and I, locked away in his college room, would indulge in sexy talk—heterosexy talk, after which discretion could be thrown to the winds. But when it was over, the talk would turn to anything but the topic before us. We never kissed, hugged, or, when parted, wrote love letters. Scott is long dead now, and I don't know if he ever turned out to be what he or I would regard as gay.

I didn't realize it then, but what I sorely needed in my love life was what I needed in religion and politics: a belief to which I could be committed. In all areas I was now a hollow vessel, and I was on my own. I had abandoned one country without adopting another. I had less and less religion; politics were now a mere vestige of an era that had passed; no women, having rejected my mother and not having approached anyone else; no male lovers, except for a few minutes on a few occasions with Scott; no friends. I made several stabs at friendship and worked up a crush on someone clearly heterosexual, who never figured out my "strange" behavior. How I behaved towards Richard Ellmann I cannot accurately remember. Evidently he thought I had made a pass at him and delivered himself of a homophobic diatribe. Correction: I did make one real friend, Arnold Kettle. Arnold also picked up his Ph.D. at Yale and went on to write two of the best volumes extant on the nineteenth- and twentieth-century English novel.

I wonder if MI5 knew whom the Commonwealth Fund was bringing to the United States as young ambassadors of imperial Britain? Of the small group, one (myself) was a pacifist who had, so to speak, stood on soapboxes to declare that he would never fight for king and country; another had kept no secret at Cambridge earlier, and would keep no secret at Yale now, that he was a member of the Communist Party. Arnold was a conspicuous member of the Party in the United Kingdom until the 1970s. My qualms about my pacifism being still secret, in conversation I inevitably espoused the cause I'd belonged to in the 1930s, and there were some harsh exchanges in the early days. Later we learned to keep the talk out of the danger area. Arnold's temperament was propitiatory: it was gentle and flexible, and his sense of humor embraced all the shadings from subtle irony to a broad sense of the ridiculous. He was tolerant, too, and I remarked that this was strange in a Communist. "No," he said, "you believe in tolerance because you're not tolerant; I don't because I am."

Arnold and I were able to make common cause: neither of us supported the war or the prospect of America's entry into it. This meant we were making common cause also with people who appalled both of us. We even turned up one evening at an America First Rally on the Yale campus. The chief speaker was Colonel Charles A. Lindbergh, whose fear that Slavic hordes might be about to pour in through Alaska did not appeal to Arnold. However, he continued to abet the crowds who cried: "The Yanks are not coming!" until Hitler invaded the Soviet Union.

That event sent Arnold rushing back to the United Kingdom and into uniform. It made no difference to me. Or did it? I kept no diary or other record and can report only from the perspective of nearly half a century later. Spiritually, I endured a black night of the soul for all of two years at Yale, but this was a secret I shared with no one, no one I'd left behind in England, no one I had met in America. Arnold could only have supposed I stayed to avoid the war, a pacifist unwilling even to volunteer for ambulance service.

I was stuck. There was no turning back, but I had no idea in which direction to move forward. Was there any movement at all by mid-1941? In order to write this Postscript I dug up the doctoral thesis I submitted to Yale in the spring of 1941, the one to which they gave a prize. Mostly, it is busy keeping up the appearances: I had learned to come on as the star student of the year. Intellectually, though, there *had* been movement since 1939. Although detachment from the war is announced as appropriate to the thinking writer, the ideas analyzed and lingered over are those I was not even acquainted with before the war. Fatalistically, I say that what is happening in our time is best exhibited in Alfred Rosenberg's book *The Myth of the Twentieth Century*! The mind behind *my* mind throughout most of the manuscript is that of Friedrich Nietzsche.

Looking for the ideological roots of Nazism, I had become fascinated with the enemy. That was the meaning of my remark about Rosenberg. I addressed a letter to him, via his German publisher, to ask if I could translate parts of his book into English. I read other Nazi writers and a number of their forebears. But then I fell in love with the enemies of the enemy, beginning with Nietzsche and, of course, culminating, for me, in Brecht. Meanwhile I was living more and more among German refugees. I married one. It is no slight to that entrancing Austrian-Jewish girl that in marrying her I felt I was marrying into Central Europe. And I became very close to the Viennese poet Berthold Viertel, who belonged to the inner circle of Brechtians. Then it was Brecht himself.

This was later. But already in that 1941 thesis, it was clear that the naïveté of my prewar pacifism was gone, and I was now approaching an abyss: belief in nothing. Though in the thesis I affirmed a belief in the intellectual who stands *au dessus de la mêleé,* even my negativism was ambiguous. Picking up the manuscript today, the first thing I notice is two epigraphs. One is a series of remarks by Heraclitus, along the lines of "War is the father of all." The other is a quotation from *The Brothers Karamazov,* beginning with the Grand Inquisitor's words: "We have taken the sword of Caesar and, in taking it, of course have rejected Thee and followed him."

When I was cramming for my finals at Oxford in 1938, I reached for a book to distract me for half an hour. The one book in my room that seemed to fill the bill was *Crime and Punishment.* I hadn't killed an old woman, but the tale drew me in as if I had. I didn't put the book down till I'd finished it. Now I had not only lost the vital hours that should have been given to cramming, but I found an author who spoke directly to me. Three years later, Dostoevsky made a second visitation, and this time it was *The Brothers Karamazov*. From it, I tore the quotation that seemed to confirm the nihilism toward which I was tending. What Dostoevsky was doing, both times, was interrupting my progress, reminding me of my Christian origin. For if I had rejected God, Jesus of Nazareth was someone I remembered and would continue to remember. If I had rejected Christianity, there is something, I now believe, that one can call the Christian spirit, which is not to be rejected.

When Arnold sailed back to England to fight for the Empire and the Soviet Union, I asked the United States for a resident visa. I still felt I had nothing to offer either the army or any pacifist resistance, but something must turn up to fill the terrible void within me or I would cease to exist: I saw things in terms as simple as that.

It turned out that, though Arnold had not won me over to communism, he had helped to make me more realistic about political power and more willing to accept, with whatever reservations, those centers of power that are the warring nation states. Had I felt that Russia was "the future, and it works" I would have gone there. Having left my motherland, I was free to choose any country that would take me, and in 1939, the United States happened to be the country that offered me a fellowship. But even before that I had been known to some, at Bolton School, as the American: I had played one in a production of Galsworthy's *Little Man*. But it contained a germ of further truth. The fellowship did not come out of thin air. I had asked previous fellows what America was like, and I did most deliberately choose New England as the best replacement for Old England. In 1941, even expecting something to turn up was a step forward.

At the same time I remained, and remain, European, and I surrendered the last vestige of my pacifism upon studying a very

European document, *Man's Hope,* by André Malraux. The book was written in the late 1930s when he was still in his quasi-Communist phase. But it wasn't communism I got from the book. It was the feeling that one could no longer, in the world of Hitler and Franco, decline to meet force with force. My pacifism had been a tactic to avoid war. Once war raged, I could not, with Gandhi, advocate lying down in the path of the invading panzers. Whether or not I'd be assigned to combat duty I now felt I should offer myself to the armed forces. My first choice—a sort of irrational compromise between Britain and the United States—was the Canadian Army. A Canadian colonel interviewed me in Ottawa, following through with a letter in which he wrote: "The projects on which your services might be used have not yet sufficiently crystallized... and I am unable to take advantage of your kind offer..."

Back in the States I had only to await the call, since, as a resident alien I was subject to the draft. The call came in December 1942. It was an anticlimax. At the induction center in New York, clad in just my jockey shorts, I was confronted by a bespectacled psychiatrist in tie and three-piece dark suit. When he asked if I was attracted to persons of my own sex, I thought it would be odd, as well as mendacious, to say no, even though at the time I was engaged to be married. My reply, however, made him very nervous, and he quickly turned me over to uniformed officers. One of them was aggressive, eager to check out if I was lying to evade the draft. Where did I find partners? What exactly did I *do* with them? I thought he wanted to put me in jail or a mental home, but he handed me over to a colleague delegated to try the opposite approach: coaxing and suspiciously androgynous, he seemed to caress my shoulders while calling me Eric and asking if the sight of a good-looking young man gave me an erection. I replied, "Not usually." The androgyne put his arm round me and said in a melancholy voice, "Well, I don't think the Army can use you at present," and I was released. I had, however, to be formally allowed through a military checkpoint where the clerk put a capital *H* against my name, while his friends, crowding around him to read his papers, cried: "Homo, another Homo!" I was staggering uncertainly as I left the building, and when I reached the sidewalk outside I had to lean on the wall for support. My attempt to join the war on political grounds had been coolly (or hotly) rejected by the war makers on sexual grounds.

Arnold's persuasions did, belatedly, have some effect. When I took the United States for my country, I let myself be drawn into the now widespread enthusiasm for its ally the Soviet Union. Within a few months of the invasion of Russia, many of us were seeing a film called *Moscow Strikes Back* on Times Square. Little did we know that in the Ukraine Hitler's armies had been received with open arms. We took the word of Churchill and others that Marshall Stalin was in the forefront of resistance. The period 1942 to 1945 is the only one in my life when I knew what it was to be a Soviet sympathizer. My first translation published in book (booklet?) form was a tract called *The Thugs of Europe*, written, probably under a pseudonym (I don't have a copy to consult), and without my name on it anywhere, by Albert Norden, a Party functionary later to be a prominent member of the East German politburo. Did I know he was "that kind of person" at the time? Well, once, when I was spouting the Party line in his small apartment on the West Side of New York, he shut me up fast, looking nervously over his shoulder: "Sh! You don't have to convince *me*." At least one commentator has concluded that in all this I showed myself a Brecht protégé. But when I met Brecht in the spring of 1942, it was because I was already in the Soviet camp. I was taken to Brecht by the movie director Herbert Kline, very much a fellow traveler except in the period of Stalin's pact with Hitler, as a sympathetic person to work with him. Had I been moving in a contrary direction—say, towards the circle that wrote for Dwight MacDonald's antiwar magazine *Politics*, which I diligently read—no one would have offered to introduce me to Brecht, nor would I have wanted to be introduced.

Thus the young man whom Brecht met in the spring of 1942 was a political sympathizer, though far from being a Communist. As a sympathizer, he would often be *called* a Communist. "You're a Communist!" Sidney Hook shouted into my face the first time we met, in 1944 or 1945 on Thompson Street in the apartment of Jeanne Wacker, who had been my student and disciple and was now his. Hook had himself been a sympathizer twelve years earlier and was still able to think along Communist lines: "Objectively, Bentley's a Communist, just hear him talk about Russia." But it was only the Russian war effort that appealed to the sympathizers of that time. We were not Marxists. We had no intention of joining the American Communist Party. My first book, *A Century of Hero Worship*—a rewrite of my thesis—was reviewed by Hook in *The Nation,* and he noticed the Stalinist tendency of one passage in it. The *New Masses* (Communist) reviewer noticed it too, but where Hook was almost ready to cry, "Communist!" (something he likes to cry anyway), the Communist reviewer noted that I had, from his point of view, some distance to go.

As I said in the Memoir, Brecht did not seem particularly aware of my passing enthusiasm for the Soviet Union, so naturally he was not aware of the passing itself. In my political development, acceptance of power, even of what is now called superpower, was the first phase of my attempted self-reconstruction. After the disenchantment of 1939 to 1942 came a certain excessive, even bumptious, fatuous enchantment with the world. That had to stop. And if a single individual had much to do with my Russophile phase (and this was Arnold Kettle, not Bertolt Brecht), a single individual had much to do with my ending it. This was Lionel Trilling.

I have led not just one type of double life but several. A double life I cultivated during World War II had these parts: I consorted with Brecht and his Communist associates; and at the same time I sought out scholars and critics in the academic world in which, after all, I made my living. (A fool has offered his guess that my motive in taking up Brecht was money. But the Brecht enterprise never helped me to make my living until after Brecht was dead.) My scholarly friends were never leftists. The first had been C. S. Lewis at Oxford. My relationship with him was delightfully dialectical. He would roar with merriment at my outrageous heresies. An unbeliever in his eyes, and beyond recall, I was accepted as a debating partner, a highly flattering role for the slightly precocious boy I was at the time. I learned a lot about Christianity from remarks of his that were above and beyond the call of duty, for he was only hired to teach me English literature.

In America the two academics whose brains I wished to pick were Jacques Barzun and Lionel Trilling. I read their books, wrote them of my interest, and proposed that they serve as examiners at Black Mountain College, which was not allowed to provide examiners of its own. They agreed. I got to know them, and it was *their* non-Communist philosophy, not the Sidney Hook variety, that brought me into conflict with my commitment, albeit limited, to the ideas of Arnold Kettle and Bertolt Brecht.

From 1943 to 1945 I was a frequent contributor to *The Nation,* the liberal journal that Barzun, Trilling, and Diana Trilling then wrote for. The magazine at that time led a double life somewhat as I did, politically speaking. The front matter was in the Communist orbit, the back keenly if somewhat quietly anti-Communist. Given my tendency always to assert the *A* part of myself if my interlocutor was asserting the *B* part, it was inevitable that I would take the Communist side when dealing with the literary editor who was a fierce anti-Stalinist. That got me dropped from *The Nation,* as a sequence of events not dissimilar later got me dropped from *Partisan Review.* But this little bit of journalistic history is worth remembering after all this time only because it caused Lionel Trilling to give me a piece of his mind in several letters. The first of them ran to eleven pages.

This was in 1946, the year in which I set out my idea of Brecht's theater in *The Playwright as Thinker,* the year in which he read the book and agreed to embark on a publishable correspondence about

Epic Theater and the like. Several years later, Brecht was to describe me as virtually the only champion of his theories. I mention this here to indicate the extent to which I lived in Brecht's world while, in Trilling's world, where also I lived, I was reading such words as these:

> I live with a deep fear of Stalinism at my heart. A usual question at this point which I know you would never ask is: And not of Fascism? Yes, of Fascism too, but not so *deep*—in one's fantasies one can imagine going out to fight one's Fascist enemies quite simply; but whenever I fantasy fighting an enemy that has taken all the great hopes and all the great slogans, that has recruited the people who have shared my background and culture and corrupted them, I feel sick. I am willing to say that I think of my intellectual life as a struggle, not energetic enough, against all the blindnesses and malign obfuscations of the Stalinoid mind of our time.

These remarks come from a rather bulky correspondence between Trilling and me that was prompted by my annoyance at Sidney Hook's review of *A Century of Hero Worship*. Trilling detached himself from Hook by stating that he knew I was not committed to Stalinism, but he went on to deplore that I would only go as far in the other direction as to cry: "A plague on both your houses!" As for Stalinist writers, none of them was any good. Brecht's work, he admitted, he did not know. Malraux's *Man's Hope* was a fraud.

The years following World War II find me moving far away from Stalin. In 1948 I became an American citizen, and I'm sure the Brecht circle took for granted that I supported their candidate for the American presidency, Henry Wallace. My colleague F. O. Matthiessen, with whom I had a number of friendly talks that summer, was prominent in the Wallace campaign. I took no part in it and did not vote for their man. The tactic that I felt I had to adopt towards Brecht was that of quiet listening. But I was open in what

I published. Mostly he never saw nor heard any of this. As reported in the Memoir, when he did hear something, there was trouble.

I can never forget the face or the vocal style of Wolfgang Harich, an East German intellectual last mentioned in the newspapers when he was jailed for subversion in 1956. The face and voice I remember belong to 1949, when young Harich was Stalinism's latest convert in East Berlin. Lunching at Die Moewe (The Seagull), the elite artists' club, I was able to listen in on many conversations, as well as take part in a few. Clearest in memory is a tirade by Harich on the subject—a sensitive one for me, as I have explained—of Dostoevsky. Our friends in the West, he said, are surprised that Dostoevsky is not favored in the Soviet Union. But how right the Russians are! This author must be totally banned. His works are *REINES GIFT* (pure poison). At which Harich's voice, already high and touched with hysteria, cracked...Was this, for me, a third visitation? Surely Dostoevsky's ghost was whispering in my ear: "Behold, the possessed!"

I am offering these fragmentary notes on my political history to help trace the evolution of the author of the Memoir in the very years when he was seeing Bertolt Brecht. And what we find in the years 1942 to 1946 is yet another duality. The zeal of the war effort, headed by Churchill, Stalin, and Roosevelt, rescued me from philosophic nihilism and perhaps from absolute self-destruction. On the other hand, this zeal had itself a large corrupt component. By the time Brecht invited me to work at the Berlin Ensemble, in the 1950s, I realized that my listener's, learner's stance would entail a good deal of hypocrisy if I was to last out the proposed year in East Berlin. And by the time Brecht died, I was ready to describe myself in the obituary as an anti-Communist.

I had not become an integrated personality, free of contradictions. I had merely got rid of one particular set of illusions. During my last meeting with Brecht, two months before his death, I continued to be a fairly silent partner, and never came near reporting to him the depth of my antipathy to the whole East Berlin enterprise. From the outset our relationship had been founded on misunderstandings, and if from time to time it changed, the change was from one misunderstanding to another. But when people find me arrogant in my studies of Brecht, I have to agree. The seemingly diffident observer, quietly concealing fundamental disagreement, did implicitly claim to understand Brecht's work better than those who agreed with him, or congratulated him on agreeing with them, in loud voices, a dogmatic tone, and an officially approved lingo.

I hope that this Postscript has filled the gap left by the Memoir, but it is possible that Bertrand Russell was right when he wrote, "The things one says are all unsuccessful attempts to say something else."

E. B.
New York, 1988

Answers to a Questionnaire

What follows is self-explanatory. I got no reply, so I had to assume that my refusal to let them edit me led to their refusal to publish.

January 9, 1964
Questions submitted by ADN, East German news agency, to Eric Bentley. Eric Bentley hereby permits publication of his answers but *only in their complete, unedited form.*

1. What meaning does Brecht have for your own work?

ANSWER: Translating Brecht is a part of my work, and an important part. Sometimes there has to be adaptation too, as when we brought *Mann ist Mann* closer to the American public by some changes and interpolations made in the spirit of Brecht.

Often when I work on another author, I work in the spirit of Brecht. For example, I made a new libretto for Offenbach's *Orpheus in the Underworld* for the New York City Opera Company, which was Brechtian enough to annoy the old-line opera critics.

I am also a university lecturer, and Brecht is prominent in my courses at Columbia University.

2. What role does Brecht play in your country's cultural life?

ANSWER: He plays no role to speak of in America's official theater, the Broadway theater, where apparently the Brecht heirs wish to install him. Bertolt Brecht wrote me he preferred the college performances to those on Broadway, and in principle this preference was probably a wise one. In any case, it is certain that while Brecht plays no role in the Broadway, Hollywood, and television world, he has a firm place in the college theaters—and in college courses. In a somewhat diluted form, he also has a place in the off-Broadway theater. Whether this is of value I cannot say. I value more highly a production of *The Caucasian Chalk Circle* by the Actors' Workshop of San Francisco, where it was just directed by Carl Maria Weber, or of *Mother Courage* at the Goodman Theater in Chicago, where it opens in May 1964, with Eugenie Leontovich as the mother. And how should this role of Brecht in our schools and theaters be summed up? He is a ferment: chiefly that. His influence, by the way, if he has one, is probably less Communist than pacifist. The youth here is less communistically inclined than in the 1930s. But there is a strong pacifist movement. Also there is a strong vein of sheer undirected dissidence—which finds itself reflected in the early works of Brecht. These early works have more resonance in America today than the late ones.

3. What are the reasons for Brecht's worldwide success?

ANSWER: An unfair question, since the reasons are not the same in every country, nor are they the same for every Brecht work. And for that matter, some phases of Brecht's work are not world famous. But to do what I can with the query: some works have a pacifist resonance, some a dissident-cynical one. Brecht's success in France has much to do with his left-wing orientation. His success in America has not. One reason he is successful is that he is good: after all, most artists of his stature do achieve world fame, though often all too slowly. Hence I would see it as in the first instance a matter of sheer, mere talent. Then there is the question of audience sympathy, which, as I say, is not everywhere the same. Since Brecht is not everywhere (in his works) the same either, he is able to please a Communist audience by his Communist works, and a non-Communist audience by his non-Communist works. To a degree, he is "all things to all men." What some people do not like in Brecht—that he was not very consistent and not all of a piece and not a very good Communist or a very good anything-ist—has its advantages when his works are sent out by publishers to find their audience: they find lots of audiences, some of which are not on speaking terms with some others. A young Russian can fall in love with "Praise of Communism," and a young American with the anti-Communist poem "Ballad of the Red Army Soldier."

A Bibliography of Other Works on Brecht by Bentley

This bibliography is simply a chronology of Bentley publications on Brecht not to be found above. Excluded, however, are translations into foreign languages (in such periodicals as *Spandauer Volksblatt, Sipario,* and *Il Dramma*) and various Letters to the Editor (published in such places as the *New Leader,* the *New York Times,* and the *Times Literary Supplement*). Included are one or two items that bear on Brecht even though he is not the ostensible subject.

1943

"German Writers in Exile." *Books Abroad,* October.

"The Status of Contemporary German Poetry." *Rocky Mountain Review,* Fall.

1946

Untitled review of *Furcht und Elend des dritten Reiches. Books Abroad,* Spring.

"German's Plots Interest Ordinary Folk." *Chicago Daily News,* December 4.

1948

"Brecht Translator Lauds *Chalk Circle*." *The Carletonian* (Northfield, Minnesota), May 18.

"Brecht on the American Stage." *Bulletin of the National Theatre Conference*, July.

1949

"A Traveler's Report." *Theatre Arts*, January and June. [The June report was reprinted in *In Search of Theatre*.]

"World Theatre 1900–1950." *Theatre Arts*, December. [Reprinted in *In Search of Theatre*.]

1952

"Notes to *Galileo*." In *From the Modern Repertoire*, vol. 2. [The 1946 contract for a collected works of Brecht had gone by the board, and his plays were appearing one at a time in successive volumes of *From the Modern Repertoire*.]

1956

"Bertolt Brecht, 1898–1956." *New Republic*, August 27. [This obituary was made the subject of a column by Joseph North in the *Daily Worker*, September 2. A German translation appeared in *Der Monat*.]

"Brecht's Good Woman." *New York Times*, December 16.

1959

"Brecht from the Outside." *New Statesman*, March 21.

"Perspective on Brecht." *New Statesman*, November 28. [These two *New Statesmen* articles were reviews of Willett and Esslin respectively; as reprinted in the *Tulane Drama Review*, they earned the author a Longview Award.]

1962

"*Mother Courage*." *Theatre Arts*, June. [Later the preface to a Methuen paperback edition of *Mother Courage*.]

"Letters over the Wall: Helene Weigel and the 'Crime' of Peter Palitzsch." *Theatre Arts*, June.

"Are Two Brechts Better Than One?" *New York Herald Tribune*, September 9.

"Says Bentley *A Man's a Man* Is a Magnificent Play." *Village Voice*, October 4.

1963

"Epic Theatre Is Lyric Theatre." In *The German Theatre Today*, ed. Leroy R. Shaw.

"Bertolt Brecht: Songwriter." *Sing Out!* October–November. [The same magazine published a Bentley piece on Eisler that year.]

"Bertolt Brecht Before the Un-American Activities Committee: An Introduction." Folkways Records. [Album notes printed in a booklet with the text of the recording itself. The same material was reprinted later in slightly different form in (a) *Getting Busted*, ed. Ross Firestone, 1970; and (b) *Thirty Years of Treason*, 1971.]

1964

"Brecht." In *The Life of the Drama* (New York: Atheneum). [Written four years earlier for the Norton Lectures at Harvard.]

"Songs of Hanns Eisler." Folkways Records. [Album notes printed as a booklet.]

"Are Stanislavsky and Brecht Commensurable?" *Tulane Drama Review*, Fall.

Preface to Grimmelshausen's *Runagate Courage*. [Earlier there was a Bentley preface to the same author's *Simplicissimus*.]

1965

"Notes on Bertolt Brecht." *New Politics*, Fall. [Two pieces that had originally appeared in German translation in the West Berlin newspaper *Spandauer Volksblatt*.]

Foreword to *The Jewish Wife and Other Short Plays*.

Introduction to *The Salzburg Dance of Death*. Reprinted from *Portfolio* 8 (1964).

Introduction to a new edition of *Parables for the Theatre*.

"Bentley on Brecht." Folkways Records. [Album notes printed in a booklet. Some of the same material had been printed on the envelope of this record when originally issued by Riverside Records two years earlier.]

1966

    Preface to *Manual of Piety*.

    "Two Notes on Roundheads and Peakheads." In *Jungle of Cities and Other Plays*.

    A contribution to "Brecht in the World." World Theatre, 15. [Answers to questions put to various directors, abridged without the author's knowledge.]

1967

    Foreword and Notes to the Songs. In *The Brecht-Eisler Song Book*.

    The Theatre of Commitment and Other Essays. [None of these essays is directly about Brecht but his presence is felt throughout.]

1968

    "An Imaginary Interview with Eric Bentley by Jerome Clegg." *The Drama Review*, Winter.

1976

    "Portrait of the Critic as a Young Brechtian." *Theatre Quarterly*, Spring. [An interview with Eric Bentley by Catherine Itzin.]

1981

    "Notes on *Arturo Ui*." *BTC Program*, June 5–20.

1982

    "Two Hundred Years of Macheath." *The Threepenny Review*. Reprinted later that year in the Limited Editions Club edition of *The Threepenny Opera*. Reprinted in 1987 in *Thinking About the Playwright* (Evanston, IL: Northwestern University Press).

1985

    "Remembering Brecht." *New York Times*, March 10.

1997

    "Mixing Brecht with the Brighter Colors of Milhaud." *New York Times*, January 19.

1998

"Bertolt Brecht, Werke, Eine Auswahl." *Kurt Weill Newsletter,* Spring 1998.

2003

Eric Bentley interviewed by Vera Stegmann, *The Brecht Yearbook* 28.

Another Bibliography: Bentley Translations of Brecht

Some idea of when Bentley translations of Brecht first appeared in print is provided here. Within the limited space it was not possible to list subsequent appearances or indicate when revised or adapted translations were later issued. This is not a discography, so the Bentley record albums are not included, nor is the material tape-recorded for the fifty Brecht programs Bentley produced for radio station WBAI in New York (Pacifica Radio). One item should perhaps be cited here because, although finally not published, it came very close to publication. This is the play *Happy End*, book translated by Leo Kerz and lyrics translated by Eric Bentley, which was scheduled to appear in *German Drama Between the Wars*, edited by George Wellwarth and published by E. P. Dutton in 1972.

1943

    "The Jewish Wife." *Nation*, September 11.

    "To the Germans on the Eastern Front." *Rocky Mountain Review*, Fall.

1944

    The Private Life of the Master Race (five scenes). *Theatre Arts*, September.

    The Private Life of the Master Race. [Reprinted in England in 1947.]

1948

Parables for the Theatre: "Good Woman of Setzuan," "The Caucasian Chalk Circle." [With Maja Bentley.]

1949

"A New Technique of Acting." Theatre Arts, January. Reprinted in England in New Theatre, March.

"A Model for Epic Theater." Sewanee Review, Summer.

"Chinese Acting." Furioso, Autumn.

The Threepenny Opera (with Desmond Vesey). In From the Modern Repertoire, vol. 1.

1954

The Exception and the Rule. Chrysalis, 7: 11–12.

1955

Mother Courage. In Modern Theatre, vol. 2.

1956

"Early Morning Address to the Tree, Green." Village Voice, March 21.

"Song of the Starlings." Village Voice, June 20.

"Visiting the Exiled Poets." Village Voice, August 29.

"Ballad of the World's Kindness." New Republic, September 24.

"The Measures Taken." Colorado Review, Winter.

1961

In the Swamp and A Man's a Man. Both in Seven Plays by Brecht.

"Hymn of the Red Army Soldier." Encounter, October.

1963

Nineteen poems in The German Theatre Today, ed. Leroy R. Shaw.

"About Poor B.B."

"Ballad of the Dead Soldier"

"Memory of Marie A."

"Orge's Hymn"

"Of the World's Kindness"

"Early Morning Address to a Tree Called 'Green'"
"Hymn of the Red Army Soldier"
"Doomed Generations"
"Swarms of Starlings"
"A Visit to the Exiled Poets"
"Easter Sunday, 1935"
"Ballad of Marie Sanders"
"To the Little Radio"
"The German Miserere"
"Song of a German Mother"
"Homecoming"
"The Solution"
"To My Countrymen"
"Three Elegies (To Those Who Come After)"

1964

The Salzburg Dance of Death. Portfolio, 8. Reprinted in England in *Encore*, September.

Baal (with Martin Esslin) and *The Elephant Calf.*

1965

"Notes to *Mother Courage*" (with Hugo Schmidt). *Encore*, May–June.

1966

Edward II.

Manual of Piety.

"Are the People Infallible?" *Nation*, April 18.

"The Other Germany." *PL* [*Progressive Labor*], March–April. [This was a piece Bentley had translated when Brecht sent it to him during World War II, but no publisher had then been found for it. It has survived only in Bentley's English, from which the German text in the twenty-volume Suhrkamp edition of Brecht is translated.]

1967

Forty songs published in The Brecht–Eisler Song Book.

"Coal for Mike"

"The Gray Goose"
"Solidarity Song"
"Song of the United Front"
"All or Nothing"
"Peace Song"
"Ballad of the Soldier"
"To the Little Radio"
"And the Times Are Dark and Fearful"
"The Homecoming"
"Easter Sunday"
"A Hollywood Elegy"
"To Those Who Come After"
"Abortion Is Illegal"
"The Mask of Wickedness"
"The Sprinkling of Gardens"
"On the World's Kindness"
"The Poplar Tree on Karlsplatz"
"How the Wind Blows"
"Happy the Man"
"Change the World It Needs It"
"Song of the Rice-Barge Coolies"
"Come Out and Fight"
"Supply and Demand"
"We Are the Scum of the Earth"
"Praise of Illegal Work"
"Praise of the USSR"
"Praise of Study"
"On Suicide"
"There's Nothing Quite Like Money"
"The Love Market"
"The Tree and the Branches"
"Ballad of Marie Sanders"
"Do Not Cry, Marie"
"The German Miserere"
"Song of a German Mother"
"A German at Stalingrad"

"Song of the Little Wind"

"And What Did She Get?"

"Song of the Moldau"

"On *The Caucasian Chalk Circle*" (with Hugo Schmidt and Jerome Clegg). *The Drama Review*, Fall. [Since at the time the Brecht estate would not authorize translations with Bentley's name on them, that name was left off.]

1970

"The Prince of Homburg: A Sonnet." In *The Great Playwrights*, vol. 1.

1971

"Resolution: A Song." *The Listener*, December 9.

1995

Happy End. English lyrics by Eric Bentley; drawings by Ilse Schreiber. Privately printed.

Index to Brecht Works and Characters

Index